The IT as a Service (ITaaS) Framework

Transform to an End-to-End Services Organization and Operate IT like a Competitive Business

Justin Mann, CCIE No. 27040

Cisco Press

800 East 96th Street

Indianapolis, Indiana 46240 USA

The IT as a Service (ITaaS) Framework

Transform to an End-to-End Services Organization and Operate IT like a Competitive Business

Justin Mann

Copyright © 2018 Cisco Systems, Inc.

Published by:
Cisco Press
800 East 96th Street
Indianapolis, IN 46240 USA

Printed in the United States of America

1   18

Library of Congress Control Number: 2017962383

ISBN-13: 978-1-58714-501-8

ISBN-10: 1-58714-501-4

Warning and Disclaimer

Trademark Acknowledgments

Special Sales

For information about buying this title in bulk quantities, or for special sales opportunities (which may include electronic versions; custom cover designs; and content particular to your business, training goals, marketing focus, or branding interests), please contact our corporate sales department at corpsales@pearsoned.com or (800) 382-3419.

For government sales inquiries, please contact governmentsales@pearsoned.com.

For questions about sales outside the U.S., please contact intlcs@pearson.com.

Feedback Information

At Cisco Press, our goal is to create in-depth technical books of the highest quality and value. Each book is crafted with care and precision, undergoing rigorous development that involves the unique expertise of members from the professional technical community.

Readers' feedback is a natural continuation of this process. If you have any comments regarding how we could improve the quality of this book, or otherwise alter it to better suit your needs, you can contact us through email at feedback@ciscopress.com. Please make sure to include the book title and ISBN in your message.

We greatly appreciate your assistance.

Editor-in-Chief: Mark Taub

Product Line Manager: Brett Bartow

Alliances Managers, Cisco Press: Arezou Gol

Executive Editor: Michelle Newcomb

Managing Editor: Sandra Schroeder

Development Editor: Ellie C. Bru

Project Editor: Mandie Frank

Technical Editor: Robert Roffey

Editorial Assistant: Vanessa Evans

Designer: Chuti Prasertsith

Composition: codeMantra

Indexer: Ken Johnson

Proofreader: Larry Sulky

Americas Headquarters
Cisco Systems, Inc.
San Jose, CA

Asia Pacific Headquarters
Cisco Systems (USA) Pte. Ltd.
Singapore

Europe Headquarters
Cisco Systems International BV Amsterdam,
The Netherlands

Cisco has more than 200 offices worldwide. Addresses, phone numbers, and fax numbers are listed on the Cisco Website at **www.cisco.com/go/offices**.

Cisco and the Cisco logo are trademarks or registered trademarks of Cisco and/or its affiliates in the U.S. and other countries. To view a list of Cisco trademarks, go to this URL: www.cisco.com/go/trademarks. Third party trademarks mentioned are the property of their respective owners. The use of the word partner does not imply a partnership relationship between Cisco and any other company. (1110R)

Foreword

Ready or not, we are living in a digital world. And with digital, change has come at the most rapid pace we have seen in our lifetimes. I always like to remind myself and my team(s) that change will happen—by us, with us, or to us. I have learned throughout my career that it's much better to be in a position where change happens by us and to set the foundation to drive change continuously. In the following pages, we will share details of a critical part of Cisco's journey that has led us to becoming a digital organization; allowing us to stay ahead of our industry and, very importantly, ensuring we are moving faster and more securely. But it is not only technology and process that changes; one of the hardest shifts is with the culture, the people who have to make all this happen. In our journey to become digital, technology has been the accelerator, but the power has been in the culture. Thus, establishing a strong and enduring foundation is extremely important and, for us, that foundation has been a culture we call "Architecture-led, Services Everything."

Operating an IT organization for an Enterprise, which happens to also be a worldwide leader in IT solutions, presents a unique mix of challenges, incentives, and opportunities. Our first job as Cisco IT is to ensure that our business is running at optimal levels. Thus, being a service provider and having the mindset of "Services Everything" has been the catalyst for running our business. Cisco has entrusted IT with an investment portfolio to help run our world-class operation and transform its business using world-class technology. Thus, we needed to run IT as a business, our business, and display the value and outcomes of the work we perform on behalf of Cisco. This culture is based on Empowered Accountability driven by a framework of personal accountability and empowered general managers of services known as our world-class Service Owners.

Our Accountability Framework anchored by IT as a Service is actually an Architectural strategy. It is the vision, point of view, and ultimately roadmaps that describe the future state of where we want to be in terms of our business, technology, and organization. Simplifying our own processes, such as how we run our own business infrastructure, was the catalyst in laying our foundation and changing our mindset to be service-oriented. Understanding dependencies, and then accelerating through the use of technology— especially showing the value of driving a large enterprise using Cisco's own architecture to automate much of our business infrastructure—was a game changer in continuously driving our own improvements and innovation. Using the framework to align our business and technology architectures ensured that all our investments and activities were supporting the same roadmap aligned to enabling our corporate strategies and desired outcomes.

Broad adoption of "Architecture-led, Services Everything" has allowed us to accelerate the transformation toward digital using an agile Continuous Delivery operating model and Extending the Cloud for continuous automation. It ensures we are building the right things and building them correctly with speed, quality, and security embedded. However, this can't be done alone within IT. Driving the pervasive agile mindset across Cisco and building dynamic teams with business and IT working together, irrespective of reporting lines, has ensured that we are laser-focused on outcomes. We are relentlessly improving based on a fast feedback loop and providing constant value to our customers through continuous innovation. Being agile in the way we think and do our work is a fundamental cultural shift that needed to be embraced by everyone in the organization but it was, and is, the only way to stay competitive: speed and agility while ensuring security.

As an IT professional, starting out on the journey to achieve these outcomes can seem daunting. The key is to start with a solid and enduring foundation. Evolving Cisco IT to be the service provider that it is today did not happen overnight; it began with a critical first step. That first step was to establish our services management approach, which enabled our architectural maturity and led us to become a strategic partner. In this book you will find key insights about this critical first step, and how you can pursue your own journey. Good Luck!

Guillermo Diaz
Cisco Chief Information Officer

About the Author

Justin Mann, CCIE No. 27040, is a senior Business and Technology Architect with Cisco's Advanced Services. Throughout his technical career that began in his teens, he has remained dedicated to understanding the business of his customers, even going so far as attending Sea-Survival and Helicopter Underwater Extraction Training (HUET) in support of oil and gas customers. This background allowed him to successfully lead the earliest Cisco engagements with customers seeking to transform their own IT organizations by following the work pioneered by Cisco IT. By working across IT and business teams at all levels, and over time across different industries and enterprises, Justin developed and refined the now-formal ITaaS framework and Services Transformation Program, allowing IT organizations to transition to end-to-end Services organizations and truly begin to operate IT like a competitive business.

During his free time, Justin is an adventure-traveler, book collector, and comic-book and videogame geek; he can be found on most weekends riding trails on his horse, Lucas. Whenever possible, Justin leverages his passion for travel and horseback riding to work with special-needs children both internationally and locally through a therapeutic horseback riding stable, ManeGait. A portion of the author's proceeds will be donated to ManeGait, and we actively encourage, welcome, and sincerely appreciate donations from interested readers.

About ManeGait

ManeGait Therapeutic Horsemanship is a PATH Premier Accredited Equine Center located on 14 beautiful acres of rolling pasture in McKinney, Texas. ManeGait's nationally recognized equine therapy programs help clients achieve individual goals while focusing on quality of instruction and the active engagement of the North Texas community.

As a result of ManeGait programs, riders are reaching milestones they once thought impossible. They are learning to move, walk, and connect with others and their environment in new and exciting ways. The great strides we celebrate in the arena translate to a better quality of life for our clients and their families.

"We have seen riders take their first steps, say their first words and achieve an emotional connection for the first time, all because of the power of riding the horse."

—Pris Darling, Co-Founder

ManeGait Therapeutic Horsemanship
3160 North Custer Road
McKinney, Texas 75071
(469) 422-6374
manegait.org

Dedication

This, my first published work, is dedicated to the only individuals it could rightly be, my mom and dad, who sacrificed so very much, assured me continuously of their love and support regardless of circumstance, and asked in return only ever that I use their sacrifices and support as a platform to achieve my own happiness. The freedom to pursue my own passions and dreams without fear or influence allowed me to fill my life with people, adventures, hobbies, and work that I love. Thank you, guys; there is nothing in my life that I don't cherish, and I am truly happy thanks to the two of you. If only every child could enjoy the same freedom and support in pursuit of their own happiness...

About the Technical Reviewer

Robert Roffey is currently a director in the Public Sector Advanced Services Team at Cisco, leading our Cloud Advisory Practice. Previously, Robert has represented Cisco at the Department of Defense as a participant in the IT Exchange Program. While working with the Department of Defense, Robert also took the lead in developing our IT Transformation Journey Map and the accompanying go-to-market strategy to support our clients.

Previous to his current role, Robert was the director of strategy and planning for the Regional IT teams. In this role, Robert was responsible for developing and implementing a unifying strategy and operating model that aligns the four regional leaders and their globally distributed teams. The primary objective was to improve the client experience of the IT consumers in the regions through adoption of a common Services model. Prior to this role, Robert worked as the strategic planning and operations leader in two other Cisco IT organizations. In those roles, he was responsible for finance, HR, planning, vendor management, and so on, and led various corporate IT initiatives such as our Services Transformation.

Prior to joining Cisco, Robert spent eight years with Deloitte Consulting leading SAP, Oracle, and Ariba implementations across a diverse client set. Virtually all of Robert's consulting engagements were business-facing roles, leading major organizational transformations enabled through technology. Robert's experience includes work within high-tech manufacturing, semiconductor, mobile telecom, service provider telecom, media and entertainment, oil and gas, healthcare, and pharmaceuticals.

Prior to consulting, Robert spent ten years leading procurement organizations in the networking and semiconductor industries. Robert has a bachelor's degree in business and a master's degree in management.

Acknowledgments

Foremost acknowledgment belongs to the large and talented Cisco IT team who pioneered the work that the content of this framework and resulting book was initially based on. I truly believe that this team created something that will become an integral element of all successful Enterprise IT organizations in the future. Although the ITaaS framework and Services Transformation Program contain differences large and small from Cisco IT's original work, they simply would not have existed without their first envisioning and putting this work into practice. I'm simply working from ideas given life by true industry visionaries, and after much consideration have still not found a proper combination of words to express my respect and appreciation for the work and efforts of the Cisco IT team.

I must also thank a great many friends and coworkers across the wider Cisco team, far too many to even begin to name, many of whom are no doubt unaware of their specific influence or support but nonetheless helped shape the now formal framework for IT Service delivery that resulted from initial Services engagements with customers. Foremost among these, however, is an English gentleman by the name of Tony Court. In a world where consultants increasingly only act to arrogantly and aggressively pander high-level "advice" regarding concepts they have little real-world experience with, Tony represents a dying breed of true consultants who believe their job incomplete until they have contributed a value impact to the business and achieved a series of desired outcomes alongside their customer. My concept of what it means to be a successful consultant changed completely after working with Tony, and of the many hopes I have for this book, one of the more idealistic is that it grants us a platform in which to advocate for this approach to business consulting and to guide a new generation of consultants focused on business outcomes. While other consulting teams "advise," our place will always be in the trenches with our customer.

Of the many other Cisco team members who deserve a few rounds on me, Keith Weaver was instrumental in gathering and then piecing together material for the "Behind the Scenes of the Cisco IT Services Transformation" feature. Special thanks also go to Guillermo Diaz, Eleanor Tullis, Terry Clark, Alice Saiki, Kory Nguyen, and many other Cisco IT leaders who shared their experiences throughout Cisco IT's Services Transformation.

Thanks also go to the team at Pearson, my editor, and technical editor Robert Roffey, all of whom no doubt exercised extensive patience in reviewing and guiding my efforts while allowing this book to take a significantly different approach from that of any previous Cisco Press book. They worked through a series of rough submissions, especially times when I attempted to inject my own brand of humor, which I happen to know Robert supports, but only after his second vodka martini.

And finally to Toby Everett and her team at BP's Lower-48 Shale subsidiary, who recognized the opportunity before so many others to leverage Cisco ITaaS framework as an opportunity for their IT organization to not only remain relevant but to excel as a critical part of an enterprise business, even in the most dire of market conditions. Toby and her team constantly pushed for this framework to do more, whether it was enabling strategic levers for navigating a challenging marketplace, or rethinking components of Cisco IT's original work to make it effective for an agile 1200-member shale oil company. Working with this team led to many of the stories featured in this book and made for a lot of great times and laughs along the way.

Contents at a Glance

Contents

Reader Services

Register your copy at www.ciscopress.com/title/ISBN for convenient access to downloads, updates, and corrections as they become available. To start the registration process, go to www.ciscopress.com/register and log in or create an account*. Enter the product ISBN 9781587145018 and click Submit. Once the process is complete, you will find any available bonus content under Registered Products.

*Be sure to check the box that you would like to hear from us to receive exclusive discounts on future editions of this product.

Command Syntax Conventions

The conventions used to present command syntax in this book are the same conventions used in the IOS Command Reference. The Command Reference describes these conventions as follows:

- **Boldface** indicates commands and keywords that are entered literally as shown. In actual configuration examples and output (not general command syntax), boldface indicates commands that are manually input by the user (such as a **show** command).

- *Italic* indicates arguments for which you supply actual values.

- Vertical bars (|) separate alternative, mutually exclusive elements.

- Square brackets ([ ]) indicate an optional element.

- Braces ({ }) indicate a required choice.

- Braces within brackets ([{ }]) indicate a required choice within an optional element.

Introduction

Beginning my career as a teen in small town West Texas, I never could have imagined that more than 20 years later I would be authoring a book focused on understanding the value IT organizations create for their business and shifting the culture of IT to focus on business outcomes rather than purely technology. Although it could be argued that the industry should have accepted years back that creating value for a business entailed much more than simply reducing the yearly IT budget, the reality is we've now reached a point where it can no longer be ignored; and all it took was completely re-thinking how we go about designing and delivering IT Services.

The foremost goal of this book is to provide a true resource for IT organizations to transform to an End-to-End Services Organization and realize the value outcomes associated with the adoption of Cisco ITaaS framework for themselves. That is to say, I want to provide not only theory but also experience-based guidance for putting these concepts into practice and achieving a set of desired outcomes.

With that in mind, I should note here that neither I nor the Cisco team pretend to have all the answers or that the contents of this book represent the only answer to the various drivers and challenges we face in today's industry. Instead, we simply offer an answer, albeit one backed by an already large and now rapidly growing body of real-world success.

Finally, I want to share the sobering realization that I've now had to slowly accept over the course of writing this book, which is simply that these topics are of a type that could never be fully explored in the clearest manner possible even if I were to spend years refining a book many times the size of the one you now have. As you progress through the contents of this book, you will no doubt find at least some questions unanswered and topics not addressed. Entire sections on strategic levers and other valuable topics were reluctantly left behind as I juggled the numerous responsibilities, and I had always planned for the final chapter of Fast IT to dig into so much more than it will.

In response to this consideration I want to stress that this book represents only one of many avenues Cisco has leveraged to share knowledge on these topics and that our teams are ready and ever eager to provide additional guidance for you and your organization, but nonetheless beg your understanding on those areas where the content of this book falls short of your anticipation.

Who Should Read This Book?

My sincere hope is that this book becomes valued reading for IT professionals in all areas and at all levels of an IT organization well into the future. As you will shortly find, the ITaaS framework is just as much about the culture of the IT organization, reestablishing the purpose and obligation of IT to the parent enterprise, and establishing a structure for communicating the value of IT Services, as it is about designing Service Portfolios and catalogs. In this regard, I truly believe the contents of this book to be of value for every member of the IT organization.

CIOs and senior IT leaders play a critical role in shaping framework and then utilizing a series of strategic levers to steer the IT organization in an agile and competitive way. IT Service Management and enterprise architecture teams will play a significant role in the Services Transformation Program, forming the bulk of any potential IT transformation team. From there, the success of the ITaaS framework will hinge on the successful introduction of Service Roles such as Service Owners, Service Executives, and more taken up by professionals across the IT organization. Finally, a true End-to-End Services Organization requires every member of the organization, even those not facilitating a Service delivery Role, to recognize how their daily activities ultimately contribute to the delivery and resulting value of IT Services. In short, while this book will initially be of greatest interest to CIOs, senior IT leaders, and Service management teams, the successful adoption of the ITaaS framework as a foundation for Fast IT requires support and familiarity with the new approach to IT Service delivery from every member of the organization.

Features in This Book

In support of this book's intended focus on supporting IT organizations in tailoring and implementing Cisco ITaaS framework, it became critically important to consider unique approaches to share all the information and experience Cisco had accumulated. This resulted in two distinct features you will find throughout each chapter, providing additional background, insight, and real-world experience on relevant topics.

"Behind the Scenes of the Cisco IT Services Transformation" features relay the stories and experiences of several Cisco IT leaders who were instrumental in the original Services Transformation at Cisco IT. It is an endlessly interesting story, and opportunities abound for you to relate Cisco IT's own challenges and successes to your own Services Transformation effort.

"Diary of an ITaaS Consultant" features act as opportunities for me to provide additional context by directly relating stories from my past several years of experience in guiding Cisco Services customers through their own transformations. As I progressed through later chapters, I found myself looking forward to the inclusion of these segments as they allowed me to not only drive home points through real-world scenarios but also to highlight the realities of working with large teams of people on a highly complex and visible initiative that likely contradicts their established culture for working with technology. In practice, this means these segments begin to reflect my natural personality and approach to introducing concepts to customer teams through references that span late nineteenth-century French plays to classic '80s movies. My hope is that these features offer an enjoyable break from the traditional straightforward approach to content found in these books while also stressing the need to not only understand theories for IT Service Design but how to work with different people across complex organizations to truly achieve implementation of a successful framework for IT Service delivery.

How This Book Is Organized

Chapter 1, "The Case for IT Transformation and IT as a Service (ITaaS)": This chapter makes the case for Fast IT, and the transition to an end-to-end Services organization as a critical foundation for Fast IT and vehicle for driving cultural change.

Chapter 2, "Introducing Cisco ITaaS Framework and Services Transformation Program": This chapter provides a high-level overview of Cisco ITaaS framework and Services Transformation Program.

Chapter 3, "Change Leadership and Ensuring a Successful Transformation": This chapter stresses the importance of change leadership to successful Services Transformation, along with sharing key best practices.

Chapter 4, "Service Delivery Taxonomy and Definition of a Service": This chapter discusses the definition of Service adopted by each transition team and how it will ultimately impact the final Service delivery framework. This chapter also goes over the various characteristics of an IT Service.

Chapter 5, "Mapping Enterprise Technical Capability Requirements": This chapter guides the development of the Enterprise Technical Capabilities map, a key input for the design of IT Services that facilitate business operations.

Chapter 6, "Service Design and Building the IT Service Portfolio": This chapter leverages previous topics to design a portfolio of Services end-to-end.

Chapter 7, "Service Delivery Roles and Responsibilities": This chapter defines the Service roles and responsibilities that act as the foundation of the ITaaS framework.

Chapter 8, "Measuring IT Service Performance": This chapter introduces a complete strategy for creating a well-rounded view of IT Service Performance that resonates with business customers.

Chapter 9, "Modeling the Total Costs of IT Service Delivery": This chapter introduces a strategy for modeling the total costs of delivering an IT Service along with best practices and basic finance concepts.

Chapter 10, "Communicating IT Service Value": This chapter provides the tools included in the Cisco ITaaS framework that provide a support structure for effective communication and constructive review of the value an IT Service provides.

Chapter 11, "Completing the Services Transformation": This chapter discusses the final phase of the Services Transformation, including the End-to-End Service Reviews, the Service Delivery Optimization, and the End-to-End Services Organization.

Chapter 12, "Fast IT—The Mandatory Future for Enterprise IT Organizations": The final chapter provides an initial introduction to Fast IT strategies and examines more closely how a Services Transformation creates a foundation.

Chapter 1

The Case for IT Transformation and IT as a Service (ITaaS)

The role of Enterprise IT organizations is changing faster than it ever has, and it is time for the industry to reevaluate the fundamental purpose, relevance, and value of an IT organization to the Enterprises of tomorrow. Today's Enterprise businesses have little choice but to rely on their IT organization to help them embrace the digitization of the business, navigate digital disruption, and develop transformative capabilities that can allow their business to become the marketplace disruptor. IT is now more central than ever to daily business operations, and the execution of processes that achieve critical business outcomes. We are nearing a point in which a determining factor in marketplace leaders will be which enterprise has the fastest and most efficient IT organization. This means IT needs to move at the pace of the various lines of business, rather than anchoring enterprise-wide opportunities to the speed of the IT organization. To prepare for this eventuality IT organizations need to become fast in all aspects of their operation. Speed, agility, efficiency, the ability to support business outcomes through delivery of IT services, and a clear understanding of the value those services provide to the enterprise represent the most significant capabilities for tomorrow's IT organizations. Many industry thought-leaders agree that in order to accomplish this a complete transformation of today's IT organizations is required—IT Transformation with a goal of becoming Fast IT.

While the theory of Fast IT is now a common and trendy topic there are few details on how exactly a Fast IT organization operates in practice or how to transition today's IT organizations to a Fast IT operating model. At the same time, many of today's IT organizations continue to struggle by varying degrees with the ever-present historical challenges of justifying investments, managing operational costs, and aligning complex technical architectures to the support of business strategies. These same organizations also face emerging challenges from combinations of "Shadow IT" and cloud-based services that could allow business leaders to completely bypass their own internal IT organizations. The underlying culture of today's IT organizations presents yet another challenge, as the mindset of many IT professionals remains fixated on the adoption and operation of complex technical architectures with little regard for the business outcomes those technical platforms exist to enable.

To date, there has been no practical guide based on real-world experience for IT organizations seeking to finally resolve these challenges and to initiate and sustain a cultural change; no proven path and first steps for today's IT organizations to begin their transformation to Fast IT. Until now.

Cisco's own massively complex, global IT organization is widely recognized as one of the industry's premier leaders in the adoption of Fast IT and related practices. Interest in Cisco IT's real-world experience with these principles continues to grow in public forums such as Cisco Live and requests for informational sessions with Cisco IT leaders. These pioneering leaders continue to stress that becoming a Fast IT organization requires much more than adopting trendy practices like DevOps, rolling out programmable infrastructures, or updating your Cloud strategy; although these things all help to increment the speed and agility of IT operations. Fast IT requires a foundation, and that foundation is an Architecture-led, end-to-end Services organization or IT as a Services organization (ITaaSO). Architecture ensures overarching alignment to a strategic roadmap, while end-to-end Services allows IT for the creation of a Service-based view of it's operations; clearly demonstrating how IT resources, assets, and budgets support Services that deliver capabilities and outcomes required by the business.

Based closely on the work pioneered through Cisco IT's own Services Transformation, Cisco's IT as a Service (ITaaS) framework is a proven solution for transitioning real-world IT organizations to end-to-end Services organizations. Its development was focused on achieving two key value outcomes: establishing the IT organization as a trusted advisor of the enterprise business and providing mechanisms for operating the IT organization as a relevant, agile, cost-effective, and highly competitive "business within a business."

The framework reexamines existing strategies, processes, and tools for the design and delivery of IT Services, and also introduces a complete strategy for measuring the value of those Services. The ITaaS framework defines Service value as a consideration of the total costs of delivering a required set of technical capabilities at a desired level of performance, weighed against the impact of those capabilities on business outcomes. It also includes mechanisms to qualify that consideration of value across individual Services. This includes processes for reporting the total costs of Service delivery using an easy-to-understand model and strategies for measuring Service performance leveraging concepts that resonate with business leaders and can spotlight the impact of Service performance on business outcomes.

Services Transformation based on the ITaaS framework also initiates and sustains a cultural shift in the IT organization. The framework is built on a foundation of people, including a broad community or resources acting as general managers of an individual Service. These Service Owners are responsible for considering all aspects of Service performance, managing operational costs and demonstrating the value of investments, and proactively facilitating future requirements for capabilities and scale. They are ultimately accountable for the value delivered by a Service.

The ITaaS framework is paired with Cisco's Services Transformation Program, capable of tailoring the framework to a specific industry and enterprise, and guiding the adoption of the ITaaS framework based on best practices and lessons learned from prior transformations. The goal of this book is not to simply share a conceptualized methodology for IT Service design, but to provide you with every means available for putting this framework into practice and ensuring it achieves its intended outcomes, widespread adoption, and continuous value creation for the IT organization and its parent enterprise business.

This first chapter makes the case for IT Transformation and Fast IT, and in doing so establishes a Services Transformation and the transition to an end-to-end Services organization as the foundational first step for today's enterprise IT organizations. It begins with a review of the drivers for IT Transformation and the historical and emerging challenges hindering the successful transformation of most IT organizations. From there, the basic, fundamental purpose of IT organizations and the obligations to the enterprise are reexamined. Although these topics may at first seem painfully simplistic, the purpose is to encourage you to consider the IT organization from the outside in, as a business resource relying on the availability and performance of capabilities delivered by IT for their own success. These principles will be referred to regularly throughout the book in relation to the culture of the IT organization. The final sections of the chapter establish how these drivers and challenges for IT Transformation can be addressed through the adoption of the ITaaS framework and transition to an end-to-end Services organization.

My intent in this chapter is not to convince you that Cisco's ITaaS framework is the only solution for Services Transformation capable of providing a foundation for Fast IT—only that it *is an* answer. It is an answer, however, that has now been so thoroughly tested in practice that my fundamental understanding of what makes it successful has changed. Over the past several years spent developing the ITaaS framework and guiding Cisco Services customers through their own Services Transformations, I have come to realize the real secret to fostering strong relationships between IT and the enterprise business all along was that single element that is so critical to the success or failure of any relationship: communication.

That is the real opportunity that Cisco's ITaaS framework creates for your IT organization—*the ability to communicate the value of IT Services.*

The Drivers for IT Transformation

The drivers for IT Transformation and Fast IT are many, so covering all relevant topics could easily represent a book in and of itself. At the same time, many of these topics represent significant interest and have received extensive dedicated discussion through numerous resources across the IT industry; I encourage you to seek out and review these for further background. Rather than duplicate these efforts, the following sections briefly highlight only the most significant drivers before examining the resulting implications for today's IT organizations.

Digitization

Digitization within the context of an enterprise business refers to the transition of assets, information, and processes to digital platforms, typically resulting in significant improvements in efficiency. As an example, consider a field maintenance team moving from pen and paper to data entry via a business app on a mobile device. While digitization has arguably been taking place across enterprise businesses for years, the term primarily refers to the recent spike in digitization of business processes, leveraging combinations of multiple new technologies to achieve significant benefits. The key is that Enterprises now have to effectively and aggressively embrace trends in digitizing, growing segments of their business to maintain efficiencies across their operations. Otherwise, they risk being left behind. So what does this mean for the IT organization?

First, it means that businesses are looking to their enterprise IT organizations to both manage and accelerate, if not lead, digitization. It also means that growing numbers of critical business processes across an enterprise now rely on the technical capabilities delivered by the IT organization for successful execution. For many business leaders today, this idea is often met with varying levels of apprehension rather than strong enthusiasm.

Digital Disruption

The most commonly referenced example of digital disruption is the e-book revolution. This particular disruption did not begin with the availability of books in digital format as the name implies, however, because we have for years been able to view and exchange digital files of novel-length text. (In fact, emails from some of my coworkers could be argued to constitute e-books.) Instead, it was the combined introduction of several capabilities that led to a digital transformation. In this case, it was a combination of books in digital format, devices such smartphones, tablets, and e-book readers purpose-built for the function, and connectivity to digital stores that could serve up books on demand. The historical industry-standard processes for the publication, consumption, distribution, and sharing of e-books were completely upended, and it all happened fairly quickly.

Within the context of an enterprise business, digital disruption primarily concerns the threat of ongoing digitization drastically transforming industry operations and marketplaces with little to no warning, leaving an enterprise scrambling to adapt to remain relevant, much less competitive, in the newly-transformed marketplace. Enterprise businesses struggling to embrace trends in digitization are most at risk, but it can even impact an enterprise that simply chose an alternate solution than the one that proves to be truly transformative.

I will be the first to admit that the threat of digital disruption has on occasion been overdramatized to the point of fear mongering, typically just prior to pitching a flashy new technical platform or poorly scoped consulting engagement. At the same time, the threat of significant industry disruption is very much real, and it is possible for instances of digital disruption to leave longstanding market leaders suddenly irrelevant within an industry they once controlled. These sudden and, in some cases, seismic-level shifts to the accepted ways of doing business can come from any sector. They will continue coming, which leaves the enterprise business relying on its IT organization to help quickly navigate and adapt to rapidly changing marketplaces.

The Internet of Things

The Internet of Things (IoT) embraces the concept of a connected world, where everything from kitchen appliances to wearable devices can connect and exchange data. The concept of IoT is concerned with more than simply what can be connected and is equally focused on "what can we do with all this data?" Going forward, we reference a pool of connected devices and the collection and value application of information from these newly connected devices as an IoT solution, which are a specific form of digitization and possible sources of digital disruption.

IoT solutions offer significant opportunities to enterprise businesses. Most often, they enable businesses to transform critical processes to achieve new levels of efficiency, establish access to newfound levels of actionable intelligence, or both. These solutions, however, present some unique challenges.

Consider first that most enterprise IoT solutions are often deeply integrated with business operations but often rely on complex technical architectures to achieve full capabilities and level of scale. Business-led IoT solutions may limit or completely avoid IT involvement. This can result in scenarios where a solution performs well in early proof-of-concept and limited pilot stages, but, because it was developed in isolation from IT's architectures and standards, can be difficult or impossible to incorporate and scale to desired levels. On the other hand, IT-led solutions often fail to deliver the proposed level of value due to a lack of knowledge of the operations they were intended to benefit. Also consider that many organizations struggle to accurately understand, report, or plan the total costs of operating a technical solution over time. Organizations often further inflate the costs of developing an IoT solution by duplicating technical capabilities already available within the enterprise.

An enterprise strategy capable of developing and scaling IoT solutions will be a major component of Fast IT for many organizations. Developing efficient and successful IoT solutions require operational capabilities and a close partnership with lines of business that simply aren't present in many of today's organizations. Managing delivery of these solutions requires the same visibility of performance and understanding of total costs required for but lacking in today's service management strategies.

IT Transformation Challenges

In reality, most IT leaders know they need to transform how they operate their organization in order to embrace digitization and prepare to navigate instances of digital disruption. These leaders are impeded however by a series of significant challenges, old and new, that act to distract from, impede, and ultimately defy any and all efforts at transformation. These topics represent significant considerations that could constitute a book of their own and, as such, here again we highlight only the most significant topics and encourage you to leverage additional resources for further background.

Historical Challenges Facing IT Organizations

Enterprise IT organizations have been restrained on multiple levels in their support of the parent enterprise as a result of numerous historical challenges present within most any enterprise IT organization today and for which the IT industry as a whole has struggled to identify proven solutions. These issues have developed over many years, persisted just as long, and will not be solved overnight. At the same time, they all must be addressed in order for the IT organization to remain relevant and transition to Fast IT.

Aligning IT Services and Value to Customer Requirements

A Service should deliver capabilities or outcomes required by a given customer base and take into consideration the value of the Service from the perspective of the customer. Many IT organizations today designate Services that reflect only a small segment of the capabilities they deliver and have little visibility to the value created by those Services for the enterprise business.

Most IT services designated today only reflect requirements for productivity such as personal computing, email and office applications, and communication and collaboration platforms. This means that numerous capabilities delivered by today's IT organizations to enable business processes, such as through an IoT solution, are never associated with a Service. For those capabilities that are aligned to a Service, Service design and management philosophies focus more on the technical platform than the capabilities it enables, which is the element consumed by the customer. If an IT organization does not have an end-to-end view of the landscape of technical capability requirements it is tasked with delivering, how can it demonstrate that its assets, resources, and budgets are fully aligned to supporting those requirements?

Delivery of a Service is always associated with a consideration of the value it provided. Value considers not only the costs associated with a Service, but the performance, customer experience, and other factors. Also remember that while value is ultimately determined by the customer, it is important that the Service Provider understand the customer perspective of value, and adopt a strategy to measure and report an initial view of value. The value of technical capabilities delivered by IT, from the perspective of the business customer, is a complete blind spot for today's IT organizations. Without a strategy to measure Service value, how can an IT organization improve?

Understanding the Customer Perspective of Service Performance

It will always be important for IT organizations to maintain extensive visibility to the operational performance of the complex systems, platforms, and infrastructures they manage. Today's enterprise IT organizations have access to near limitless amounts of technical metrics and analytics, and this data is critical to the successful operation of the underlying systems and platforms they operate. The challenge is that these metrics seldom support an understanding of whether various technologies operated by IT successfully combined to deliver the specific capabilities required by a customer at the desired level of performance. Determination of Service value requires an understanding of the desired levels of performance from the customer and an understanding of how the final delivery of the Service either met, exceeded, or failed those requirements.

The key consideration is that while the underlying performance of these platforms can impact the resulting capabilities and customer experience, that is not always the case and, in some scenarios, can even paint a false narrative. Consider those instances where a customer escalates concerns regarding a Service, but IT performance monitoring shows nothing but green lights. The reality is that system uptime and other measurements of the platform may have little do with the capabilities it is in place to enable. That is why technical metrics alone do not represent the ideal measurement of the capabilities they enable through a Service.

As an illustrative example of this concept, consider submitting a request for a taxi or ride-sharing Service to reach a destination by a designated time. In this case, the Service fails your requirements if the vehicle never picks you up, takes too long to pick you up, or follows an inefficient route that prevents you from reaching your destination on time. The fact that the oil pressure, engine temperature, and tire pressure were all within operating parameters does not change the fact that the Service failed to deliver the required capability or outcome within conditions that made the Service valuable to you. Enterprise business customers continue to prioritize and look to IT to deliver specific capabilities, while IT continues to focus on measuring the underlying systems and infrastructure.

Accurately Communicating the Total Costs of Delivering IT Services

IT leaders have for years faced growing levels of concern and frustration from their customers around IT costs. These pressures have led to intensified processes for the justification and prioritization of IT investments. While important, the reality is that investment costs traditionally represent only 20 to 30 percent of an IT budget, and IT organizations traditionally struggle to understand and effectively manage the daily costs of running the organization that makes up the majority of the budget.

It is also important to acknowledge that the ongoing pressures on IT spending have resulted in a widespread atmosphere of pure focus on cost cutting, regardless of the consequences. Consider that without visibility to the way technical architectures enable capabilities and outcomes for the business, or an understanding of the desired performance from the customer perspective, cutting costs may further impact the customer experience. It is imperative that today's IT leaders remember that cutting costs does not necessarily equate to value for the IT organization or enterprise business.

I honestly believe that many concerns around IT spending result from business customers who are simply trying to understand the value they receive from the significant costs associated with IT. Illustrating the size of a budget tied to an organizational team rarely provides insight to the total costs of delivering capabilities to the customer, and cost is a key component for consideration of value. What results instead is a type of negative feedback loop where enterprise business customers struggle to understand the value the IT organization creates and then express concerns specific to IT spending. This leads IT to slow investment and cut operational costs. Without a framework to align Services to customer requirements or measure performance from the customer perspective, this results in still further degradation of the capabilities, performance, and customer experience. This finally leads to further frustration and escalation of concerns, then further cost reductions, and so on.

Understanding Organizational, Operational, and Procedural Challenges

IT organizations are responsible for managing multiple complex, shared architectures, which in many cases leads to equally complex organization of assets, resources, and budgets. Enterprise business customers often feel that these things hinder their operational success. In reality, a customer should never even be presented, much less impacted, by these elements of a Service Provider's organization.

Consider a scenario in which a business team identifies a rare, limited-time opportunity in the marketplace but requires IT's support in quickly developing and implementing the solution. In many cases, these opportunities fail to be supported in the time allowed due to combinations of budgeting cycles, change control, and other operational processes, or they are even passed back and forth between different IT teams. Too often the complexity of IT assets, resources, processes, and budgets combine to constrain rather than enable capabilities and value for the enterprise business.

Emerging Challenges for IT Organizations

As technology and industry marketplaces change, so do the challenges driving a wedge between IT organizations and the businesses they support. Unlike any time in the past, however, emerging challenges facing IT and the expectations for how businesses leverage technical capabilities are pushing IT organizations to a tipping point. Otherwise, they risk becoming irrelevant to the businesses they support and bypassed altogether. This section introduces the most significant of these emerging challenges and how they combine to allow business leaders an option to completely bypass their IT organizations.

Shadow IT

Shadow IT is a loosely defined concept across the industry, regarded as enterprise resources taking on the delivery and support of their own technical capabilities. They range from simple applications to large and complex systems, outside of and typically without the knowledge or formal support of the enterprise IT organization. These scenarios emerge from a perception that the IT organization is unable to deliver important technical capabilities required by a business unit to be successful, leaving business leaders with no choice but to sanction their own team's efforts to develop and deliver these capabilities.

Concern for Shadow IT stems from the inherent risks it can introduce to an enterprise. Consider that development of a solution often ignores numerous architectural, operational, and security standards mandated by the IT organization. This means increased risk of outages or even security breaches even as reliance on a successful solution grows across a business team. It also creates scenarios in which a popular solution creates significant or even impossible interoperability and support challenges for the IT organization when the solution reaches a point that it has to rely on IT for scale and long-term support.

From the Diary of an ITaaS Consultant

Cisco Services regularly partners with Cisco customers to guide Services and IT Transformation initiatives. These Cisco Services teams leverage the same ITaaS framework and Services Transformation Program that are the focus of this book, but are also able to lean on an extensive pool of additional intellectual capital and years of real-world experience. This allows Cisco Services teams to provide a level of insurance that the value outcomes for Services Transformation are realized in the target time frame.

These "diary entries" located throughout the chapters of this book aim to share insightful stories from my experience leading these engagements over the past several years. While I have obviously omitted customer-specific details, the hope is that by correlating chapter topics to real-world context, they can more accurately perceive the practical decisions and challenges they will face when conducting their own Services Transformation.

Chapter 2, "Introducing Cisco ITaaS Framework and Services Transformation Program," introduces the Services Transformation Program, which begins with a "discovery and design phase" intended to gather and review a wide range of IT and business considerations to refine an ideal target future framework for Service delivery. A key activity in this phase, and one in which Cisco Services teams acting as neutral outside parties often have great success with, is to evaluate instances of Shadow IT across the enterprise. Uncovering and understanding the occurrences of Shadow IT and the circumstances that led to them can provide strong indicators for areas of the business where IT support is struggling and trust and patience for working with the IT organization have become strained to the point of complete avoidance.

In one such effort, our teams were immediately inundated with stories from both IT and business contacts regarding a recent and ongoing challenge stemming from an incredible innovation developed through an instance of Shadow IT. An assortment of resources across various business functions had tied together a series of previously isolated data sources and then created a highly customizable front end, allowing for informational maps to be created. In effect, they had created a transformative new source of information, and demand for access to the tool quickly skyrocketed.

The challenge was that the enterprise and its industry were subject to extensive regulatory oversight and higher security requirements than most Enterprises, resulting in the IT organization deploying highly secure and restricted operating system images across all standard customer devices. The Shadow IT tool, however, had been developed in a highly customized VM environment using a later browser and plug-ins, extensions, and configurations far beyond what the standard images would allow. This meant it could not be supported by current device standards.

Escalations and broad requests (complaints) pushed IT to fast-track the rollout of updates to the browser environments and other features on the standard images. Unfortunately for all involved, this led to widespread issues when it was discovered that a number of existing critical business apps across the enterprise, including finance billing portals, had their own dependencies that were broken by the upgrades. IT teams felt they had been pulled into an unfair, no-win situation, while business teams perceived the IT organization as struggling yet again to simply manage a platform that their own teams had proven could be delivered successfully.

Real-world situations like this are common, and can ultimately be dealt with and managed through the ITaaS framework and IT Transformation. However, they illustrate the many unintended consequences that can result from cases of Shadow IT.

While many IT leaders actively attempt to ferret out and eliminate instances of Shadow IT as a result of the risk it can introduce to the business, Cisco actually recommends embracing Shadow IT. While it can introduce risk, instances of Shadow IT can also initiate significant, even transformative opportunities for the enterprise. Business-led development of technical capabilities can provide a significant amount of insight to areas where the IT organization is struggling to support the business.

IT leaders instead should seek to understand where pockets of Shadow IT exist, why they persist, the potential risks and opportunities for the enterprise, and how the IT organization can best optimize their Service delivery strategy before then inviting businesses to transition solutions to a long-term partnership with IT. The Cisco Fast IT recommendations evolve this concept even further, leading to a concept I call "Customer-Initiated IT," which is explored in Chapter 12, "Fast IT—The Mandatory Future for Enterprise IT Organizations."

The Cloud

Business leaders frustrated for years by their IT organization but with no alternative can now consume a complete range of enterprise-class technical capabilities from growing numbers of cloud-based vendors. While these capabilities were initially limited to general productivity, such as email, they now span platforms that can Service complete sets of technical capability requirements for entire corporate business functions common to Enterprises, such as sales, HR, or finance. Instead of relying on the enterprise IT organization to execute a complex and lengthy project to implement a large-scale enterprise resource planning (ERP) platform and then manage it over time, business leaders can simply subscribe to the capabilities. What's more, many business leaders will consider this approach to consuming technical capabilities to be far superior to working with the enterprise IT organization. Public cloud Service Providers represent the image of IT Service delivery that business leaders have for so long sought from their own IT organizations.

The real threat to today's IT organizations from these emerging challenges is the inevitability of business leaders combining Shadow IT efforts and public cloud vendors to completely bypass the IT organization for virtually any capabilities they require. Rather than awaiting the inevitable outcome of irrelevancy, IT organizations need to begin their transformation to Fast IT, beginning with how they design and deliver IT Services across the enterprise and communicate the value of those Services.

The Purpose and Culture of IT Organizations

The following sections encourage readers to reconsider the fundamental goals of an enterprise business and the purpose and obligations of an IT organization within that enterprise, followed by a candid examination of the culture common to today's enterprise IT organizations. Contrasting these concepts highlights a number of considerations informing the need for a cultural shift in the organization to support a transition to an end-to-end Services organization.

Getting Back to the Basics of Business

Many of the upcoming chapters in this book begin by clearly establishing a purpose and goal for the topic of the chapter. This is true whether the chapter in question focuses on Service taxonomy or principles for communicating IT Service value. Over my years of consulting, I've found that this approach not only helps to proactively address questions and concerns that tend to emerge throughout the life of a challenging effort but also helps to align a team from the earliest point possible. Here I want to encourage you to forget about IT organizations for a moment, and especially technology, and instead consider the fundamental purpose of an enterprise business.

The purpose of an enterprise business is to participate in one or more industries and marketplaces through the production of goods or services, with a goal of accomplishing a set of outcomes such as maximizing profits. While many businesses focus on profit as the primary outcome, others such as public sector and nonprofits pursue a different but equally important set of outcomes.

An enterprise business achieves these outcomes through the execution of major functions or groups of related business processes. Execution of these processes, and support for business outcomes, is facilitated through any number of departments, teams, and resources. There are numerous possible organizational structures found across enterprise businesses today, and these can be further influenced by the particular industry and the size and complexity of the enterprise. To simplify things throughout the remainder of this book, I want to distinguish between two specific types of enterprise business departments, or organizations.

Lines of business (LoB) are those organizations within an enterprise that perform the functions that directly enable the desired outcomes of the business. These teams and their operations are unique to the industry and marketplaces they participate in. As an example, those teams within an oil and gas company that find and extract petroleum and natural gas, or the teams that manufacture vehicles for an auto manufacturer, each represent an LoB.

In contrast, some organizations perform functions common across industries, such as HR, finance, legal, and IT organizations, which I refer to going forward simply as business units (BUs). These BUs deliver critical capabilities to the LoBs and the enterprise itself, such as enabling a manufacturing department to train and pay its resources or the enterprise business to file its taxes, and in doing so either directly or indirectly support the desired outcomes of the business. Enterprise IT organizations are just another example of a BU, and they share a similar purpose.

The purpose of an IT organization, then, is to deliver technical capabilities required by the enterprise for productivity and the execution of processes that support business outcomes.

Obligations to the Enterprise Business

There are two fundamental obligations to the Enterprise business shared by all enterprise organizations (both BUs and LoBs):

■ Supporting business outcomes

■ Ensuring efficient operation

These obligations are applicable at all times and to all enterprise business organizations, regardless of the functions supported by a given team or department.

The previous section described how BUs like the IT organization support business outcomes, either directly or indirectly, by supporting the execution of processes and functions. Now consider that whenever a BU repeatedly fails to support those business outcomes, it negates its purpose and value to the enterprise business. The key consideration for IT and business leaders then becomes, "Is the operation of today's enterprise IT organization aligned to the support of business outcomes, or to the adoption and operation of technology?" Always remember the fundamental purpose of the IT organization is not the operation of technical platforms but is instead to deliver capabilities that support business outcomes through the operation of those platforms.

All enterprise organizations are also equally obligated to continuous, efficient operation. Failing to operate efficiently in any area ultimately constrains the successful achievement of desired outcomes like maximizing profits. Even a critical LoB must operate efficiently or risk draining precious enterprise resources. Again, this highlights an important consideration for IT leaders. How efficient is the operation of today's IT organizations?

Looking back at the challenges highlighted in previous sections provides evidence that today's IT organizations are struggling with their obligations to the enterprise business.

Addressing these issues requires a transformation designed with the purpose and obligations of the IT organization at the forefront.

A Reminder About the Nature of Service Providers and Customers

Many IT organizations today have not only forgotten who their customers are but that they have customers at all.

Customers are the teams and individuals that ultimately require and consume the goods and Services produced by an enterprise business. Enterprise businesses live and die by how effective they are at providing Services that their customers require and delivering superior value compared to offerings from competitors. For an enterprise company, the customers make up the market(s) in which the enterprise participates in the sale of goods and Services. For enterprise business organizations whose purpose is providing capabilities to the enterprise, they are in effect a Service Provider, and their customers are those resources across the enterprise who require and consume those Services. *An enterprise IT organization is a Service Provider within an enterprise business, whose customers are those resources across the enterprise who consume technical capabilities delivered by IT for daily productivity and the execution of business processes.*

Note that the IT organizations' customers include resources and teams not only from other business units but also from their own organization. IT resources leverage many of the same technical capabilities for productivity and collaboration as the rest of the enterprise, and they consume technical capabilities to execute business processes for managing support cases, operating infrastructures, and even delivering and then communicating the value of IT Services. Also consider that some IT organizations may serve customers outside the enterprise business, such as providing technical capabilities to partners or external contractors.

This is an incredibly important and foundational principle of IT organizations for today's IT professionals and IT leaders to revisit. Whenever you consider enterprise resources that leverage collaboration infrastructures, request devices and applications, and open and escalate support cases, how do you refer to them? As "customers"? Or as something else? Maybe as "users"?

There is a very real set of implicit obligations, priorities, and expectations associated with the relationship of Service Providers and customers. Service Providers operate to provide Services their customers want and prioritize customer satisfaction. They actively seek to understand the customer base and its requirements, now and in the future, and evaluate opportunities to provider higher levels of value. Above all, they are expected to be responsive, if not apologetic, whenever the customer base is not satisfied with the Services and value they are receiving. Referring to your customers as anything other than customers acts to delegitimize this relationship and its implicit expectations. Whenever the whole of your IT organization continuously refers to its customer base as "users," it devalues the obligations IT has to its customers. Resources within a Service Provider respond differently to concerns from a "customer" than they do from a "user."

From the Diary of an ITaaS Consultant

A major focus of Cisco Services teams supporting Services Transformations for Cisco customers is on fostering and then reinforcing at all times the cultural shift of the IT organization. While presentation of the topics highlighted in this chapter is important, the ideal behaviors are reinforced through continuous coaching by the Cisco Services consultants, and I have used any number of creative means to drive these points home.

Specific to the topic of reestablishing users as the customers of IT Services, I have used a range of tactics to highlight for IT professionals the many instances they refer to their customers as anything else, even banging on distracting bells during mock Service Reviews. That said, happy hours are always common, and rounds are provided for those who repeatedly demonstrate the ideal behaviors.

To demonstrate the importance of this concept, I will not use the term *user* again in this book, and the rounds are on me if you can prove otherwise.

A Candid Look at the Culture of Today's IT Organization

Based on the obligations established in the previous section, you might assume that a given enterprise organization would include a community of resources with knowledge of the desired outcomes of the business and who were capable of describing how their organization supports those outcomes. Take a moment to consider how well resources across your own IT organization could respond to the questions below:

- What are the desired outcomes of the enterprise business, such as maximizing profits?

- What are the current enterprise strategies to support those outcomes?

- How does the IT organization support those outcomes and strategies?

- Can you provide a basic description of the enterprise industry, value chain, and marketplace?

- Can you describe how technology is impacting the industry and any trends in the marketplace?

- Can you describe the major functions of the enterprise business and identify specific IT Services or capabilities that support those functions and processes?

Note that later chapters provide further details on the target ideal culture of an ITaaSO, along with Service delivery roles and change leadership strategies to support the shift. The key to understand now is that there is likely a gap of some degree between the culture of today's IT organizations and the ideal culture needed to support the purpose and obligations of the IT organization, which creates a significant challenge for moving to Fast IT.

From the Diary of an ITaaS Consultant

Another workstream of the Services Transformation discovery and design phase focuses on an in-depth assessment of an IT organization's existing strategy for Service delivery. This strategy assessment also attempts to gauge the current culture of the IT organization through various interviews. During one such interview for a major oil and gas firm, a long-time member of the company and IT team shared an eye-opening observation:

> During the late '80s and '90s every member of this organization knew they worked for an oil company, had a basic knowledge of the different business departments and their operations, followed industry news, and had at least a loose sense of how their role ultimately helped the company to find and get oil out of the ground and into the markets. But then from the early 2000s onward, a technology-centric view of the business set in and quickly took over the IT organization entirely. Adoption of technology became our sole focus and before long, we were driving technical projects simply for the sake of the technology itself. It was as if, without realizing it, our mentality completely shifted to the idea that we were a technology company which had to do small side-ventures in something called the "oil industry" in order to help fund all of the IT projects we had to drive.

Remember also that today's IT organizations are constituted largely by resources who were hired and promoted based purely on technical expertise. Consider that the easiest way for IT professionals to grow their value (and related compensation) within the industry is by demonstrating expertise in the implementation and operation of complex technologies, which in turn drives many IT teams to prioritize adoption of complex technologies.

This topic has not been completely ignored by IT leaders. Many IT organizations have instituted roles intended to bridge select IT resources to various business teams and operations. These resources often leveraged a level of industry background in an attempt to understand customer perceptions of the IT organization and respond to their concerns and priorities. In most cases, however, these roles were limited in scope and their intended goals, constrained by a lack of strategies for measuring and communicating Service value with relation to business outcomes, and lacked the authority needed to advocate effectively across the IT organization.

Next, while many enterprise IT organizations today include small Service management teams, they often leverage standards for Service design that reflect only a segment of IT's operations, and more importantly have little in the way of strategy or tools to correlate those Services to the support of business outcomes. Successful Services Transformation requires not only a framework for end-to-end Services and strategies for measuring Service value, but also an extended community of IT resources who understand how these Services support the purpose and obligations of the IT organization.

Customer Perceptions of IT

Another important practice for a Service Provider is to maintain an understanding of how it is viewed by its customer base. Ideally, the various priorities, concerns, and opportunities on the minds of the customer base should be shared by a community of resources within the Service Provider in order to continue aligning Services and creating value, as well as shaping future Services and offerings.

How many IT organizations today have adopted a well-rounded strategy to understand the customer perception of IT, and if more did, how do you think those customers would describe their IT organizations? As a trusted advisor, or purely as an order taker and unnecessarily expensive Service broker?

From the Diary of an ITaaS Consultant

While each enterprise we engage with often offers unique nuggets of feedback, many comments recur from one business to the next, becoming well-known and anticipated themes. While IT professionals no doubt retain their own opinions regarding the circumstances and the challenges that led to these perceptions from their customer base, it is critically important that IT organizations, as Service Providers, acknowledge and maintain an ongoing understanding of how their customers view them.

When conducting interviews with business teams across enterprise lines of business and BUs, these are some of the comments we generally expect to hear:

- We couldn't afford to wait on IT any longer and finally had to take care of the issue ourselves.

- IT pushes technology at us that never works like we need it to and then charges us huge amounts of money after having forced us to adopt their chosen platform rather than allowing us to guide the decision on the best platform.

- We needed to upgrade our systems, but IT informed us we would also have to fund the costs of a data center and network upgrades but couldn't clearly explain why our business unit had to absorb costs ten times above what our system license and support costs amounted to.

- It feels like IT regularly makes important decisions that result in a significant impact in the technology we leverage for our operations, but it never seems like our business operations teams or senior leaders are ever involved in these decisions.

- We know that IT outsourced a wide range of their support to some vendor, and now it's even more difficult for us to get the type of support we need and it doesn't seem to have saved the company any real money.

- IT support is overly focused on SLAs, which seem to have become an end in and of themselves, and refuses to acknowledge that these SLAs have little to no correlation to how the technology impacts our business processes.

- IT keeps showing us tons of metrics that don't mean anything to us, our priorities, or our business operations and doesn't seem interested in understanding our actual performance requirements for the capabilities we need them to deliver.

- We receive significant chargebacks to our department from the IT organization, but IT has never been able to provide justification for the costs themselves or explain why they are so high.

A dedicated and ongoing effort to understand the customer perception of the IT organization will often surprise many IT teams because the customer base points to a series of priorities that may at times be completely inverted from those of the IT organization.

From the Diary of an ITaaS Consultant

Perhaps one of the most impactful comments I've received during interviews aimed at understanding current IT and business alignment came from a VP of Operations:

My primary concern with IT is that they don't deliver the technical capabilities my teams need to operate. When they do, they don't work when we need them or how we need them to, and then they charge us an exorbitant amount for having dealt with the headaches of using them. Whenever we raise these concerns, IT only responds by trying to reduce the costs, which seems to make things worse. The reality is that if the capabilities were made available to us and worked, I might be okay with those costs, and might even support investment to add additional capabilities.

Remember to forget technology and IT organizations, but instead think about this feedback purely in the context of a customer's perception of a Service Provider they are effectively forced to use. The customer is stating that the Service Provider failed to deliver several of the capabilities he needed, and those that were delivered failed to perform at a level required to be of any value, and then charged the customer an exorbitant amount for these "Services."

To put this in context, consider entering a bar while on a date and placing an order for a vodka martini (stirred rather than shaken so that it does not bruise the ice), a margarita for your date, and an appetizer. The bartender delivers a cheap beer, alongside separate shots of tequila and lime juice, and no appetizer. You immediately ask, "Is this my order!?" to which the bartender replies "Why, yes, that will be $300." This type of Service delivery is unacceptable for bars and business Enterprises alike.

Welcome to IT Service Delivery Club

The feedback from this VP had a significant impact on the ITaaS framework, along with how I coached enterprise IT teams throughout a Services Transformation, in particular establishing a new set of priorities for Service delivery. I began to talk about Service delivery teams within an ITaaSO as a club, and just like any club, we have a set of club rules. These rules must be adhered to sequentially for successful Service delivery, in other words accomplishing the last two rules but missing the first means you failed the customer. The IT Service Delivery Club rules are:

- **1st Rule of Service Delivery Club:** Deliver the technical capabilities required by your customers to be productive and achieve business outcomes such as maximizing profits.

- **2nd Rule of Service Delivery Club:** Deliver the technical capabilities required by your customers to be productive and achieve business outcomes such as maximizing profits!!!

- **3rd Rule of Service Delivery Club:** Understand the requirements for Service performance from the customer perspective, measure the appropriate things, and improve over time.

- **4th Rule of Service Delivery Club:** Understand the total costs of delivering the required capabilities at the desired level of performance.

While these rules may not represent great technical literature, they have proven effective at reminding IT professionals of the priorities for Service delivery within an ITaaSO.

The Implications for Today's IT Organizations

This chapter has laid out a series of drivers for Fast IT, alongside both historical and emerging challenges preventing successful transformation of today's IT organizations. It has also reestablished the fundamental purpose and obligations of the IT organization to the parent enterprise and contrasted these considerations with the culture present across many of today's IT organizations. Now it is time to explore how the transition to an end-to-end Services organization or ITaaSO can help today's IT organizations address these challenges and lay the foundation for Fast IT. Chapter 2 presents an overview of the ITaaS framework, and in doing so further details how it resolves these challenges and support the purpose and obligations of IT to the business.

One of the most important topics to acknowledge first, however, is that the answer to these challenges for becoming a Fast IT organization does not involve the adoption of a new technical tool or platform. I want to be clear on this point: *today's IT organizations have all the technology they need to function as Fast IT organizations.* IoT-ready sensors, control devices, even wearables are widely available, proven, and often inexpensive. Scalable cross-platform development frameworks allow teams to quickly build and deploy tools across corporate computing devices, smartphones, and tablets in parallel. Fully programmable infrastructures allow for rapid adaptability and agility in historically complex and difficult-to-change infrastructures. The tools for Fast IT are ready, proven, and available. We just don't know what to do with them all or how to align them to the support of business outcomes.

Continuing to operate and invest in technology provides value to the enterprise business only when it improves the support of business outcomes. In fact, committing major investments before resolving this linkage can actually make any disconnect between IT and business and the perceived inefficiencies of the IT organization that much more visible. That's where the designation of IT Services end-to-end comes in.

Services provide an organization the opportunity to link business outcomes to different elements of their operations.

Consider the basic concept of a Service and the value of leveraging it. Services are nothing more than a logical construct, but they provide the benefit of establishing a zone of management. Designation of a Service allows an organization to frame a group of related customer requirements into a single area and then provide dedicated support for the delivery of those requirements. The Service can additionally cater specifically to the priorities, concerns, and opportunities of the associated customer base. Establishing a Service creates a center of leverage for delivery teams to manage the customer experience and value to the business that simply would not exist otherwise.

Contrary to popular belief, there is a great deal of flexibility in how a Service is defined and structured. Different Service design philosophies determine the capabilities and outcomes that a Service can support.

While designation of individual Services can benefit select customers, addressing the challenges highlighted in this chapter requires moving an organization to an end-to-end Services framework. Doing so requires first that the organization understand all of the capabilities and outcomes it's operations are required to deliver to the enterprise business, and then designate a complete set of Services to facilitate these requirements. Next, the organization associates all of its assets and resources to one or more of those designated Services. Note that this does not mean that existing organizational structures or the ownership of assets or budgets is changed—simply that a second, parallel view of the organization is established with these elements aligned to Services. This Services-based view of an organization establishes a clear link between the assets and resources and the Services understood to be delivering required capabilities and outcomes for the enterprise business. For example, Service costing creates a parallel view of an organization's budget distributed across all designated Services, allowing each cost element to be associated with delivery of a required Service.

For enterprise IT organizations, designation of an IT Service establishes a logical connection between the capabilities required by a customer to facilitate business outcomes, through a Service delivered by IT, then all the way down through application, network, and compute stacks and even the resources operating those assets. Once IT Services have been established, Service delivery teams can focus on understanding the customer perspective of value, and develop strategies to measure Service performance that resonate with customers. These same teams can now understand and manage the total costs of delivering a Service, such as optimizing operational costs or leveraging investments to drive Service value. Service delivery teams can now advocate for their Service across different IT functional teams, processes, and budgets, rather than allowing these things to constrain the support of business outcomes.

The operation of IT as an end-to-end Services organization, or an ITaaSO, focuses on three things:

- Business-value-driven (prioritizes support of business outcomes)

- Customer-centric (prioritizes customer satisfaction)

- Efficient operations

Initiating a Services Transformation and driving support across these focus areas, in turn, initiates the cultural shift of the IT organization. With the proper strategy and support from senior leadership, this cultural shift can be fostered and sustained over-time.

While the value outcomes of Services Transformation are many, three strategic value outcomes are associated with the adoption of Cisco's ITaaS framework that are commonly referenced:

- Establishing the IT organization as a trusted advisor to the enterprise business

- Implementing a series of mechanisms, including strategic levers for facilitating desired outcomes, that allow the IT organization to be operated as a relevant, agile, cost-effective, and highly competitive "business within a business"

- Initiates and sustains a cultural shift across the IT organization

The pursuit of these strategic outcomes is referenced regularly throughout the book, but I should stress that simply completing the activities in Cisco's Services Transformation Program does not guarantee these outcomes. While doing so means that all the core strategies for the framework are now operational, they will have to be optimized. It also relies on the underlying shift in the culture of the IT organization to be effectively leveraged in a manner that will support these outcomes, which will take time. The key is that the transformation will have been initiated.

Behind the Scenes of the Cisco IT Services Transformation

The ITaaS framework is based closely on the work pioneered in previous years by innovative leaders in Cisco IT. These industry thought-leaders developed, then implemented and refined over time, a completely new approach to IT Service delivery. This approach differed significantly from many emerging standards of the time but has now proven itself capable of addressing the historical and emerging challenges facing today's IT organizations and supporting Fast IT. Because they were the first, there was no well-tested framework or program to follow, no established image of success to look to. This also means the story of Cisco IT's Services Transformation is one filled with many great stories, lessons learned, and insightful knowledge from looking back across the transformation.

Similar to the "Diary of an ITaaS Consultant" feature found throughout chapters of this book, the goal of this feature is to provide an additional source of knowledge gleaned from real-world, practical experiences in hopes that it might allow these complex topics to better resonate with you. The material shared in this feature was primarily derived from a range of interviews held with various Cisco IT leaders, and conveys their direct experience, feedback, and opinions on key topics at times presented in a free flow of statements. In truth, these sections represent only a fraction of the many thought-leaders and the extensive knowledge available from Cisco IT, and I encourage you to leverage the multitudes of additional information available relating the incredible insights of this transformation.

Prior to establishing itself as one of the industry's earliest Fast IT organizations, Cisco IT, like many of today's enterprise IT organizations, originally thought of itself as a technology organization. It focused on the adoption and operation of technology rather than on supporting business outcomes. Instead of working to understand the customer requirements, customer experience, or ideal level of adoption, teams were instead focused on the latest hardware or software release. Cisco IT considered CCIE's and industry certifications to represent the value created by a resource instead of focusing on the value a person created in support of business outcomes.

These common challenges for IT organizations were amplified by the explosive growth of Cisco as a business with regular acquisitions, and entries to new markets driving constant requirements for new capabilities, and a widespread proliferation of applications resulting from a client-funded model. This model meant that different functional groups, or business units, funded by the business would engage Cisco IT for support in a manner one leader described as "Here is my money, here is what I need, here is what I want you to do." This model reinforced an order-taker mindset and a servant-oriented organization versus a Service-oriented organization. As a result, there were a lot of disparate apps and lot of heavy lifting from Cisco IT, even while many of these apps duplicated the capabilities of one another.

Cisco IT began its transformation in much the same manner many enterprise IT organizations will—by realizing that this mix of historical and emerging challenges had to be resolved and that doing so would require a complete transformation of the IT organization. It needed to put a stake in the ground. It had to reposition itself as a Service Provider to the company. Whether it was how Cisco IT funded programs, interacted with clients, or architected Services—it needed to be thought about differently.

The transformation was initiated with a strategic vision from the full Cisco IT leadership team for the IT organization to become two things: architecturally led and Services everything. *Everything that Cisco IT did going forward would be within the context of delivering a Service and would align to an architecture roadmap.* While the messaging was fine, Cisco IT leaders quickly realized that the strategy would require more than simply new processes and tools, and would rely on a fundamental transformation of the culture of the IT organization. Not just the culture within IT, but the overarching culture of priorities and how IT interacted with the business. IT needed to prove it was capable of more than just reacting to outages, and that it could be more proactive and be tied to the value drivers of the company. For Cisco IT, this also meant centralizing the IT organization and moving away from the decentralized teams funded directly by separate functions that drove significant levels of duplication and an order-taker mindset.

Services were identified as the opportunity to align to the requirements of the business, understand the business value delivered by a Service, and transform the customer experience. Cisco IT leaders viewed a transition to an end-to-end Services model as the foundation for addressing the many challenges they faced, which could then support additional practices enabling Fast IT. Services as a foundation stands in contrast to many philosophies for Fast IT that have become overly focused on transitioning everything to the cloud.

As one Cisco IT leader described it, "A lot of people think that Fast IT is only about moving things to the cloud. The problem with that is if you haven't truly defined your Service, then you likely have not aligned to the requirements, performance, and costs requirements of the customer. If you don't do that first, then what you end up doing is sort of just lifting and shifting your stuff over, and you really never solve the real issue of delivering business value and driving customer experience." This led to fundamental changes in how Services were aligned, measured, costed, and supported by the underlying organization and processes. Once Cisco IT began to truly understand the foundational value of the capabilities they were delivering to their customer through Services, it was then able to simplify, automate, and optimize from the top of the stack at the application level to the bottom-of-the-stack platforms and infrastructures.

One person described the moment that the concept of a Services organization clicked for him. During a worldwide IT management offsite workshop, a presenter highlighted the mindset of operating as a competitive Services organization by comparing Cisco IT as an organization to a rapidly growing company providing enterprise capabilities through a cloud Service. At the time this company was valued at around $1.5 billion, while the budget Cisco IT was attempting to centralize and manage was multiple times larger. He stated, "Now, don't you think they know how many customers they have? Do you know when they upgrade? When there is a glitch in the customer experience! Don't you think they know how often a customer uses their Service? Don't you think they know what everyone pays to access similar offerings from competitors? Now think about us; do we know these things? We as an organization have customers and an obligation to provide competitive value Services just like they do, and we are several times larger than this company—but we can't even begin to answer these questions. That's why we need to become an end-to-end Services organization."

Considerations for Services Transformation

Before progressing further, it is important that we acknowledge several fundamental considerations for Services Transformation and the successful adoption of Cisco's ITaaS framework. While many of these topics are explored in greater detail throughout later chapters, I felt it best to highlight key considerations for you early on.

Adoption of the ITaaS framework does not require a reorganization of the IT organization's designated teams or departments. The framework is organizationally agnostic. The only consideration I would highlight regarding organizational structure is the recommendation for a single, centralized organization. De-centralized IT presents many challenges, especially wide scale duplication, and any perceived value even for quasi-decentralized organizational structures will be achieved by the transition to an end-to-end Services organization.

You should anticipate that Cisco's ITaaS framework will introduce new concepts for IT Service delivery, in particular a set of strategies for measuring and reporting the value of IT Services. You should also anticipate that realizing the value outcomes associated with the ITaaS framework will require teams to revisit previously established strategies, processes, and tools for Service delivery such as Service portfolios, catalogs, and more. Upcoming chapters lay out detailed justification for revisiting these established concepts, and highlight how the new approach enables greater value potential.

You should also expect to find surprises regularly throughout the ITaaS framework, whether it is Cisco's unique approach to Service definition and design, or the priorities for Service delivery needed to prioritize customer satisfaction. Whenever this occurs, first keep an open mind and then continue reading, because each chapter strives to always justify the purpose and goals for a given topic and the justification for its design and use within the framework. Next, remember that the ITaaS framework was developed to facilitate IT Service delivery for future Fast IT organizations, and the culture and mindset of IT professionals who support those organizations, so there will obviously be conflicts in the approach to Service delivery that you are accustomed to today. Finally, remember to consider the many concepts highlighted in this chapter. Reminding yourself of the goals of an enterprise business, the purpose and obligations of the IT organization, and the culture required to support an ITaaSO will help to rationalize the direction that the ITaaS framework takes for IT Service delivery.

Transitioning to an ITaaSO will impact more than just the strategies and tools for Service delivery. It will require many aspects of the IT operating model that are not today to become "Services-aware." This means updating various IT processes, tools, and especially reporting to reflect Services, for example adding a Services field to map reporting information to Services. Consider how IT can truly become an end-to-end Services organization or ITaaSO if the majority of it's operations are completely unaware of Services? Chapter 11, "Completing the Services Transformation," provides full details on the steps and considerations for ensuring all required aspects of the IT operating model become Services-aware.

This chapter has already stressed the importance of fostering a shift in the culture of the IT organization to a successful Services Transformation, and this approach continues to be highlighted throughout practically every chapter of this book. Always remember that the ITaaS framework and its Services Transformation Program act to initiate this cultural shift, but equally rely on this cultural transition for its successful adoption and ability to create value for the enterprise. The two are irrevocably linked.

Even without consideration for the need to foster a cultural shift in becoming an ITaaSO, a Services Transformation is a lengthy and complex initiative. The Services Transformation Program can be expected to last from 16 to 24 months for most IT organizations, and require broad engagement across the IT organization as well as quite often across the enterprise business. Note that Cisco's Services Transformation Program was designed to deliver incremental value, so the IT organization and enterprise business will realize value outcomes throughout the program rather than only at completion.

The length and complexity of Services Transformation, along with many other reasons that are explored in Chapter 3, "Change Leadership and Ensuring a Successful Transformation," require that the program be supported by the CIO and senior IT leaders. There simply is no chance for realizing the intended value outcomes of Services Transformation without the complete backing of the IT organization's most senior leaders.

Finally, remember that transitioning to an end-to-end Services organization is not the final step for enterprise IT organizations; it is only the foundation to support Fast IT. While the ITaaS framework can establish the IT organization as a trusted advisor to the enterprise business, Fast IT can solidify enterprise IT organizations as a "transformative enabler" of the business.

Summary

Enterprise businesses have to embrace digitization to be successful in tomorrow's marketplaces. The growth of enterprise digitization, and the risk of digital disruption, mean that enterprise businesses will rely more than ever on technology to operate and achieve business outcomes. IT Transformation to Fast IT is required for today's enterprise IT organizations to remain relevant to the enterprise business, accelerate digitization, and quickly navigate instances of digital disruption. Cisco considers the transition to an architecture-led, end-to-end Services organization to be the foundation for Fast IT, and the ITaaS framework is a proven model for transitioning IT to a Services organization (ITaaSO).

Enterprise IT organizations face historical and emerging challenges impeding transformation. Many IT organizations only designate Services reflecting a segment of the capabilities they deliver, and have no strategy for measuring the business value of those Services, the performance of the Service from the perspective of the customer, or the total costs to support business outcomes.

The fundamental purpose of an enterprise IT organization is to deliver technical capabilities required for enterprise productivity and to enable the execution of business processes. IT shares two fundamental obligations to the enterprise business with all other enterprise organizations: the support of business outcomes and efficient operation. The underlying culture of today's IT organizations is often not aligned to the purpose and obligations of IT, and a cultural shift will need to be initiated and fostered alongside the transition to an ITaaSO.

The ITaaS framework, and associated Services Transformation Program, was designed to transition an IT organization to an end-to-end Services organization (ITaaSO) and achieve three strategic value outcomes:

- Establishing the IT organization as a trusted advisor to the enterprise business

- Implementing a series of mechanisms, including strategic levers for facilitating desired outcomes, that allow the IT organization to be operated as a relevant, agile, cost-effective, and highly competitive "business within a business"

- Initiates and sustains a cultural shift across the IT organization.

Chapter 2

Introducing Cisco ITaaS Framework and Services Transformation Program

The adoption of Cisco's ITaaS framework allows today's IT organizations to transition to an end-to-end Services organization while initiating and sustaining a cultural shift, and establish a foundation for Fast IT. In this chapter we will introduce the ITaaS framework and the elements that allow it to support these value outcomes.

First, we briefly review IT operating models and a series of major functions common to all IT organizations. This includes an explanation of the Service delivery function and its components, along with how it interacts with other common IT functions such as IT technical operations and enterprise architecture practices.

With the Service delivery function clearly established, we introduce the ITaaS framework and review its foundational components, key strategies, and how they support the intended outcomes for Services Transformation. We also justify the adoption of the "as a Service" label to a framework for enterprise-wide IT Service delivery and examine how Services in the ITaaS framework create a layer of abstraction and simplification capable of transforming the customer experience. The goal is to provide you with an overview of the framework, before expanding on each of the topics in full detail in subsequent chapters.

Finally, while a framework for IT Service delivery may create significant value in theory, it is in fact completely useless unless it can be successfully adopted and put into practice by real-world IT organizations of different sizes and across different industries. With this in mind, Cisco's ITaaS framework is paired with a Services Transformation Program, a proven progression of work packages and activities capable of guiding an IT organization's adoption of the framework and ensuring that the value outcomes for Services Transformation are realized.

IT Operating Models

Before we introduce Cisco's ITaaS framework, it is important that you have a high-level grasp of IT operating models and how a framework for IT Service delivery complements other major functions of an IT organization. The goal here is not to recommend or review any particular IT operating model in depth, but we do recommend that you explore common standards for operating models in place today. By looking at legacy IT operating models and considering the drivers and challenges for IT Transformation outlined in Chapter 1, "The Case for IT Transformation and IT as a Service (ITaaS)," you are able to further appreciate why the ITaaS framework is so effective at achieving its intended outcomes for the IT organization and enterprise business and how it builds a foundation for future operating models tuned to enable Fast IT.

An IT operating model is a logical representation of how an IT organization operates, typically providing an informative, high-level, graphical overview of the many hundreds of functions and processes the IT organization conducts on a daily basis. There are numerous IT operating models in existence today, and they can vary in complexity from demonstrating only the most significant functions of the organization to highlighting various key strategies and processes that IT leaders are seeking to emphasize. They may include segments for governance, organization, and management of resources or project lifecycle management.

All IT operating models, however, have common components, and we can designate three major functions shared by all enterprise IT organizations:

- **IT Technical Operations:** A broad set of standards, practices, and processes informing the day-to-day operation of technical platforms and architectures that enable IT Services, including processes for change control and incident and problem management.

- **IT Service Delivery:** A set of frameworks, processes, and tools that support and inform the design, delivery, and management of technical capabilities in the form of IT Services delivered by the IT organization. Cisco's ITaaS framework also introduces a strategy for measuring and communicating the value of IT Services to the enterprise business.

- **Enterprise Architecture:** The standards and methodologies for developing and then managing architecture models capable of illustrating the alignment of technical architectures to business operations and strategies, including the processes for leveraging these models for investment prioritization, acquisition planning, and other strategic decision making.

Figure 2-1 illustrates some of the many components, processes, and tools associated within each of these functions. Note that some are already well known, whereas others, especially within the IT Service delivery domain, are introduced or revisited as part of Cisco's ITaaS framework.

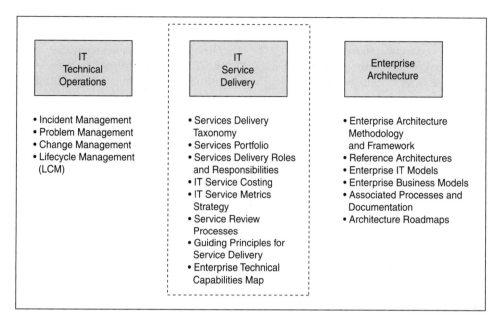

Figure 2-1 *Common IT Operation Functions*

I've adopted this approach to distinguishing between the major functions of an enterprise IT organization for several reasons. The first is that it establishes a unique purpose and intended outcomes for each domain, and also creates discernable boundaries for each, along with logical intersection points. The primary reason, however, is that it allows an IT organization to apply a much-needed focus on how it designs and delivers IT Services independent of how it operates technical platforms, in contrast to many standards today that often combine IT operations and IT Service delivery into a single function commonly referred to as IT Service management.

These IT Service management standards are popular and commonly familiar to many IT professionals. They have introduced practices for technical operations that have led to significant improvements in the management of complex infrastructures. These standards have also introduced now-common concepts for IT Service delivery, such as Service portfolios and catalogs, and in doing so have introduced foundational Service delivery concepts to the IT industry. By focusing on IT Service delivery as a unique function of the IT organization, we can better understand where historical practices for the design and delivery of IT Services can be improved, and in doing so hopefully resolve many of the numerous challenges facing IT organizations today and prepare them for IT Transformation and Fast IT. This is why Cisco's ITaaS framework revisits a number of historical concepts for IT Service design and delivery, while also introducing completely new strategies, such as those with a goal of measuring and communicating IT Service value.

The upcoming sections expand on each of these major functions of an IT organization's operations. We also look at their purpose and outcomes along with how they link to and augment one another in support of the goals of the IT organization in providing value capabilities to the enterprise. Finally, Chapter 12, "Fast IT—The Mandatory Future for Enterprise IT Organizations," provides another view of how these functions, once matured and actively complementing one another, must evolve further in support of enabling a Fast IT organization.

IT Technical Operations

The IT technical operations function focuses on best practices, tools, and processes for ensuring the stability and availability of technical architectures across an enterprise. The function ensures that changes can be safely conducted in a complex environment without impact. It also ensures that when impact does occur, the incident and problems are managed effectively and that steps are taken to safeguard from impact in the future. In other words, this domain of an IT operating model focuses on the operation and management of technical platforms and infrastructures that enable technical capabilities, which are then delivered and managed by IT Services.

Note that an enterprise IT organization must first achieve and then maintain a high level of maturity within the technical operations domain before the benefits of a Services Transformation can hope to be realized. Put simply, you can't make a case for the value delivery of IT Services required by the business if the various technical platforms they rely on are constantly unavailable or unusable due to performance issues or outages.

Fortunately, most enterprise IT organizations today are already well on their way to becoming highly mature technical operations thanks in no small part to numerous industry standards and practices that have emerged over the past decade. These standards have led to proven strategies for change control, lifecycle management, and incident and problem management becoming common across many IT organizations and enabling increased stability across the many complex technical platforms and architectures found in today's enterprises.

The purpose of the technical operations function of an IT organization is to manage and operate technical infrastructures effectively and efficiently, with a goal of ensuring that technical capabilities delivered by IT Services are available and perform according to their unique requirements. The outcome of performing this function successfully is the facilitation of requirements on behalf of IT Services, the IT organization, and the broader enterprise business.

Input and requirements for the IT operations function are provided by IT leaders and especially from IT Services, which directly convey the requirements of IT customers for capabilities. These capabilities must then be translated to the operation of the underlying technologies and infrastructures. This is an important consideration because many IT organizations historically set requirements for IT operations with only limited input from the customer base, and have tended to focus on adopting technology and platform-specific SLAs that were simply common across the industry. Within the ITaaS framework, Service Owners and Service Executives act as an extended community of IT leaders who advocate for their Service across the IT organization and especially the technical operations function. Likewise, this function of the IT organization is also expected to provide a great deal of information back to the Service delivery function in support of measuring and reporting IT Service performance. Achieving high levels of interaction between these functions is key to successful Service delivery, thus building trust with IT's customers over time, and provides a foundation for much sought-after Fast IT strategies like continuous delivery and Dev/Ops/Sec.

IT Service Delivery

The IT Service delivery function of an IT organization is focused on the design, delivery, and management of IT Services across the enterprise. Cisco's ITaaS framework is entirely focused on this domain of an IT operating model, and does not include recommendations for strategies, processes, or tools associated with technical operations or enterprise architecture. However, it does provide extensive consideration to the interoperation and exchange of information with these functions.

Unlike technical operations, it may be challenging to quickly identify a purpose, goal, and outcome of the Service delivery function of an IT organization's operating model. The reason is that although you may be familiar with popular tools associated with Service delivery, such as Service portfolios and catalogs, it has never received a great deal of focus from many IT organizations or IT leaders. If the IT organization hopes to establish itself as a trusted advisor to the enterprise business, however, this domain of an IT operating model needs to be completely reevaluated from the ground up and given top priority by IT leaders going forward.

Consider for a moment that the strategy for IT Service delivery ultimately determines how enterprise customers view the IT organization. An IT organization's strategy for IT Service delivery makes up the overwhelming majority of its interaction with its customer base, and as such, no other function of the IT organization will have so significant an impact on how IT and the Services that it provides are perceived. Strategies for Service delivery shape the customer experience, and provide a vehicle for demonstrating value and driving increasing levels of customer satisfaction. This interaction is illustrated in Figure 2-2.

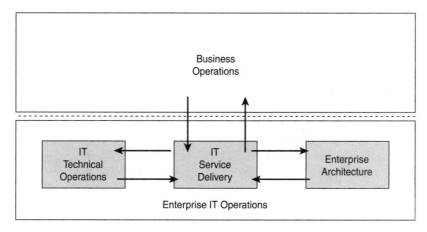

Figure 2-2 *IT Service Delivery Interactions*

The purpose of the Service delivery function is to designate and manage IT Services associated with the delivery of technical capabilities end-to-end across the enterprise with a goal of driving continuous value for the IT organization and enterprise business.

This means that the IT Service delivery function encompasses the strategies, processes, and tools that primarily support the delivery and management of Services. To date, this has entailed the development of IT Service portfolios, catalogs, and even the provisioning and management of e-stores. Cisco's ITaaS framework retains all these elements but reexamines the purpose and value of each and, in some cases, adopts a new approach to these existing processes and tools. At the same time, the ITaaS framework introduces new elements to the design and management of IT Services, such as the IT Service taxonomy, which establishes a multilevel hierarchy for the strategic management of the Service landscape and making a set of strategic levers available to IT leaders for use in facilitating desired outcomes.

One of the most significant contributions to this function made by Cisco's ITaaS framework is a complete strategy for developing an understanding of the value the Service delivers to the enterprise, and then communicating and refining that value assessment with customer stakeholders. Cisco defines Service value as a consideration of the total costs of delivering a Service at a desired level of performance, weighed against the impact of that Service on business outcomes. From this definition in value, you may correctly infer that the ITaaS framework includes strategies for Service performance and modeling the total costs of Service delivery, but it also includes a strategy for communicating IT Service value. This is accomplished through structured, formal conversations called Service Reviews, led by IT Service Owners who understand the operations, concerns, and priorities of the business stakeholders.

While strategies such as these for the measurement and communication of Service value introduced in Cisco's ITaaS framework are not yet common across today's IT organizations, the reality is that without them, the value an IT Service provides and its impact on business outcomes is left to question; and unlikely to ever be clearly understood by either the IT organization or business teams. In effect, this means that many enterprise companies today have a strategic blind spot; after all, virtually any decision regarding the delivery of technical capabilities without a clear understanding of the value it provides to supporting business outcomes is simply guesswork at best. This is why Cisco's view is that a framework for enterprise IT Service delivery simply isn't complete without a proper strategy and supporting tools and mechanisms for facilitating the ongoing communications of Service value between IT and business.

The Service delivery function interacts with many different elements of an IT operating model, including the other two major functions common to IT organizations. For IT technical operations, this information exchange involves Service delivery passing requirements for availability and performance to the operations function, and also relying on significant levels of information from the operations function to report on IT Service performance. Enterprise architecture practices are likely to contribute valuable information during the initial design of IT Services, and then provide critical prioritization and oversight for the introduction of new Service capabilities. This ensures they align to the enterprise business plan and do not duplicate capabilities already available elsewhere.

From the Service delivery function side, the Services Transformation Program associated with Cisco's ITaaS framework includes development of an Enterprise Technical Capabilities (ETC) map as a critical input for Service design. This, along with the resulting Services portfolio, can inform or even link directly to elements of the EA model. From there, IT Services act at a tactical level to plan future Service capability requirements and, when possible, respond in an agile manner to opportunities for the introduction of transformative capabilities. The Service delivery function must share these rapidly evolving capabilities with the EA practice to ensure that duplication of capabilities does not occur.

While the Service delivery function has historically received less focus than other domains in IT operating models or even been grouped with technical operations, Cisco's ITaaS framework isolates and prioritizes this function, revisiting existing elements and introducing a number of new strategies. Remember that how an IT organization approaches and prioritizes a framework for Service delivery within its operating model will have a significant impact on the customer experience and will act as either a bridge or barrier between the IT organization and the enterprise business.

Enterprise Architecture

Fast IT requires an architecture-led, end-to-end Services organization as its foundation. While a detailed introduction to enterprise architecture is far beyond the scope of this book, it is still important to understand the purpose of this critical practice and how it differs from and augments the Service delivery function of an enterprise IT organization.

Enterprise architecture methodologies grew in popularity in response to the widening disconnect between IT organizations and the priorities of the enterprise business they were meant to support. The goal was to establish a practice within the enterprise that could link technical architectures to the operations and evolving strategies and priorities of the enterprise business.

Imagine for a moment that you have in front of you a three-dimensional model of the enterprise business with multiple levels, almost like a model of a building. The topmost level of this model illustrates the core elements of the enterprise business, such as the value chain, products, and Services that the enterprise produces; various customers and markets it participates in; and also the organization of resources across the enterprise. It also models the relations between each of these elements. At the bottommost level of the model is a representation of the different technical architectures that the IT organization manages. The level above this models how these various technical architectures work together to enable complex systems and platforms that enable specific technical capabilities and perhaps how these technical capabilities are organized into IT Services. From there, links are made to specific business processes in the next level up, which are then associated with major functions, operations, and even projects across the business, with many of these elements finally linked back to elements in the topmost level of the model.

With an asset such as this, you could ensure that the technical architectures deployed today are ultimately required to support business functions on an ongoing basis. Proposed business strategies could be fed into the business level of the model allowing business and IT to proactively ensure the required components are in place at each level to support the business strategy throughout every section of the model. This, in turn, helps drive better investment planning, ensuring prioritized support for those projects and initiatives that are closely tied to formal business strategies. All of this can be achieved only if the models are complete and accurate, which is a complex effort and requires extensive support from both IT and enterprise business teams.

The purpose of enterprise architecture practices is to develop and maintain these models and then leverage them to conduct informed technology and business planning. EA practices enable the IT organization and business leaders to prioritize investments and evaluate the readiness of technical platforms to support new business strategies. Highly matured EA practices can even be leveraged to conduct predictive modeling exercises in support of acquisition planning.

Service Architecture and Enterprise Architecture

Being architecture-led still allows flexibility for individual Services to evolve quickly with the needs of the customer base, but requires all Services to follow an overarching strategic architecture roadmap. Service architectures are a part of the broader enterprise architecture, but functioning at a different level and likely different pace.

As an analogy, consider the difference in citywide planning and that of individual city zones such as neighborhoods and business centers. Retaining the planning and execution for development of these individual zones at the city planning level only constrains the pace at which required changes can be made while also distracting from the core citywide planning activities. At the same time, the development of individual city zones must always adhere to the broader citywide plan, and realize they are dependent at times on major infrastructure projects and expansions for their own success.

This same dynamic plays out with enterprise architecture (citywide planning) and Service architecture (zone-level planning). The goal is to allow Services to evolve with customer requirements, while always aligning to and prioritizing investments against a broader enterprise architecture. This allows IT Services to keep pace with customer requirements for digitization and transformative capabilities. At the same time, we must recognize that moving too quickly or broadly at the Service level can risk duplication of resources and assets and eventually even large-scale divergence from the highest-level enterprise planning, priorities, and strategies.

After the ITaaS framework is in place, IT Services are designated end-to-end, allowing the overarching enterprise architecture roadmap to drive specific areas of individual Services, even while allowing Service architecture to evolve at its own pace so long as it supports the EA roadmap. Chapter 7, "Service Delivery Roles and Responsibilities," introduces the role of Service Architects and further discusses this topic. These roles act as a key bridge between these EA and Service delivery domains and partner with the Service Owner on development and management of Service capability roadmaps detailed in Chapter 5,

"Mapping Enterprise Technical Capability Requirements," and the linkage of each through Service architecture to a broader enterprise architecture strategy.

Behind the Scenes of the Cisco IT Services Transformation

The shift to Cisco IT being architecturally led began in earnest when a line was drawn, establishing that all funding would require architecture approval going forward. Cisco IT had previously been funded by siloed functional teams. The shift to Architecture-led investment planning meant that the roadmap and associated programs, or bundles, were approved instead of one-off investments. Numerous Cisco leaders regularly emphasize that it wasn't until we had EA-defined bundles and (architecture) roadmaps that the funding model started to really work.

As one Cisco IT leader put it, "It's not until you put the money behind it that behavior starts to change."

Making Capabilities Available "as a Service"

You may be wondering why a framework for the design and delivery of IT Services across an enterprise business was designated by a label most commonly associated with various cloud platforms. In truth, the "as a Service" label has led to some confusion in the past regarding exactly what ITaaS is. With this in mind, it warrants a quick examination of the "aaS" label and why its association with Cisco's framework for Service delivery is actually quite fitting.

Over the past decade, "as a Service" has become a popular label most commonly associated with platforms and capabilities made available through cloud architectures and the introduction and growth of virtualization technologies. Virtualization introduces a layer of abstraction between hardware and software, removing complex historical dependencies between these two levels that drastically simplifies the operation of the systems. Advances in data center and network technologies, along with solutions for orchestration and management of these environments, complemented the now-virtualized infrastructures and resulted in a wide range of core technical capabilities capable of being provisioned, scaled, and managed at levels previously unheard of.

This led to the complete transformation of the customer experience for consuming these core technical capabilities because they could now be delivered using models that were subscription-based and could be scaled on demand, along with a host of other benefits. "As a Service" became the term associated with this new approach to delivering these capabilities, and the label quickly reached a point of automatically attributing a well-known set of advantages to the delivery of technical capabilities for any platform it was applied to:

- Subscription-based access to technical capabilities that could scale on demand.

- Rapid provisioning and delivery of required capabilities in a fraction of the previous time.

■ Consumption-based cost models that allowed customers to pay only for what is consumed, with overhead spread over a much larger consumer base.

■ High volumes of meaningful data and metrics available to both IT and customers allowed for informed decision making and right-sizing of environments.

■ Highly efficient use of underlying infrastructure resources operated to deliver the capabilities.

■ Greatly increased ease of management.

The customer experience associated with capabilities associated with the "as a Service" label was transformed. Customers were now able to quickly access the capabilities they needed with little-to-no hassle, understand the associated costs, and receive enough information to confirm the value of the Service they were consuming. The key consideration is that "as a Service," or aaS, is now a well-recognized and popular label that implies the delivery of capabilities in a way that provides a number of benefits for both the customer and Service provider, with a significant emphasis on transforming the customer experience.

The goal of Cisco's ITaaS framework is to deliver IT Services end-to-end, achieving the simplification and benefits associated with "as a Service" models for delivery of capabilities. An upcoming section will examine how Cisco's approach to IT Service design focuses delivery on capabilities required by the customer and establishes a Service as a layer of abstraction and simplification between the customer and complexities of the IT organization. The combination of IT Services as a layer of simplification, along with other strategies for Service delivery and understanding the value of those Services introduced by the ITaaS framework, acts to create the same highly sought-after customer experience historically associated with technical capabilities delivered from the Cloud; hence the name.

Introducing Cisco IT as a Service Framework

The purpose of Cisco's ITaaS framework is to provide IT organizations with a proven, real-world framework for moving to an end-to-end Services organization, or ITaaSO, alongside strategies for understanding the value those Services create for the enterprise business. The goal of this framework is to establish the IT organization as a trusted advisor to the enterprise business, enable mechanisms allowing the IT organization to be managed like a competitive "business within a business," and foster a shift in the culture of the IT organization to one focused on supporting business outcomes and driving customer satisfaction.

Figure 2-3 provides a graphical representation of the ITaaS framework and its core strategies and components. I developed this as a means of quickly introducing the framework and presenting its key aspects, often quickly drawing it on whiteboards as an architectural structure with a foundation and pillars supporting a pinnacle.

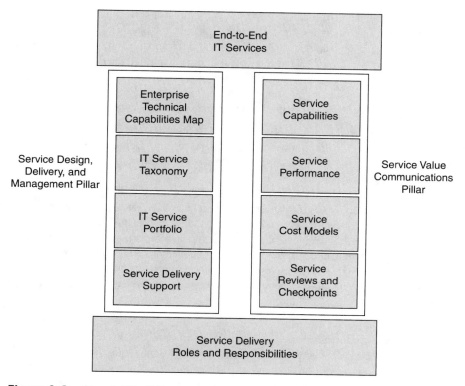

Figure 2-3   *Cisco's ITaaS Framework*

As expected, Services represent the pinnacle of our framework, the topmost level that delivers technical capabilities up to IT's customer base to facilitate productivity and enable business outcomes. Although a great deal of focus is paid to the design and delivery of IT Services, it is important that any introduction of the ITaaS framework begin with its foundation.

Cisco's ITaaS framework is built on a foundation of people. It establishes a set of Service delivery roles and functions carried out by a community of IT resources responsible for facilitating Service Delivery across the Enterprise. The goal of Service Delivery roles is to distribute accountability for efficiency and the creation of business value across a broad community of resources. This same community of resources will also share in the responsibility for managing risk and security end-to-end. This foundation of people will also act to initiate and sustain the cultural shift of the IT organization, required for achieving the value outcomes of a Services Transformation and eventual transition to Fast IT.

Moving up from the foundation, the ITaaS framework is supported by two key strategies, or pillars, that support IT Service delivery and the goals of the framework. The first pillar—the Service Design, Delivery, and Management strategy—ensures the continual alignment of

Services to the requirements of the business through the Enterprise Technical Capabilities map and other tools and processes. Next, it enables the strategic management of the entire Services landscape through a unique approach to the Service portfolio and the introduction of a Service taxonomy. It also includes processes and tools that guide the delivery and availability of Services through a unique approach to Service catalog design and recommendations for customer portals such as corporate e-stores. This strategy also considers the need for the many operations of the IT organization to become Services-aware.

The second pillar and strategy is unique to Cisco's ITaaS framework and introduces a set of building blocks critical to understanding IT Service value from the customer's perspective, and measuring and managing that value over time. It also ensures that the value of IT Services is communicated effectively. As discussed in Chapter 1, IT organizations regularly deliver significant value to the enterprise business, but IT has historically struggled to qualify value for Services in a way that resonates with their customers, which is the focus of most of the building blocks in this pillar. Once a view of IT Service value has been established, however, it is important that the initial view of value be communicated and then refined in partnership with senior customer stakeholders. That is why this strategy also establishes and provides a structure for regular three-party conversations between Service Owners, IT leaders, and business leaders to review IT Service value and plan future requirements.

Note that these are only the most significant building blocks of the framework and that there are numerous supporting strategies, processes, and tools that make up each and need to be adopted and leveraged successfully to realize the value outcomes of the ITaaS framework. The following sections expand on each of these components of the framework further—enough to provide a reference-level overview—while later chapters delve into the complete details of each and provide best practices for adopting them in real-world IT organizations.

Service Delivery Roles and Responsibilities

The ITaaS framework relies on people, rather than processes or tools, to act as the foundation for fulfilling the obligations of the IT organization to the enterprise business through the delivery and management of valued Services. It does so by establishing a set of Service delivery roles, each with a unique set of responsibilities and accountability for supporting different aspects of the ITaaS framework. Chapter 7 provides complete details on each of these roles and their responsibilities, along with guidance for identifying the best candidates. Brief descriptions of each are shown here:

- **Service Owner:** Responsible for the end-to-end delivery and efficient management of a Service; solely accountable for the value the Service provides to the enterprise business.

- **Service Executive:** Responsible for supporting executive-level business relationships and providing a strategic level of oversight, planning, and strategy for a set of related IT Services. They are additionally accountable for facilitating target outcomes across the Service group as directed by the CIO or customer stakeholders.

- **Service Architect:** Responsible for the end-to-end architecture of a Service or Service group and the alignment of that Service architecture to the broader enterprise architecture, planning and development of Service strategy alongside the Service Owner, and accountable for enabling systemic Service capabilities as directed by the Service Owner.

- **Service Offering Manager:** Sometimes referred to as Service managers, responsible for supporting a Service Owner via tactical operation of specific aspects of a Service, commonly aligned to a Service offering, and held accountable for outcomes as directed by the Service Owner.

It is important to note the difference between these roles and formal job definitions. Although this may seem confusing, think of job definitions as a term associated with a level of responsibility, general organizational alignment, and compensation structure related to an individual's position within the enterprise. This is different from a "role," which is an abstraction from a job definition, referring to a logical grouping of tasks and responsibilities. This means that a job can fulfill multiple roles, and also means that a role can be fulfilled by resources assigned different jobs. This allows flexibility in selecting the best resources for fulfilling the responsibilities of a Service delivery role and contributes to the ITaaS framework's capability to be leveraged by any IT organization regardless of its organizational structure; and large-scale reorganizations to be carried out without impacting the Service delivery function.

Another key concept is that ownership of the Service does not imply responsibility for managing and operating the various assets and resources used to make the capabilities delivered by the Service available. Rather, a Service Owner and other Service delivery roles advocate across application owners, system administrators, and support teams to ensure that the requirements for their Service capabilities are achieved on an ongoing basis. The success of this approach obviously requires that the broader IT organization recognize the significance of requests made by Service delivery teams and prioritize them appropriately.

Of the roles defined by the ITaaS framework, Service Owners play the most significant role in Service delivery and forging trusted relationships with business stakeholders. One Service Owner is assigned to every Service defined in the portfolio. The Service Owner is expected to act as the general manager or CEO for that Service in every way, ensuring the Service continues to deliver a value to the customer base while operating efficiently. The Service Owners are responsible for understanding their business customers' goals and priorities along with the specific business outcomes and underlying processes supported by the technical capabilities delivered by the Service. They are additionally responsible for representing and championing the needs of their customers within the IT organization, across potentially multiple technology domains and functional IT teams. In time, they will lead the development and introduction of transformative capabilities. Service Owners leverage the building blocks of the IT Service Value Management pillar of the framework to lead Service Reviews with senior IT and business leaders and will ultimately become the "face" of the transformed IT organization to the enterprise business.

IT Services

Services obviously represent the pinnacle of a framework for Service delivery; they are what the foundation and pillars exist to support. When considering Service delivery it is important for IT organizations to understand how it impacts the customer experience, and how the adoption of the ITaaS framework can fundamentally transform that customer experience. A key goal of the ITaaS framework is to leverage an IT Service as a layer of abstraction between the customers who are consuming the capabilities and the complex technologies that teams, processes, and budgeting cycles use to deliver the Service. In the transition to an end-to-end Services organization, customer engagement takes place through the Services and associated Service delivery teams rather than specific elements of the organization behind the Services. In other words, designating a Service within the ITaaS framework creates a type of beach-head for IT to centralize, manage, and improve the customer experience.

Consider how the customer base interacts with IT Services today. Today's IT organizations recognize the concept of a Service but seldom leverage it as a formal or significant element within the IT operating model. Use of the term often differs wildly across the organization, and it is associated more closely with either a technology domain or a very tactical and specific capability found on a corporate e-store. This means that many of the capabilities delivered by today's IT organizations are not reflected in IT Services, and those Services that are defined are heavily focused on technology rather than the capabilities a technical platform enables. This leaves a given customer base, such as a business unit that relies on a set of technical capabilities to enable its operations, in a situation in which it has to escalate requirements for capabilities across any number of IT teams and resources as illustrated in Figure 2-4.

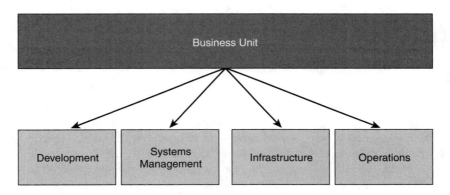

Figure 2-4 *Historical Customer Interaction with IT*

One problem with this approach is that customer requirements are seldom communicated across all the teams that can impact the delivery of a set of capabilities. There is simply no IT function focused on the capabilities rather than the various underlying technologies. Further, each one of these teams is juggling requests from other customer stakeholders and often responds by highlighting the challenges of facilitating the requests across various technologies, processes, and budgets. The customer experience is nothing more than a confusing and frustrating chain of engagements.

The ITaaS framework seeks to transform the customer experience and how IT interacts with its customer base to facilitate their requirements. It begins by first grouping a logical set of technical capabilities into an IT Service and then developing a view of the value delivered by the Service by associating it with a well-rounded view of Service performance and the total costs of delivery. Then it assigns a Service Owner with an understanding of the business unit's operations to facilitate continuous engagement with the customer base, and of who is responsible for working across the IT organization to ensure these requirements are met. The Service is focused on the delivery of capabilities rather than operation of technical platforms, provides a singular interface for customers, manages a view of Service value from their perspective, and removes any need for them to concern themselves with the complexity of the IT organization. This concept is illustrated in Figure 2-5.

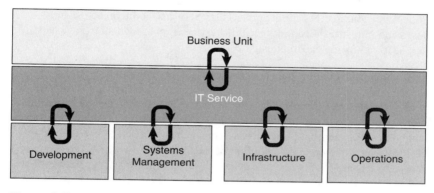

Figure 2-5   *IT Services as an Overlay*

These concepts are expanded on in Chapter 4. Note that these examples refer to the exchange of capability requirements from the customer to a Service Owner and then across the IT organization. Requests for technical support or placing an order for a specific capability would still be conducted through relevant IT customer portals and teams that then provide Service Owners with detailed information on these requests. The key is to understand how the foundation and pillars of the ITaaS framework create an opportunity to fundamentally transform the customer experience by leveraging Services as a layer of abstraction and simplification between customers and the complexities of the IT organization. Doing so is the first step toward recognition as a trusted advisor to the enterprise business.

In Chapter 4, "Service Delivery Taxonomy and Definition of a Service," the ITaaS framework revisits a fundamental consideration that many IT professionals likely assume to be already well finalized: how exactly do we define an IT Service? It is important that we consider exactly what conditions constitute the designation of an IT Service, what characteristics we want to associate with a Service, and how our definition of a Service and its characteristics serves the broader purpose and goals of the framework.

While teams may choose to tailor the definition of a Service or the characteristics associated with them it is important to understand the ITaaS framework's distinction of three different, explicit Service types. Understanding the Service type best associated with a Service helps anticipate design and management criteria, customer base, and other key elements for successfully delivering a Service.

■ **Business Operations Services:** Services that deliver specialized sets of technical capabilities that enable business processes and outcomes, potentially unique to the industry or the enterprise itself, and primarily consumed by a specific enterprise business unit. Examples include Services that directly enable line of business (LoB) operations such as manufacturing or design processes.

- **Enterprise End-Customer Services:** Services providing technical capabilities consumed by end customers all across the enterprise, common across most enterprises and industries. Examples include Services that enable productivity and collaboration capabilities such as email or video-conferencing across the enterprise.

- **Technology Foundation Services:** Services that primarily enable core technical capabilities which indirectly support other ITaaS Services, common across most enterprises and industries. Examples include Services providing data storage and cloud application hosting capabilities.

Another important consideration is the ITaaS framework's recognition of relationships between Services, through a concept known as Service chains. Each Service is focused on the delivery of a unique set of technical capabilities and may consume technical capabilities from another Service to deliver its own capabilities. Whenever an IT Service consumes technical capabilities from another IT Service, a Service chain is formed. Two-and three-level Service chains are common in the adoption of the ITaaS framework. As an example, consider a Business Operations Service that delivers a series of technical capabilities that enable several key business processes for a line of business. These specific capabilities are made available through a set of applications directly associated with the Service; however, these applications need to be hosted, and the data that these systems leverage has strict requirements for availability, backup, and security. Rather than attempt to manage these capabilities within the Service, the Service Owner instead consumes these capabilities from several Technology Foundation Services, as illustrated in Figure 2-6.

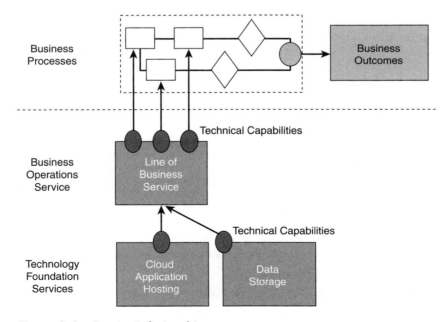

Figure 2-6   *Service Relationships*

This is a powerful concept for a Service delivery framework. Service chains provide a foundation for constructing an accurate model of the total costs of Service delivery and can even be used to chain performance metrics to drive improvements. Service chains also clearly establish the widespread dependency of different Services, rather than viewing technology-focused efforts as being siloed.

Service Design, Delivery, and Management

As the name implies, Service Design, Delivery, and Management is all about determining exactly what the right set of Services are for an IT organization to deliver, how to make these capabilities available to customers, and how best to organize them for management and delivery at all levels. Completing this pillar of the ITaaS framework successfully not only ensures alignment of enterprise IT Services to documented requirements of the enterprise but also provides Service Owners, senior IT leaders, and even the CIO with a set of levers for the strategic management of the IT organization.

As a part of this strategy, teams will develop an IT Services delivery taxonomy, which acts to establish a hierarchy for the complete Service delivery function and define each of its levels, with a goal of enabling the strategic management of the Service landscape. Hierarchies have been used throughout history to simplify the definition, organization, and management of complex concepts ranging from militaries to scientific classifications of species. The scope of technical capabilities that today's IT organizations are expected to deliver is immense, and we cannot hope to manage them effectively without introducing a taxonomy to the Service delivery framework.

The Service taxonomy is also leveraged to align key components of the Service delivery framework, such as various Service delivery roles, and also establishes capabilities allowing Service delivery teams to more easily manage individual Services. The various levels of the Service taxonomy and the linkage between each often lead to profound impacts on IT's perception of Services, shifting its orientation from technology silos to a broader contemplation of how Services required across the enterprise and different levels of the taxonomy relate to each other. This is why establishing the Services taxonomy and carefully considering how the IT organization will define an IT Service are considered a crucial phase of work that must be completed in the earliest stages of the Services Transformation Program.

Cisco's ITaaS framework includes a reference taxonomy shown in Figure 2-7 suitable for most enterprise IT organizations. As you can see Services represent the pivotal level of the Taxonomy. The levels that sit above Services support the categorization and aggregation of Services, allowing for the strategic management of the Service landscape. The levels resting below Services provide Service delivery teams with mechanisms for organizing and managing individual Services.

While the reference taxonomy has proven itself an ideal solution for most enterprises, the final taxonomy adopted by an IT organization should ultimately reflect the size and requirements of the enterprise and underlying goals for Service delivery. In some cases, a simple name change in a level of the reference taxonomy can act to link the new framework for Service delivery to previous initiatives and support more positive change leadership efforts. Chapter 4 provides a detailed look at the IT Service taxonomy and how and when an IT organization should consider tailoring aspects of the reference taxonomy.

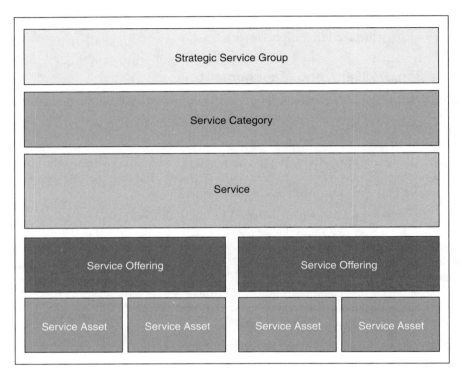

Figure 2-7   *Cisco Reference Taxonomy*

Before IT Transformation teams begin to design Services, there is another key set of information that must be made available in order to support the design of Business Operations Services. Remember these Service types act to enable various business processes, which means in order to designate the Services teams will need to understand technical capability requirements of the processes across the enterprise. The Enterprise Technical Capabilities map is created to document these requirements. This tool maps the correlation from technical capability requirements and the assets currently in use today, to a business process, and finally to a desired business outcome. This information is critical to proper design of Business Operations type Services, and allows Service Owners to clearly understand how the technical capabilities that their Service delivers impact business outcomes.

Most IT organizations are able to leverage information from EA practices, or even obtain business process information from enterprise BUs, to expedite the development of this crucial artifact for Service delivery. In some cases, they can even help to revalidate and update existing intellectual capital for these teams. Those with limited information available can leverage templates from Cisco's ITaaS framework to develop the same level of information, which can then be passed on to EA practices or enterprise BUs for additional value. Note that although its purpose is foremost to support successful design of Business Operations Services, the ETC map creates a number of significant value opportunities for IT organizations. The ETC mapping process and its uses are explored in full in Chapter 5.

Finally, with these important elements and sources of information in place, IT Transformation teams begin designing Services to meet the various requirements of the enterprise end-to-end. The result of this effort is the creation of the IT Services portfolio. This artifact is the central nexus or heart of a framework for IT Service delivery, and as the "heart" its health is crucial to the performance of IT Services delivery across the enterprise. Too small, and the framework will likely struggle and fail to support the requirements of IT's customers. Too large, and the operation and management of the IT Service delivery function itself can grind to a halt, leading to the same outcome on enterprise operations. Rather than a flat listing of nonrelated Services, the ITaaS framework's approach to portfolio design leverages the taxonomy model to categorize and aggregate Services, allowing for the strategic management of the Services landscape at different levels of the organization. Chapter 6, "Service Design and Building the IT Service Portfolio," provides an in-depth look at designing an IT Service portfolio and long-term management strategies.

This pillar of the ITaaS framework also considers how technical capabilities are ultimately made available to customers for consumption. A key aspect of supporting the desired outcomes for the Service delivery function is to ensure that the many processes and tools leveraged by the IT organization are Services-aware, so that mappings to Services are maintained for all aspects of IT operations. Whenever a customer submits a request through a corporate e-store or for support of a specific capability, IT leaders need to understand which Service each of those requests maps to. We must also consider the many different variations now available and often expected by customers for requesting technical capabilities. Historically, corporate e-stores and portals for IT Services and support represented the extent of customer expectations, but now those expectations have grown to include business app stores, provisioning portals, and many more. Chapter 11, "Completing the Services Transformation," examines a new approach to the designation of IT Service catalogs that can enable a wide range of customer request portals well into the future while maintaining all-important Service mappings end-to-end.

Service Value Communications

A series of strategies for measuring and then communicating the value of Services is an integral part of shifting the customer perception of IT to that of a trusted advisor. An IT organization must have the ability to qualify the impact that IT Services have on business outcomes. It also must be able to develop an initial view of the value the Service creates for the enterprise, which it can then refine in partnership with customer stakeholders. This concept represents a significant priority for Cisco's ITaaS framework, and the building blocks associated with this pillar of the framework help IT organizations to begin successfully measuring and communicating Service value, and improve over time.

The first step in developing a view of Service value is to understand how best to define *value*. We established previously that Cisco's ITaaS framework defines *Service value* as a consideration of the total costs to deliver a Service at a required level of performance, weighed against its impact on business outcomes. This provides us with a target set of building blocks to develop in order to qualify Service value: capabilities, performance, and then costs.

One final element to consider for developing an understanding of Service value is that it must be understandable and also relatable to the customers consuming the Service. In other words, an effective strategy for Service value cannot simply consist of technical metrics that provide no meaning to the customer alongside a report on costs so complex that it takes hours to review and understand. The goal instead is to develop an informative measure of Service value that resonates with the customer-base, rather than solely with IT professionals. This initial view of value is presented as part of a formal communication strategy; is refined as necessary; and should ultimately achieve widespread agreement among the Service delivery team, IT leaders, and business leaders regarding the value a Service provides to the enterprise. Going forward, Service delivery teams continue to build stronger and broader relationships with lines of business and other customer bases, leveraging information gleaned from those relationships to further improve Service value qualification.

Over time the Service value communication strategy leads to a shift in how the enterprise business views IT Service delivery and the IT organization itself. Table 2-1 highlights how the view of IT shifts as a result of an effective Service value communication strategy.

Table 2-1   *Views of IT Pre- and Post-ITaaS Adoption*

Business and IT Relationship Pre-ITaaS Transformation	Business and IT Relationship Post-ITaaS Transformation
IT is viewed as a burdensome "order taker."	IT is viewed as a proactive, trusted advisor.
IT and business have different goals and priorities.	IT Service delivery teams understand the goals and priorities of the customer base, and advocate across the IT organization to facilitate outcomes.
IT and business speak different languages.	IT Service delivery teams can clearly articulate and demonstrate how IT Services impact business activities.
IT struggles to articulate the reason for costs assigned to a Service, frustrating business leaders.	IT can demonstrate an easy-to-understand model of the costs based on consumption of technical capabilities.

To accomplish this shift in how the business views IT, the value communication strategy initiates a formal series of Service Reviews between three parties—IT Service Owners, IT leaders, and senior customer stakeholders—structured to review all key aspects of Service delivery and Service value along with planning future Service requirements. This approach fundamentally transforms how IT Service planning is conducted in many of today's IT organizations, where customer stakeholders often describe feeling left at the mercy of significant Service planning decisions made by IT in a vacuum. Figure 2-8 illustrates this shift in how Service value is reviewed and future planning is conducted within the ITaaS framework.

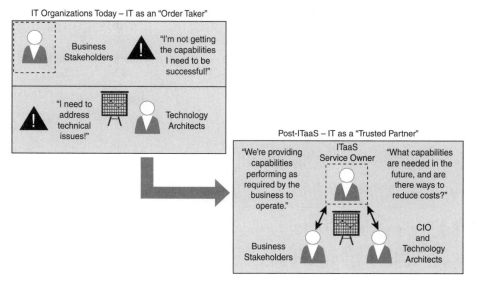

Figure 2-8   *Transitioning to Three-Party Service Reviews*

Note that the customer stakeholders vary depending on the Service type. Because Enterprise End-Customer Services provide technical capabilities across the entire enterprise, the CIO or senior IT leaders often advocate on behalf of that broad base of stakeholders. However, senior leaders from across the enterprise may still participate when key decisions are being discussed. Service Reviews for Technology Foundation–type Services can be especially tedious for Service Owners, because their customers are made up of fellow IT leaders in the role of Service Owners managing Services that rely on the capabilities provided by the Technology Foundation Service. Three-party Service Reviews primarily refer to Business Operations Services, where a Service Owner and senior IT leaders, potentially including the CIO, meet with senior business leaders. For these Service types, Service Reviews act as a bridge between IT and business teams. Figure 2-9 illustrates how the Service value communication strategy runs parallel to Service delivery strategies to engage these stakeholders.

Chapter 10, "Communicating IT Service Value," provides full details on strategies for communicating IT Service value and how to structure successful Service Reviews. It also explores how these Service Reviews should continue to evolve over time to continue strengthening the value of the conversations and the relationships they foster.

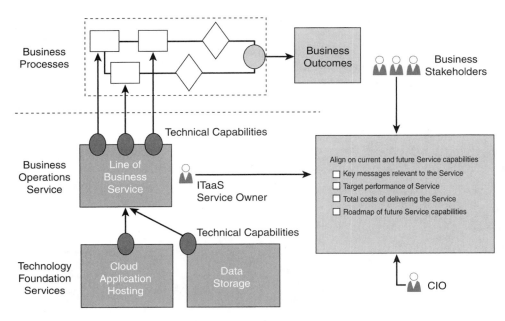

Figure 2-9 *Service Review Strategy Example*

In order to qualify an initial view of IT Service value to present in a Service Review, Service Owners must have visibility to each of the elements that contribute to the customer perception of value, beginning with set of technical capabilities delivered by the Service. Service Owners must also understand how those capability requirements will change over time. A key aspect of Service Reviews includes joint development of a Service capability roadmap. Rather than project timelines or lifecycle roadmaps for technical assets familiar to most IT professionals, these roadmaps reflect a rolling multi-quarter view of changes to the Service capabilities. Detailed further in Chapter 5, the goal is to illustrate when capabilities will be discontinued, scaled, or introduced and to confirm these proposed changes and timeline from senior stakeholders.

Understanding the performance of a Service is key to qualifying its value. The ITaaS framework's strategy for Service performance is broken into two key steps. In the first step, Service Owners aggregate all applicable metrics into a series of strategic Service Metric Categories that coincide with concepts familiar to business leaders. These categories are as follows:

- **Quality:** Provides an overall measurement of the operational performance of the Service and the effectiveness and efficiency of the technical capabilities it delivers

- **Leverage:** Measures the scale and utilization of technical capabilities

- **Speed:** Measures the time to respond to customer requests for technical capabilities already delivered by the Service, as well as the time to develop and make new capabilities available

■ **Risk:** Measures overall risk to the ongoing delivery of technical capabilities and ensures that Service delivery continuously manages risks associated with the IT organization and enterprise business operations

■ **Customer Experience:** Establishes a measurement of the performance of a Service from the perspective of the customer stakeholders consuming the technical capabilities

This strategy supports a conversation of Service performance that begins with concepts familiar to nontechnical stakeholders, rather than starting a conversation with an intimidating set of technical metrics. Specific key performance indicators (KPIs), technical metrics, and data points can still be evaluated if required. However, doing so is easier due to their alignment to a category and concept familiar to the customer stakeholder.

Another key advantage to these Service performance categories is that they establish a complete, well-rounded view of the performance of the Service. It forces both IT and business leaders to consider aspects of Service performance they may not have considered or prioritized previously and to also understand how changes in one category can affect the others.

The next step in the Service performance strategy is to correlate specific metrics to their impact on business outcomes. Remember that based on the capability set associated with their Service and the information available in the ETC map, Service Owners have a complete view of the processes and business outcomes enabled by their Service. This level of information enables Service Owners to understand and translate specific performance metrics to their impact on business outcomes.

There is a great deal more to the Service performance strategy, including the development of dashboards, importance of trending, leveraging of benchmarks and baselines, and prioritizing of KPIs. Chapter 8, "Measuring IT Service Performance," expands on all these topics, but a key consideration now is that the requirements for Service performance should be a joint effort between IT and customer stakeholders. This ensures that performance targets are not overprovisioned and consuming unnecessary resources, or underprovisioned and failing to facilitate the needs of the customer base or leaving the enterprise at risk.

The next step in understanding Service value is determining the costs to deliver a Service at the required levels of performance. When senior leaders understand these costs they can better partner with IT leaders to support informed investment planning and management of operational expenses. In some cases, this may mean business leaders are supportive of further investment, or it may lead them to carefully reconsider their requirements for Service performance. In other cases, once they truly understand the costs involved, they may determine that the value of the Service does not warrant the costs to the enterprise business and therefore decide to discontinue the Service until it can be delivered at a lower cost threshold. These types of decisions can be made only when both IT leaders and customers understand the total costs to deliver a Service.

Note that there are a significant number of considerations for IT finance, differentiating views of the IT budget, cost types, and the impact of each on IT Service cost modeling. These are explored in full detail in Chapter 9, "Modeling the Total Costs of IT Service Delivery." The goal here is to understand the key principles and considerations for cost modeling.

The ITaaS framework's strategy for Service cost modeling establishes a parallel view of the IT budget in which cost elements are distributed to Services. We are not replacing or overwriting existing views of the IT budget.

For modeling the total costs of Service delivery, the ITaaS framework once again adopts a two-step strategy. In the first step, 100 percent of the IT budget is distributed to Services. These costs are designated as either "Run the Business" (RtB) costs or "Change the Business" (CtB) costs and together represent direct Service costs.

RtB costs represent the costs of day-to-day delivery of the capabilities at the desired levels of performance. These costs often represent the most significant block of costs in a Service's total cost of ownership (TCO) model. As such, they will receive a great deal of consideration by IT and business stakeholders, resulting in Service Owners dedicating a great deal of attention toward understanding, optimizing, and reducing the broad range of cost elements associated with this cost block. The ability to understand and begin focusing on operational cost reduction is yet another valuable capability afforded by adoption of Cisco's ITaaS framework, because these costs represent a significant portion of IT budgets but can be optimized only through an effective Service-based view of the IT budget.

CtB costs represent investment leveraged to increase Service performance, scale or transform existing capabilities, or introduce new capabilities. They also include investments made to reduce RtB costs. Isolating and trending these costs over time to evaluate the impact of approved investments is an important responsibility for Service Owners.

In the second step of the cost modeling strategy, any Service that delivers technical capabilities consumed by another IT Service as part of a Service chain is required to develop a process for chaining out costs based on consumption. These processes are unique to each Service and often are refined and optimized over time. A key consideration for the development of these processes is that Service Owners are not required to chain out 100 percent of their direct Service costs, but instead only those costs that fairly represent consumption of capabilities they delivered. This point is important because it ensures that Service costs are not unnecessarily inflated by Services operating large-scale infrastructures attempting to zero out their own costs. When these costs are received by a Service, they represent indirect Service costs. Cost chaining and indirect Service costs are crucial to developing an understanding of the total costs for delivery of a Service.

These three cost blocks—direct Service costs including RtB and CtB, along with all applicable indirect Service costs—represent the total cost of ownership model for a Service. By allocating costs to three well-known blocks, Service Owners, along with IT and business leaders, can qualify the value that a Service creates for the enterprise and begin making informed decisions about the costs associated with delivering a Service to improve that value.

Introducing Cisco Services Transformation Program

A framework for IT Service delivery is valuable only if it can be successfully adopted by real-world IT organizations of different sizes and across different industries. Conceptualized frameworks often lose a great deal of their theorized value by the time they meet the many and varied challenges presented by a specific IT organization.

Cisco's ITaaS framework is complemented by a proven Services Transformation Program that can guide IT organizations in tailoring and adopting the framework, putting it into practice, and achieving its value outcomes. This is the same program followed by Cisco Services teams that regularly partner with Cisco customers to guide Services Transformations. The program emphasizes change leadership from day one, and engages business stakeholders early and often. The program begins with a Discovery and Design phase, focused on understanding gaps in current IT and business alignment, refining a series of guiding principles for Service delivery, and finally designing a target future model for IT Service delivery capable of addressing these considerations.

Cisco's Services Transformation Program is shown in Figure 2-10; the different phases and workstreams of the program can generally be expected to require between 12 and 24 months to complete.

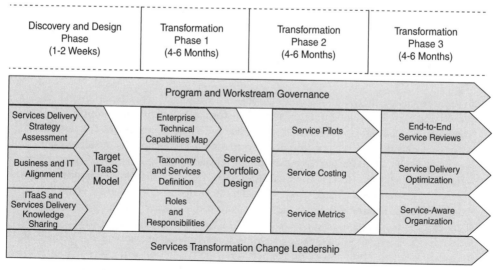

Figure 2-10 *Cisco's Services Transformation Program*

The time, effort, and complexity of each phase, workstream, and work package contained within a given phase vary significantly between enterprises, depending on the size and complexity of the business operations, availability of existing key information and artifacts, previous work conducted for Service delivery and its alignment to Cisco's ITaaS framework, and numerous other factors. I've learned from experience that leading these programs is far different from a technical program, because politics, resistance to change from key participants, and many other challenges present themselves but must be navigated to achieve the desired outcomes. Think of the Services Transformation Program as a large-scale art project that happens to contain a number of complex science projects, but always remember that this program has been leveraged successfully before and by a growing number of IT organizations.

A key aspect of Cisco's Services Transformation Program is its focus on delivering incremental value. Cisco's guidance for IT Transformation teams is to demonstrate significant value outcomes early in the transformation program, and then consistently after that as the organization progresses across the different phases of transformation. With this in mind, each of the following sections detailing the transformation program also provides a summary of the value outcomes that can be realized.

The transformation program is not overly prescriptive with regard to the make-up of teams and resources conducting the effort within each phase and work package. Other than to recommend instances when IT executives and senior leaders should be engaged, the work is assumed to be conducted by a core IT Transformation team. This team is typically made up of an existing enterprise IT Service management team and EA practice, but may also include a selection of participants from across IT functions (and possibly various business teams); it should also include program and project management professionals. Chapter 3, "Change Leadership and Ensuring a Successful Transformation," stresses the importance of a change leadership function within the broader IT Transformation team and resources within the IT Transformation team responsible for developing and driving related strategies. Key stakeholders and subject matter experts should be engaged as necessary—for example, IT finance teams during the IT Service costing workstream.

In order to ensure the value outcomes are realized within a desired timeframe IT leaders should also consider augmenting these IT Transformation teams with support from third parties. Cisco Services teams are equipped with a library of templates, standard processes, change leadership material, and other intellectual capital; consultants are highly experienced and often have a working knowledge of the customer industry and operations. They can also call upon a deep pool of resources within the broader Cisco Services team and even engage Cisco IT leaders to share experience and guidance directly from the teams that are leveraging the framework today. Rather than leveraging a small army of consultants focused on creating a set of deliverables related to Service delivery, Cisco Services leverage small teams of two to three consultants who embed themselves with the IT organization and guide the Services Transformation while focusing on developing the organization's ability to leverage the framework successfully. This combination of deep experience and intellectual capital offered by Cisco Services teams allows

IT leaders to ensure that the value outcomes of Services Transformation are achieved within the desired time frame.

Program and Workstream Governance

While it is one of the most straightforward workstreams in the program, if not facilitated entirely and with care, the Program and Workstream Governance phase can allow the entire Services Transformation to falter and even fail entirely. As shown in Figure 2-10, this workstream stretches across the entire program, with its primary goals considered to be as follows:

- Work with the broader transformation team to structure workflows and timelines.

- Establish internal and external communications, including stakeholder engagement, and facilitate engagement of sponsors and senior leaders for decision making and issue resolution.

- Provide extensive support wherever necessary to ensure progression of the program, such as scheduling support, assignment, and follow-up on action-items, and escalations if needed.

- Track and report successful completion of work packages and communicate value outcomes.

Teams should note that the complexity and level of effort associated with this workstream is often minimal to moderate in the Discovery and Design and first Transformation Phase of the program. The complexity and effort rise significantly during Phase 2 of the program, as the program governance team must facilitate significant collaboration and scheduling between the individual work packages, allowing the Service pilots to act as test grounds and critical resources for feedback on the validity of design decisions being made in the other work packages. Phase 3 broadens the potential complexity and effort even further as larger numbers of smaller teams are aggressively building numerous supporting tools, documenting processes, and automating activities for Service delivery, all of which must be aligned still to the broader transformation plan and timelines.

Strong resources in this workstream can contribute to a significant reduction in timelines. As a common example, consider that many milestones in the transformation program require review and sign-off by the CIO or other senior IT leaders. Their calendars may be booked solid for weeks, potentially stalling an entire work package until completed. Also consider that while the IT Transformation team is fully dedicated to the program, many of the most critical and highest-effort work packages require significant participation from stakeholders across the IT organization that are unlikely to be fully dedicated to the program. This leads to delays in scheduling meetings and potentially for completing action items. As with any large-scale enterprise program, selecting and then empowering strong resources in support of this effort are critical elements of completing the program on time and within budget and ensuring all the planned value outcomes are achieved.

Services Transformation Change Leadership

Services Transformation Change Leadership is a workstream so critical to the transformation program that a chapter is dedicated to its discussion. Because Chapter 3 provides robust guidance for supporting a successful Services Transformation through change leadership, this section comments primarily on the need for robust and exhaustive change leadership, and understanding the level of effort that grows quickly as the transformation program moves outward from the Discovery and Design phase.

During the Discovery and Design phase, change leadership teams are closely involved with the development, refinement, and final adoption of the guiding principles for Services Transformation and immediately afterward should begin work on developing a number of different value proposition messages. From there, these teams can provide critical support in developing introductions and initial messaging for teams conducting interviews in support of the business and IT alignment work package. They also can leverage the ITaaS knowledge-sharing work package to establish initial repositories and processes for knowledge content archives. Note that these archives will grow in the amount of content and resource access as the program progresses.

After the target ITaaS framework and value messaging from the Discovery and Design phase are completed, change leadership teams develop an initial set of content for the purpose of conveying the importance of, value outcomes of, and support by the CIO and senior IT leaders for Services Transformation. This content may range from previously prepared "elevator pitches" for use by transformation teams to posters, handouts, and other promotional material for use in building a broader awareness of and support for the upcoming transformation. Capturing, retaining, and then facilitating the long-term education of the details for the Phase 1 work packages is also key during this time.

Phase 2 of the transformation requires the change leadership team to begin broadening their messaging beyond the core transformation teams, with an emphasis on building support and buy-in for successful pilot Services and the first-ever Service Reviews. The team develops onboarding material for Service Owners and supports teams in development of knowledge content that is spinning out of the work packages for IT Service performance and costs.

The final phase of the transformation program leverages all the effort to date by the change leadership teams at scale across the whole of the IT organization as well as across broad sections of the enterprise business units. Teams also are required to capture training modules for future IT professionals, ensuring that the purpose, value, and messaging associated with Services Transformation, along with the culture it influences, are preserved well beyond the end of the transformation program itself.

Discovery and Design Phase

The initial Discovery and Design phase of the transformation program evaluates existing strategies for Services delivery against the principles of the ITaaS framework, assesses the impact of those strategies across both IT and the enterprise business today, and begins expanding a deeper knowledge of the ITaaS framework to key stakeholders. It also creates a set of guiding principles for the future of IT Service delivery across the organization.

The primary outcome of this phase is a target future model for IT Service delivery, its key capabilities and value proposition, and a detailed view of the scope and effort of the transformation phases of the program.

Guiding principles for IT Service delivery shape the framework and set the tone for the future culture of the IT organization. It acts as a type of foundational constitution for IT Service delivery that guides all the future design decisions and implementation efforts, the "true north" for IT leaders when in doubt. The ITaaS framework begins with a set of reference principles, as shared in Table 2-2, but each IT organization is encouraged to customize these principles and ultimately receive sign-off from the CIO and all senior IT leaders.

Table 2-2 *Guiding Principles for IT Service Delivery*

Category	Guiding Principle
Image of Success	The IT organization will become an end-to-end Services organization, or ITaaSO.
	IT Service delivery will prioritize creating business value, and customer satisfaction.
	Going forward, the IT organization will drive value on behalf of its customers rather than acting solely as a "Service broker."
	Going forward, the IT organization will be managed as a competitive and efficient business.
Change Leadership	Change leadership is required to ensure widespread adoption of the new framework for Service delivery, and that it continues to deliver value for IT and the business.
	Responsibility for driving change is shared by IT leaders and the broader organization, rather than being limited to the change leadership team.
	Services Transformation must be championed by the CIO along with buy-in and endorsement from IT and business leaders.
	The value proposition will be clearly documented and communicated.
	Transforming the "culture of IT" is a top priority and will require consistent support from the change leadership function.
Service Roles and Responsibilities	Service delivery roles are the result of explicit resource activities required for the function and value outcomes of Service delivery on a regular, recurring basis.
	Roles are defined by the work to be done in support of Service delivery, not based on an organizational structure.
	The CIO holds ultimate responsibility for Service management and performance.
	Service Owners are the singular role accountable for the delivery of a Service and its resulting value to the enterprise, customer satisfaction, and managing the operational excellence of the Service.

Category	Guiding Principle
Service Design, Alignment, and Management	The IT Service taxonomy is designed with the goal of aggregating and categorizing IT Services to enable strategic management of the Service landscape.
	Services focus on the processes and outcomes they support rather than technology and are defined to reflect the capabilities being delivered and in terms that resonate with the consumer rather than IT.
Service Capabilities	Services deliver capabilities that have an associated performance level and cost.
	Services will maintain an alignment of capabilities to current and future business operations and customer requirements that are expected to change over time.
	Service Architects are accountable for the alignment of an IT Service to business strategies over time.
Service Performance Metrics	Service performance strategies measure the capabilities being delivered, rather than the operation of the technical platforms used to deliver them.
	Service performance is intended to enable fact-based decision making around the desired impact of technical capabilities on business outcomes.
	All Service metrics will be assigned a target and benchmark.
	All Services will share the same Service metric categories, but there will be customization and differentiation of the data points grouped into each category based on the Service type.
Service Costs	Target 100 percent of IT spend allocation across IT Services.
	Going forward, the total costs of delivering IT Services will be completely transparent.
	Designing an easy-to-model and- understand transparent view of the total costs of IT Services delivery is the priority over 100 percent cost allocation accuracy.
	The TCO for a Service is made up of all accumulated costs for delivery of technical capabilities at desired levels of performance.

Transformation Phase 1

With a clear view of the target ITaaS based Service delivery framework and a set of guiding principles to inform the design of future elements, teams now begin work in earnest on Services Transformation and becoming an end-to-end Services organization. The significance and long-term impact of the design decisions made during this phase to the long-term success of the transformation program cannot be understated. Transformation teams have to strike a careful balance between broadly vetting their design proposals across various IT and business interests to ensure the model works end-to-end across the enterprise, while at the same time avoiding "analysis paralysis," or serialized vetting of proposals that leads to never-ending feedback and change loops. These risks and best practices for mitigating are discussed in detail in Chapter 3. Besides the foundational components of the ITaaS model, there is a significant strategic value outcome associated with this phase of the transformation, namely an IT Service portfolio completely aligned to the delivery of technical capabilities required by the enterprise business to operate and drive outcomes such as maximizing profits. Creating this portfolio requires significant effort and careful decision making on top of the outputs of the first work packages in this phase.

Teams begin by building the Enterprise Technical Capabilities map detailed in Chapter 5. This invaluable tool helps align Business Operations type Services and is key to understanding their impact on business outcomes, along with creating many other value opportunities for the IT organization.

In parallel, transformation teams review and finalize a Services delivery taxonomy. The ITaaS framework includes a reference taxonomy, and while substantial design changes are rarely needed (and undertaken at risk), a careful review can identify opportunities to better align it to the organization's goals through minor refinements. Transformation teams should also carefully consider the names, descriptions, and definitions included at each level of the taxonomy hierarchy to ensure that the result resonates with their organization and enables the right level of strategic management of the portfolio for the CIO and senior IT leaders. Clear definitions of each component in the taxonomy, with a major focus on the definition of a Service, are critical outputs passed to change leadership teams and leveraged for quality assurance checks against the draft portfolio.

Closely related to the taxonomy work, transformation teams also finalize a set of IT Service delivery roles and responsibilities. Depending on the size of a company and other factors, some roles included in the ITaaS framework may not be needed, at least initially. Roles such as Service Executives and Service offering managers are typically not needed in small enterprises and can be introduced at a later date if required. It is important to note, however, that while roles may change, the responsibilities identified by the ITaaS framework must all be accounted for, even if they are conducted by a single role. Transformation teams also designate where each role aligns to the Service taxonomy—for instance, aligning Service Executives to the Strategic Service Group level of the taxonomy.

With these foundational components of the framework for IT Service delivery in place, transformation teams now begin designing the IT Services portfolio. Chapter 6 takes you through the best-practice-based approach to designing a portfolio end-to-end. At key points in development, sections of the portfolio are vetted with teams closest to the customers and also teams supporting the technologies.

Transformation Phase 2

The second phase of the transformation program represents the transition of the transformation team's activities from "theory" to "practice." Teams begin building out the Service value communication strategy (the second ITaaS pillar) and putting it into practice. In doing so, they initiate the earliest steps in the transformation of the IT organization's culture beyond the IT Transformation team.

In parallel to the design and implementation of strategies for Service performance and cost modeling, IT organizations and transformation teams kick off a series of Service pilots and the first-ever IT Service Reviews. This process involves selecting and training the first-ever wave of IT Service Owners, and then supporting and empowering each through the initiation of their pilot Service, including the initial outreach and conversations with the associated customer base. The careful selection of these Service Owners cannot be stressed enough. We established earlier that Cisco's ITaaS framework is built on a foundation of people, and the pilot Service Owners selected in this phase set an example for all future Service Owners and other Service delivery roles as the first stewards of the cultural shift of IT.

The transformation teams with support from senior IT leaders should also carefully select actual Services to be piloted. The piloted Services should also represent a selection of each Service type so that strategies and elements of the Service delivery framework can truly be tested and refined across all types of Services.

It is this Service pilot work package that often creates the most angst for leaders. After all, they've likely just begun work on IT Service costing and metrics, which many IT veterans consider to be the most critical components of an IT Service. The reality is that the design of these complex strategies and related processes for measuring IT Service performance and modeling IT Service costs can't be completed successfully in a vacuum or without thoroughly testing across all Service types. The three Phase 2 work packages create a feedback loop between one another, with pilot Services acting as a "test bed" for design decisions in the other work packages to provide critical feedback to transformation teams. The Program Management workstream can play a valuable role in linking these work packages at the proper time as Service Owners get an initial handle on their responsibilities and accountability, and the many facets of their initial Service in time to begin participating in the testing of initial design decisions for performance and costing strategies.

Transformation Phase 3

The final phase of the transformation program brings the onboarding of all IT Services defined within the portfolio through fruition, and seeks to fully optimize the now-completed ITaaS framework. By the close of Phase 3, all IT Services are now active and associated with a view of the value they provide to the enterprise business.

Phase 3 also represents the largest and broadest shift in the culture of the IT organization because the earliest part of Phase 3 sees more and more IT professionals add the role of Service Owner to their commitments and adopt the new focus on creating business value and customer satisfaction. By the end of Phase 3, virtually every member of the IT organization, even those most deeply focused on pure technology enablement, should understand that their IT organization is now an end-to-end Services organization and focused on enabling business outcomes through Service delivery and efficient operation.

This phase requires the creation of numerous additional tools and processes that help optimize the long-term delivery and consumption of IT Services. Cisco's best practices for the design of an IT Service catalog ensure an enterprise can quickly launch successful corporate e-stores, regional and specialized e-stores, business app stores, and self-provisioning portals while maintaining Service mappings. In addition to these and other tools, processes for the long-term management of the framework for Service delivery are finalized and published. Additional Service roles, such as the Service Executive and Service Architect, are introduced in this phase if they have not been introduced already.

Further optimization of the Service delivery model is often realized in this phase because all remaining aspects of the enterprise IT organization become "Services-aware." Asset databases, change management databases (CMDBs), ticketing systems for help desks, and any number of existing processes across the enterprise need to become Services-aware in order to map information back to Services.

Finally, optimization is continued through the automation of IT Service performance and cost modeling strategies, replacing potentially clunky manual qualification of Service value and allowing Service delivery teams to actively monitor and manage value and the customer experience.

Summary

IT operating models illustrate a high-level representation of the operation of an IT organization and its key functions and initiatives. While these models may vary, all IT organizations share a common set of major functions:

- **IT Technical Operations:** A broad set of standards and practices for processes informing the day-to-day operation of technical platforms and architectures that enable IT Services, including processes for change control and incident and problem management.

- **IT Service Delivery:** A set of frameworks, processes, and tools that support and inform the design, delivery, and management of technical capabilities in the form of IT Services delivered by the IT organization. Cisco's ITaaS framework also introduces a strategy for measuring and communicating the value of IT Services to the enterprise business.

- **Enterprise Architecture:** Standards and methodologies for developing and then managing architecture models capable of illustrating the alignment of technical platforms to business operations and strategies, including the processes for leveraging these models for investment prioritization, acquisition planning, and other strategic decision making.

Cisco's ITaaS framework is a model for enterprise IT Service delivery designed to enable an "as a Service" style of delivery for IT Services end-to-end across an enterprise. This framework is built on a foundation of people, defining a set of Service delivery roles fulfilled by resources who have adopted a culture that prioritizes creating value for the business and customer satisfaction. From there, the framework is supported by two key strategies, or pillars. The Service Design, Delivery, and Management strategy reexamines historical IT Service management practices, creates a map of technical capability requirements as a key input for Service design, and introduces a Service taxonomy model that enables the strategic management of the Services landscape. The second, IT Service Value Communications strategy, is unique to Cisco's ITaaS framework and focuses on strategies for measuring, communicating, and then refining a view of the value provided by IT Services in partnership with senior stakeholders. This pillar includes strategies for modeling the total costs of Service delivery along with establishing a view of Service performance that resonates with the customer base.

The ITaaS framework leverages Services as a layer of abstraction between IT customers and the complex technical architectures, teams, processes, and budgets used to deliver the Service. This approach transforms the customer experience, enabling many benefits for IT Service delivery commonly associated with "as a Service" models of delivery and consumption.

Cisco's Services Transformation Program provides a proven method for tailoring the ITaaS framework to a specific industry and enterprise and then putting the resulting framework into practice successfully. The program emphasizes change leadership from day one, engages business stakeholders early and often, and delivers incrementally for the IT organization and enterprise business.

Chapter 3

Change Leadership and Ensuring a Successful Transformation

Cisco's Services Transformation Program relies on a strong change leadership program to successfully achieve the value outcomes associated with the adoption of Cisco's ITaaS framework and transition to an end-to-end Services organization. Change leadership plays a critical role in ensuring the widespread adoption of the ITaaS framework and that it continues to create value for the IT organization and enterprise business long after the final phase of the program is completed. It also plays an important role in instigating and then fostering the cultural shift across the IT organization to one focused on delivering business value through Services and customer satisfaction.

Some IT leaders and teams may be apt to overlook or marginalize this function of the Transformation Program, potentially failing to provide proper support in terms of senior resources or authority. After all, it's likely that some IT organizations have successfully conducted large-scale multiyear programs before where formal change leadership was not utilized. None of these programs, however, relied on fundamentally shifting the culture of the organization for successful adoption. Only a strong, robust, and consistent prioritization of change leadership throughout the entirety of the Services Transformation Program and beyond can support an IT organization in achieving this outcome.

Before progressing to any specific recommendations, I want to acknowledge that change leadership and change management represent a large and varied field of professional expertise, for which significant volumes of invaluable material have been created and which countless professionals have dedicated their careers to. The goal of this chapter is not to educate you in detail on this extensive field of knowledge, but instead to share a set of principles, strategies, and best practices that have been leveraged previously in successful Services Transformations.

First, we consider the change leadership function and how the resources within the IT Transformation team support it. Following that, we establish a set of critical success factors for Services Transformation and guide transformation teams in gaining a commitment of support to each from the IT leadership team. We present the change leadership activities across the Services Transformation Program as a set of overarching strategies, alongside recommendations for specific tactics in support of each strategy that will vary based on the circumstances. A section is also dedicated to providing a detailed look at the ideal future culture of an end-to-end Services organization. Finally, we share a set of best practices specific to the management and execution of the Services Transformation Program itself, based on real-world experience, ensuring your own transformation has every chance of success.

Building the Change Leadership Team

It is important to understand the difference between change leadership as a broad, critical function of the Services Transformation Program and the core change leadership team responsible for developing the strategies for driving change. The responsibility for change leadership is shared by the IT Transformation and IT leadership teams and, over time as Service delivery roles are introduced, a broader community of IT professionals until eventually the whole of the IT organization can be considered as playing an active role. Believing that change leadership is the responsibility of a small team of resources means the risk of failure is high.

Whenever we refer to the change leadership team, we are referring to a small team of resources within the IT Transformation team who will initiate and shepherd the overarching change strategies, develop supporting material, and monitor change over time. This team acts as points of leverage for the growing community of resources facilitating change.

In general, an enterprise IT organization should identify candidates within its ranks, consider soliciting across the broader enterprise, or even consider funding external resources to fulfill a small number of roles made up of senior professionals in the field of change leadership. From there, the change leadership team is often best rounded out by a small subset of the core transformation team, with those resources volunteering to dedicate all or a portion of their time in support of the change leadership workstream and related efforts. The overall size of the change leadership team, similar to the transformation team, varies depending on the size and complexity of the enterprise and may even be required to scale to larger or smaller sizes throughout the transformation program.

Identifying Services Transformation Critical Success Factors

The first major effort undertaken by the change leadership team is to ensure that the conditions for a successful transformation are acknowledged and supported by the leaders of the IT organization prior to initiating the Services Transformation Program. This task is accomplished by reviewing a series of critical success factors (CSFs) with the IT leadership team and obtaining their commitment of support. The broader IT transformation team also needs to review and understand these success factors, and adhere to each as they make various design decisions and execute specific work packages within the transformation program. These critical success factors are

- Obtaining executive sponsorship
- Championing a new culture of IT
- Willingness to engage the business
- Assuring complete/end-to-end IT Services delivery transformation
- Using a top-down/business-first Service design approach
- Recognizing a centralized transformation authority

The foremost goal of the change leadership team with regard to these critical success factors is essentially to provide a clear understanding of each to the IT leadership team, including the CIO, and their commitment of support for each throughout the life of the transformation program. Let's be candid and clear on this: no transformation program can be completely successful if even one of these factors for success is disregarded by either the transformation team or the most senior leaders of the IT organization. Consider these to be the most foundational and unquestionable requirements for a successful Services Transformation.

The transformation program's dependence on the support of these critical success factors does not cease once it has kicked off. Even the most talented transformation teams will be hamstrung at key junctures of the Services Transformation Program if they do not have support for each and every one of these requirements for success throughout the life of the program. Change leadership teams need to ensure ongoing support for critical success factors across all the transformation phases while at the same time expanding the supporting audience as the program progresses.

Getting sign-off on these critical success factors requires change leadership teams to develop a set of material that can communicate the details and potential impact of each. This material can largely be built from the following sections, which describe each success factor in detail and provide real-world examples of IT organizations that have both proactively leveraged and also ignored these critical factors for success. Also consider that successful presentation of these success factors builds confidence across the IT leadership team that the newly formed IT Transformation team has a firm understanding of the effort and commitments for Services Transformation and are capable of achieving the value outcomes. The IT Transformation team, along with the CIO and senior IT leaders, must understand and agree that the Services Transformation is not capable of providing the value outcomes described in Chapter 1, "The Case for IT Transformation and IT as a Service (ITaaS)," without the commitment to support each of these critical success factors throughout the life of the Services Transformation Program.

Executive Sponsorship

A true Services Transformation will lead to far-reaching changes across every part of the IT organization and impact how business units and IT customers across the enterprise consume technical capabilities and interface with the IT Services. Considering the extent of this impact, the reality is that it's unlikely for an enterprise CIO not to be heavily involved in the Services Transformation. In fact, the most successful Services Transformations are those where the CIO plays a regular role in guiding and championing the transformation across the IT organization and broader enterprise business.

The advantage for transformation and change leadership teams is that many enterprise CIOs are already actively aware of and contemplating Services Transformation as a result of the growing drivers and potential opportunities for Fast IT organizations discussed in Chapter 1. In cases where the CIO is actively aware of, supportive, and potentially even responsible for initiating the Services Transformation, the job of a change leadership team at this stage is made easy. In most cases like this, the team can simply summarize and finalize the support of the CIO on the remaining critical success factors. In cases where the CIO is not proactively championing the Services Transformation, teams will likely be required to present the ITaaS framework and Services Transformation Program along with its value proposition to the CIO and senior leaders via an investment board or similar type of initiative proposal process specific to their enterprise. Regardless, a transformation team should not proceed with the transformation program until executive sponsorship is obtained.

The exact type of executive sponsorship can take many forms and degrees. The most basic and limited type is a statement of support and commitment from the CIO for the Services Transformation Program, captured and then leveraged by the change leadership team throughout the life of the program. While limited, this explicit commitment of support may be challenging enough for some teams to obtain. Opposite from this example, however, are those cases in which an enterprise CIO personally champions the transformation of IT Service delivery across the organization, taking steps to announce the launch of the Services Transformation Program and providing regular updates on the successful progress and outcomes across numerous forums, including organizational all-hands meetings and town halls. In these cases, the support of the CIO for the program becomes implicit across the IT organization and acts to quickly address what may otherwise be long uphill battles for change leadership strategies focused on evangelizing the Services Transformation across resistant teams. Additional potential scenarios include sponsorship from a CIO, who then assigns a member of her staff as dedicated point of contact.

So why is the support of a CIO so critical to a successful Services Transformation? The implications are many. First, the commitment of support from the CIO grants the ITaaS transformation a mandate for the program. Consider this a clear announcement and statement from the highest authority within an IT organization effectively saying, "Our organization will transform the way we deliver IT Services, it will become an end-to-end Services organization, and I expect every member of the organization to collaborate constructively with the team leading the transformation program, which has my full support." Note that the upcoming section for change leadership strategies contains recommendations for just such announcements by a CIO or senior IT leaders during various organization-wide meetings, all-hands, or town halls.

Transformation teams will ultimately face a broad range of resistance not only from within their own IT organization but potentially from external teams as well. This mandate, or sign-off and support, for the critical success factors grants the transformation team a badge of authority, or "hall pass" of sorts, that is key to enabling the transformation team to lead and host likely trying conversations with both internal and external stakeholders throughout the life of the transformation program.

As the IT Transformation team begins engaging a wide range of IT and business teams, this mandate proactively communicates the clear support of the highest authority within the IT organization for whichever efforts the transformation team may be progressing at any given moment, proactively encouraging the support of these various teams. Transformation teams with such a mandate can often expect unassuming collaboration from the teams they engage with. Much of the resistance so often on display from teams can be reduced to only the most legitimate of concerns, which the transformation and IT or business team in question can then work through in a constructive manner.

Dedicated executive support can also encourage IT leaders and their teams across the organization to make time in their existing schedules to lend productive support to transformation team efforts. An end-to-end Services Transformation is a complex program even in the best of scenarios, challenging many ingrained notions for how IT Services are designed, delivered, and operated. Without the acknowledged support of the CIO, these various teams whose input and guidance will be critical in helping the transformation team shape key components of the ITaaS framework are just as likely to dig in their heels and resist proposed changes rather than provide constructive guidance.

The purpose of executive sponsorship is to proactively ensure that the entire IT organization understands that the Services Transformation initiative is a program personally championed by the CIO. This ensures teams are flexible in dedicating time to provide value support to the transformation team and also marks the first big win in the larger change leadership strategy for rallying the broader IT organization in support of Services Transformation.

From the Diary of an ITaaS Consultant

I have now personally witnessed (and done my very best to support in every way I could) a number of enterprise IT teams' attempts to tackle end-to-end Services Transformations without the full support of senior IT leaders and the CIO. In all cases, the teams leading these programs find their work constantly inhibited by the lack of support or participation from IT and business teams, leading to timelines being pushed and increased complexity and effort across even the most simple of tasks, ultimately constraining to a large degree the potential value outcomes of a given activity or work package. Eventually, with the various efforts limping along and often failing to demonstrate significant value outcomes, these programs were ultimately shut down.

I've even known some enterprises to repeat these failed attempts at Services Transformation on an almost yearly basis. Teams may alter the basic approach and scope of the program, but always without the explicit support of the CIO, leading to yet another failed attempt at Services Transformation. Teams in such an enterprise may at best hope to make tactical wins, updating existing or introducing new components of the ITaaS framework and potentially realizing some value outcomes. But they never truly are able to undertake the type of end-to-end transformation that results in the value outcomes we discussed in Chapter 1.

On the other hand, I've also worked with enterprise customers where the CIO takes a personal interest in Services Transformation, playing an active and recurring role in championing the transformation across the IT organization as well as outside the organization to senior leaders of enterprise lines of business and business units. In these scenarios, I regularly witnessed these efforts:

- ITaaS transformation teams were recognized across the IT organization as shepherding a strategic program mandated directly by the CIO rather than being viewed as a limited-time project team attempting to pull together a tactical, self-mandated activity that lacked strategic significance for the organization outside the project team.

- IT teams actively volunteered their time and input to support the transformation instead of ignoring requests from the transformation team.

- IT teams identified potential issues and then worked constructively with transformation teams to identify opportunities to address within the ITaaS framework instead of citing potential challenges as a reason to disengage.

- IT teams actively accelerated timelines through prompt replies and detailed follow-up instead of treating action items from the transformation team with an "as time allows" mentality that leads to program milestones and timelines being overrun on a recurring basis.

I have yet to work with a customer enterprise within which the CIO personally championed the transformation that did not achieve the value outcomes of having an IT organization capable of being operated like a competitive business and recognized as a trusted partner to their enterprise business.

As a final consideration, remember that the CIO's support should be based on a firm understanding of the ITaaS framework and its value proposition, as well as an understanding of the remaining critical success factors. It is critical that the change leadership team within the larger core transformation teams be ready to build and share a clear understanding of each of these concepts at the executive level. Without the explicit support of the CIO and commitment to these critical success factors, transformation and change leadership teams should likely begin asking themselves the difficult question of whether launching an ITaaS transformation program is even warranted and to what degree. Initiating a Services Transformation with executive-level support does not ensure its success, but initiating one without executive support will ensure its failure.

Championing a New Culture of IT

For the value outcomes of Services Transformation to be achieved, the culture of the IT organization itself must be transformed, and this will not be accomplished without the ongoing support of the CIO and senior IT leaders. Without fostering a widespread cultural change, adoption of the ITaaS framework simply amounts to a lot of effort to build a framework that will likely never be leveraged to its full extent. An upcoming section examines in detail what that culture should look like, which can be used to assess the current culture and then inform the ideal strategies and tactics for cultural change. At this point, change leadership teams must communicate the need for a cultural change and obtain the committed support of the CIO and senior IT leaders prior to kicking off the broader transformation program to actively support the cultural shift.

Fostering a shift in the culture of the IT organization is not an easy task. Almost every IT organization will face some level of resistance, and it can happen at any level of the organization and is likely to take many forms. The only way such a shift can be accomplished is by the most senior leaders in the organization acknowledging the necessity of cultural change and committing their support to it from the very beginning.

Engaging the Business

It is impossible to implement a framework for Service delivery capable of establishing the IT organization as trusted advisors to the business without ever actually engaging the business during the design of the framework. While this might sound like common sense, many IT organization attempting Services Transformation do everything they can to not engage the business, and in some cases even the broader IT organization, until the work is completed. Consider this question for a moment: how can a Service portfolio intended to reflect Services providing all technical capability requirements end-to-end across an enterprise be accurate without gathering input firsthand from the teams that consume those capabilities to operate and execute business processes? How can IT begin to qualify the value that an IT Service provides from the customer perspective without understanding directly from the customers who rely on the underlying set of technical capabilities to accomplish their day's work?

IT leaders must understand that these Service value conversations between IT and business don't result from a transformation team designing a Service delivery framework within the IT vacuum and then overnight suddenly kicking off well-rounded and highly polished conversations with business leaders that include considerations of how technical capabilities impacted business outcomes. Achieving such a state of constructive conversations requires extensive collaboration throughout all phases of the transformation program. The transformation team needs to solicit input and feedback from business teams in multiple phases of the transformation, while also effectively trialing likely imperfect Service Reviews across a selection of business teams, each with its own priorities, concerns, and preference of engagement styles, and gathering critical feedback from each.

In other words, the transformation team needs to engage business customers with an initially imperfect solution to test and identify opportunities for improvement. Change leadership teams should not be surprised to uncover some level of hesitation on the support of this critical success factor from senior IT leaders.

To obtain support for this critical success factor, change leadership teams should demonstrate a concern for ensuring consistently positive engagement of business teams. They should communicate to IT leaders a strong and clear approach to engaging the business successfully with a desire to foster their support and anticipation for the Services Transformation.

For the value outcomes of Services Transformation to be realized, the IT organization has to be willing and eager to engage their business customers. Senior IT leaders must be willing to support this level of business engagement, but to win this support, change leadership teams must be clear that care will be taken to ensure the success of these early engagements.

From the Diary of an ITaaS Consultant

I've had the opportunity to work with and witness the efforts of enterprise customers in the midst of Services Transformation Programs, including both those that partnered and collaborated closely with the lines of business during the transformation as well as those that instead chose to conduct the entirety of the design within the IT organization. Even worse, some have attempted to design the majority of the Service delivery framework completely within an IT Service management team.

In one such case, the engagement of business teams was facilitated by the CIO, who expressed to fellow business executives a desire to transform how the IT department delivered IT Services to focus more on enabling business outcomes. These business leaders then instructed their respective teams to support the IT Transformation teams whenever needed. This meant the framework for Service delivery was shaped from the earliest phases by leveraging key input and guidance from across the enterprise. Every component of the resulting framework resonated "business enablement" from the makeup of the Service portfolio to the Service-specific performance strategy. Pilot Service Reviews quickly progressed from imperfect trial to well-oiled forums for direct conversations around the current and future value of IT Services to the enterprise business.

Contrast this with a multiyear effort by one customer in which the bulk of the design was conducted purely by an IT Service management team who would, on limited occasions, solicit feedback on their approach from a limited set of teams within the IT organization. A point was reached whereby this team was called on by senior leaders to share their work to date with a selection of business customers. The result was a complete lack of understanding by these business customers as to how the efforts of this IT Service management team in any way changed how their teams consumed technical capabilities, much less facilitated any value outcomes that the business teams could look forward to. The sense of "looks like nothing new here" then shifted to confusion as business teams were unable to identify any of the newly defined Services and then raised one concern after another with regard to the proposed new approach to Service delivery that the IT teams were unable to answer. While the event was soon forgotten, so were all the Service management team's efforts to date, and the program was quietly abandoned soon after.

Top-Down/Business-First Services Design

It's not enough for ITaaS transformation teams to simply engage the business when adopting Cisco's ITaaS framework; they must begin with the business. The framework for IT Service delivery that results from Cisco's ITaaS framework and Services Transformation Program should be aligned completely to the delivery of technical capabilities required by the enterprise business. This outcome is facilitated by the ITaaS framework's approach to Service design that begins with Business Operations Service types. All remaining Service types are created only when they are required to provide capabilities that support these top-level Services. Services are not created simply because IT infrastructure, resources, or costs exist today. If they can't be mapped to a requirement, a Service is not designated.

By leveraging this approach, virtually every enterprise IT organization today can be assured of identifying a number of ways in which to optimize the organization, often by realigning pools of resources, infrastructure, and investments that aren't encompassed by any Services after completing the top-down development of Services. Not only is it common for enterprise IT organizations to be left with pockets of IT assets and resources without alignment to a Service, but most can expect both significant cost savings and opportunities to drive efficiency in those Services that were established through these realignments.

Note that not only do most IT organizations not follow this top-down or business-first progression of Services design, but most actually design Services from the bottom up, or from inside the IT organization out. We can assume this approach is typically taken with a concern for optimizing a Service delivery strategy in-house prior to engaging customers external to IT. What happens instead is that every IT asset, resource, or cost element that exists today is magically tucked into any number of Services, resulting in Services that are bloated with assets and resources that have no real alignment to enabling business outcomes. If your IT organization wants to ensure its infrastructure, resources, and assets are optimized and justifiably associated with Services aligned to the support of business outcomes, the way to accomplish this is with a top-down Service design approach.

Complete/End-to-End IT Services Transformation

The value of the ITaaS framework, and a Services Transformation, lies in becoming an end-to-end Services organization which also means that designating Services across only a portion of the organization's operations limits or even outright prevents much of the value potential. Not only does an IT organization forfeit the opportunity to achieve many of the most impactful value outcomes by electing to implement only pieces of the framework, but it also condemns itself to significant levels of rework and added complexity to all future efforts. This is the result of key components of Cisco's ITaaS framework design taking place in a linear and sequential fashion and the linkage between work-specific packages and their resulting artifacts, tools, and processes.

This is a mistake committed by many organizations who often choose to only designate IT-internal Services, what the ITaaS framework recognizes as Technology Foundation Service types. While these plans often intend to progress outward to Services delivering to the broader enterprise business the challenge is that the development of tools, strategies, processes, and even roles that work for IT-internal Services often fail to support these other Service types. Imagine spending months developing a Service costing strategy, only to find it has to be completely reworked in order to support a new wave of Services.

This does not mean that Cisco's ITaaS framework encourages teams to simultaneously launch hundreds of new IT Services at once. Instead Services are piloted in waves, typically increasing the number of Services in each wave until each Service defined in the portfolio has been onboarded, something a close friend often refers to as "rolling thunder." The key is that the first Service pilots launched include Services of each type and across the organization. This allows for every element of the framework from strategies for performance and costing to Service delivery roles to be tested and then refined across all Service types.

By implementing Cisco's ITaaS framework in its entirety and following the transformation program through sequentially, an enterprise can minimize complexity. It also can mitigate any need for extensive rework as additional strategies for Service delivery are implemented and ensure the quality of every component of the Service delivery framework while still accomplishing all the major value outcomes associated with the Services Transformation.

Centralized Transformation Authority

Successful Services Transformation requires the broad engagement of not only the IT organization but also business stakeholders at all levels of the enterprise, from operational teams to senior leaders. Without a centralized team recognized and supported by the CIO and senior IT leaders to make final decisions in the design and implementation of a new model for IT Service delivery, the IT organization can expect significant delays and timeline extensions for milestones throughout the transformation program. It also can expect a general dilution of the value that many work packages and the resulting strategies and tools are intended to deliver to the enterprise as numerous compromises to core aspects of the ITaaS framework are accepted simply to progress the effort.

These challenges result from transformation teams that must leverage engagement and input from IT and business stakeholders to derive key design decisions for the Service delivery model. All of these stakeholders present the potential for holding fast to their view of the proper course of development for a design decision, designation of a Service, or input to other components of the ITaaS framework. It is not uncommon for these design decisions to result in complete stalemates. Alternatively if transformation teams acquiesce to parties too readily while trying to prevent the design effort from hitting a roadblock, they can find themselves sacrificing long-term value of the transformation. Transformation teams can also easily find themselves in a looping state of serialized revalidation of decisions, with recommendations from one stakeholder group being overwritten by the next. This means the final direction of a critical design decision may result from either the last set of stakeholders solicited for input or from the stakeholders that most aggressively champion their input during the review process. Neither guarantees the best direction is adopted or that the final decision is in line with the long-term goals of an ITaaS framework and transformation program.

With regards to IT stakeholders, transformation teams should remember that these resources are a product of the current IT organization's historical culture of IT Service delivery, which may be poorly aligned with the future culture and associated mindsets that transformation teams are seeking to foster. Also, consider that these IT resources may base their input on previously established philosophies for Service management, resulting from any number of industry standards or legacy practices that may only align partially or not at all to Cisco's ITaaS framework.

The next section details a complete set of change leadership strategies for proactively educating IT and business stakeholders prior to engaging for design input in response to these considerations. Fully addressing these situations, however, requires nothing less than the recognition and empowerment of a central authority, typically a subset of the transformation team, to make the final decisions in hotly contested design decisions. To convince senior leaders to support this level of authority requires change leadership teams to communicate a commitment from these resources to evaluate all stakeholder input in detail. They must weigh this input carefully against the transformation guiding principles and long-term vision of success for the adoption of the framework before making a final decision that ensures the value outcomes of Services Transformation can be achieved.

Establishment and recognition of a centralized design authority within the transformation team by the CIO and senior IT leaders is required to ensure the best direction on key design decisions for the long-term outcomes of the Services Transformation are adopted and that stalemates between stakeholders won't pose a recurring risk to transformation program timelines.

Employing Change Leadership Strategies and Tactics

Earlier in this chapter, we established that change leadership teams supporting the ITaaS transformation are primarily concerned with two key goals: ensuring widespread adoption of the ITaaS framework and that the framework itself continues to create value for the enterprise. In this section, we review a series of overarching strategies that the change leadership function must drive to accomplish these two main goals. The topics presented here should remain constant considerations for change leadership teams across every phase and work package of the transformation program, and for every interaction with the broader IT organization and business teams.

Managing Services Transformation Messaging Strategies

A large part of the change leadership team's job is to act as the "public relations" arm of the Services Transformation Program. By this, we mean acting to drive key messages across the IT organization and enterprise business regarding the Services Transformation:

- The necessity for transforming to an end-to-end Services organization

- The goals and guiding principles for the Services Transformation

- The value that will be created for the enterprise through Services Transformation

This messaging strategy entails developing and updating various messaging content throughout the program ensuring all members of the IT Transformation team communicate a consistent theme and accurate, impactful message. Chapter 1 provided a great deal of background detail that change leadership teams can leverage to build their message from, and a later section in this chapter shares a range of tactics that change leadership teams can employ. Change leadership teams should tailor this background to best reflect considerations for IT Service delivery for their industry- and enterprise-specific goals, challenges, and opportunities. Clearly establishing relevance to a specific industry and to the enterprise itself serves IT Transformation teams especially well in efforts to win the support of stakeholders across the enterprise.

Think of the resulting Services Transformation messaging strategy and associated materials and artifacts as an effort at branding the Services Transformation Program. This is done to support the transformation team and other stakeholders in actively sharing the value message while ensuring that the messaging is accurate and consistent with the goals of the transformation. Consider for a moment the challenges that would result from members of the transformation team passing along incorrect or inconsistent messaging regarding the transformation to various stakeholders. While business stakeholders could quickly become frustrated or hesitant to contribute their input, the IT organization itself could become a major hurdle in its own right with mixed or inaccurate messaging. This is why it is critical that a core group of resources like the change leadership team proactively develop a formal messaging strategy to support IT Transformation teams and other resources in sharing the case for Services Transformation across a broad spectrum of stakeholders with an accurate and consistent message. Note, however, that the message should flow in specific directions and has to be tailored, including level of detail, style of content, type and length of the communications, and even who delivers it, all depending on the audience.

Directionally the messaging should begin with the CIO and then progress downward, top-to-bottom, eventually perpetuating across the whole of the IT organization. Change leadership teams should seek to evangelize the message through this top-down alignment of IT leaders who, in turn, encourage the leaders and teams under them to align to the goals of the transformation. The more committed a given leader is to the necessity and vision for Services Transformation, the more likely they are to initially inspire their teams to fully support any changes the transformation may mean for them. This also encourages

IT leaders to work through any concerns raised by their teams. Without the top-down alignment of IT leaders, it's possible that pockets of the IT organization will forgo adopting the framework or even actively hinder its development without the appropriate leaders taking action.

The starting point and direction of messaging for business stakeholders across the enterprise can and will likely vary. In some cases, the CIO may kick off awareness of the pending Services Transformation through announcements to peers. This is always an ideal opportunity to pursue because it allows the messaging to traverse enterprise business units in a top-down fashion, with business leaders convinced by the value creation potential for their departments and then encouraging their teams to lend their support and guidance to the IT Transformation teams whenever possible. In some cases, however, business stakeholders may learn of the plan for Services Transformation only when engaged for input and direction on components of the framework by the IT Transformation team.

Regardless of when the transformation team engages the stakeholders, it is critically important that they be prepared with a clear and strong message for Services Transformation. It is completely acceptable that the path of the messaging for Services Transformation across enterprise business units be fluid. The direction and timing of Services Transformation messaging for business stakeholders are less critical than for the IT organization. The important point is that the messaging itself be ready and appropriate for whichever level and whatever timing stakeholders are engaged. This flexibility is allowed because business stakeholders aren't required to adopt a new culture type and are impacted only by receiving technical capabilities better aligned to their needs, alongside a clear view of the value that the Services delivering those capabilities is providing to the business. As such, the stakeholders are likely to be much more receptive of the transformation program and supportive in providing input and direction for the design and implementation of the ITaaS framework than some members of the IT organization may be.

Next, change leadership teams should take care to consider updating the Services Transformation messaging based on the timing and progression of the transformation program. At times, this may include highlighting or developing further messaging details in support of specific efforts either recently completed or soon to be initiated, addressing particular concerns or challenges, or spreading the news of value impacts of the transformation on specific business units. Early in the program, the CIO and transformation team may prefer to minimize detail and instead repeatedly drive messaging around a small number of key value statements, and only to senior business leaders and stakeholders engaged in early phases of the transformation program. As the program progresses, the messaging may grow more robust, with details on specific efforts such as the Service portfolio design, and all shared to a wider group of recipients. The key is that change leadership teams remain proactive and considerate of the shifting requirements for value messaging based on the progression of the transformation program.

While the change leadership team should largely lead the development and management of the value message and branding for the Services Transformation, this does not necessarily mean that they will be the ones to deliver the message. In reality, a number of resources—from the CIO, broader IT Transformation team, and even IT managers providing updates to their teams—are likely to leverage the Services' transformation messaging content maintained by the change leadership team.

Ultimately, it is a combination of the progression and timing of the transformation program, the messenger, and the intended recipients of the message that will inform the style and type of content leveraged to deliver the message. Proactively managing a strategy for the development and readiness of a set of material that brands the Services Transformation is a proven method for fostering support at all levels of the IT organization and enterprise business.

Now that we understand the goal of a messaging strategy and some considerations for its implementation, we can consider specific activities or tactics that can be leveraged to support the strategy. The change leadership teams can and should consider specific types of material for development in support of the strategy for evangelizing the Services Transformation.

Sets of ITaaS and Services Transformation Program overview material can be prepared to support 15–90-minute overview presentations from the CIO, transformation team, or IT leaders when introducing the program. More detailed versions of these can be prepared for distribution to interested parties with the intention that they provide deeper context than a presentation would allow for but can be reviewed by stakeholders as their time allows.

"At a glance" material, or "one-pagers," can be incredibly effective at driving home the most critical points of the Services Transformation message in a way that is easily consumable and memorable. This material is most often leveraged in the form of handouts and even posters and other forms of promotional material that can be widely distributed. While highly effective for sharing an overview and case for becoming an ITaaSO, the concept of one-pagers can be employed for specific components and activities of the framework as well, such as IT Service performance or Service cost modeling.

Change leadership teams should also actively provide progress tracking for the Services Transformation to any and all interested parties. Just as important as sharing progress, however, is an explicit effort to identify, document, and then communicate the value outcomes achieved by the program's progress over time. Today's enterprise environments provide change leadership teams with a range of options for sharing this information at varying frequencies and level of detail, depending on the interested party. A corporate intranet page dedicated to the Services Transformation effort can offer updates on demand for parties, and newsletter- or flyer-type communications can be distributed by email on a subscription basis.

From the Diary of an ITaaS Consultant

I've enjoyed getting to witness various customers employ a wide range of Services Transformation messaging material. Some of the most effective materials included a "one-pager" employed by a company that clearly illustrated the goals of the Services Transformation, including highlights for the intended development of strategies for Service costing, Service metrics, and Service capabilities roadmapping, all resting under the bold text of the attention-grabbing title they had given their future Service delivery framework. This one-pager was then copied onto handouts with foldout stands and widely distributed across the IT organization and eventually business teams. It was also copied onto a poster and then proudly displayed outside the CIO's office. In one of the most memorable uses of this material, I was surprised to find these small handouts in the customer's office restrooms and even overheard positive comments on the posters while washing my hands. The result of this calculated and creative effort was an IT organization as well as a wide range of IT customers who were aware of and actively anticipating the implementation of this new framework for Service delivery and the value it would bring.

Optimizing Stakeholder Engagement

A successful framework for Service delivery is unlikely to prove much value to the enterprise business if it is designed in a vacuum. Transformation teams must engage both IT and business stakeholders for input and direction regularly throughout the transformation program. Recall that engaging the business is a critical success factor that should have the blessing of IT leaders prior to launching the program. With the ITaaS framework relying so extensively on the input of such a varied group of stakeholders, it becomes critically important that these resources understand the necessity of transitioning to an end-to-end Services organization, the value it enables for IT and the enterprise, and that they are willing to contribute quality input and direction to its development. Costing, metrics, and the design of Services are just a few examples of efforts and activities within the transformation program that necessitate stakeholder engagement to ensure the framework is capable of successful adoption and value creation.

With the need to engage a broad set of stakeholders established, we want to encourage change leadership and IT Transformation teams not to fear these interactions but rather to anticipate them as an opportunity to simultaneously ensure the validity of the in-development framework and build a broader base of awareness and support for the transformation program. To do so, however, requires that transformation teams be adequately prepared.

The first and most important strategy is the adoption and use of the Services Transformation messaging content developed by change leadership teams detailed in a previous section. Transformation teams should review the latest messaging and branding while considering their intended audience. The goal is for transformation teams to be able to quickly explain, in the early minutes of a meeting with stakeholders, the key messages supporting the necessity, goals, and value outcomes of Services Transformation.

General rules for stakeholder engagement with any type of project also apply here. Transformation teams should ensure they carefully consider and communicate the input they need and ensure they are engaging the best stakeholders possible for the desired input. They should be clear from the beginning in their descriptions of the Service delivery framework and the components for which they need input from the stakeholders to avoid having to revisit stakeholders on numerous occasions to refine their input. Finally, teams should ensure that they make the most of the stakeholders' time and actively leverage in-person meetings, remote web and audio conferences, and email while also remaining flexible around stakeholder availability. Previously established good will and support for the program can be quickly lost if transformation teams book time on calendars with incorrect resources, don't make effective use of stakeholders' backgrounds and availability, or poorly communicate their questions and inquiries at first, resulting in the need for multiple stakeholder follow-ups to fully validate the input.

Resources assigned to the program governance and project management workstream can lend assistance to transformation teams or even play active roles in maintaining the quality of stakeholder engagements by providing agendas proactively and following up with stakeholders on action items. After all, stakeholders and transformation teams have to reach some agreement on the timing for finalization of input to move ahead with the transformation program.

One of the most valuable tools that change management and transformation teams can develop in support of successful stakeholder engagement strategies is an interview protocol or strawman script for leading stakeholder conversations. These scripts can then be leveraged by transformation teams as they kick off communications with stakeholders; they ensure the teams are ready to facilitate a clear overview of and value message for Services Transformation in the opening minutes of a conversation and then clearly communicate the specific component of the framework they are seeking input on. Whenever possible, these scripts should be rehearsed prior to leveraging with actual stakeholders, and transformation teams should know that these scripts can and should be updated as they are tested with actual stakeholders. Note that the intent is not necessarily for the scripts to be read verbatim, or that they can't be translated into the style and words of the person delivering the message; rather they are intended as supportive outline and reference for guiding a meeting or prompting a speaker.

Clever use of material from the Services Transformation messaging strategy can also support successful stakeholder engagement. For example, a transformation team may use one-pagers or overview material to introduce the topic or provide overview content ahead of time.

Changing the Culture of IT

How can you truly influence and foster a cultural shift across a business organization? Or as one customer asked me, "Sounds great in theory, but how do we really get this thing started?" Think of an actual shift in an organization's culture as a large wave, moving from one end to the other until it has washed across and impacted every part of the organization. The change leadership team's job is to initiate and power that wave until it becomes self-propelled. We can do this by starting small, leveraging a strategy that encourages an ideal mindset and behavior at the individual level, and working outward from change leadership and IT Transformation teams with the support of IT leaders until a growing number of individuals have fully embraced the ideal mindset and become influencers themselves.

Change leadership teams play a crucial role in initiating this cultural wave by shaping the strategy and tactics leveraged to keep it moving. They begin by evaluating the existing cultural landscape of the organization, then developing and evangelizing a vision of the ideal future culture of the organization and how its widespread adoption is capable of evolving IT's relationship with the enterprise. After considering gaps between these two cultures for IT Service delivery, the change leadership team can lead the development of a strategy and underlying tactics to facilitate the cultural change by influencing the mindset of a growing number of professionals until it becomes a self-propelled wave moving across the organization.

Evaluating the Culture of the IT Organization Today

To best facilitate a shift in the culture of an IT organization, change leadership teams need to first understand the culture of the IT organization today. The underlying culture of any IT organization today differs from the ideal future mindset of an end-to-end Services organization; the goal is to understand just how far apart they are in order to shape the best strategy, proactively identify and manage challenges, and adopt the best tactics.

Below are some of the considerations a change leadership team may want to gauge in order to develop an informed understanding of the culture of their IT organization today:

- What is the general level of knowledge of the enterprise industry and markets, value chain and line of business operations, and corporate strategies across the IT organization?

- What is the landscape for IT resources with knowledge and experience relevant to the industry and line of business operations? What about corporate function BUs such as HR or others?

- What is the general opinion of IT resources with regard to who customers are, and the purpose and obligations of the IT organization to the enterprise business?

- How do various IT resources describe the value of IT Services; how does this differ from the customer-base?

- What is the general sentiment of business stakeholders at different levels and across different functions of the enterprise business toward the IT organization and its approach to Service delivery?

- Are there any existing considerations for recent events or characteristics of the IT organization that could impact, positively or negatively, the adoption of a new culture for IT Service delivery and partnership with the business?

This information can be gathered in a number of ways, from surveys to interviews that carefully sample each part of the IT organization. Whenever possible, leverage senior leadership support to bolster participation. Besides simply gauging the potential resistance to cultural change within the IT organization, the data gathered by change leadership teams here can inform the need for learning programs and knowledge-transfer initiatives later in the transformation program.

The best approach to capturing and documenting the information gathered should also be considered. Scaled measurements can provide an easy method for illustrating a surveyed characteristic of the organization's culture. For instance, when considering an IT organization's readiness to support a new approach to IT Service delivery, a scale of 1 to 10 could be used, with 10 reflecting a very high level of understanding and support. Multiple-choice responses offer another alternative; for example, when gathering input from business customers regarding their views of the IT organization, consider having them select from four descriptive responses.

It is important to consider any major events, either recent or even years past, that may influence the mood of the IT organization or business. Large-scale outsourcing, layoffs, or leadership changes could all sow resistance. Characteristics of the IT organization, such as large numbers of contractors or large numbers of resources new to the industry, can also present opportunities or challenges.

Another important factor to consider is the presence and number of resources within the IT organization today that already perform and share a mindset closer to that of the ideal future culture of IT. Some enterprises have already made attempts at establishing roles for IT resources that focus on dedicated engagement of business stakeholders and developing knowledge of their operations. While these roles vary widely between enterprises, are not always common, and may have been met with mixed success, they still represent opportunities for change leadership teams to identify and leverage. Another possible opportunity are resources in the IT organization who actually transitioned into IT from another business unit or have prior industry or business unit expertise. Note that IT resources with experience outside the IT organization are often more common in managerial roles due to historical approaches to rotations for management resources across various business units of an enterprise. At the individual level, change leadership teams need to assess a candidate's willingness to learn about and share a customer's goals and priorities versus a desire to focus purely on technology.

Envisioning the Future Culture of IT

What does it mean to say that an IT organization has adopted the ideal mindset in support of an end-to-end Services organization? What are the daily behaviors and attitudes of a given group of resources that manifest and sustain such a culture? In other words, what does good look like?

Change leadership teams should be able to describe the ideal future mindset of IT professionals and the culture they will cumulatively create. They should be able to provide strong examples of how a resource who has adopted this mindset would impact interactions with their customers and their view of the value technical capabilities create for the enterprise business. Change leadership and broader IT Transformation teams should be the first to exemplify those behaviors themselves, acting as the earliest role models for the future culture of IT. They should be the first to "walk the walk." Developing the abilities to describe and demonstrate these behaviors, guide the development of supporting training material, and act as early role models are all key activities for the change leadership function.

To begin, first consider those traits that should be shared by every member of the future IT organization. For starters, every IT resource should have general knowledge of the enterprise that the IT organization is supporting, such as its industry, relevant markets, value chain and major functions of the lines of business. Every resource within the IT organization should also understand the top corporate initiatives and, obviously, how the major goals and strategies of the IT organization support those initiatives. These resources should also acknowledge the various considerations described in Chapter 1, such as the fundamental purpose of the IT organization, obligations for supporting business outcome and operating efficiently, and the relationship and expectations associated with Service providers and their customers. Every resource should understand that IT is an end-to-end Services organization and focused on creating business value and customer satisfaction through the delivery of Services that enable business outcomes. Furthermore, each member of the IT organization should have a high-level familiarization with the organization's framework for Service delivery. Remember, these characteristics are true of every resource in the future IT organization, regardless of whether they act in a Service delivery role or focus purely on supporting a specific technology domain.

Characteristic requirements for IT resources facilitating Service delivery roles such as a Service Owner go even further. These resources should demonstrate a strong desire to partner with their customers and strive to be recognized as trusted advisors. Service Owners need to demonstrate an intimate knowledge of the operations, concerns, and goals of their customer base. For Business Operations Service types, this often requires developing knowledge of the business processes executed by the business unit and the business outcomes that these processes enable. This is required in order to understand the impact that technical capabilities have on the processes and to identify opportunities to leverage new technology platforms to improve the execution of those business processes. These resources have a thorough understanding of the Service delivery framework and constantly seek to drive value through the Services they support. Chapter 7, "Service Delivery Roles and Responsibilities," expands on the ideal candidates and behaviors for these Service delivery roles.

Once the change leadership team has developed an initial view of the IT organization's future culture, they can compare it with the culture that exists today. In doing so, they can identify gaps and challenges that become critical inputs while shaping change leadership strategies, identifying opportunities, and informing the development of training material.

Using Strategies and Tactics to Facilitate the Cultural Shift to an ITaaSO

Developing a strategy and a series of corresponding activities to foster a shift in the culture of an organization is another important activity for the change leadership team. Although the change leadership team is responsible for the initial strategy, it is key that the IT Transformation and IT leadership teams review and help refine the proposal because they will be equally responsible for executing it over time.

The strategy and resulting tactics are heavily influenced by careful consideration of the current and ideal future culture of the IT organization. Based on these considerations, the strategy should illustrate a plan for shifting the underlying culture of IT overlaid with the Services Transformation Program, highlight significant opportunities and challenges, and recommend specific activities. The strategy should also consider methods for qualifying the progress of the cultural shift and effectiveness of the strategy.

Some of the first activities applicable for all change leadership teams to support a strategy for cultural change are to prepare a set of materials that describe the target future culture of the IT organization and mindsets of the individuals who make it up. The shock of the intended cultural shift can be lessened through strong onboarding practices for Service delivery roles, regular training and knowledge-sharing sessions such as lunch-and-learns, and continuous learning programs that equally serve the Services Transformation value messaging effort. In fact, much of the materials that make up the Services Transformation messaging effort can likewise prepare IT resources for the cultural shift and raise the visibility of role models.

Some of the most impactful tactics for influencing a shift in the culture of an organization are to incentivize behaviors through rewards alignment and recognize those individuals who demonstrate the ideal behavior and mindset. The principle is simple: explicitly describe and encourage the adoption of new behaviors and mindsets, and then reward and recognize those who best demonstrate those characteristics in practice. Consider spotlighting top-performing individuals and leveraging their leading mindset for Service delivery roles. Reinforce the organization's commitment to the new culture over time by maintaining visibility and recognition. Proactively ensure that leadership approval and programs are in place to support these tactics.

Finally, the content of this section would not be complete until we share with you a hard truth of the implementation of the ITaaS framework and transformation of the culture of the IT organization: not all IT resources present today will thrive in the future IT organization. The change leadership team and IT leaders should make every effort to encourage and support every resource in the organization, but we cannot ignore that the IT organization post-Services Transformation is a completely different organization than the one that exists today. Some resources simply may not appreciate or enjoy how the organization operates, whereas others simply may not be capable of facilitating a role required in this new end-to-end Services organization. IT organizations committed to facilitating a new culture for IT Service delivery must prepare for these inevitabilities, while change leadership teams shape strategies and supporting activities to guide resources through the changing landscape. Note that this is not meant to imply in any way that a large portion of the organization will not be needed or will be unable to adopt the new mindset of an ITaaSO. Rather, our intent is to highlight the eventuality that the priorities of the organization will be much different. As a result, the top performers today may not be the top performers of tomorrow, some resources will struggle to adopt the new mindset and will need support to adjust, and in some limited cases, professionals may not be willing or able to adjust to the new culture of the IT organization.

Services Transformation Program Best Practices and Lessons Learned

The following topics relate to the overall management and successful execution of the Services Transformation Program rather than specifically to the change leadership function and its related strategies. Similar to the transformation critical success factors, making sure IT Transformation and IT leadership teams remain aware of these considerations represent a key activity to change leadership. Chapter 2, "Introducing Cisco ITaaS Framework and Services Transformation Program," provided a brief introduction to a lengthy and complex Services Transformation Program. Despite a growing successful track record, a Services Transformation that realizes the outcomes discussed in Chapter 1 is a difficult task to achieve, and there is no reason for your IT Transformation team to repeat the mistakes of previous organizations.

Show Value Early

Realizing valuable outcomes for the IT organization and enterprise business is not limited to the completion of the Services Transformation. In fact, there is substantial opportunity to demonstrate value outcomes stemming from the transformation program within even the earliest phases and activities.

The Discovery and Design phase of the transformation program offers some of the earliest opportunities to provide value outcomes to the IT organization and its customers. In the Business and IT alignment work package, transformation teams conduct interviews across a range of both IT and business teams from operational, management, and senior management levels. While the bulk of this feedback informs the target ITaaS model for Service delivery and its desired capabilities, these interviews often uncover a lengthy list of issues that can be quickly addressed by the IT organization. Change leadership teams should quickly inform IT leaders of the opportunities and then make sure to track and share the results of any activities stemming from the feedback collected in the interviews. Examples of these low-hanging fruits commonly include IT teams quickly developing scripts or other means of automation in support of pesky repetitive tasks for business operations teams or by reprioritizing and escalating challenges that business teams had previously given up on. Other examples include IT managers making changes to policy or temporary concessions, allowing IT operational teams to better address the needs of the business where they may have previously been constrained. There is no reason to wait until these capabilities have been framed into a formal IT Service by the transformation program to support the customer. Note that similar value outcomes can be derived from the other work packages within the Discovery and Design phase again by maintaining a sharp eye for opportunities to engage and support IT customers. Value will be created; the goal of the change leadership team is to recognize, communicate, and track it.

Demonstrating value early can benefit the transformation team in a number of ways, from bolstering change leadership efforts at spreading the word about the Services Transformation, to encouraging constructive support from key stakeholders, to quickly solidifying the support of IT and business leaders who may have at first hesitated to formally back the program. There's also just something to be said for getting a complex, multiyear program that seeks to fundamentally change the way IT interfaces with its customers off on the right foot.

Show Value Often

Show value early, and then keep it up throughout the life of the transformation program. The goal here is to develop a regular cadence for communicating value outcomes stemming from the Services Transformation, often referred to as incremental value.

Every work package and underlying set of activities provides the opportunity for a range of value outcomes—minor and major—for both the IT organization and the enterprise business. Some of these are the direct result of the work to adopt the ITaaS framework, whereas other instances of value outcomes are indirect, such as the identification of gaps in delivery of technical capabilities or cases where IT processes are constraining business operations. Whenever such a gap is identified, IT Transformation teams should communicate these and other opportunities to IT leaders who can engage the appropriate teams to address. Uncovering and reporting key information to relevant parties is itself a value outcome.

Whether directly or indirectly, relevant to IT or business stakeholders or to both, value continues to be created throughout the Services Transformation. Change leadership teams who make an effort to identify, capture, and actively communicate the value stemming from the transformation can be sure of support for their efforts throughout the program rather than simply at the beginning.

Engage the Business Early

The sooner change leadership teams engage key business stakeholders, the better. Although we established that a willingness and support for engaging the business throughout the transformation are critical success factors in an earlier section, this consideration is intended to encourage transformation teams to do so as early as possible. Engaging business stakeholders for input to the development of the framework and sharing details of the planned transformation aren't tasks that should be withheld until later phases of the transformation but instead should be done as early as possible. This is especially true for IT organizations that have found themselves in strongly unfavorable positions with their business customers.

The earliest opportunity for doing so is within the Discovery and Design phase work package for business and IT alignment, which encourages teams to conduct interviews with a range of business stakeholders. These interviews not only provide valuable input for the target ITaaS model design but also communicate that IT is eager to listen to its customers and to change its approach for Service delivery. Soon after this activity, as transformation teams complete an initial "to-be" design for the Service delivery model, change leadership teams should be strongly positioned to begin actively sharing a wide variety of value messaging. The sooner the change leadership team shares the message that the IT organization is seeking to align and partner with the business and to transform its culture to one focused on enabling business outcomes through technology, the better.

General Transformation Program Best Practices

While they may not require extensive explanation or detail, transformation and change leadership teams at some point in the future truly will appreciate this set of general best practices for conducting a Services Transformation. Consider these a compilation of tough lessons learned from Cisco Services teams dedicated to guiding customers of all sizes and varying industries through their own Services Transformations.

Respect the Realities of "Theory versus Practice"

As a creative spin on a quote intended for combat environments, I like to tell IT Transformation teams, "No business plan survives first contact with the customer." Business teams regularly conceptualize innovative, high-value business plans that just don't quite work out or create the level of value they had intended when put into practice, or in some cases cannot even be put into practice within real-world enterprise businesses. IT organizations and historical standards for IT Service management have struggled with the same challenges for translating theory into practice.

This principle means that IT Transformation teams need to emphasize from the earliest stages of the program that the capacity for putting a proposed design into practice trumps any other aspects of a proposal. This requires demonstrating high confidence that a proposed element of the framework can work in practice. The question that should be at the top of any IT Transformation team's design deliberations is "Can this approach be implemented successfully across different Service types and for different customer bases?" Don't make the mistake of overriding thoroughly tested design philosophies with seemingly big, innovative designs that have never been tested.

Cisco's ITaaS framework and the corresponding transformation program are a reflection of Cisco's focus on the ability to successfully implement a framework for Service delivery and achieve adoption end-to-end across the enterprise. Success is accounted for only after the Service delivery framework has achieved widespread adoption and value outcomes have been realized, not when the transformation team completes the design of a conceptual Service delivery framework.

Adopt the 80/20 Rule and Avoid Analysis Paralysis

Transformation teams hoping to progress components of the Service delivery framework to perfection prior to implementing or reviewing with stakeholders quickly find themselves in a quagmire, or state of "analysis paralysis." Striving to be perfect right out of the gate just leads to increased timelines for milestones as well as frustrated transformation teams as they hit one roadblock after another.

Rather than striving for perfection, transformation teams should be reminded that they are working with incredibly complex strategies expected to work across different areas of the enterprise. There is no way these strategies can be 100 percent perfected without testing them.

At a more tactical level, transformation teams should consider adopting an "80/20" approach to their design work before then trialing the solution with the intent to monitor and improve over time. This practice involves transformation teams progressing a strategy to the point where they have a confidence that 80 percent of their design decisions are likely to stand up to widespread implementation. The remaining 20 percent have been developed to the best of the transformation team's abilities, leveraging all available input, but have the potential to be refined after they are tested across different scenarios.

Be Willing to Engage at All Levels

Transformation teams engage stakeholders across both the IT organization and the enterprise at large, and these teams can be easily be distracted in such a way as to shift almost all their focus to collecting input solely from managers and senior leaders across the enterprise business units. Doing so is a mistake, resulting in an incomplete picture of the true day-to-day requirements of a business unit to operate and achieve business outcomes. Ultimately, this means a diluted Service design and the potential to miss out on any number of opportunities to truly impact the daily execution of business outcomes by those individual contributors that perform the activity.

A model for IT Service delivery has to address the requirements of all IT customers. The best way to accomplish this is for transformation teams to talk with everyone. Whenever possible, transformation teams should collect input from junior and senior individual contributors, first- and second-level management, and senior leadership. Talk with resources who have been with the company for decades, and talk with recent hires who may bring fresh ideas.

The goal of transformation teams when engaging stakeholders—whether for the purpose of validating proposed Services, testing an approach to Service performance metrics dashboarding, or working through early Service Review pilots—is to paint a *complete* picture of how the IT Services impact and create value for the enterprise business.

Remain Open to New Ideas

As transformation teams engage a complete range of IT and business stakeholders, they must always remain open to evaluating new ideas that these resources may propose. As they progress through the transformation program, it is not uncommon for transformation teams to develop a detailed view of the direction that certain components of the Service framework should take. The potential issue this raises is the prospect of transformation teams sometimes neglecting a careful and thorough evaluation of stakeholder input simply because it fails to align perfectly with their preconceived plans for the resulting framework.

Embrace, Don't Fear, Service Review Pilots with Business Stakeholders

Many enterprise IT organizations make the mistake of waiting too long to launch a series of Service Review pilots. Change leadership teams should set expectations, emphasizing the "pilot" status of these sessions with stakeholders who are invited and to encourage constructive criticism and feedback. Even with these precautions highlighted, however, many teams refrain from including Business Operations Service types requiring the presence of business stakeholders in the pilot phase. Doing so effectively means ignoring a wide range of Services within the portfolio during crucial design and development phases. This can lead to major components of the framework design being finalized after significant effort only to fail to work effectively, or at all, for those Services that directly interact with business stakeholders.

Stick to the Program

Earlier in this chapter, we established a commitment to the implementation of the ITaaS framework in its entirety as a critical success factor for successful Services Transformation. We also highlighted that the Services Transformation Program depicted in Chapter 2 is very high level, allowing for some flexibility in the efforts and activities within any given work package. That flexibility should never be extended outside the transformation phases themselves. The reason is that so much of the complex work conducted in a work package is likely to build off earlier work packages. As an example, IT organizations that try to develop an IT Service costing strategy without first developing a robust taxonomy and detailed and consistent approach to Service definition and design are complicating an already-difficult task and are faced with a strong likelihood of having to conduct significant rework at some point in the future. Also, consider that work packages within a specific transformation phase often provide opportunities for feedback and testing between one another. For example, in Transformation Phase 2, as teams develop an initial approach to demonstrating IT Service performance and IT Service costing, the Service Review pilots provide an ideal test ground and constructive feedback arena with IT customers for these strategies across different types of Services.

Again, the transformation program illustrated in Chapter 2 is very high level and offers transformation teams flexibility for conducting activities within a specific transformation phase. There is a great deal of risk and no long-term value to tackling work packages outside their designated sequence and transformation phase.

Just stick with the program.

Behind the Scenes of the Cisco IT Services Transformation

For Cisco IT, there was never a change agent or change leader, but a change organization; and it was one of the first things initiated in support of the Services Transformation. The change organization was made up of resources from various groups that came together to drive what we needed to, which was the framework of change and how to measure the organization's adoption of it.

The change team relied heavily on support from the CIO. It takes a leader who is clear and adamant that "THIS IS WHAT IS GOING TO HAPPEN!" The CIO drove accountability and a constant "make it better" mentality, along with the message that "We are all on this bus together." Everyone had to get on board, and people had to understand it. It was clearly established that within the first year, "We will know we are a Services organization by certain things: Instead of ops reviews, we will have Service Reviews, etc." That sent terror through the organization initially, but everyone knew it was being driven by the CIO. The leaders and messaging acknowledged that this was a difficult task, but also tangible. The CIO empowered the change organization and made them powerful and public. You have to make the change organization into "a big stinkin' deal" if you really want to change or transform yourself, so the question is "How bad do you want it? How serious are you about achieving these outcomes?"

The change organization also understood quickly that this was a cultural change and that successful change leadership would require tenacity. You just don't quit. It's going to go slower than you think it should; you are going to hit roadblocks and unseen challenges. You are going to want to give up. There will be a tipping point where it's cool to be disparaging. Then one day it's not cool any more to disparage; instead, it's cool to be doing it. There's no way to project when that tipping point will happen.

The change team at Cisco started by looking for basic tenets: What's the urgency? What's the vision? What are the things that will help get this mass of people to move in this direction? The entire organization, from interns to VPs, all have to see what the Services Transformation means to them. If you only have a small percentage of people to shoulder the load because a job description is forced on them, then you are not going to succeed. You have to spend a lot of time, energy, and effort on that. Change team members presented topics, answered questions, and addressed concerns over and over again. At times they had to reach out there and grab the person by the collar and go, "This is YOU! I'm talking to YOU!" and when you've got that for 3,000 people, and every single one of them has felt that tug: "Oh, you mean me? I have to do something?" That's what you have to get to.

As one person stated, "In the early days, I remember hearing about the end-to-end Services mantra and thought it was pie in the sky." There was resistance across the organization around what this even meant. So, one of the first things the CIO did was create a change team. These people where handpicked from across the organization at different levels—a very diversified group. The CIO considered them the "listening team." These were influential folks who could bring the message back to senior staff (to avoid dilutions as messaging moves up the stack). And they heard the concerns coming from rank and file about why we were doing this.

Next, they created IT cohorts. The idea was that people would watch each other's back. There was a group of peers (no one reported to the leader). Once a month or so, they would meet for two hours on big changes happening in IT. People in the cohort would have their own opinion on why it would work or why it was stupid. It was a safe place you could voice concerns and work through them. I remember two of the big problems. The first was that people just didn't understand what it really meant, and people were wondering if it was "the flavor of the month." "Is this another fad that will die?" The other was that there was a lot of additional work being put on people. We had the cohorts set up so that we could discuss these problems, and it helped people understand that this was happening across the organization. It helped people understand it wasn't just me or my group; this is not the flavor of the month. This was real.

Historically, as part of change management, senior leaders would dream up the new thing. Then the rank and file were chomping at the bit to get to work on the new thing. But then the middle (middle management, etc.) were there primarily because they were successful with the *old* way. So, they didn't want to change (they were frozen). The cohorts helped the change team thaw the "frozen middle."

Ideal behaviors had to be demonstrated and then fostered and rewarded. Think of this process as a change wheel. You need to reward, celebrate quick wins, define crisp destination, and have a listening team, and repeat. Create cohorts that let resources at all levels talk freely about the frustrations, know they are not alone, and know that their frustrations are being addressed.

Summary

The importance of change leadership to achieving the value outcomes of Services Transformation and fostering the cultural shift of the IT organization cannot be understated. Without a dedicated and consistent prioritization of change leadership, the transformation program is exposed to risk from all directions and is likely to fail.

Responsibility for change leadership is widespread but is driven by a core team of resources within the IT Transformation team. Their purpose is to shape the overarching strategies for change leadership and supporting material, acting as leverage points for IT leaders and transformation teams. The goal of the change leadership is to ensure the widespread adoption of the ITaaS framework for Service delivery and ensure that it continues to create value for the IT organization and enterprise business.

Change leadership teams need to win the commitment and support of the enterprise CIO and senior IT leaders for a series of critical success factors that must be supported throughout the life of the transformation program:

- Obtaining executive sponsorship

- Championing a new culture of IT

- Engaging the business

- Assuring complete/end-to-end IT Services delivery transformation

- Using a top-down/business-first Service design approach

- Utilizing a centralized transformation authority

Change leadership teams need to shape a strategy capable of addressing the following, along with the tactics to support the strategy, such as creation and distribution of materials and other activities:

- Developing Services Transformation value messaging

- Supporting the optimization of stakeholder engagement

- Guiding the cultural change of IT

- Preparing for the future

Finally, as the IT organization progresses through the Services Transformation, change leadership teams should remain conscious of and actively share with transformation teams a series of best practices for conducting the Services Transformation Program successfully:

- Show value early.

- Show value often.

- Engage the business early.

- Be mindful of general best practices.

Chapter 4

Service Delivery Taxonomy and Definition of a Service

Now we begin our review of Cisco's ITaaS framework in earnest, and it must start with a detailed and well-rounded examination of exactly how an IT organization defines an IT Service. Although consideration for defining a well-known term may seem trivial, as you will see, its impact on the Service delivery framework's capabilities, resulting customer experience, and ability to achieve desired outcomes is quite significant.

If you have a background in existing IT Service management standards and practices, which include their own definition of Services, you will find some similarities in Cisco's definition. But you will also find that the ITaaS framework takes an equally simpler and more strategic view of a Service that is ultimately quite different from existing standards. This unique approach to the definition and subsequent design of Services can result in a starkly different landscape of Services for an enterprise, and the mechanisms available for managing them, than previous Service management practices.

While their impact to the framework is far reaching, Services represent only one of several levels designated by a Service delivery taxonomy, leveraged to create a hierarchy for strategically managing the Services landscape. The taxonomy creates a range of capabilities for the Service delivery function of an IT organization and, as such, must be purpose-fit to the IT organization. With this in mind, we introduce a reference taxonomy included as part of the ITaaS framework and also discuss the considerations for altering the reference model.

Service Definition Considerations

As an initial consideration, recall back in Chapter 1 where we discussed the purpose of leveraging the concept of a Service. A Service allows us to collect a set of customer requirements into a zone of management, creating a focal point for delivery and improving customer satisfaction along with measuring and improving value of the Service.

With so many existing definitions and descriptions already widely perpetuated across the industry, you may be eager to understand Cisco's justification for introducing still another designation of what constitutes an IT Service as part of the ITaaS framework. Rest assured, there is a reason, and it is far more than a simple desire to establish itself from existing standards. Rather, it is the direct result of Cisco's goals for the capabilities of the Service delivery framework, which in turn necessitated a complete reassessment of previous approaches to defining IT Services, their characteristics, and the resulting set of Services they would create. Many IT teams often accept a simple definition and example of a Service with little consideration, and immediately begin work designing Services for their IT organization. This is a significant oversight as the definition of a Service has far-reaching consequences for the eventual adoption and effectiveness of an IT organization's Service delivery function and resulting customer experience.

When applied to the same enterprise, variations in the definition of a Service, even minor in detail, can result in a completely different landscape of Services. One definition of a Service may result in a set of 100 Services for an enterprise but when subjected to minor changes could result instead in a portfolio of 300 Services for the exact same enterprise. The same minor change to a definition could also drastically alter how the Service is managed, and how a determination of value can be evaluated through the amount of costs or the type of performance strategies that could be measured and associated with it.

Perhaps most significantly, the adopted definition of a Service will influence what the resulting Services will focus on. Historical IT Service design is often technology-centric, focusing specific consumables or requests such as those found on a corporate e-store. Some IT Service management teams have even attempted to associate an IT Service with an application in a one-to-one type approach, so an IT organization managing 50 applications would designate 50 Services. Although these approaches may allow for quick and direct association of a range of common technical metrics meaningful to most IT practitioners, it also results in a large set of several hundred or even far more Services for even a medium-size enterprise. In a large-size enterprise, these technology-centric approaches to designating IT Services could result in portfolios exceeding well over 500 or more Services.

Another consideration to remain conscious of is the careful balance of management overhead that results from the designation of a Service and the value the effort invested in managing it creates. In other words, does the underlying definition of a Service result in the creation of IT Services that are worth the effort to manage?

The goal of the ITaaS framework's definition of an IT Service is to focus on the delivery of capabilities consumed by IT customers, rather than the technical platforms used to enable them, and to create a point of leverage for Service delivery teams to measure and improve the customer experience and value the Service creates for the business. In other words Services are intended to be customer-centric, and designed in a manner that warrants the effort of managing a series of strategies associated with each and every Service that can in turn enable informed decision making.

The following sections will take you through a step-by-step build-up to the ITaaS frameworks definition of a Service. While this may seem unnecessarily tedious, the intent is to minimize the complexity of Service design, while also protecting the integrity of the resulting Services. The practice of designating Services end-to-end across an IT organization holds significant potential for confusion and deviation from what was originally intended. By following the build-up of a definition for IT Services Transformation teams are better prepared to navigate the perplexing and heated debates likely to result from applying a consistent approach to Service design across a complex organization.

The ITaaS framework also associates a set of characteristics to its definition of an IT Service. Here again the purpose in attributing characteristics, or traits, with our definition is to proactively influence the proper use of the term, and to provide clarity for potential points of confusion that are sure to arise.

A Step-by-Step Approach to Defining a Service

Conducting an online search for "definition of Service" will return a limitless number of sources, each providing largely similar definitions for the term used as both a noun and verb. If we were to quickly review and summarize these sources, we would likely arrive at something similar to the following simple definitions for a Service:

- **Simple Definition of a *Service* (noun):** A designation for a logical organizational unit encompassing the resources, material, and processes required to provide or deliver goods, commodities, utilities, or capabilities

- **Simple Definition of *Service* (verb):** The act of providing or delivering goods, commodities, utilities, or capabilities

With these simple definitions in mind, let's next consider some basic characteristics that we could associate with the generic concept of a Service:

- A Service is delivered by a provider to a customer.

- A Service should deliver goods or capabilities that are required/desired by customers.

- The delivery of goods or capabilities should provide a value to the customer.

The first point seeks to add additional detail to the definition while the following two establish some qualification criteria that help distinguish between what constitutes a Service and, just as importantly, what does not. After all, if the delivery of a set of goods or capabilities fails to add value—for example, a utility fails to be available when required or a consumable is broken or otherwise unusable upon receipt by the customer—then we wouldn't highlight the provider as having provided a Service. Additionally, we would not want to highlight examples where a provider delivered goods or utilities that customers never even needed in the first place. Arguably, in both cases, a provider made an effort at delivering goods or utilities, and you could easily debate the fact that this is in line with our definition of a Service, but while accurate, the fact would yet remain that it wasn't an ideal implementation or use of the term Service.

Next, because we know the ITaaS framework is concerned purely with the delivery of Services from the IT organization, we can refine this definition further. What is it exactly that we deliver from within an IT organization?

Referring back to Chapter 1, "The Case for IT Transformation and IT as a Service (ITaaS)," we know we are focused on the delivery of technical capabilities leveraged across the enterprise business for productivity (such as through email or computing devices) or to enable processes that achieve business outcomes (such as a large-scale platform that enables management of the supply chain). It could be argued that some IT Services, for instance a Service for "IT Technical Support," deliver outcomes as well, such as the restoration of certain operational capabilities. In reality these cases represent a small portion of the whole, and IT Services will largely focus on delivering technical capabilities, and for that reason that ITaaS framework most often simply refers to IT Services as delivering capabilities.

Besides specifying that technical capabilities are being delivered, we can also change the reference to *materials* (likely to invoke thoughts of manufacturing a consumable of some type) and replace it instead with *assets*, which is a more appropriate reflection of the various applications, servers, and networking equipment that support the provisioning of technical capabilities. Now we have an initial, simple definition for an IT Service:

> Simple *IT Service* Definition: A designation for a logical organizational unit encompassing the resources and assets supporting the delivery of technical capabilities by the IT organization.

That's it. At its core, there's really no more to the basic concept. We're just adapting our previous definition of the term and specifying that rather than generic goods, utilities, or commodities, we are specifically delivering technical capabilities through a logical grouping of resources and assets managed by the IT organization.

While they each still apply, we can also refine the characteristics we associated earlier to our definition, helping them to better reflect the elements of Services delivered by an IT organization. We should also begin presenting these as bold statements, or declarations, regarding the use of the term *Service* as we are anticipating the need to reference these to address questions, concerns, and potential points of confusion from various stakeholders:

- The IT organization is a Service provider, responsible for the delivery of Services to its customers end-to-end across the enterprise.

- An IT Service should deliver technical capabilities required by IT customers.

- The technical capabilities delivered from an IT Service should provide value to the customer.

We can add further detail to our definition through additional context such as the capabilities support of business outcomes and emphasizing aspects of how we intend Services to be managed.

> Detailed *IT Service* Definition: An IT Service is a logical collection of technical capabilities, delivered by the IT organization, required to support business outcomes, managed in a cost-effective manner while seeking to proactively innovate, transform, and improve business outcomes through the application of technology.

That is a strong candidate for a final, detailed definition of a Service, and adding additional text would likely detract from the points we have successfully emphasized. At the same time, we should consider rounding out our definition with additional characteristics that could help ensure the use of the term *Service* is supportive of the outcomes and behaviors we wish to drive.

To begin with, we know that our goal is to focus on the delivery of Services that drive value from the customer's perspective, so we should describe a given individual Service in terms that resonate with the customer. We can also highlight the ITaaS framework's definition of value, which in order to qualify requires that each Service be associated with a strategy for measuring performance and a total cost of delivery. We also know from the ITaaS framework that each Service represents one of three implicit Service types. Further, we know that we will list each Service in the portfolio and that the Service taxonomy (detailed later in this chapter) will influence the organization of the portfolio. We also know that we want to associate a Service Owner with each Service and can highlight the responsibilities the role will contribute.

We should also consider for a moment what elements we do not want to impact our Service designs. Many teams will create Services reflecting each and every activity they carry out, or to house existing resources or assets with no. I regularly witness IT leaders insisting on the establishment of Services in order to tuck numerous IT cost elements away in. The fact is these things no longer warrant the designation of a Service in the ITaaS framework, and we should explicitly address that in one of our characteristics.

Once our set of Service characteristics reflects these considerations then we have effectively built up the ITaaS framework's definition of a Service.

The ITaaS Framework's Definition of a Service

Now that we have taken the time to build up our definition and understand the background and many considerations that influenced its development, we can present it in its entirety. This is the ITaaS framework's definition of a Service and associated characteristics that will be leveraged going forward.

> *IT Service* **Definition:** A set of technical capabilities delivered by the IT organization, required to support business outcomes, managed in a cost-effective manner while seeking to proactively innovate, transform, and improve business outcomes through the application of technology.

- The technical capabilities delivered from an IT Service must provide value to the customer, with value defined as a consideration of the impact on business outcomes achieved by the Service weighed against the cost of delivering the Service at the required performance levels.

- All Services are associated with a set of technical capabilities, performance levels of those capabilities, and a model of the total costs of ownership for delivery of the Service capabilities at the performance levels achieved.

- A Service is defined in terms that resonate with the customer.

- Each Service represents one of three implicit Service types: Business Operations Services, Enterprise End-Customer Services, or Technology Foundation Services.

- A Service is listed in the Service portfolio and organized by the Service taxonomy.

- A Service is managed by a Service Owner responsible for end-to-end delivery, innovating on behalf of the customer, operating the Service in a cost-effective manner, and accountable for the value it provides to the enterprise.

- A Service is technology-agnostic, and may span several technology platforms or architectures and IT functional teams in order to avoid duplication.

- A Service is not created as a result of a specific application, IT functional team or activity, or cost element.

Behind the Scenes of the Cisco IT Services Transformation

Looking back, one Cisco IT leader stressed, "It's important how you define and structure a Service. You don't want to let the existing IT organization and culture drive how you define your Service. You define and structure your Services in a way that can support the desired outcomes, and you drive the organization to accommodate that. The Service should stand the test of time."

For Cisco, the first phase of Service design resulted in everything as a Service. People equated every activity to an individual Service. One of the earliest Service proposals was huge, upward of 2,500 Services, stemming from an initial concept of tying Services to applications in a one-to-one relationship. As the ideal definition and structure of a Service was refined over time, this was rationalized down to about 800 before refining to the low 100s which became the sweet spot for the initial ITaaSO. We had to look at our own backyard and define what a Service really meant. There was significant debate about what was and wasn't a Service. After triaging some of the initial Services, they up-leveled the Service definitions to something much, much more strategic than earlier proposals.

The goal shifted to defining a Service as not just the capabilities that were consumed, but as something substantial enough that could be measured across multiple aspects, including total costs, rate of adoption, and more. We knew the more strategic approach was right when the teams naturally shifted to then debating how best to measure a Service. We started measuring costs (costs weren't that important in the past) and benchmarking against other similar Services. Before, we never worried about that (we cared about availability).

Considerations for IT Services

An IT Service represents an interface between IT and its customers and plays a major role in driving the customer experience. To ensure our framework supports the best customer experience, it is important to consider which elements of an IT Service are appropriate for the customer to be presented with versus those that may only concern the provider of the Service. We should also consider the different Service types recognized by the ITaaS framework, and consider the different customer bases and other characteristics associated with each.

It is also important that we consider how Services interact with one another within our framework to facilitate some of the desired capabilities for the Service delivery function. This includes understanding the implicit Service hierarchy and the concept of Service chains. While many of these concepts were introduced in Chapter 2, the following sections expand on each, ensuring that you have a well-rounded and in-depth understanding for all aspects of an IT Service.

IT Services as a Layer of Abstraction

In Chapter 2, we introduced the concept of leveraging IT Services as a layer of abstraction that would effectively decouple the customer base and the various aspects of the IT organization's operations. Rather than linking customer stakeholders consuming technical capabilities directly into different, complex functions of the IT organization, we instead insert a Service between the two. In theory, this should create the opportunity for an entirely new and simplified customer experience, as shown in Figure 4-1.

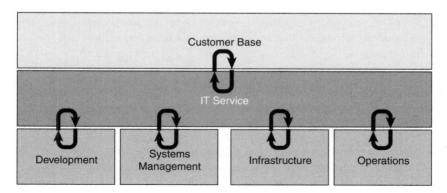

Figure 4-1 *IT Service as a Layer of Abstraction*

The success of this concept relies on the strategies and capabilities we outfit our Service with in order to effectively interface with the two very different elements of the enterprise. Cisco's ITaaS framework not only accommodates the required strategies and capabilities of a Service but also assigns several Service delivery roles, including that of a Service Owner. The methods by which a Service Owner leverages the strategies and capabilities of a Service afforded by the ITaaS framework ultimately drive the customer experience, and that is the topic of this section.

The most significant opportunity created by the ITaaS framework to transform the customer experience is the chance to reevaluate the most applicable views of an IT Service. In other words, what types of information does a Service Owner maintain visibility to in order to manage the Service, and what types of information should the customer base be presented with?

To effectively manage a Service, Service Owners are required to work across many different elements of an IT organization's operations. First, they engage a group of customer stakeholders to understand the requirements for technical capabilities and the conditions for these to create value, such as a required level of performance or a threshold for the total cost of delivery that, when exceeded, causes the value proposition for the Service to be impacted. Then they work across the necessary elements of the IT operating model in order to facilitate these outcomes. This requires Service Owners to maintain informative views of and continuously evaluate several overarching elements of IT operations:

- **IT Architectures:** What are the major systems, platforms, and infrastructures involved in the delivery of the technical capabilities associated with the Service? Are there any upcoming changes to these architectures that could impact the Service capabilities? Are the architectures capable of enabling the capabilities at the proper scale required today and in the future?

- **IT Organizational Teams:** What are the various functional teams within the IT organization that operate the technical systems and infrastructures that enable technical capabilities delivered by the Service? Are these teams aware of and capable of supporting the specific customer requirements for these Service capabilities and performance?

- **IT Processes:** What are the various processes that could impact the Service? Do these processes potentially constrain the customer base, and is there an established mechanism for escalating or bypassing a process if required?

- **IT Budgets:** What are the various budgeting cycles and processes, and how can they impact current and future capability requirements? What level of investments in direct Service costs require approval, and what are the processes and timelines associated?

Each of these represents high-level categories of information the Service Owner must maintain awareness of and elements of the IT organization's operations they must work across. They also represent the many complex aspects for how technical capabilities are made available. The key consideration for the ITaaS framework's approach to Service delivery, however, is that there is rarely a need for the customer base to be presented with any of this information.

Instead, IT Service customers should be presented with an informational view of the Service that is appropriate to their concerns and priorities. Most often this amounts to

- Am I getting the capabilities I need?

- Are the capabilities performing at the level I require?

- Does the total cost of delivering these capabilities justify their ongoing delivery?

- Is the Service prepared to deliver the capabilities I need at the scale required in the future?

These elements make up the informational view of an IT Service appropriate for customers. Additional details regarding the delivery and management of the capabilities can always be provided if required or requested but are typically managed behind the scenes on behalf of the customer. The key is that customers are not burdened by information that has no relevance to their considerations for the Service or are beyond their realm of expertise to interpret or provide guidance to. The Service Owner, as the middleman, has two separate views of the Service, and architects, engineers, and managers across the IT organization can maintain a siloed view of the IT organization's operations with the understanding that each plays a critical role in the delivery of various IT Services. These different views of a Service are illustrated in Figure 4-2.

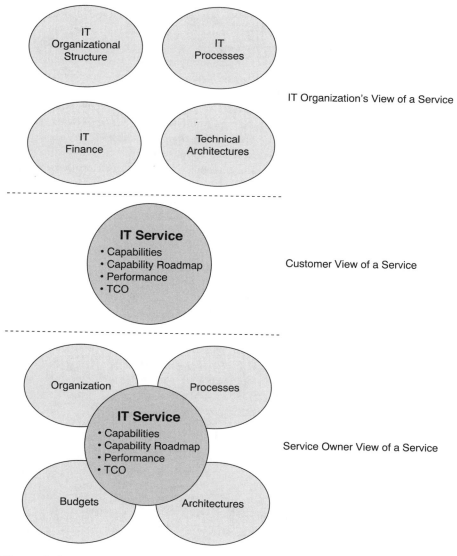

Figure 4-2   *IT Service Views*

The concept of different views of an IT Service applicable for the customer and the Service Owner is effective only when they are actually leveraged. While this may seem like common sense, remember that many IT professionals have historically only leveraged information that we would associate with the IT view of a Service. Newly initiated Service Owners must develop a habit of leveraging the ITaaS framework's strategies and capabilities to develop and present the appropriate view of the Service to the customer. Service Owners must lead with and emphasize the information relevant to the customer, while keeping technical information under the Service level.

Look again at the illustration of the Service Owner's view of a Service in Figure 4-2. Think of an IT Service in the ITaaS framework as a table top, on which the IT organization places a number of technical capabilities for use by their customers when needed. We know that a table must be supported by a number of legs to be able to stand and maintain stability. In this case, those legs are made up by the various teams, architectures, processes, and budgets managed by the IT organization. Assume that customers of a Service want to know that the items (technical capabilities) they need are sitting on the Service "table top" when required, but seldom care a great deal about the number, type, or style of the legs used to support that table top. In other words, Service Owners seek to minimize the need for customers to be presented with or to understand the many complex technical details involved in delivering the Service. Instead, they first make sure the capabilities are available and then present the customer with an informational view of the Service that allows them to partner with the Service Owner and refine an accurate view of the value provided by the Service to the enterprise. *Within Cisco's ITaaS framework, IT Services are supported but not defined by the IT organization's functional team structure, operational processes, budgeting cycles, or technical architectures leveraged to enable the technical capabilities associated with a Service.*

From the Diary of an ITaaS Consultant

A major part of any engagement with a Cisco Services customer is mentoring resources across the IT organization as they take on the role of Service Owner and reinforcing over time specific behaviors that ensure the Services Transformation is successful and that a true cultural shift is initiated. While the contents of this section are reviewed with customer transformation teams, a good deal of coaching and guiding initial presentations is inevitably required as newly indoctrinated Service Owners make their first passes at customer engagements and Service Reviews.

Following is a sample of my most common feedback from these early sessions:

- Your customers don't need to know that onboarding this new capability requires activity from five different IT teams; they just want to know when the capability can be made available.

- As Service Owner, you will need to coordinate with all of the teams necessary for onboarding a capability in your Service, not your customer.

■ The customer should not be obligated to maintain an understanding of the IT organization's change-control processes and timelines; as a Service Owner, you are responsible for ensuring that all required changes are conducted according to process and in the timeline agreed with the customer.

■ Your customer does not want to hear that a critical capability for their operations will be delayed because the network team's budget is gone.

■ You are obviously very proud of the detail displayed in that architectural diagram and the information it presents to you, but does your customer really need to see it or even understand it?

I even regularly find myself invoking the classic '80s movie *Top Gun*, where fighter pilots were instructed to never engage "below the hard deck." Within the ITaaS framework and for Service Owners engaging business customers, the Service level is the hard deck, and you do not engage your customer there. The reference paints an effective visual, and calling out to Service Owners during mock Service Reviews that the data they are presenting is "below the hard deck" makes for a few laughs but is something the presenter easily remembers. Just as important, it also represents the only time in my professional career when I can shout, "Get your butt above the hard deck and return to base" at clients.

IT Service-Types

The ITaaS framework acknowledges three different implicit Service types, which we review here. Although they are not part of the Service taxonomy or regularly leveraged for organizing the Service portfolio, understanding—and recognizing—the different Service types is invaluable to the design of IT Services, while also informing the best value management strategies and the likely customer base.

The three Service types found within the ITaaS framework are

■ **Business Operations Services:** Services that deliver specialized sets of technical capabilities directly enabling business processes and outcomes, potentially unique to the industry or the enterprise itself, and primarily consumed by different enterprise business units. Examples include Services delivering technical capabilities that enable processes supporting the sales function of an enterprise.

■ **Enterprise End-Customer Services:** Services providing technical capabilities that directly enable productivity for end-customers across the enterprise, common across most enterprises and industries. Examples include Services that enable productivity and collaboration capabilities such as email or video-conferencing across the enterprise.

■ **Technology Foundation Services:** Services that primarily enable core technical capabilities indirectly supporting other ITaaS Services, common across most enterprises and industries. Examples include Services providing data storage and cloud application hosting capabilities.

Service types represent a key input for Service design and creation of the IT Service portfolio, as detailed in Chapter 6. Based on the descriptions listed, we know that to designate Business Operations Services, we need to understand the technical capability requirements of business processes across the enterprise, which is discussed in Chapter 5, "Mapping Enterprise Technical Capability Requirements." The design of Enterprise End-Customer Services depends on visibility to the requirements for technical capabilities that enable productivity and collaboration across the enterprise. Finally, Technology Foundation Services are designated as requirements are established for systems and infrastructures to support other IT Services. This follows the top-down approach to Service design highlighted in Chapter 3, "Change Leadership and Ensuring a Successful Transformation."

Beyond informing the type of information we will need as inputs for eventual Service design, these Service types also provide a significant level of information about the resulting Service and its characteristics once it has been designated. As their name implies, Business Operations Service types are most often aligned to the support of operations for a specific enterprise function or business unit, and as such require the appointment of Service Owners capable of engaging that specific customer base. These Services also leverage a three-party Service Review strategy, where a Service Owner and CIO or other senior IT leader engage customer stakeholders. These Services require performance strategies to take the added step of correlating metrics to business outcomes, and their TCO models often contain indirect Service costs, chained from Technology Foundation Services.

Also consider that the capabilities delivered by Business Operations Services represent those that can have the most impact on business outcomes and the success of the enterprise business in the marketplace. As such, these Services often prove ideal candidates for identifying and developing transformative capability opportunities.

Out of the three Service types, Enterprise End-Customer Services engage with the broadest range of customers. In many cases, every member of the enterprise business represents a part of the potential customer base; for example, consider a Service that delivers email and calendaring, or laptops and desktops. These capabilities can be used by anyone, so the customer base for these Services would be spread across the enterprise, independent of any organizational or functional alignment.

There is no underlying requirement for Service Owners to understand a set of business processes when dealing with Enterprise End-Customer type Services. Instead, the primary focus of these Service Owners is the effective designation, alignment, and management of Service Offerings that can support the requirements of a diverse customer base. Service offerings are reviewed in detail in the upcoming taxonomy section of this chapter; fundamentally, they allow for the differentiation of capabilities without large-scale duplication of resources. Also note that the capabilities delivered by these Services are seldom unique, resulting in reduced focus on innovation and an emphasis on managing a wide range of capabilities in the most cost-effective way possible. This widespread customer base means that Service Reviews often take place between Service Owners and a selection of IT leaders, representing the interests of the large customer base. Customer stakeholders external to the IT organization should still receive information about these Services and should have the option of participating in Service Reviews if they wish to provide input on the Service; for example, providing feedback on capability roadmaps.

Technology Foundation Service types are designated last in the Service design phase, in order to support the requirements of Business Operation and Enterprise End-Customer Services through the delivery of capabilities enabled by large-scale systems, platforms, and infrastructure. Technology domain focus is actually emphasized here, because Service Owners attempt to drive out costs while simultaneously scaling complex technical architectures. That is not to say these are purely technology Services, however—quite the contrary. These Services often participate in Service chains, meaning that Service Owners are often responsible for developing processes to chain out consumption-based costs to other Services and even performance metrics. These Service Owners also share the same requirements for leveraging Service Offerings to support differentiation of capabilities in the most efficient manner possible. While the capabilities supported by these Services have the potential to impact every corner of the enterprise business, and therefore share the widespread customer base of Enterprise End-Customer Services, the stakeholders they interface with are often regarded as the most difficult and demanding—fellow IT Service Owners. In fact, while these Services may initially seem more technology-focused and familiar to IT leaders, and attract the most initial interest for candidate Service Owners, in many cases they can present the most demanding Service management challenges of any Service type.

As you can see, Service types can indicate a significant level of information regarding the resulting characteristics of a designated Service. At the same time, remember that these are simply aids for Service design and development, and do not represent final designations for a customer base, strategy, or ideal Service Owner candidate. IT Transformation teams should take care not to get too hung up on the assignment of a proposed Service to a Service type, and instead look to Service types as loose rather than strict guidelines for the way many IT Services will be shaped and function.

Service Hierarchies and Service Chains

In addition to Service types, an implicit hierarchy of Services also exists within the ITaaS framework. This hierarchy is a reflection of the Service chaining mechanism of the framework, in which one IT Service may consume technical capabilities from one or more additional IT Services. Figure 4-3 illustrates these concepts.

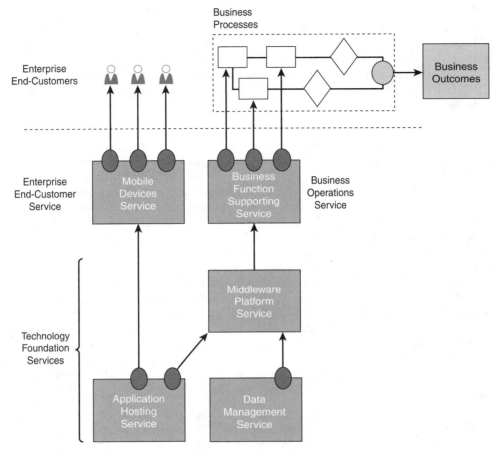

Figure 4-3 *Service Hierarchy and Service Chaining*

Service chains are a powerful mechanism within the ITaaS framework and are key to building accurate total cost of ownership models by chaining costs that reflect the consumption of capabilities and demonstrating how the performance of one Service can impact other Services. As illustrated in Figure 4-3, Service chains can be made up of two Services or, in some cases, even three or more Services.

Service chains create an implicit, logical two-level hierarchy of Services. In this hierarchy, the top-level Services, often Business Operations or Enterprise End-Customer Services, consume capabilities from the bottom-level Services that are typically Technology Foundation Services. Service Owners for Services chaining capabilities upward in the hierarchy carry the additional responsibilities of developing and managing the processes for chaining costs and metrics. Note that there is no requirement for a Service of any type to form or participate in a Service chain; rather, these chains are created only when required.

The processes and strategies for chaining costs and performance metrics between Services are explored in their respective chapters. For now, understand that Service chaining is an important mechanic of the ITaaS framework and the implicit hierarchy of Services that results from its presence in the Service delivery function.

Service Ownership

Technical capabilities delivered by a Service are enabled by any number of IT resources, assets, processes, and budgets; however, that does not imply that these assets are necessarily owned, operated, or funded by the Service and Service Owner. Resources and assets continue to be aligned to organizational and functional teams and cost centers while the Service delivery framework develops a parallel view of how these elements come together in support of individual IT Services.

Service Owners may, as a matter of coincidence, also fulfill another role that has responsibility for some or all of the assets enabling their Service, but this is a result of the additional roles they facilitate and those associated responsibilities. An example would be a network infrastructure manager who also accepts the Service Owner role for the corporate network Service. These instances are not as common you may suspect and primarily occur within Technology Foundation Services.

The same is true for Service costs. A Service Owner is responsible for managing the Service TCO, which may reflect cost elements from multiple cost pools, investment projects, and budgets, each with its own responsible party. As you will learn in Chapter 9, "Modeling the Total Costs of IT Service Delivery," IT Service cost modeling establishes a parallel view of IT spend rather than replacing historical views of IT finance.

Impact of Services

While the number and type of Services can and should evolve over time as the IT organization maintains alignment with the enterprise business and transitions to Fast IT operating model, it is important to understand the impact of introducing or discontinuing a Service. Chapter 9 details strategies for distributing costs from the IT budget to Services, highlighting the likelihood for single cost elements to be distributed across multiple Services. If one of the Services involved in the cost distribution is discontinued, the remaining Service costs will rise as a result of the cost element being divided across a smaller number of Services. Likewise, if a newly introduced Service were determined to receive a distribution of those costs, the cost assignment to existing Services would again fluctuate. Besides, potentially impacting cost distribution changes to the Service landscape can additionally impact Service performance strategies and other aspects of Service delivery. While it is necessary for the Service landscape to evolve, it is equally necessary for IT leaders and Service executives to understand and remain conscious of the impacts that these changes bring.

The IT Service Delivery Taxonomy

The Service delivery function of an enterprise IT operating model is large and complex, often entailing a landscape of dozens or even hundreds of Services along with any number of related strategies and processes. The only way an IT organization can hope to manage a large Services landscape strategically is to establish an order and classification of Services through the introduction of a Service delivery taxonomy.

We already completed the designation and definition of one major segment of our taxonomy when we carefully refined our definition of a Service; now we simply designate and define additional levels that create additional Service delivery capabilities for the framework. By designating additional levels in a taxonomy hierarchy, we can enable aggregation of Services capable of supporting the strategic management of vast segments of the Services landscape and even provide Service Owners with mechanisms for successfully managing complex individual Services in a highly efficient manner.

This section begins by highlighting the many benefits for leveraging a taxonomy in a Service delivery framework and its significance in enabling the value outcomes of a Services Transformation. From there, we introduce a reference taxonomy included in Cisco's ITaaS framework and describe best practices for tailoring and adopting a taxonomy purpose-fit to your own IT organization.

The Benefits of a Taxonomy

The purpose of the taxonomy is to order and classify IT Services with a goal of enabling the strategic management of Services and the Service delivery function of the IT organization. This includes designating each level of classification, as well as considering the relationships between levels.

Designating and then defining each level within a multilayer taxonomy can be associated with a number of beneficial traits for a Service delivery framework:

- Enables alignment of major components of the ITaaS framework to a hierarchy model

- Provides organization and management of Service groups

- Provides organization and management of individual Services

- Enables strategic levers for managing the IT organization

Establishing a taxonomy creates a multilevel hierarchy within the Service delivery framework. This allows us to align components of the ITaaS framework to individual levels of the hierarchy, such as specific Service delivery roles and Service value strategies. Doing so enables IT Transformation teams to illustrate clearly what things happen at each level of the taxonomy, providing clear distinction for the proper use and implementation of the many strategies, roles, processes, and tools that will be leveraged within the ITaaS framework. Introducing these numerous elements for Service delivery without aligning to a taxonomy often leads to widespread duplication of efforts, confusion, and even volleying of responsibilities. Instead, we want to provide order and distinction to our Service delivery framework from day one.

Enabling the strategic organization and management of the Services portfolio is directly aligned to one of the strategic value outcomes of the ITaaS framework, allowing the IT organization to be operated as a relevant, agile, and competitive business within a business. Whenever IT Service management teams employ standards that simply create a portfolio that is nothing more than a flat listing of Services managed by the IT organization, they create a significant barrier to ever managing that Services landscape strategically. Consider that the ITaaS framework's approach to Service design can result in over 100 Services for large-scale enterprise companies, far too many for a CIO to analyze in a strategic manner, with the same true even of a hypothetical mid-size enterprise with 40–60 Services. Instead, Cisco's ITaaS framework leverages the taxonomy to aggregate and classify Services. This approach establishes multiple levels of categorization, each with its own unique purpose, which allow IT leaders to engage and operate at the appropriate level.

The taxonomy and resulting hierarchy also allow for the general organization of the Service portfolio, making it easier to navigate and manage. For example, simply imagine for a moment that you are a newly appointed Service Owner seeking out details associated with your Service in the portfolio. Rather than searching through a long, unordered, unrelated list of IT Services, you can instead quickly find your Service by simply looking under its relevant classification. Chapter 6 provides complete details on developing a Service portfolio, along with best practices for ensuring it becomes a strategic tool rather than simply a record of data.

The concept of a taxonomy is often associated with the classification and organization of specific elements, in our case IT Services. We can add to this, however, the classification of IT Service components or the elements that make up a Service. Consider for a moment the management of an IT Service from the Service Owners' perspective. Delivery of the Service likely involves any number of IT resources and assets, relies on numerous strategies, and potentially supports large customer bases with varied requirements. At the same time, the Service must be managed efficiently. IT leaders often call upon the Service to facilitate specific outcomes, such as reducing operating costs by 5 percent, while continuing to deliver capabilities that meet the customer requirements. This ultimately represents unrealistic expectations for Service Owners and the Service delivery framework.

Cisco's ITaaS framework solves this dilemma by leveraging the taxonomy to introduce and classify elements of an individual Service. This provides Service Owners with a mechanism for organizing and managing an individual Service more easily, and even the capability to provide differentiated capabilities to a customer base without large-scale duplication of resources.

The final benefit of developing and leveraging a taxonomy within an enterprise IT Service delivery framework is one likely to receive the most attention from CIOs and senior IT leaders. Cisco's ITaaS framework for Service delivery creates a set of strategic levers for IT leaders that can be leveraged to facilitate desired outcomes. This is a complex topic that leverages multiple aspects of the ITaaS framework, but the availability of these levers is closely tied to the introduction of a taxonomy and resulting hierarchy to the Service delivery function.

Taxonomy Considerations

Before we begin designing a taxonomy for our Service delivery framework, we need to review a number of considerations. The design of the taxonomy, including the number and classification of levels in the resulting hierarchy, can have significant impacts on the resulting framework.

First, IT Transformation teams should understand that although tailoring a taxonomy to purpose-fit their IT organization and goals for Service delivery is required, one level of the hierarchy is effectively untouchable—Services. Services act as the central level of the taxonomy. The taxonomy is, after all, a hierarchy for a Service delivery framework, and we have already invested a significant level of effort in carefully defining associated characteristics to the term *Service*. Our purpose now is to designate new levels of classification above and below the Service level that can enable the various benefits reviewed in the previous section.

Next, always remember that levels of classification introduced above the Service level of the hierarchy create options for aggregating Services. Levels of classification designated below Services create leverage points for managing individual Services. This concept is illustrated in Figure 4-4.

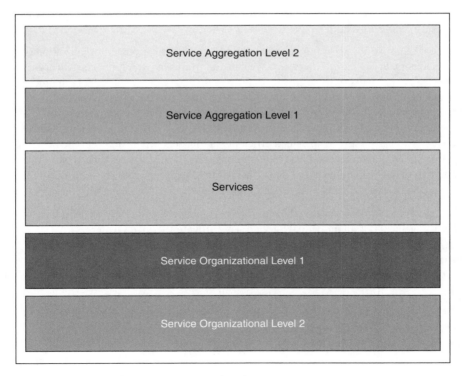

Figure 4-4 *Sample Taxonomy Levels*

Our next consideration is for the appropriate number of levels to introduce both above and below the Service level. Figure 4-4 demonstrates a taxonomy that provides two levels of aggregation for the organization and management of the Service portfolio and two levels of organization and management of individual Services. While IT Transformation teams may be tempted to continue introducing additional levels to the hierarchy, this can dilute the value of existing levels and can quickly result in these elements of the taxonomy being ignored. Each level of the hierarchy should be associated with a specific functionality and desired value outcome for the Service delivery framework. Cisco's reference taxonomy is a five-level hierarchy, suitable for most enterprise IT organizations. Upcoming sections also detail best practices for four-level models more applicable for small enterprises.

The IT Transformation team's efforts are not limited to designating levels of the taxonomy. They must also carefully define each level of the hierarchy, similar to the way we did Services. In doing so, they must consider the relationship of a level of the hierarchy to those above or below it. Note that although we will continue to emphasize the designation and presentation of Services in terms that resonate with the intended customer base, with regards to the taxonomy, the primary stakeholders are IT leaders and the eventual community of professionals who fill the various Service delivery roles defined by the ITaaS framework. In that regard, the taxonomy should be defined and described in terms that resonate with these IT-internal stakeholders.

Finally, we should stress that the taxonomy and resulting hierarchy are intended to enable the strategic management of the Service landscape that results from best-practice-based Service design and is not intended to inform Service design. Many IT Transformation teams make the mistake of creating overly specific taxonomy levels and then creating Services to fit in these levels. The taxonomy is intended to organize the Service portfolio, not drive Service design.

The ITaaS Framework's Reference Taxonomy

The reference taxonomy included as part of the ITaaS framework is the same as that which has been leveraged successfully by Cisco's own IT organization for years. While it is intended to be customized, this reference taxonomy has served as an ideal starting point for IT organizations of all sizes and across a growing number of industries. Leveraging this proven taxonomy can save IT Transformation teams countless hours of effort and avoid frustrating and often impassioned debates.

Cisco's five-level reference taxonomy is shown in Figure 4-5.

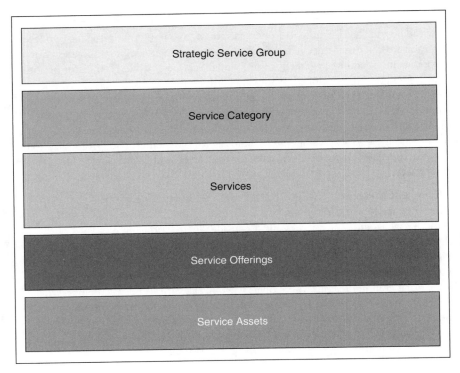

Figure 4-5   *ITaaS Reference Taxonomy*

Following this taxonomy, we see that a Service is made up of Service Offerings, which are enabled by a pool of Service assets. From there, Services are aggregated first into Service Categories and finally into Strategic Service Groups. The definition and intended purpose of each level of this taxonomy are reviewed in the following sections. While examples of each level are provided, note that designation of and resulting numbers of elements within each level are considered to be part of the portfolio design effort detailed in Chapter 6. For now, you need only understand the definition and intended use of each level in the hierarchy. These sections also highlight the recommended alignment of various Service delivery roles defined by the ITaaS framework. While the role of Service Owner has been briefly introduced, many others have not, and all are fully detailed in Chapter 7, "Service Delivery Roles and Responsibilities."

Strategic Service Groups

As the name implies, Strategic Service Groups (SSGs) are intended to provide the CIO and senior IT leaders with a strategic view of the Services landscape and enable informed planning and decision making. The elements designated at this level should represent strategic significance to IT leaders and, as such, should be reviewed and approved by these same leaders. The role of Service Executive, adopted by senior leaders in the IT organization, is often aligned to this level of the hierarchy. Informational roll-up views of costs and performance across Service groups are made available at this level, allowing the CIO to task Service Executives with high-level outcomes, such as reducing the operational costs of an entire Strategic Service Group by 5 percent.

The primary consideration for this level of the hierarchy is how exactly to designate strategic aggregations of IT Services. Senior IT leaders need strategic visibility that they can share with their peers and that enables them to make informed planning decisions that can be translated to desired outcomes that one or more IT leaders such as Service Executives are responsible for facilitating. As an example, consider the advantage of grouping all Business Operations Service types into two designated Strategic Service Groups: one for those Services delivering capabilities to common corporate function BUs such as a finance or human resources department, and the other delivering capabilities to enterprise lines of business that execute the core business. This aggregation of Services would provide IT leaders with a great deal of information and planning capabilities. Investment could be shifted to the Strategic Service Group supporting the enterprise lines of business, allowing Service Owners to develop and introduce transformative capabilities capable of accelerating business operational capabilities far ahead of marketplace competitors. The corporate function Service group delivers technical capabilities that are common across almost any enterprise and could focus on adopting trends and strategies for reducing operational costs while maintaining capabilities.

Service Categories (Service Architecture Groups)

With Strategic Service Groups aggregating large numbers of Services for the purpose of enabling strategic planning, it is important that the taxonomy support an option to group smaller numbers of Services with a more tactical purpose, which is where Service Categories come in. Service Categories may be used to aggregate Services for different reasons, such as by technology domain or architecture group, or simply by the enterprise business units that consume their capabilities. Teams may even create Service categories using different justifications, all within the same portfolio and IT organization. As an example, consider a grouping of Services for corporate network, data center network, and secure remote connectivity into a Network Services category, while another may group a set of business operations Services that each enable processes executed by the finance department.

Many recent adoptions of the ITaaS framework have begun to group Services at this level by architecture and have even renamed this level of the taxonomy as "Service Architecture Groups." This initially stemmed from the alignment of the Service Architect role to this level of the taxonomy, which allowed a single resource to oversee the architecture for a group of related Services. Dedicating a level of the taxonomy to the categorization of Services with related architectures also provides the IT organization with a strong point of information exchange between Service delivery and an Enterprise Architecture practice.

Note that for IT organizations opting for a four-level taxonomy, this is the level that is removed. The reason for this is that if the total number of Services supports the presence of only a single level of aggregation, the functionality of Strategic Service Groups is the one that should be retained for all Service delivery frameworks.

Whether Services are grouped at this level in support of a specific function of the IT organization such as architecture or to provide value in multiple other ways, they act as an important step between Strategic Service Groups and a large landscape of Services. The only real requirements are that the proposed grouping of Services facilitates visibility, planning, or management of Services desired by a segment of the IT organization that is not addressed by the Strategic Service Groups.

Services

A great deal of detail was provided earlier regarding the Services level of the taxonomy, its definition, and its various characteristics. In this section, we simply highlight that Services will be grouped into Service Categories, which are then grouped into Strategic Service Groups and are made up of Service Offerings that are enabled by a pool of Service assets.

Service Offerings

Service offerings are the first level of the taxonomy provided purely for the support of a Service Owner in the organization, delivery, and management of an individual Service. They provide Service Owners with a highly flexible mechanism for managing different aspects of an IT Service in a tactical manner. This means a Service still enables the strategic management and visibility for a set of related technical capabilities and the value they create for the enterprise, while also ensuring the Service can respond quickly to the shifting needs of the customer base.

Service offerings can allow Service Owners to provide differentiated capabilities to stakeholders while minimizing resources, organizing and compartmentalizing aspects of Service delivery for ease of management, and even creating strategic levers that can be utilized to facilitate desired outcomes. Perhaps most significant is that they can be employed for any of these value purposes with little overhead, no impact to the broader Services landscape, and without requiring review and approval from Service executives or IT leaders.

Recall that the designation of a Service carries with it a degree of overhead associated with managing the Service, including development and maintenance of a Service performance and cost modeling strategy, among other activities. Also recall that the introduction or discontinuation of a Service can have a broader impact to the Service delivery framework, potentially affecting cost distribution or performance processes across the broader Service landscape, and as such should be carefully reviewed by IT leaders, Service executives, and the Service management office. Service offerings, however, do not entail a significant level of overhead or potential impact. In fact, they can be introduced or removed in large numbers within a Service virtually at will by a Service Owner without impacting other Services and with little to no increase to the overhead for managing the Service. Changes to Service offerings also do not require review and approval by Service Executives or other IT leaders.

The most common implementation of these organizational units is to allow for differentiation of capabilities. In other words, Service offerings may reflect the presence of various styles, or "flavors," of core technical capabilities. For example, the Service Owner of a "Corporate Email" Service may create Service offers for standard and encrypted email. This is an important mechanism for the IT organization and Service Owners to leverage because it allows the efficient delivery of similar capabilities with minor distinctions in requirements, without the need to replicate significant amounts of IT resources and assets. Broad and active adoption of Service Offerings for this purpose supports the intended outcome of allowing the IT organization to operate efficiently.

Differentiation of technical capabilities is not the only way in which a Service Owner can leverage Service Offerings, however. Some Service Owners simply leverage Service Offerings as an opportunity to categorize different elements of their Service. For example, Service Owners of Business Operations Services can often find themselves overseeing a large pool of applications and will group these into various offerings for ease of management and reporting. They can also be used to compartmentalize capabilities by customer base or the underlying Service assets leveraged to enable the capabilities. In some cases, Service Owners may be able to organize the technical capabilities by the type of associated costs; for example, offerings for both capital expenses (CAPEX) and operating expenses (OPEX). This last example actually provides the Service Owners and IT leaders with a lever for facilitating desired outcomes for Service costing.

They can also be used as a distinction between legacy and current infrastructures, allowing Service Owners to influence consumption of capabilities by demonstrating the costs and challenges associated with legacy technologies associated with a Service offering. A common example is a Service providing capabilities for application hosting, with clear advantages for IT organization and business customers for transitioning their application from "bare-metal" server infrastructure to cloud environments (public or private). In this scenario, the Service Owner can create a Service offering for each and demonstrate cost and performance discrepancies in an effort to encourage rapid transition to cloud-based offerings.

Service offerings are a flexible, multipurpose tool that provides Service Owners with a range of options for managing and communicating the value of their Service in the most efficient manner possible without significantly increasing overhead or impacting the broader Services landscape.

Service Assets

It is important that our Service delivery taxonomy acknowledge the many resources, processes, assets, and budgets that combine to enable technical capabilities delivered by an IT Service. The purpose of the Service asset level of the taxonomy is to ensure Service Owners maintain awareness of these many components and can then work across the segments of the IT organization that own and manage each in order to facilitate the desired outcomes of the Service. Think of Service assets as the most basic level of building blocks within an IT organization that are combined to enable a set of technical capabilities for a Service.

Note that the intent of this level of the taxonomy is not to develop a complete listing of every asset that could directly or indirectly impact the Service. This function is provided by asset databases, application portfolios, or other platforms and documentation commonly already in place within the IT organization. In practice, elements designated in this level of the taxonomy are a reference or mapping to these platforms, informing Service delivery teams of the types of assets involved with enabling Service capabilities and allowing them to quickly navigate to relevant details. Chapter 6 provides further guidance on designating Service assets within the IT Service portfolio.

The Reference Taxonomy in Practice

To ensure readers are provided with a clear understanding of the ITaaS framework's reference taxonomy, we should consider its application in full with some examples. Note that Chapter 6 provides additional examples of the reference taxonomy in practice as it describes how to designate specific elements within each level of the hierarchy. First, Figure 4-6 provides examples of each taxonomy level against each of the ITaaS framework's potential Service types (including two examples for business operations Services).

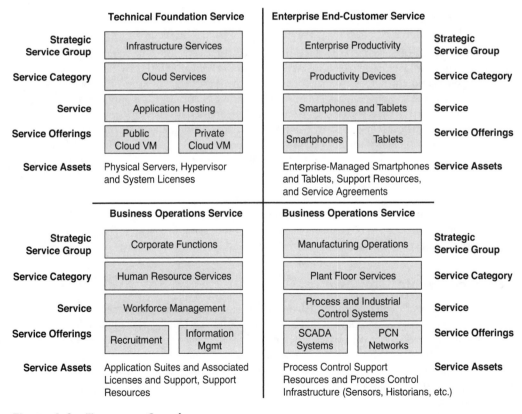

Figure 4-6 *Taxonomy Samples*

Next, Figure 4-7 illustrates the recommended alignment of Service delivery roles and other elements of the Service delivery framework.

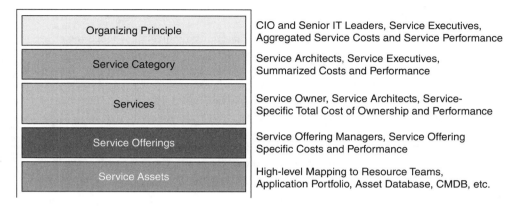

Figure 4-7   *Taxonomy and Service Role Alignment*

Finally, Figure 4-8 demonstrates how the reference taxonomy is leveraged to organize Services and to then aggregate Services for different levels of management.

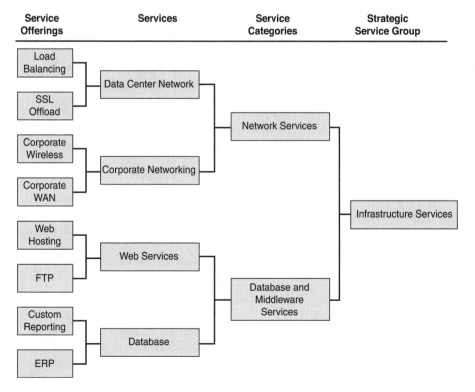

Figure 4-8   *Taxonomy Aggregation Example*

Tailoring a Taxonomy

Cisco's ITaaS framework and Services Transformation Program acknowledge the need for enterprise IT organizations to adapt the taxonomy to various degrees for optimal alignment to their company size, industry, and goals for their Service delivery framework. In some cases, IT Transformation teams may find that levels of the taxonomy can be tailored to reflect or even loosely map to existing IT Service management initiatives, potentially achieving both a reduction of effort in later activities and quicker acceptance and adoption of the framework as a result of stakeholder familiarity with existing strategies. In some cases, all of this can be done simply by changing the name of one of the reference taxonomy levels, while still maintaining the core definition and functionality.

Many transformation teams begin by considering how many levels are appropriate for their taxonomy, which will be driven primarily by the number of Services present in the portfolio. You may be curious as to how you can determine the appropriate number of levels to include in your taxonomy when you have likely not yet determined the number of Services present in your portfolio. Luckily, the most optimal updates to the taxonomy from small- to large-scale enterprises and resulting Services landscapes are historically only one level of difference, which can be added or removed as the initial Service portfolio nears completion.

The ITaaS framework recommends a four- to five-level taxonomy for all implementations. Taxonomies for smaller enterprises or, in some cases, even medium-sized enterprises with a smaller set of Services work best with only a single level of aggregation above the Service level, in other words by removing the Service category level of the reference taxonomy. In practice, IT Transformation teams organizing a small Service portfolio can struggle to effectively leverage two levels of organization and find that their highest levels of aggregation often hold only a single unit of the first level of aggregation. For instance, if using the reference taxonomy as an example, teams may find themselves with several Strategic Service Groups that each contain only a single Service category and varying Service categories in turn containing only one to two Services. In these cases, a four-level taxonomy provides the optimal opportunity for Service aggregations.

On the high side of a set of Services, however, it is highly unlikely that transformation teams will need to introduce a sixth level or higher to the taxonomy. Five taxonomy levels should be sufficient for even the largest and most complex of IT organizations, as transformation teams will find themselves struggling to clearly differentiate the functionality and purpose from one level to another. As with the IT organization itself, there is a point where there are simply too many levels of management and organization for each to deliver differentiated value.

For taxonomy levels below Services, Cisco recommends that transformation teams retain the two-level approach and the functionality provided at each level. Every model for Service delivery should provide a means for Service Owners to both organize their Services and maintain a view of the assets capable of impacting the Service. In short,

Cisco's ITaaS framework is prescriptive in its recommendation of two levels for the organization of Services and one to two levels of organization for the portfolio, along with the Services level, resulting in a taxonomy model of four to five levels.

While the ITaaS framework is prescriptive on the number of levels attributed to a taxonomy and, to a large degree, the functionality of the levels contained within the reference taxonomy, it is not prescriptive at all with regard to the designation or naming of those levels. We could even say that the Services Transformation Program anticipates and encourages IT Transformation teams to update these names. Never underestimate the potential level of impact a name can have on the success or failure of an effort. The best-designed taxonomy levels may struggle to achieve widespread adoption and recognition if the various names it is associated with fail to resonate with stakeholders or to convey its role and function in a logical manner. Numerous IT Transformation teams have also found that carrying the names of previous taxonomies or prior Service delivery efforts across to the ITaaS taxonomy can aid in quickly winning support of the Services Transformation and act as a preemptive measure for avoiding resistance to the newly proposed framework.

Over the years of supporting customer transformations, Cisco has seen the Service categories level of the taxonomy renamed to "Functional Service Domains," "IT Architecture Groups," and more. In each case, the name accurately reflected the manner in which Services were aggregated and the mechanics of how those groupings were then used for strategic management and planning. Also note that Cisco IT's original Services Transformation designated the top level of the taxonomy as Organizing Principles, and this continues to be used in Cisco IT-specific material.

Closely related with the name assigned to a level of the taxonomy model would be further consideration for the function of the level in question. IT Transformation teams should carefully consider any desire to remove or omit the functionalities described in the reference taxonomy but can easily add to the functions of a given level with additional mechanics. Deliberations for augmenting the mechanics for a taxonomy level are welcome and common when updating the names associated with each level.

Sample Tailored Taxonomy

The diagrams in Figure 4-9 demonstrate potential customizations of the reference taxonomy in both four- and five-level hierarchies. Note that the Service level is always present and that only one sample taxonomy has updated the names of the Service organizational levels. In each case, we can assume that although the names have been updated, the basic purpose and functionality of each level remain largely the same.

Five-Level Tailored Taxonomy

Figure 4-9   *Sample Tailored Taxonomy Models*

Summary

The definition of a Service adopted by an IT Transformation team has wide-ranging impact to the final Service delivery framework. These implications include the number and type of Services that result as well as the capability for effectively managing and then measuring and communicating the value of those Services.

The ITaaS framework defines a Service as a set of technical capabilities delivered by the IT organization, required support business outcomes, managed in a cost-effective manner while seeking to proactively innovate, transform, and improve business outcomes through the application of technology.

Characteristics of an IT Service:

- The technical capabilities delivered from an IT Service must provide value to the customer, with value defined as a consideration of the impact on business outcomes achieved by the Service weighed against the cost of delivering the Service at the requested performance levels.

- All Services are associated with a set of technical capabilities, performance levels of those capabilities, and a model of the total costs of ownership for delivery of the Service capabilities at the performance levels achieved.

- A Service is defined in terms that resonate with the customer.

- Each Service represents one of three Service types: Business Operations Services, Enterprise End-Customer Services, or Technology Foundation Services.

- A Service is listed in the Service portfolio and organized by the Service delivery taxonomy.

- A Service is managed by a Service Owner responsible for end-to-end delivery, innovating on behalf of the customer, operating the Service in a cost-effective manner, and accountable for the value it provides to the enterprise.

- A Service is technology-agnostic, and may span several technology platforms or architectures and IT functional teams in order to avoid duplication.

- A Service is not created as a result of a specific application, IT functional team or activity, or cost assignment.

The ITaaS framework recognizes three different Service types:

- **Business Operations Services:** Services that deliver specialized sets of technical capabilities that directly enable business processes and outcomes, potentially unique to the industry or the enterprise itself, and primarily consumed by different enterprise business units. Examples include Services delivering technical capabilities that directly enable line of business operations.

- **Enterprise End-Customer Services:** Services providing technical capabilities that directly enable productivity for end customers across the enterprise, common across most enterprises and industries. Examples include Services that enable productivity and collaboration capabilities such as email or video-conferencing across the enterprise.

- **Technology Foundation Services:** Services that primarily enable core technical capabilities which indirectly support other ITaaS Services, common across most enterprises and industries. Examples include Services providing data storage, and cloud application hosting capabilities.

The introduction of a Service delivery taxonomy allows for the strategic management of the Service landscape. It creates a hierarchy for the Service delivery framework, which allows alignment of roles and strategies. Cisco's ITaaS framework includes a five-level reference taxonomy that can be purpose-fit by IT Transformation teams to a specific IT organization and goals for the Service delivery framework.

Chapter 5

Mapping Enterprise Technical Capability Requirements

This chapter guides IT Transformation teams in mapping a specific set of technical capability requirements that will be leveraged as input to the design of Business Operations type Services. Recall that these Service types deliver technical capabilities required to execute business processes across the enterprise. This means that to design these Services, we need to understand the major functions taking place and how each is enabled and impacted by technology. While this information could be collected and assembled in a number of ways, Cisco's ITaaS framework and Services Transformation Program include a process for the development of an Enterprise Technical Capabilities (ETC) map. This artifact not only captures the information required to support best-practice-based design of Business Operations Services but also creates significant value for Service Owners and even for IT organizations outside the Service delivery function.

This chapter begins by examining the purpose and goals of the ETC map and then examines the value and opportunities it creates. From there, we review several considerations for the ETC map, as these efforts can easily deviate off-course and consume significant levels of effort with little added value in exchange. Luckily, substantial amounts of information are commonly already present in most enterprises—for example, from enterprise architecture practices or from process mapping documentation managed by various business units. In fact, a key consideration is whether an existing EA practice may have a full set of documentation available that closely matches the information sought by transformation teams. This chapter guides transformation teams in structuring the ETC map and then compiling the required information from available sources or engaging different business teams to document it. Finally, with a mapping of the technical capability requirements that exist today, we introduce the ITaaS framework's Service capability roadmaps, which help Service delivery teams partner with their customers to understand and prepare for future capability requirements.

The Purpose and Value of a Technical Capabilities Map

As with all things in Cisco's ITaaS framework and Services Transformation Program, it is important that IT Transformation teams understand and be capable of communicating the value of the activities they are undertaking. Development of an ETC map requires a dedicated effort from the transformation team, even with varying sources of information commonly available within an enterprise that can be leveraged. For that reason, teams should clearly understand the purpose, goals, and value of their efforts.

The primary purpose of the ETC map is to document the technical capability requirements of major business functions and processes end-to-end across the enterprise. This includes the functions performed by lines of business, corporate function BUs such as a finance department, and also the functions performed by the IT organization such as Service delivery and support, and enterprise architecture.

The goal of the capabilities map is to create an input for the design of Services that deliver these capabilities and support Service Owners with the information they need to correlate the availability and performance of technical capabilities on business outcomes. Service Owners should have visibility to the processes that their Service enables, and the business outcomes associated with these processes that are impacted when the capabilities fail to be made available or perform as required.

These goals represent the most obvious value justification for the development of an ETC map. Proper design and alignment of IT Services to the support of business functions are fundamental requirements for Cisco's ITaaS framework. The IT organization has to designate Services focused on the delivery of these capabilities that enable enterprise functions and business outcomes, and the information collected in the ETC map by IT Transformation teams is how we accomplish that.

The information collected also allows Service Owners to effectively manage the Service, maintaining alignment while continuously driving further value creation, and even innovating solutions capable of transforming these processes and outcomes. They can't do this without an accurate view of how the technical capabilities delivered by their Service impacts these business functions. In short, the development of an ETC map is directly linked to enabling the first strategic value outcome of the ITaaS framework: establishing the IT organization as a trusted advisor to the business.

Another value opportunity associated with the ETC map is that in order to build and finally vet the information within it, the IT Transformation team is required to engage the various business units that support these functions. This process provides the IT organization with one of its earliest opportunities to begin formally engaging the business and fostering their interest and support in the Services Transformation, and the IT organization's desire to understand their processes and align Service delivery to their needs going forward.

Later in this chapter, we describe the data elements within the ETC map, including both optional and required data fields. The data elements that Cisco recommends can provide significant value opportunities for the IT organization, even beyond the visibility they create for Service Owners.

For starters, the IT organization will quickly learn of any gaps in delivery of technical capabilities. If teams identify instances of technical capability requirements for enabling a business process, they should act on them immediately. There is no reason to wait for the Services Transformation to complete. The required capabilities can be provisioned and made available to address a gap in customer requirements as soon as possible, and then associated with a proper Service during the Service design effort. Identifying and then responding quickly to these cases should better position the IT organization with business customers and demonstrate value for the Services Transformation Program while still in its infancy.

Next, by following Cisco's recommendations for which data elements to gather as part of the ETC map development, IT Transformation teams are likely to identify instances of duplication. Upcoming sections that detail the design of the ETC map stress the differentiation between technical capability requirements and the IT assets currently leveraged to deliver them today. What many transformation teams find is the presence of the same or very similar technical capability requirements across the enterprise, but delivered by completely different assets. Upon completion of the ETC map, IT Transformation teams are encouraged to review for cases of duplication and develop a report for IT leaders. Leaders can then ensure the proper teams investigate and take advantage of opportunities to consolidate assets and infrastructure.

Cisco's recommended data elements also help the IT organization in understanding the business processes most critical to each function and the performance of the enterprise business in the marketplace. As transformation teams map the linkage of technical capabilities to specific processes and business outcomes, they are encouraged to understand which capabilities are considered a competitive advantage. These processes that can directly impact the enterprise's competitiveness with industry peers are highlighted and provide IT leaders and Service Owners with clear visibility for focusing investment and innovation efforts.

Finally, remember the recommendation from Chapter 3, "Change Leadership and Ensuring a Successful Transformation": show value early and often through the Services Transformation Program. As teams develop the ETC map and demonstrate any of the value outcomes or opportunities discussed in this section, they should be sure to pass this information to the change leadership function for documentation and messaging.

Considerations for Mapping Technical Capabilities

Before IT Transformation teams begin pursuing the value outcomes and opportunities presented in the previous section, they should carefully evaluate a series of considerations. These considerations can have a significant influence on the value potential of the ETC map, along with the level of effort required to develop and manage it over time.

The first consideration is an acknowledgment of the potential overlap in the information recommended for inclusion in the ETC map and that of business process documentation managed by enterprise business units or technology and process mappings already established by an enterprise architecture practice. In fact, it is possible that a significant amount of the information required by transformation teams already exists. While it is a possibility, we strongly recommend that IT Transformation teams thoroughly review the following section on designing the ETC map and understand key differences in the information sets for each. The reality is that, while similar, there are some key distinctions in the information that are important for IT Transformation teams to collect in support of Service design and eventual management of the Services.

The similarity of the desired information does present most IT Transformation teams with ample opportunity to leverage existing intellectual capital that can help quickly complete the core elements of the ETC map, leaving them with a substantially reduced effort to compile the remaining recommended data. Transformation teams should review their requirements and partner closely with enterprise architecture practices and any teams or business units responsible for business process documentation to identify and leverage existing documentation. Care must be taken, however, to ensure that this information is accurate.

Regardless of the level of information available, IT Transformation teams need to engage stakeholders to complete each of the data elements for the ETC map. Remember that this includes stakeholders across the enterprise business units, including the IT organization. Also, remember that any stakeholder engagement represents an opportunity to foster interest and support for the broader Service's transformation, and as such the change leadership function of the program should be leveraged. As we discussed in Chapter 3, change leadership teams develop messaging material that can provide transformation teams with value messaging for the Service's transformation that can be leveraged to quickly introduce the effort and show how the information gathered for the ETC map supports its desired outcomes. Teams should take care that they are engaging the right stakeholders and have a firm understanding of the information they need to gather. Interview protocols or outlines can help guide these conversations and ensure the right data is collected.

It's also important that IT Transformation teams not overdevelop this tool and unnecessarily extend or complicate the effort of developing it. Data gathering efforts associated with the ETC map have a tendency to stray, and it is important that teams remember that they are not responsible for creating detailed business process documentation where none exists. Cases in which detailed documentation of dozens of processes are available to leverage are ideal, but when not available, teams should focus on identifying known technical capability requirements and working with stakeholders to verify the major processes and functions they are linked to enabling.

Another key consideration is how the information in the ETC map is maintained over time. While the final artifact can be managed by an IT Service management team or EA practice, updates are primarily driven by the Service Owner but should be limited in practice. Major business functions and related processes are unlikely to change often unless the enterprise enters new markets or fundamentally transforms its operations. Also, always remember that neither the IT Transformation team nor broader IT organization is taking on responsibility for business process documentation beyond, obviously, the IT organization itself. Instead, the goal of the ITaaS framework and ETC map is to develop an initial alignment of Services and then partner Service Owners with senior customer stakeholders to maintain this alignment of technical capabilities to requirements. A later section introduces Service capability roadmaps, leveraged by Service Owners and stakeholders to develop a view of future technical capability requirements.

Finally, as the IT Transformation team completes the ETC map, they should make sure to dedicate time to reviewing and vetting the final document with relevant stakeholders and senior business leaders. The last thing the team wants to do is to kick off a lengthy IT Service design effort leveraging information gleaned from outdated documentation or input from a limited sample of the stakeholder community.

Creating the Enterprise Technical Capabilities (ETC) Map

Now that IT Transformation teams have a firm understanding of the value created by the ETC map and its importance to the Service delivery framework, along with an awareness of key considerations, we can begin looking at the effort of actually building the map. This section looks at the design of the ETC map, including a recommended graphical overlay of the likely extensive information it will collect, and also guides you through Cisco's three-lane development approach to gathering and compiling the required data.

Designing the Enterprise Technical Capabilities Map

The first task for IT Transformation teams is to establish the data fields they feel are relevant to the ETC map they wish to build. Then they can carefully define each and potentially even consider providing examples of the information that could be associated with a given field. Next, teams need to consider what data fields and associated information might already be available from existing documentation and also carefully consider the overlap of these fields with information managed by other teams and how it is differentiated if at all. The best way to determine the relevant fields is to think through the structure of the enterprise business operations and the information transformation teams need.

Enterprise business operations are commonly described as a series of major functions. These functions typically represent a series of processes executed to achieve one or more desired outcomes. Sometimes referenced as process groups in documentation, they are managed by one or more organizational departments or business units. For example, an enterprise may designate functions for "Workforce Analysis and Planning," "Recruitment," and "Employee Performance Management." Transformation teams need to identify these functions, along with the business units involved, and then understand the existing technical capability requirements, which can be the most confusing information field to effectively populate for most teams.

The first guideline for documenting technical capability requirements is to differentiate between the requirements and the IT assets currently leveraged to deliver the capabilities. Documenting these data fields separately is a mechanism by which IT teams can identify and work to minimize duplication in instances where similar capability requirements are captured across the enterprise but each currently leveraging different assets. Transformation teams must be sure to capture a brief summary of the capability requirement and then separately document any systems or platforms currently in use.

The second guideline for capturing technical capability requirements in the ETC map is not to allow the exercise to become a fully detailed requirements document. Instead, transformation teams should strive to document a brief summary of the technical capabilities that are required. As an example, an "Employee Career Development" function managed by an enterprise HR department may require a system that allows HR admins to develop and publish training modules to employees and track their completion. The "IT Technical Operations" function of an IT organization would likely require a system capable of generating and managing problem tickets, with additional requirements for advanced reporting functionality and a dependency for interoperating with the corporate e-store platform to allow for automation of ticket creation. That is not to say that transformation teams should ignore gathering or linking to existing requirements documentation because they could prove quite helpful to the future Service Owners. Note that a given function or process may have multiple unique technical capability requirements, which could currently be enabled by technical assets operated by different IT departments.

After IT Transformation teams have considered the information they need, they can develop an initial proposal for the data fields present in their ETC map. The following are Cisco's recommended data fields for the ETC map:

- Business Function or Process Group

- Managing/Operating Business Unit or Organizational Department

- Business Process

- Business Process Description

- Business Process ID# [OPTIONAL: if linked to separate documentation]

- Primary Stakeholder List

- Business Outcomes

- Technical Capability Requirements Description

- IT Assets Currently Leveraged

- Competitive Advantage [Yes/No]

- Reference to Relevant System/Solution Requirements Documents

Transformation teams are obviously welcome to tailor this list of data fields. They should be careful, however, to remember the underlying purpose and goal of this effort, which is simply to understand the functions and processes of the enterprise, the outcomes they are linked to, and the technical capabilities required to support each in order to design a specific type of IT Services.

Building the ETC Map

Filling the ETC map with the information required to support Service design should begin by engaging enterprise architecture practices, and then teams across the enterprise responsible for documenting business processes. The goal is to populate as much of the information from existing documentation as possible while at all times ensuring its accuracy. While it may be tempting to use only existing documentation, teams should take care not to sacrifice key information such as separately documenting the requirements and the current assets used to enable, and the identification of priority or competitive advantage processes, that may not be included in documentation. After they've evaluated the landscape of existing documentation, transformation teams can better gauge the remaining level of effort required and best approach and tactics for gathering the information they need.

We can assume that teams need to engage stakeholder groups across some or all of the enterprise. Before doing so, Cisco recommends clearly establishing the type of information they are gathering to ensure they engage the right contacts, and developing an agenda or interview protocol to ensure they get the best information possible.

IT Transformation teams must also ensure that they have captured process and technical capability requirements end-to-end across the enterprise. We can't achieve complete alignment of IT Services to the needs of the business if we have blind spots in our map. To support this, Cisco recommends a three-lane approach to gathering and reviewing the information in the ETC map, which allows teams to better visualize, review, and pursue stakeholder engagement for each of the functions across the enterprise. Each lane operates as follows:

- **Business Functions:** A collection of capabilities required for the execution of business processes by lines of business, such as drilling a well, manufacturing a vehicle, or providing health care.

- **Corporate Functions:** A collection of capabilities required for the execution of business processes by common enterprise business units, such as a human resources department managing the recruitment of resources.

- **IT Functions:** A collection of capabilities required for the execution of processes specific to the IT organization, such as IT Service support.

The IT organization may not have visibility to the functions across the enterprise at first and can instead leverage the likely well-known organizational departments to populate their ETC map, as illustrated in Figure 5-1.

Business Functions

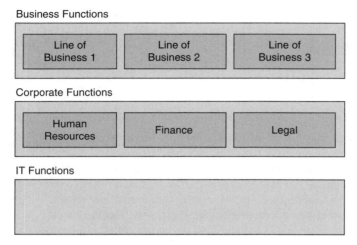

Figure 5-1   *Department-Based ETC Map*

IT Transformation teams can leverage this as a guide for which departments to engage stakeholders in order to finalize the information in the ETC map. As they identify specific functions, they can update their ETC map graphic, as shown in Figure 5-2, which includes sample potential functions for an auto manufacturer.

Business Functions (Auto Manufacturer Example)

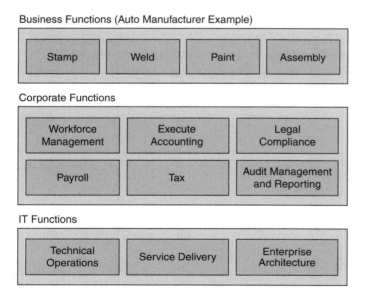

Figure 5-2   *Sample Enterprise Technical Capabilities Map—Auto Manufacturer*

Note that a graphic similar to the one shown in Figure 5-2 can be leveraged as an overlay for the extensive information contained in the ETC map, and in the future used to illustrate the alignment of IT Services to business functions. Functions illustrated in the map correlate to data fields in the ETC map document and can also include name or numeric codes that correlate to IT Services in the portfolio, allowing business leaders to quickly identify Services aligned to different segments of enterprise business operations.

Service Capability Roadmaps

To maintain alignment with the needs of the business, IT Services need to evolve over time. One of the earliest tools a Service Owner can leverage is a Service capability roadmap, which will later become part of Service architecture, which is then linked to the broader enterprise architecture.

The purpose of a Service capability roadmap is to illustrate the introduction, and in some cases discontinuation, of capabilities delivered by the Service. The ultimate goal is to refine and agree to the roadmap with customer stakeholders, allowing the Service Owner to proactively develop plans to support the required capabilities.

These roadmaps are typically presented and reviewed in Service Reviews; they represent part of a larger strategy to evolve the IT Service landscape, often informing investment and architectural planning. Cisco recommends a rolling six-quarter roadmap, but enterprise companies or Services that primarily deal with more complex and larger-scale capability sets may opt to leverage eight- or even 12-quarter roadmaps. Also note that many Service Owners find it convenient to organize these roadmaps by Service offering, as demonstrated in the same roadmap in Figure 5-3.

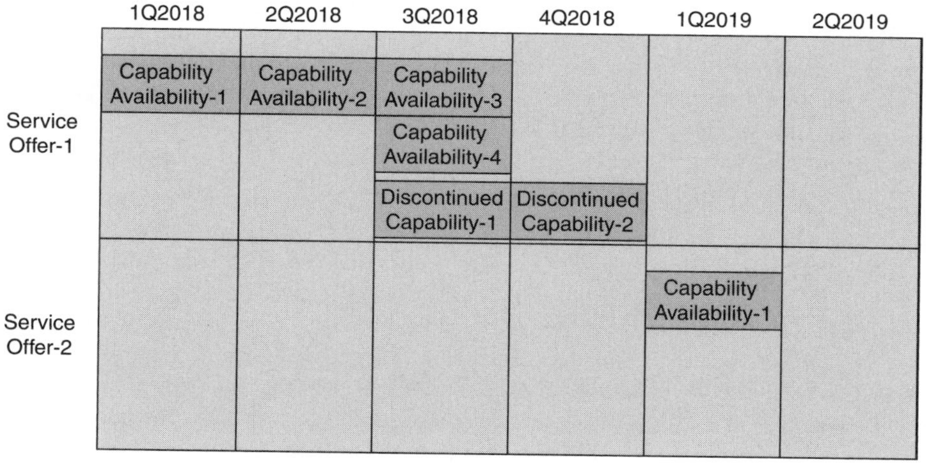

	1Q2018	2Q2018	3Q2018	4Q2018	1Q2019	2Q2019
Service Offer-1	Capability Availability-1	Capability Availability-2	Capability Availability-3			
			Capability Availability-4			
			Discontinued Capability-1	Discontinued Capability-2		
Service Offer-2					Capability Availability-1	

Figure 5-3 *Service Capability Roadmap Example*

The most important consideration for Service Owners is to ensure these roadmaps continue to reflect the quarter in which technical capabilities will be made available or discontinued, and not diverge into project or technical asset lifecycle roadmaps. Also, note that these are early tools for use in Service Reviews and Service planning activities in partnership with customer stakeholders, but over time they will become part of overarching strategies for combining enterprise architecture and Service architecture.

Service capability roadmaps provide an effective tool for engaging the customer base and inform the broader Service architecture, which aligns to the overarching enterprise architecture and roadmap. Chapter 2, "Introducing Cisco ITaaS Framework and Services Transformation Program," provided a brief introduction to enterprise architecture practices and highlighted that these two core functions of the IT organization would link to and exchange information, ultimately augmenting one another. The ITaaS framework's ETC map and Service capability roadmaps represent one of the earliest opportunities for these two domains to exchange information and complement one another.

From the Diary of an ITaaS Consultant

While I was guiding an early customer Services Transformation, a scenario played out while reviewing an initial draft Service capability roadmap that would continue to repeat itself with future customers. This customer was a shale oil company, and the scenario involved one of the first-ever Service Owners building a Service Review presentation for one of the earliest Service pilots.

The initial draft was a slide that consolidated several massively detailed project roadmaps into what could best be described as an eye-chart test for a fully equipped astronomer. The second iteration looked like more of a lifecycle roadmap for the applications involved, reflecting upgrades of various components of the platform being leveraged to deliver the core capabilities (upgrading the database from version 10.1 to 10.6 as an example).

At this point, I went through each entry asking the question "What does your customer actually get out of this?" In most cases, the answer was simply ongoing support, stability, or mitigation of known security vulnerabilities. In each of these instances, I pointed out that these were characteristics of the Service that should be maintained in the background on behalf of the customer and didn't represent a change in capabilities being delivered. In other words, the Service Owner had engaged below the Service level (using the reference I shared in the diary entry in Chapter 4, "Service Delivery Taxonomy and Definition of a Service").

At one entry, however, the future highly successful Service Owner, almost in passing, mentioned that besides ensuring ongoing support, an upgrade would also allow drilling engineers to begin evaluating wells significantly deeper than before. It was at this point I jumped out of my chair and shouted, "That's it!" calling out that "Capability for well-bore analysis up to X amount of feet" perfectly represented the type of entry we were looking for. The Service Owner emailed a final Service capability roadmap for my review just an hour after the meeting wrapped, and it was clear that highlighting such an example had served its purpose. The roadmap now reflected a series of intriguing capabilities being introduced over the next few quarters, without any unnecessary project or technical details. When shared with business leaders soon after, the slide served to completely transform the relationship between IT and this particular business unit, and joint conversations around future capabilities soon overran the allotted time.

This scenario not only provided a clear reference for all other Service Owners but also provided yet another step in the cultural shift of the IT organization as IT professionals began to think more often in terms of business capabilities rather than isolated technology details. Project and asset lifecycle roadmaps and similar details are, at best, boring to business leaders, who expect those things to be managed by the IT organization on their behalf and only reviewed when there is significant reason to. Laying out a roadmap of capabilities that can improve or change how a business unit operates, however, is a topic that will bring business leaders to the table and result in high-value joint Service planning.

Summary

Business Operations Service types within Cisco's ITaaS framework deliver technical capabilities required to enable business processes. To properly designate and align these types of IT Services, transformation teams must have clear visibility to the functions and processes operated across the enterprise, including within the IT organization, and the technical capability requirements of each.

Cisco's Services Transformation Program includes the development of an Enterprise Technical Capabilities map, which can provide this key input for Service design. The ETC map creates a number of value opportunities for the IT organization, but there are some considerations for transformation teams to review. Some of the information collected by the ETC map can be found with EA practices and teams responsible for documenting business processes, but there is likely to be some remaining data to collect and verify through the engagement of stakeholders across the enterprise.

Cisco recommends following a three-lane approach to organizing enterprise business functions to help ensure the transformation team captures information end-to-end across the enterprise. This approach can also be leveraged to develop a graphical overlay for the ETC map in support of reviewing with stakeholders and illustrating Service alignment. The three lanes are as follows:

- **Business Functions:** A collection of capabilities required for the execution of business processes by enterprise lines of business to achieve outcomes, such as drilling a well, manufacturing a vehicle, or providing health care.

- **Corporate Functions:** A collection of capabilities required for the execution of business processes by enterprise business units, such as a human resources department managing the training and education of resources.

- **IT Functions:** A collection of capabilities required for the execution of processes specific to the IT organization, such as IT Service support.

To support Service evolution and continuing alignment to the needs of the business, teams should build and manage Service capability roadmaps for each Service. These roadmaps aid Service Owners in partnering with customer stakeholders to understand future capability requirements and can be used to support architectural and investment planning.

Service capability roadmaps act as an early tool for Service Owners in support of planning future requirements for Service delivery in partnership with their customer stakeholders. These roadmaps function as part of an overarching Service architecture, which is part of a broader enterprise architecture.

Chapter 6

Service Design and Building the IT Service Portfolio

IT Transformation teams now have a clear definition of an IT Service that supports the goals of the Service delivery framework. They also have a multilevel taxonomy providing a structure for the strategic management of the target Services landscape and a complete mapping of technical capabilities required across the enterprise to enable the execution of business processes. With these and other inputs provided in this chapter, transformation teams can now begin the design of IT Services and build the Service portfolio.

Before we begin, however, we should reevaluate the purpose, goals, and value potential of a Service portfolio. The portfolio within the ITaaS framework is no longer a simple listing of IT Services. Instead, the introduction of the Service taxonomy introduces a hierarchy to the portfolio and requires us to designate elements beyond just IT Services; it also enables a number of value capabilities and outcomes for Service delivery. With this in mind, this chapter provides a complete overview of the ITaaS framework's Service portfolio, including considerations, structure and design, and even the recommended workflow for developing and finalizing.

From there, the focus shifts to designing specific elements of the Service portfolio, dedicating a considerable amount of time to reviewing the various guidelines, best practices, and lessons learned for the successful design of IT Services across the enterprise. We also cover guidance for the design of each Service type, along with the designation of elements at each level of the Service delivery taxonomy. Cisco's ITaaS framework includes a complete reference portfolio, capable of significantly accelerating this extensive effort, allowing transformation teams to focus on the design of IT Services unique to their enterprise industry and business. The reference portfolio, along with guidance for leveraging it, are included in Appendix A.

Service Portfolio Overview

Service portfolios are far from a novel concept; in fact, IT Service management standards have for years advocated for their use in managing IT Services. Consequently, portfolios can be found in place across most enterprise IT organizations. Cisco's ITaaS framework also leverages the concept of a Services portfolio, retaining its core intent as an artifact for organizing and managing IT Services while also striving for a more strategic purpose within the framework for IT Service delivery. The following sections ensure that you clearly understand the purpose, goals, and value of the Service portfolio and its impact on Service delivery. Transformation teams should remain conscious of a number of considerations, and they need to carefully review their design approach and general workflow for building the portfolio, which spans gathering all the required inputs to vetting, finalizing, and administering the IT Services portfolio.

Purpose and Value of the Service Portfolio

Many IT Service management standards leverage the portfolio solely as a tool for listing Services. While this basic function will remain the ITaaS framework leverages it as a vehicle for applying the Service taxonomy, allowing for summarization of information at each level of the hierarchy and positioning it as a strategic tool for IT leaders as well. The foremost purpose of the IT Service portfolio then becomes to support planning and execution of strategies at different levels of the Service delivery hierarchy.

As an example of this value potential, say a Service delivery team aligns summarized information for Service costs and performance at the Strategic Service Group level. Recall that Services are aggregated at this level in order to support strategic planning. Simply associating costs and performance with a portfolio listing of over a hundred individual IT Services can provide a valuable reference to specific Service delivery teams but is not conducive to strategic planning. When we summarize Service cost and performance information at higher levels of our hierarchy, however, we effectively create a strategic dashboard for IT leaders. These multilevel dashboards enable quicker assessment and even monitoring over time of strategic segments of the Service landscape, and it is the portfolio that would drive these informational views

While its use as a strategic tool receives most of our value examination, the Service portfolio serves additional purposes within the ITaaS framework. At its most fundamental level, through the application of the taxonomy it helps organize an otherwise cumbersome list of Services, making the portfolio easier to navigate and administer even for those IT organizations that choose to leverage it strictly as a basic reference for IT Services. In practice, it may exist as a reference artifact for Service delivery that additionally feeds a strategic dashboard. Regardless, it will always exist as a primarily IT internal tool. It will also be used to derive the IT Service catalog, which is leveraged to enable customer request portals, such as corporate e-stores as described in Chapter 11, "Completing the Services Transformation."

The ITaaS framework's IT Service portfolio still acts as a valuable reference for Services and related information, but it also acts as the point of execution for the Service taxonomy, allowing the portfolio to be organized and administered more easily. Through the association of carefully designed information sets at each level of the Service delivery hierarchy, the portfolio also becomes a multilevel strategic dashboard for IT leaders.

Service Portfolio Considerations

With the purpose and potential value of the Service portfolio clearly established, IT Transformation teams are likely eager to begin designing Services. Before they begin, however, they should remain conscious of a number of considerations, both general and specific, in the design and development of the Service portfolio.

The first general consideration for the portfolio is that it represents a significant effort. Design of a complete Service portfolio is complex and is also likely to represent the largest task that IT Transformation teams will face in the Services Transformation Program. Development of strategies for Service costing and performance represent significant efforts as well, and have the potential to present as much or more complexity, but the breadth of the portfolio design along with its own complexities mean it will typically represent the most time consuming effort, often far in excess of original timeline estimates of most teams. Remember that the team is not only designing a complete set of IT Services capable of delivering capabilities end-to-end across the enterprise business but is also designating elements at each of the additional levels of the Service taxonomy. Be sure that IT leaders, stakeholders, and the transformation team understand the task and be sure to not overcommit on timelines.

The complexity inherent in the effort is another consideration. There are numerous opportunities for proposed designs to veer from best practices or for teams to take different directions, resulting in discontinuity in the designation of elements within a given level of the portfolio. The length of the effort may lead some team members to fall back on historical approaches to IT Service design that contradict the ITaaS framework's definition of an IT Service and fail to support future strategies for costing and performance. Change leadership is critical in driving consistency end-to-end and ensuring that proposed Services adhere to the established definition and characteristics of a Service and best practices shared later in this chapter, and that they support the guiding principles for Service delivery.

A key advantage for IT Transformation teams is the ITaaS framework's inclusion of a reference portfolio, which is shared along with guidance for use in Appendix A. This reference portfolio provides transformation teams with an initial set of Technology Foundation and Enterprise End-Customer Services common to IT organizations across any industry. These Services act as a guide for further Service design and can be easily customized and adopted. Doing so can significantly reduce the level and complexity of the overall effort and allows teams to focus the bulk of their energy on the careful designation of Business Operations Services unique to their industry and enterprise business.

Remember that although the bulk of the effort to design the Service portfolio is carried by the IT Transformation team, it does not represent a task that can be completed solely within the team or even internally to the IT organization. The entirety of the portfolio needs to be vetted across relevant stakeholders and refined based on their feedback. Practices for vetting are detailed later in this chapter, but must leverage value messaging and Service transformation educational material managed by the change leadership function. Review and vetting of the proposed portfolio take place across three primary stakeholder groups: IT leadership, IT internal stakeholders, and business stakeholders.

As IT Transformation teams progress the portfolio and begin to review with stakeholders they should consider tactics for effectively presenting and reviewing the appropriate sections of the portfolio. The most commonly used tools for managing in-development Service portfolios are spreadsheets, which can easily capture and sort relevant data but are not always the most favorable method for reviewing a proposed set of Services for input. Cisco recommends leveraging graphical illustrations of the portfolio—for example, simple block diagrams of a specific segment of the portfolio that can be more easily presented and reviewed. An example is shown in Figure 6-1.

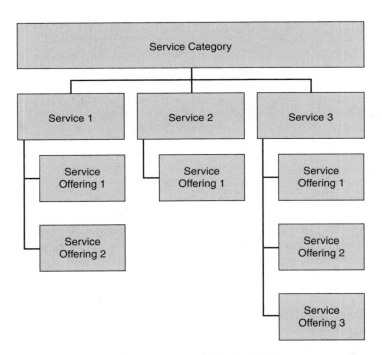

Figure 6-1   *Sample Service Portfolio Block Diagram*

Aside from managing the portfolio throughout the design phase, transformation teams should also begin actively considering the requirements and ideal platform for hosting the portfolio in the long term. Remember, the ITaaS framework presents the opportunity to leverage the IT Service portfolio as a multi-level strategic dashboard, but this requires a platform capable of summarizing Service information at different levels for IT leaders. Even if transformation teams opt to initially leverage the portfolio only as a Service reference, they still require a platform that supports remote navigation and administration because the portfolio will not remain static and must be managed over time if it is to evolve with the needs of the business.

Portfolio Design Considerations

Several of the considerations that IT Transformation teams must evaluate are specific to the design and approach to building the Service portfolio. Note that a number of these considerations will echo recommendations highlighted in Chapter 3, "Change Leadership and Ensuring a Successful Transformation."

Chapter 3 recommended a top-down and end-to-end design of IT Services to ensure complete alignment and the efficient operation of the IT organization. The top-down approach means beginning with Business Operations and Enterprise End-Customer Services types and then designating only those Technology Foundation Services that are required to support them. This approach ensures all of IT's resources and assets are aligned to justified Services and often leaves IT organizations with opportunities to shuffle or realign those that cannot be, ensuring they are operating efficiently. Portfolio design efforts that begin with Technology Foundation Service types tend to force alignment of IT assets early on and rarely achieve the level of efficiency that a top-down approach does. Separately, the end-to-end design of Services supports the transition to an ITaaSO, allowing for the creation of a parallel view of IT resources, assets, and budgets aligned to Services in a manner that cannot be reflected when only pockets of Services are designated.

The ITaaS framework's reference portfolio supports this same top-down design approach, allowing teams to focus on Business Operations Services from the beginning. Then, as they transition to Enterprise End-Customer and finally Technology Foundation Services, their work involves aligning the remaining requirements to IT Services listed in the reference portfolio, customizing where needed, omitting where requirements do not exist, and finally designating Services for any capability requirements that have not been accounted for by the reference portfolio.

Portfolio Design Inputs

Before beginning development of the Service portfolio, transformation teams should confirm they have all the relevant inputs available and take time to carefully review each:

- Service definition
- Service delivery taxonomy
- Enterprise Technical Capabilities (ETC) map
- ITaaS reference portfolio
- Guiding principles for Service delivery
- Existing Service management artifacts

While each of these should be familiar to readers, it warrants highlighting the use of existing artifacts for IT Service delivery. The ITaaS framework's unique and more strategic design of IT Services warrants the development of a new Service portfolio to support the new approach to IT Service delivery. That does not mean that existing Service portfolios, catalogs, and other data and documentation that have been previously leveraged in support of Service delivery are not useful. On the contrary, many of these assets can be leveraged successfully in the design of the new portfolio, often simply mapping to new levels of the taxonomy other than Services. For example, many elements from prior portfolios can often speed the designation of Service Offerings, especially for Technology Foundation and Enterprise End-Customer Service types, or eventually be mapped to IT Service catalog requests as detailed in Chapter 11. The key consideration for transformation teams is knowing what exists and then taking advantage of it whenever possible without sacrificing the guiding principles and future desired outcomes for IT Service delivery.

Portfolio Development Workflow

Following is the general workflow recommended for the development of the IT Service portfolio:

- **Structuring the Portfolio:** Transformation teams designate specific data elements for the portfolio, creating an initial information set aligned to each level of the taxonomy.

- **Designing the Services:** The Service definition, reference portfolio, and ETC map are leveraged to design a complete initial draft of IT Services end-to-end across the enterprise. Note that Cisco recommends conducting initial Service offering design, capturing potential Service asset information, and documenting likely Service chains during this phase as well.

- **Designing Remaining Portfolio Elements:** As the complete set of Services nears completion, the Service taxonomy is leveraged to designate elements for the organizational levels of the portfolio (Service categories and Strategic Service Groups within Cisco's ITaaS reference taxonomy).

- **Vetting the Portfolio:** Transformation teams begin reviewing the initial proposal for the portfolio across each stakeholder group. All feedback should be carefully considered for potential incorporation and refinement of the proposed portfolio.

- **Identifying Service Chains:** Teams document all Services participating in Service chains, which inform Service cost modeling and Service performance strategies.

- **Finalizing the Portfolio:** IT Transformation teams conduct an end-to-end review of the portfolio, evaluating the design consistency, support of guiding principles for Service delivery, and any remaining requirements to support the IT operating model and enterprise business.

Timeline ranges are not included because they can vary so drastically depending on variables ranging from enterprise size and operational complexity, the inputs leveraged, and the transformation team's experience and grasp of the ITaaS framework as a whole. As a general rule, the Service design represents the most significant and time-intensive step, with the design of the remaining portfolio elements often completed in one-third or even a quarter of the time. Considering the design activities requirement to span the enterprise end-to-end, even stakeholder availability to engage with transformation teams can have a significant impact on the vetting timeline, but the portfolio can typically be finalized in a matter of weeks.

Although these steps are largely sequential, transformation teams can easily stagger each phase in a waterfall approach, as illustrated in Figure 6-2. The key is to recognize that beginning the next phase in sequence too early before completion of the current phase can both jeopardize the quality of the design and lead to significant rework. As an example, designation of Service categories and Strategic Service Groups often becomes clear after the first rounds of Services are submitted but would represent pure guesswork if begun at the same time as the Service design effort.

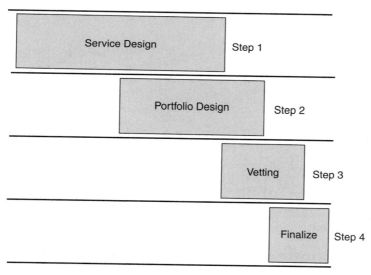

Figure 6-2 *Service Portfolio Development Workflow*

Structuring the Service Portfolio

It is important for IT Transformation teams plan the information that will be associated with the Service portfolio, both initially in support of Service design and longer term to support strategic planning. The eventual transition to strategic dashboarding depends on information from Service costing, performance, and other strategies not yet available to the transformation team, but it is important to plan for its eventual adoption into the portfolio.

Following are the most basic data elements for the Service portfolio:

- Strategic Service Group
    - Service Executive: [Name]
- Service Category
    - Service Architect: [Name]
- **Service**
- Service Description
- Service Owner
- Service Delivery Resources
    - Service Architect: [Name]
    - Service Offering Manager: [Name]
    - Service Executive: [Name]
- Service Offerings
- Service Asset References
    - Application Set
    - Product or Device References
    - Resource References
- Service Performance Information/Link to Dashboard
- Service TCO Information/Link to Dashboard
- Technical Capability Set: [Description of capabilities delivered by the Service, or link to ETC map]

At any time transformation teams engage with a stakeholder group to review segments of the portfolio, they should consider what information the meeting could be leveraged to capture and add to the portfolio. For example, a stakeholder may agree to the proposed Service and then provide an initial proposal for Service Offerings associated with the Service that the transformation team can then refine. Capturing Service Offering and Service asset references whenever possible can save future Service Owners time and help them quickly get the newly initiated Service optimized.

Vetting the Portfolio

As the portfolio nears completion, it is important to review and refine segments with specific stakeholder groups. The complete set of proposed Services along with Service categories and Strategic Service Groups should be reviewed with the IT leadership team. Groups of Services and potentially their aggregation should be reviewed with IT internal communities that ultimately support the architectures, processes, and budgets that enable the proposed Services. Remember that Service Owners and other Service delivery roles will likely be established from this same group of stakeholders. Finally, segments of Business Operations Service types should be reviewed with their associated stakeholder groups across the enterprise.

Initial proposals for Service Offerings and Service asset references can also be reviewed, but newly appointed Service Owners should be encouraged to refine them to support the most efficient management of the Service. Review and finalization of the portfolio are primarily focused on Services, and the most effective aggregation of those Services for IT leaders.

It is important for transformation teams to strike a careful balance for actively gathering input and determining how long to allow the vetting processes to proceed. The goal here is to avoid "analysis paralysis," or scenarios in which teams allow never-ending serial review of a section of the portfolio, enabling competing stakeholder groups to constantly override one another in a never-ending loop. Chapter 3 called out the "80/20" rule as a best practice for supporting a successful transformation program and also highlighted senior commitment to a "Centralized Authority for Transformation" as a critical success factor. These principles were established specifically in support of allowing transformation teams to gauge when sufficient feedback has been presented, qualified, and incorporated wherever possible and that it is now simply time to formalize a decision to move on with the program.

The general guidelines for IT Transformation teams engaging stakeholders in this critical activity are as follows:

- **Be Prepared:** Transformation teams should have not only a prepared set of material describing the approach to Service and portfolio design but also a firm grasp of the current proposal that is being reviewed, paired with an explanation for how the proposed Service would impact the stakeholder.

- **Be Patient:** Beyond the initial effort to review the Service and portfolio design principles with stakeholders and presenting the initial proposals, transformation teams likely need to host multiple rounds of review across different teams and mixes of stakeholders to collect all relevant feedback. Always listen intently to the feedback from every round of review and then make the best decision in support of the Service(s) in question as well as the broader transformation program.

- **Expect Change:** Transformation teams should never be personally invested in a proposed design but should be ready and willing to update the proposal based on quality input and qualified feedback. Also always be sure to remember that it will not be the core transformation team but likely the stakeholders in the room who will be responsible for managing aspects of the Service in the future.

- **Remember the 80/20 Rule:** Could the current proposal be considered as 80 percent right with the opportunity to optimize the remaining 20 percent in the coming months? If so, then move along and allow the best solution to take shape over time as Service delivery teams put the proposal into practice and refine. Remember that even the best designs have to adapt when put into practice; there will always be opportunity for change over time and continuous improvement. The important point is that the proposal is largely right at the moment rather than perfectly right, which it can be in the future.

■ **Leverage the ITaaS Framework's Reference Portfolio:** While the reference portfolio can accelerate the initial set of Services proposed for the portfolio, it can also be leveraged as a valuable comparison. Transformation teams should carefully consider cases in which there is little in common with reference Services.

Identifying Service Chains

As they begin finalizing the Service and portfolio design, IT Transformation teams should work to identify all Service chain requirements. Service chaining is a critical mechanism within Cisco's ITaaS framework for modeling the total costs of Service delivery and understanding the impact of Service performance to other Services. Documenting the Services participating in Service chains helps transformation teams more quickly complete the Service cost modeling strategy as well as improve strategies for Service performance, and even support Service Owners in early Service delivery.

Finalizing the Portfolio

Whenever we discuss the effort of finalizing the IT Service portfolio, we do not mean to imply that the Service and portfolio design is completed for good. As we established previously, IT Services and other elements of the portfolio must be adapted over time to drive the most value from the Service delivery function and maintain alignment to changing business needs. In fact, IT Transformation teams should expect some degree of changes to be made even prior to completing the transformation program. This is a result of putting the Service delivery framework into practice through early Service pilots and Service delivery roles such as Service Owners slowly growing more accustomed to the ITaaS framework.

IT Transformation teams finalizing the initial proposed Service portfolio should work through each of these steps:

■ Accuracy and completion review

■ End-to-end consistency and quality assurance review

■ Review against guiding principles for Service delivery

■ Review and sign-off by CIO and senior IT leaders

The accuracy and completion review is intended as a "did we miss anything obvious?" opportunity. As extensive as the ETC map and efforts to qualify the portfolio have been to this point, something potentially could have been missed, and often it represents a major focus of the IT organization or even an enterprise business strategy. As an example, consider an IT Service portfolio supporting an enterprise that relies heavily on vendors but failed to include a Service delivering capabilities for vendor management simply because the small number of stakeholders who would have identified requirements for such capabilities happened to not have been engaged. Transformation teams should use this as an opportunity to openly challenge themselves with the question "Have we forgotten anything?"

The initial proposal for the portfolio will be built by multiple groups within the IT Transformation team working to incorporate feedback across a wide range of stakeholders; the purpose of the second review is to ensure that the outcome of the design activities is consistent end-to-end. Quality assurance is also considered here—for example, holding up Service proposals against the definition of a Service and ensuring all the requirements identified by the ETC map have been addressed.

The guiding principles review can be conducted quickly but is an absolute necessity and should not be taken lightly. Here again, transformation teams should have high confidence that the outcome of the Service and the portfolio design activity are completely in line with the guiding principles for Service delivery.

Designing IT Services

Now that IT Transformation teams understand how to structure and approach the overarching development of the Service portfolio, we can examine the design of elements at each level of our Service delivery hierarchy. The following sections describe the considerations and best practices for designing IT Services end-to-end across the enterprise. The goal of the IT Transformation team is to designate a complete set of Services. The proper design of these Services will have profound implications for the long-term success of the transformation program and Service delivery framework. Limited degrees of updates and reworking of this initial set of Services should be expected as the Services Transformation progresses. At the same time, if large groups of Services fail to support the principles of the ITaaS framework from inception, then strategies for communicating Service value and achieving the desired outcomes for Services Transformation will be that much more difficult.

First, we review the general approach and best practices for Service design, and examine common mistakes and lessons learned for IT Service design within the ITaaS framework. We also consider how Service types impact Service design. Finally, we need to consider the enterprise-wide implications, such as gauging an appropriate number of Services for a given enterprise business and how the size and complexity of an enterprise business can influence Service design.

Basic IT Service Design

How does an IT Transformation team go about designing an individual IT Service within the ITaaS framework?

First, recall that we defined an IT Service as a set of technical capabilities, delivered by the IT organization, required to enable customer productivity and the execution of processes that achieve business outcomes, managed in a cost-effective manner while seeking to proactively innovate, transform, and improve business outcomes through the application of technology. This definition provides us with the ITaaS framework's recommended point for initiating the design of a Service: a set of required technical capabilities.

IT Transformation teams begin the designation of an IT Service with a logical grouping of technical capability requirements and then iterating through a series of considerations that help refine and properly size the proposed Service that will deliver those capabilities. This refinement may include adding additional capabilities or removing an overly complex capability. In some cases, transformation teams may even realize that the original set of capabilities they began working with is more representative of two or more IT Services. Note that this basic approach to Service design applies primarily to the designation of Business Operations Services, as development of Enterprise End-Customer and Technology Foundation Services can leverage the reference portfolio and rarely need to be initiated from scratch. Later sections expand on design aspects unique to different Service types.

Grouping a set of technical capabilities leveraged to enable a single business process is one of the easiest approaches to begin with. Remember, however, that some processes may have limited technical capability requirements. In these cases, consider grouping capabilities that support related business processes, process groups, or major business functions.

One of the most fundamental considerations for IT Service design is the careful balance of justifying the overhead associated with managing an individual Service against the value opportunity its establishment creates. In other words, we want to make sure that the capability set delivered by an IT Service is significant enough to warrant the effort of managing a Service value communication strategy that includes modeling a TCO and developing and maintaining a Service performance strategy. This concept was first introduced in Chapter 4, "Service Delivery Taxonomy and Definition of a Service." Service designs based too closely on underlying technologies, such as a specific application, or reflecting a request that might be submitted via a corporate e-store often struggle to develop meaningful performance strategies or TCO models. At the same time, we don't want a Service housing a set of capabilities so large or complex that understanding the associated costs or performance becomes unnecessarily difficult.

Designation of an IT Service results in Service management overhead for the IT organization. Every Service defined in the portfolio is associated with a TCO, performance strategy, capability roadmaps, and other elements that result in Service management overhead requiring a Service Owner and other Service delivery roles. Service Offerings on the other hand have no direct association to these elements or their overhead. This leads transformation teams to favor establishing fewer Services during early design efforts, because they can leverage Service Offerings to differentiate capabilities and can always split these Service Offerings into separate, standalone IT Services at a later date. Design of Service Offerings is explored in a later section, but provides a helpful option for teams struggling to group a viably significant set of capabilities to consider instead grouping as a Service Offering within another Service.

When the team feels they have properly sized a set of capabilities, they can work through several secondary considerations to help refine the Service, highlighting further opportunities to refine the capability set or potentially informing the designation of early Service Offerings. These considerations should never represent justification for initiating a Service but are leveraged instead to inform the best structure of a Service in its infancy.

Transformation teams should evaluate the customer base that is likely to result from the current Service design, and consider whether a different grouping of capabilities might consolidate the potential customers that the eventual Service Owner is required to support. Consideration of the Service assets involved in enabling the proposed set of capabilities may also lead the transformation team to update their proposal. Here again, there is the potential that minor updates to the capability set could help streamline the assets involved, which in turn aid Service Owners in managing Service delivery.

When IT Transformation teams consider naming their newly established IT Service, remember that the Service should resonate with the customer and reflect what is being consumed, rather than the underlying technologies leveraged to enable the capabilities. For example, while a large-scale software platform may be leveraged to deliver a wide range of capabilities enabling a business process like "Product Design," we would not want to name the Service after the platform. Instead, teams should consider a name more descriptive of the actual capabilities the platform is delivering, or even use "Product Design Technologies" or a similar Service name to begin with. The goal is to ensure the customer base is immediately familiar with the capabilities that the Service delivers, independent of any familiarity with the IT assets that may be currently leveraged to deliver the Service.

As a final reminder, we want to once again encourage transformation teams to always refer back to the definition and characteristics of a Service and the guiding principles for Service delivery. IT Services should be initiated only in response to vetted technical capability requirements, and never as a result of the presence of IT resources, assets, processes, or costs.

From the Diary of an ITaaS Consultant

One of my biggest challenges when leading some of Cisco's earliest ITaaS engagements was properly sizing Services in a way that facilitated the type of strategic evaluation and planning for a Service that I knew Cisco IT had achieved. Perhaps as a result of my technical background, or a combination of this and the impressions left by earlier standards and practices for IT Service management that I had been exposed to, I simply kept steering Service designs back to a more tactical and technology-focused approach.

I soon realized that this approach led to even more complexity and effort to manage an individual Service while also multiplying the resulting number of Services in the portfolio. Performance dashboards and attempts at modeling the costs were tedious and resulted only in inconsequential data. Worse, the scope of the Service itself, along with its impact on business operations, simply wasn't enough to justify getting senior IT and business leaders into a room to discuss its value.

Finally, after much wasted effort and little value in return, I tested the more strategic approach that reflected Cisco IT's work and now represent the principles of the ITaaS framework. Suddenly, the Services meant something. The tradeoff in overhead for managing a Service was justified by a clear understanding of the impact and value the Service had on enterprise operations. Performance dashboards and TCO models reflected a level of significance that was missing before. There was now a justified reason to bring senior IT and business leaders together in a room to jointly agree to the value of a Service and plan its future.

While I can relay extensive experiences with the value outcomes of this approach to IT Service design, I have also witnessed firsthand how quick IT leaders can be to establish Services for the sole purpose of tucking away various assets for cost elements simply because they exist today. Services designated in this manner are incapable of demonstrating value-add to the enterprise business, and exist primarily to house resources that could not otherwise be aligned to a Service that was delivering a required set of capabilities. Allowing even one such IT Service to exist in the portfolio can create challenges for costing and performance strategies, and add confusing variables to strategic views of the Service landscape used for planning and steering the IT organization. Worst of all, the existence of these superfluous Services robs the IT organization of the opportunity to achieve new levels of efficiency and actively devalues the rest of the IT Services.

IT Transformation teams have to remain vigilant throughout the entirety of the Service design effort, and ensure they adhere to the principles for Service design across every segment of the portfolio. If they wish to realize the highest level of efficient operation through adoption of the ITaaS framework for Service delivery, they must resist the temptation to establish Services for any reason other than to deliver a required set of technical capabilities.

Service Design by Type

Each of the three Service types referenced by the ITaaS framework can be associated with specific design considerations that can provide invaluable guides for IT Transformation teams. The considerations range from how best to leverage the reference portfolio and the general design approach, and even the likelihood a Service will participate in a Service chain.

The ITaaS framework's reference portfolio primarily designates Enterprise End-Customer and Technology Foundation Services because many of these are common across industries. This means that Business Operations Services most often need to be created from scratch, leveraging the ETC map as a primary input and closely following the approach to basic Service design described in previous sections. These Services are unique to a given industry and enterprise and are shaped in response to the scale and complexity of the enterprise operations. As such, it is impossible to include them in a reference portfolio such as the one included in the ITaaS framework.

Remember that these Services will participate in three-party Service Reviews and are the most impactful for establishing the IT organization as a trusted advisor to the business. Consideration for the resulting customer base can and should influence the design of these Services, with transformation teams grouping capabilities to support a focus on specific stakeholders, while at the same time ensuring duplication is not allowed into the portfolio for non-unique capability requirements. As an example, technical capability requirements for execution of project management may be specified within an overarching business function, but similar requirements may appear numerous times across the enterprise. These capabilities can be more efficiently delivered by a single IT Service that could leverage Service Offerings to provide differentiated capabilities to different teams.

Service assets associated with these Service types are typically applications, or groups of applications. Hardware assets and infrastructure supporting process control systems and industrial control systems (PCS/ICS) for manufacturing, production, and operation processes may also appear. These Services often participate in Service chains, typically consuming technical capabilities from other IT Services, usually for storage of data and application and platform hosting. Transformation teams can expect names associated with these Services to most often reflect capabilities or technologies delivered to specific processes or functions.

Unlike Business Operations Services, the design of Enterprise End-Customer Services providing productivity and collaboration capabilities directly to end customers across the enterprise is not strictly limited to the presence of documented requirements. While this may seem to abandon key principles for Service design, the reality is that insisting on the designation of Enterprise End-Customer Services based on documented requirements for technical capabilities is unrealistic in today's enterprise IT organization. Mapping requirements for these types of technical capabilities from individual customers across the enterprise is impractical and unlikely to dramatically alter the resulting landscape of Services.

Instead, IT Transformation teams are permitted to designate Services based on the capabilities they deliver today, and encouraged to compare these against the ITaaS framework's reference portfolio. Justifying and right-sizing Service capabilities, ferreting out duplication, and ultimately achieving high levels of efficient operations are achieved over time as Service Owners are assigned and tasked with continuous value creation. These Service Owners will prioritize the Leverage metric category within their Service performance strategy, introduced in Chapter 7, "Service Delivery Roles and Responsibilities," to help them drive out inefficiencies.

The customer base is also less useful for informing Service design because consumers are literally spread all across the enterprise, even throughout the IT organization. Right-sizing the Service becomes a question of at what level the IT organization wants to align Service performance and costing strategies. The outcome may be limited to an educated guess initially, requiring refinement by the Service Owner at a later date as the full scope and complexity of delivering the Service becomes clear. The reference portfolio can prove invaluable in shaping these Services.

Service assets associated with these Services run the gamut from software spanning standalone to large-scale platforms, to hardware ranging from laptops and desktops, phones, and tablets. Names are easily agreed upon and reflect the grouping of capabilities being delivered, such as "Mobile Devices" or "Enterprise Computing Hardware." These Services may at times participate in Service chains, either consuming or delivering capabilities to other Services, although not as often as other Service types.

Ideally, Technology Foundation Services should be designed only after Business Operations and Enterprise End-Customer Services have been designated and there is some understanding of the technical capabilities that these Services require. By taking this approach and designating Services only in the presence of these requirements, many IT organizations today can expect to realize opportunities to drive efficiency.

At the same time, IT Transformation teams can in most cases safely assume the presence of many Services encompassing infrastructure and platforms that exist today, such as networking and application hosting. These Services are additionally reflected in the reference portfolio, which again the transformation team can leverage to vet their own Service proposals.

Enterprisewide Service Design Considerations

The size of an enterprise business, along with the complexity of its operations, can influence the design of individual Services while also informing the overall number of Services that transformation teams can anticipate for the portfolio. To begin with, Table 6-1 provides a range of Services likely to result from application of design principles within the ITaaS framework across different size enterprises.

Table 6-1   *Enterprise Size and Service Numbers*

Enterprise Size	Details	Total Number of Services
Small	100–5,000 employees, low-complexity operations in limited markets	10–40
Medium	5,000–20,000 employees, operations across multiple markets	40–80
Large	20,000–100,000+ employees, complex global operations across multiple markets and business types	80–150

We should immediately stress that the ranges for Services shown are provided as a reference for IT Transformation teams and are not intended for establishing a target number of Services before initiating Service design efforts. Proper Service design principles should never be sacrificed to result in a preconceived total number of Services in the portfolio. At the same time, if a team completes their initial proposal for the portfolio and the resulting number of Services is far outside the ranges listed, it can be a key indicator that the ITaaS framework's Service design principles have not been applied consistently. The determining factor in the ranges provided is most commonly the complexity of business operations. It is also important for IT Transformation teams to consider how the size and complexity of business operations can affect the design of individual Services.

As an example of how these factors can impact not only Services but also multiple levels of a portfolio, consider the delivery of technical capabilities supporting the procurement function at two different enterprises. The first is a medium-sized enterprise that provides consulting Services in a central region, so the processes and associated outcomes within the procurement function are narrow and not overly complex. The resulting technical capability requirements are limited and straightforward, and a single Service is established to deliver technical capabilities across the entire function. A potential portfolio including Service, Service Offerings, and aggregation of related Services for this example is illustrated in Figure 6-3.

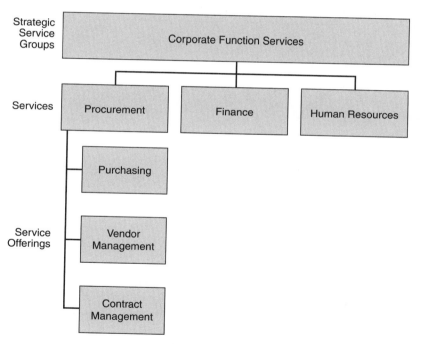

Figure 6-3   *Medium Enterprise Service Design Example*

Now consider a larger enterprise that performs manufacturing, where the procurement function is a critical component of supply chain activities that directly impact the enterprise's success in the marketplace. The processes and desired outcomes associated with the procurement function are much more complex and require a broader range of technical capabilities. The scale and complexity of the technical capability requirements drive the creation of multiple IT Services supporting specific processes within the procurement function. A potential portfolio to support the broader and more complex capability requirements for the same procurement function is illustrated in Figure 6-4.

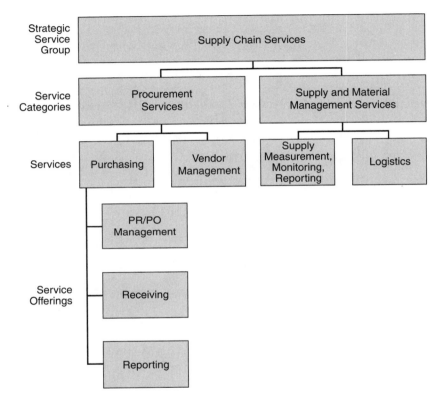

Figure 6-4   *Large Enterprise Service Design Example*

These examples demonstrate how individual Services can be impacted by the scale and complexity of enterprise operations, which in turn drive different levels of requirements for technical capabilities. In practice, even similarly sized enterprise businesses may define different Services to support similar processes, assuming that the scale and complexity of requirements for technical capabilities are different.

Designing the Service Portfolio

Chapter 4 provided details on the purpose and value of additional levels in the Service delivery taxonomy. These additional levels created a hierarchy for our portfolio and enabled the aggregation of Services (Service categories and Strategic Service Groups) along with the management of individual Services (Service Offerings and Service assets). The following sections describe the actual design and designation of elements at each level of the taxonomy and provide examples and best practices for each.

Designing Service Offerings

Recall from Chapter 4 that the availability of Service Offerings within the Service taxonomy affords Service Owners a highly flexible mechanism for managing an individual Service. They could be leveraged simply to organize and ease the management of a Service, deliver differentiated capabilities while minimizing resources and assets, and even create levers for use in facilitating desired outcomes. Even more significant was their low overhead and ability to be introduced with little impact to the Service landscape.

The level of flexibility afforded by Service Offerings, their low management overhead, and isolation from impacting the broader Services landscape provide teams with an ideal first option for facilitating delivery of new capability requirements. If it is later determined that the Service Offering warrants its own Service, the capabilities can be spun out and a Service Owner assigned, TCO model constructed, and performance strategy developed. The key is that unless there is an obvious requirement for a new Service, teams should attempt to minimize.

Cisco recommends that IT Transformation teams attempt to designate one to two Service Offerings during the Service design phase. Doing so can help potential stakeholders better envision the future focus and size of a proposed Service during vetting and support newly initiated Service Owners in getting the Service up and running. This is strictly a recommendation and not a requirement, however, because teams can sometimes struggle to define details at the offering level for some Service types and should not allow their Service design activities to be stalled. Even then, transformation teams can expect their initial proposals for Service Offerings to change dramatically through the process of vetting and finalizing the initial Service portfolio, however, and due to their flexibility and low management overhead, they can be leveraged to address the various competing requests from different stakeholder groups. Teams should also anticipate Service Owners making their own changes to proposed offerings soon after taking over a Service. Transformation teams should view this as a Service Owner having gained a working understanding of the ITaaS framework and confidently taking on the responsibilities for driving more value from the Service.

Service Offerings can often be identified by working through the various capabilities they provide for the management of a Service and considering whether they apply. For example, does the proposed Service need to provide any level of differentiation in its capabilities? Can the capabilities be grouped by customer base or underlying Service asset?

In the long term, each Service should ideally define a minimum of two Service Offerings, but this is not a definitive requirement. Remember that many Service Owners find it easier to designate appropriate Service Offerings after several months of managing Service delivery. In general, Service Owners tend to most often leverage three to five Service Offerings. In cases where more than five Service Offerings are required, the Service Owner's efforts to manage and maintain each can potentially begin to outweigh the value they add. Numerous Service Offerings can also be an indicator that one or more offerings should be considered for their own separate Services.

Capturing Service Asset References

Service assets require little to no "design" work. Instead, IT Transformation teams are required only to identify the different types of Service assets associated with a Service. From there, the real design effort involves how best to reference the often extensive array of Service assets in the Service portfolio while still ensuring that it can be leveraged as a strategic tool for steering the IT organization.

Recall that Service Assets are the various resources, assets, processes, and even budgets that actually enable the capabilities delivered by a Service. Service assets can include everything from standalone applications to large-scale application suites, to hardware spanning everything from servers, storage arrays, smartphones, laptops, network devices, and of course, IT staff (people) resources. Documenting each asset involved in the delivery of a Service would represent a major effort, and IT Transformation teams working through the design of the initial portfolio are likely eager to understand to what degree they are required to identify these many assets.

The short answer is that the IT Service portfolio should reference only the types of Service assets in use and, whenever possible, link or map directly to other platforms such as asset databases, application portfolios, configuration management databases (CMDBs), or even corporate directories. These platforms are purpose-built for the function of managing and documenting specific information, and are better suited for capturing details such as licensing information, serial numbers, or similar data unique to each. The design work focuses on reviewing the structure and organization of these platforms, and determining how best to link information to the Service portfolio, including the appropriate level of detail to associate with each. The following Service asset references might be contained in a portfolio.

- IT Staffing Resources: Level 1 Support Desk Team

- Hardware: Networking Equipment: WAN Routers

- Software: Standalone Licensed Application: [NAME]

- Software: Multi-User Hosted Platform: ERP System [NAME]:

Many IT organizations develop solutions for linking to these systems from the Service portfolio, allowing customers to navigate from one platform to a complete listing of applications associated with a Service and to locate detailed data such as cost and licensing information. Successfully linking information between platforms can accelerate multiple strategies and processes for Service delivery and other functions of the IT organization.

Designing Strategic Service Groups

Chapter 4 established the purpose of the top level of Service aggregation within an ITaaS Service taxonomy and portfolio as providing the CIO and senior IT leaders with a strategic view of the IT Service landscape. With this in mind, the specific elements that make up this topmost level of the Service delivery hierarchy depend on the aspects of the enterprise business and IT organization that IT leaders want to establish visibility to.

IT Transformation teams can begin developing an initial proposal for the elements that will populate this level of the portfolio in parallel with initiating Service design. However, they should remain conscious of several considerations. First is that the designation of Strategic Service Groups (SSGs) should not be allowed to influence the design of any individual Services to a significant degree, much less to supersede fundamental Service design principles. In other words, teams should ensure they are foremost designing Services in response to requirements for technical capabilities, and not proposing Services simply to populate a proposed Strategic Service Group. Transformation teams should also anticipate that as the Service design effort progresses and the final landscape of IT Services across the enterprise begins to take shape, they may be required to revisit an earlier proposal for Strategic Service Groups. With this in mind, they may choose to defer proposing SSGs until they have progressed the Service design effort beyond its anticipated midway point. Teams should also always remember that the final design can and should be heavily influenced by the IT leadership team.

Cisco recommends that this level of the taxonomy be populated with no more than ten elements and considers four to six to be ideal for most IT organizations. Designating fewer than four or more than ten Strategic Service Groups begins to strip this level of aggregation of its strategic significance. Cisco's reference taxonomy designates six Strategic Service Groups.

The best advice when proposing a set of Strategic Service Groups is for IT Transformation teams to consider these questions: What types of questions will the CIO and senior IT leaders have regarding the IT Service landscape? What is the most valuable view of aggregated Services information to support their top priorities and the decisions they will be faced with? Some examples of these may include

- Do we have visibility to the technical capabilities the IT organization delivers that have been deemed a competitive advantage to enterprise business operations?

- What are the total operating costs for Services supporting common corporate functions and delivering capabilities that are standard requirements across businesses, and are there any emerging trends that these Services could adopt to decrease these costs?

- What are the total costs of Services that enable the IT operating model, how have those costs changed over time, and how are they forecasted to change?

- What is the high-level performance of core Technology Foundation Services, and how is this impacting Business Operations and Enterprise End-Customer Services that directly enable our customers?

Cisco's ITaaS framework and reference portfolio contain a set of SSGs based closely on the original organizing principles of Cisco IT's portfolio and then refined across numerous enterprise businesses of different sizes and industries. As with any segment of the reference portfolio, they can both accelerate and guide the efforts of the transformation team, but should be carefully reviewed and customized when necessary to address the characteristics and goals of each IT organization and enterprise business.

- **Competitive Advantage Business Services:** Business Operations Services that primarily enable processes for enterprise lines of business, including delivery of technical capabilities identified as differentiating the enterprise business in the marketplace, outperforming competitors, or supporting strategies and outcomes driven by the leadership team.

- **Standard Business Services:** Business Operations Services that primarily enable processes for enterprise lines of business via common standard, matured capabilities common within the industry.

- **Corporate Functions Services:** Business Operations Services that primarily enable processes for common corporate functions such as human resources, legal, and finance.

- **Enterprise Productivity Services:** Enterprise End-Customer Services that enable general productivity, communication, and collaboration across the enterprise.

- **Technical Infrastructure and Platform Services:** Technology Foundation Services that enable technical capabilities consumed by other IT Services to deliver capabilities.

- **IT as a Business Services:** Business Operations Services that enable processes unique to the IT operating model and allow the IT organization to run like a competitive business.

Aggregation of IT Services across the Strategic Service Groups recommended by the reference portfolio effectively aligns Technology Foundation and Enterprise End-Customer Service types into different classes, providing IT leaders with direct visibility of and ability to focus on the unique needs of each. From there, Business Operations Service types are categorized by the operations the Service enables, establishing visibility to Services that enable common corporate function BUs, industry and enterprise unique lines of business, and the IT organization itself. For those Services enabling the lines of business, IT and business leaders can additionally distinguish those that provide capabilities that can disrupt the industry and establish the enterprise as a market leader. This differentiation allows the IT organization to subject competitive advantage Services to unique requirements, such as dedicated Service Reviews with business execs, investment prioritization, and increased scrutiny on Service performance.

Once again, the names and guidance for categorizing Services within a specific Strategic Service Group can and should be customized as required to facilitate the purpose and goals of the IT organization. Regardless of how closely the finalized Service portfolio reflects those included in the reference portfolio, the key is that teams remember the name and purpose of establishing this level of the taxonomy. If the designation of elements fails to create a strategic view of the IT Service landscape, this level of the Service delivery taxonomy has failed in its fundamental purpose.

Designing Service Categories

The common role of this taxonomy and portfolio level is to provide an initial step of aggregation for the likely significant set of IT Services defined in the portfolio. Chapter 4 described that it could be leveraged to create opportunities in various ways and for different segments of the IT organization. Services can be grouped by architecture, technology domain, or even by customer base. The key consideration for the IT Transformation team is the opportunity and value it creates for the IT organization.

Cisco recommends transformation teams consider grouping Technology Foundation and Enterprise End-Customer Service types by technology domain, and business operation Services by function. Table 6-2 provides examples.

Table 6-2 *Domain and Function Grouping*

Sample Service Categories	IT Services
Enterprise Sales Function Services	Revenue Accounting Capabilities, Customer Data Management, Partner Program Management
Collaboration Services	Email and Calendaring, Video Conferencing, Messaging Technologies
Network and Access Services	Corporate Network, Partner Connections, Home and Remote Access
Application Development Services	Enterprise Application Customization and Development, Mobile App Development, Programmable Infrastructure Development

A second consideration is to allow Service Architects and the EA practices to group Services into share architecture categories. In doing so this option creates an aggregation of Services that better facilitates architectural planning.

A Service category should contain a minimum of two to three Services, and no more than a dozen, beyond which the group of Services can become difficult to manage. Remember, for Service delivery frameworks that have adopted a four-level taxonomy, this is the level that is removed from the Service delivery hierarchy in favor of retaining the functionality of Strategic Service Groups. Transformation teams that initially chose to progress a five-level taxonomy and now find themselves struggling to populate Service categories with more than two Services should consider moving instead to a four-level portfolio.

Summary

Within the ITaaS framework, the purpose of the Service portfolio is to apply the Service delivery taxonomy and create a hierarchy for managing the IT Service landscape, with a goal of creating a strategic tool for the planning and execution of strategies at different levels of the IT organization.

IT Transformation teams begin by considering how to structure and also present the information within the portfolio. From there, they begin the design of IT Services and other levels of the taxonomy to facilitate the technical capability requirements of the enterprise. Once an initial proposal for the Service portfolio nears completion, it should be subject to several rounds of reviews and vetting with all applicable stakeholder groups. After this feedback has been incorporated transformation teams finalize the portfolio by conducting an end-to-end quality assurance review and consistency check, as well as getting sign-off from senior IT leaders.

Basic Service design begins with a logical grouping of related technical capability requirements. From there, teams iterate through a series of considerations, such as the complexity of management and resulting customer base in order to refine the initial proposal. Service types also inform Service design. Business Operations Services leverage the ETC map as a key input, while Enterprise End-Customer and Technology Foundation Services more heavily leverage the reference portfolio.

Initial Service design should also include proposals for Service Offerings, which can help shape the scope of a proposed Service and support informative review with stakeholders. Transformation teams need to review the best approach to documenting Service asset references, and should also capture initial references for each proposed Service. Once they are assigned, Service Owners are responsible for finalizing Service Offerings and Service assets.

Design of Strategic Service Groups should focus on creating strategic visibility of the IT Service landscape for IT leaders. Cisco's reference portfolio includes a set of SSGs that have been successfully leveraged by IT leaders across different industries that can be tailored by transformation teams. Service categories provide a first level of aggregation and should enable capabilities and create value for other segments of the IT organization. Cisco recommends categorizing Enterprise End-Customer and Technology Foundation Services by technology domain, and Business Operations Services by function or stakeholder group. IT Transformation teams should also consider leveraging the Service categories as architecture groups, creating a distinct point of information exchange with an EA practice.

Chapter 7

Service Delivery Roles and Responsibilities

While IT Services represent the pinnacle of the ITaaS framework—and often receive the most attention—it is ultimately the team of people who take on the deliver of Services that drive value and represent the foundation of the framework. Service delivery roles defined by the ITaaS framework put the Service delivery function into practice and act as the medium across which it delivers value to the IT organization and enterprise business. Without this community of people across the IT organization who have adopted a Services end-to-end mindset that prioritizes the creation of business value through IT Services, an IT organization's Services Transformation is little more than a flashy new set of presentation slides and documentation that has little impact on the business or the future relevancy of the IT organization.

This chapter provides even further visibility to the purpose and value these roles afford the IT organization and business. From there, we share hard truths gleaned from years of experience regarding the challenges IT organizations are likely to face when introducing these roles. As we examine each of the roles defined by the ITaaS framework, we will pay a significant amount of attention to the role of Service Owner. No other role within the ITaaS framework represents such a significant level of influence on achieving the desired value outcomes for Services Transformation. Each of the additional Service delivery roles receives its focus in turn, while also looking at how these many roles interact with and support one another to drive and achieve increasing levels of Service value and manage the overarching Service delivery framework.

Purpose and Value of Service Roles

So far in this book, we have made strong statements regarding the importance of the Service roles and responsibilities defined by the ITaaS framework. In this section, we expand on those statements to ensure IT Transformation teams understand and can communicate the extent of the ITaaS framework's dependency on these Service roles.

At the highest level, the Service roles and responsibilities component of the ITaaS framework creates several major capabilities for the future Service delivery framework and end-to-end Services organization:

- Establishes a clear structure for the operation and execution of Service delivery

- Establishes the accountability for the delivery of an individual Service

- Establishes structure for customer engagement and the cultivation of relationships

- Sustains the cultural shift of the IT organization to an ITaaSO

Structuring Service Delivery

Service delivery is a large and complex function of an IT operating model, and it is important to understand who is supposed to do what and when. The Service roles and responsibilities segment of the ITaaS framework provides the structure for executing the many strategies and processes required to deliver and communicate the value of Services. They also help determine who will manage, maintain, and leverage supporting tools and artifacts.

The ITaaS framework requires a broad set of responsibilities to be aligned to a defined set of roles. The many interconnections of roles and responsibilities establish a structure that enables the smooth, consistent operation of the Service delivery framework. Without such a structure, even the best designed strategies for Service delivery are likely to operate erratically, experiencing irregular bouts of fits and starts and long delays between progress or value outcomes. This results from large pools of individuals facilitating poorly defined roles with indistinguishable responsibilities, leading to repeating scenarios of confusion, overlapping efforts, and gaps in accountability.

Establishing Accountability

Business leaders must establish a clear line of accountability to ensure that business outcomes are supported and value creation is achieved on a consistent basis. This is as true of Cisco's ITaaS framework as it is for any business function. Without accountability, a business function can potentially achieve outcomes and deliver value at irregular intervals, but for business leaders to plan and execute strategies, they must be able to rely on a consistent state of operations and outcomes. This, in turn, requires accountability to be established.

At this point, you may be wondering, "Haven't we already established accountability by aligning a set of responsibilities to a Service role?"

Accountability and responsibility are separate concepts. Responsibility is associated with resources who are executing or carrying out an activity; and is something that can be shared across multiple resources. Accountability, however, is associated with a single individual who is recognized as the sole party ultimately responsible for an outcome.

In the context of competitive, high-visibility business environments, if an outcome fails to be achieved, it is the single accountable party, not a pool of resources with varying responsibilities, whom senior leaders seek out. The difference in the two is also evident in commonly leveraged RACI matrices that have long distinguished between responsible and accountable parties.

Accountability is not something that can simply be assigned. It is something that must ultimately be accepted by an individual resource, and this is where the Service roles and responsibilities component of the ITaaS framework comes in. When the principles and best practices in this chapter are leveraged, along with the broader ITaaS framework, the proposal for accepting accountability for outcomes that have never before been prioritized by the IT organization is seen more as a strongly supported opportunity by individual resources. In other words, the detail and structure provided by the framework means that accountability is not seen as a "push" from senior IT leaders. Instead, it is seen as a proposal backed by a significant level of support by the Service delivery strategies along with representing an opportunity for visibility in the future ITaaSO.

Cultivating IT and Business Relationships

In Chapter 1, "The Case for IT Transformation and IT as a Service (ITaaS)," we stressed that building strong relationships with the IT organization and establishing it as a trusted advisor to the business required much more than simply aligning delivery of IT Services to business operations and using some tools for performance and costing. These things ultimately provide support for a community of individuals capable of leveraging the strategies created by the ITaaS framework to initiate and cultivate strong relationships with business customers and drive business value through Services.

The IT organization can't just suddenly advance on its business customers in small armies all claiming to represent a new type of IT professional with bold ideas for Service delivery. Doing so would only serve to alarm most business customers who have likely seen and supported failed attempts to partner with IT organizations in the past. Instead, the ITaaS framework creates a structured series of Service roles with a specific purpose and goal for engaging the business, along with the strategies and tools to do so. By defining these roles, the IT organization acknowledges the need for specific roles to focus on a given line of business, supported by strategies and tools that can align and measure the value of a Service to the business, in order to build trust over time.

The structure established by the Service roles and responsibilities component of the ITaaS framework also provides a much-needed level of organization and consistency to the Services roles for engaging business customers. The roles and associated responsibilities in support of a given IT Service are the same across the enterprise, regardless of customer or Service type. When viewed by the customer, this order and consistency across all IT Service delivery assures them that IT's new model for Service delivery is mature and well established. As such, it encourages their support and provides confidence that their commitment to engaging the IT organization will be rewarded. IT's customers across the enterprise recognize and work with the same structure of Service Owners and other Service roles to review and plan Services supporting their operations.

It does so by defining roles with a sense of focus and a clear purpose and goal for engaging the business, along with the support needed to do so successfully, and providing a much-needed sense of consistency for IT Service delivery across the enterprise.

Sustaining the Cultural Shift of the IT Organization

Acting as role models, demonstrating an end-to-end Services mindset within the IT organization, and serving as an example for fellow IT professionals are responsibilities shared equally by all Service delivery roles. The individuals nominated to fulfill Service roles act as the first wave of the new culture of the IT organization.

The cultural shift of the IT organization to an ITaaSO won't happen on its own; it needs to be initiated, and the initiation of Service roles for IT Service delivery across the enterprise is the best way to do so. As the individuals acting in these roles advance the adoption and value outcomes of the Service delivery framework, their mindset for prioritizing the needs of the business and customer satisfaction become a visible reference for the rest of the IT organization.

The CIO, a few senior business leaders, and a small IT Transformation team may play the role of grand visionary for this future culture of the IT organization, but they simply cannot facilitate a complete cultural shift on their own, especially one that exists in direct opposition to many IT professionals' views of IT priorities. Instead, it is the Service Owners and other Service delivery roles that lead the way, setting the tone and priorities for the future IT organization through their own example.

Challenges and Considerations for Service Delivery Roles

As the foundation for IT Service delivery, the design and alignment of Service delivery roles and alignment of responsibilities must be as strong as possible to support the rest of the framework. This can prove to be a challenging foundation for IT Transformation teams to lay, however, so this section proactively highlights these challenges and provides guidance for transformation teams in navigating a successful deployment.

Considerations for ITaaS Service Roles and Responsibilities

Remember that Cisco's ITaaS framework was designed to be organizationally agnostic; it can be adopted effectively by any IT organization today regardless of organizational structure, and it can continue delivering value uninterrupted throughout small- and even large-scale reorganizations. To accomplish this, the ITaaS framework treats Service delivery roles as a logical set of tasks and responsibilities that can be associated with any individual, rather than being directly linked to a job profile managed by an HR department that determines organizational alignment and compensation. This distinction means a given resource can take on multiple roles, and it provides the Service delivery framework with a critical level of flexibility to leverage the best possible candidates regardless of their title or job profile.

As an example, consider a formal position within the IT organization for Director of Infrastructure. This formal job title is associated with responsibilities for overseeing several functional teams and their managers, each focused on the operation and administration of specific infrastructures (network, hosting, and so on) and for managing a department-level budget. This same individual may volunteer or be nominated to facilitate the role of Service Owner for an IT Service and would then additionally be required to manage the responsibilities and tasks associated with that Service delivery role. By taking on the particular Service delivery role, the individual accepts the associated set of responsibilities in addition to other roles or functions these roles may perform.

Leaders across the IT organization need to be aware of and plan to support this added level of responsibility. IT leaders and transformation teams should also be sure to advise potential candidates of the fact that these roles supplement their existing roles and responsibilities, but then also illustrate the visibility and opportunity the roles afford. In some cases, ideal candidates for a specific Service role may need support in sharing current responsibilities to create the bandwidth necessary to take on the supplemental responsibilities of the Service role. As the upcoming section on change leadership highlights, the IT organization needs to proactively support and provide encouragement in various forms for those individuals choosing to augment their existing job functions with Service roles.

So how much effort do the responsibilities associated with a Service role equate to in practice?

There simply is no formula for this because so many elements act as factors with varying levels of impact. Everything from the size of the enterprise and IT organization, the Service design, and the maturity of the Service delivery framework impact the amount of effort associated with a given Service role. Efforts to support the responsibilities of a Service role also are greatly impacted by the maturity of the processes and tools and the level of automation present. For example, Service Owners in a sample IT organization may at first have to perform extensive manual development of Service performance and costs, whereas in another IT organization the complete process is fully automated with dynamic information dashboards. The one rule I can confidently recommend specific to level of effort associated with Service roles is to expect it to be heavily inflated during early piloting of Services in the Services Transformation Program, and then reduced significantly over time as processes mature and higher degrees of automation are leveraged.

Finally, remember at all times that although only a subset of the IT organization facilitates Service delivery roles, every single member of the IT organization needs to adopt a Services-centric mindset in the long run. The IT organization at large has to realize that the future of the IT organization is one focused on Services that enable the business and that each individual is very much a part of this mechanism for delivering Services, even if not directly facilitating a Service role. Formal job functions such as network engineers, system administrators, and application development teams are still required after adopting the ITaaS framework. They simply now have a visible alignment to the needs of the business. In other words, many IT professionals' day jobs remain largely the same, but they should attain a broader understanding of how their activities support various IT Services and the impact those Services have on business outcomes.

How to Identify Strong Service Delivery Resources

An important step in the Services Transformation Program is nominating the first-ever individuals to facilitate the roles defined by the transformation team. For the Services Transformation to move forward and achieve its value outcomes, the first Service delivery roles need to demonstrate value creation for the IT organization and enterprise business through the framework early on. They must also act as the earliest role models for the new culture of the end-to-end Services organization.

Choosing early candidates that ultimately fail to adopt the target mindset or demonstrate value through Services can bring the future of the Services Transformation into question. Alternatively, selecting strong candidates who exemplify the ideal mindset and prove capable of demonstrating business value through IT Services will successfully lay the first bricks in the foundation of the Service delivery framework and ITaaSO.

The challenge facing transformation teams is that the criteria historically used to hire and promote individuals in IT organizations often had very little in common with the qualities that today's transformation teams are seeking to foster and prioritize through Service roles. There simply is no correlation between success as an IT manager, director, senior engineer, or architect and success in a given Service delivery role. Adhering strictly to a practice of associating a Service role with an existing organizational job profile such as IT managers is rarely successful. A best practice recommended by Cisco's ITaaS framework is to anticipate that Service roles can be fulfilled from anywhere within the IT organization and to cast a wide net. While there are some acknowledged limits to this principle—for example, Service Executives are typically facilitated by direct reports to the CIO and are unlikely to be fulfilled by a senior engineer—a focus on the qualities and mindset of the individual is key to successfully identifying strong candidates.

Each Service role is associated with a set of responsibilities, which in turn correlates to a unique set of qualities that support successfully fulfilling the role and function. As an example, Service Architects should have a background and experience with EA practices, and Service Executives should have a senior level of business acumen. In general, however, every candidate for Service delivery roles should share the following qualities:

- Understand and support the obligations of the IT organization to the parent enterprise (supporting business outcomes while operating efficiently)

- Demonstrate a strong understanding of the ITaaS framework and how to leverage the strategies, processes, and tools to deliver business value through Services

- Demonstrate the ideal mindset of the future ITaaSO

- Demonstrate a strong understanding of the Service roles and associated responsibilities

- Accept accountability for the outcomes associated with a given Service delivery role

- Ensure available bandwidth or plan for availability required to facilitate the responsibilities of the associated Service role

The best candidates to fulfill the first-ever Service delivery roles are those that "just get it," and need little to no encouragement or coaching from the transformation team. Individuals within every IT organization today already fundamentally support the goals of the ITaaS framework even if they've never heard of it. Transformation teams need only find these individuals and provide them the opportunity to support the IT organization and enterprise business in the manner they hoped to previously but lacked the strategies and tools to do so. Forget resumes and certifications; look for the right mindset and motivations.

Challenges for Service Delivery Roles and Responsibilities

The goal of this section is to highlight challenges that IT organizations and Transformation teams adopting the ITaaS framework will likely face so that they can proactively prepare to minimize or avoid them altogether. Launching Service delivery roles can represent a significant disruption to the IT organization. This disruption can be minimized, however; doing so simply requires IT Transformation and the change leadership function to be prepared, which first requires an understanding of what to expect.

One of the foremost challenges to anticipate is resistance to early signs of the shifting culture of the IT organization, it's priorities, and the individual mindset it fosters which tends to manifest soon after launching Service delivery roles. Remember that the new prioritization of a Services-centric mindset focused on enabling business outcomes through technology, rather than simply technology itself, runs counter to the philosophies developed by many IT professionals over the past decades. Some parts of the IT organization—in many cases, individuals who have attempted to drive better alignment and relationships with the business in the past but lacked the proper strategies and support—actively support and adopt the new approach. These individuals should receive the opportunity to support the first wave of Service delivery roles.

Another larger segment of the IT organization represents individuals who may not have preemptively shared the emerging vision for IT Service delivery but who can be expected to support the framework and shift their philosophies over time with the right change leadership strategies. This group of individuals should represent the second and future waves of Service delivery roles as transformation teams progress the initiation of Services end-to-end across the enterprise.

A final segment of the IT organization, hopefully representing a small portion of the whole, either openly or covertly opposes the new culture and priorities brought on by the Services Transformation. The reality is that the focus and priorities of the ITaaS framework, in some cases, simply do not merge with the DNA of some of today's IT professionals. Note that these resources do not necessarily oppose the communicated goals of the ITaaSO, but the changes it requires. Transformation teams should anticipate this opposition and avoid leveraging these individuals for early critical Service delivery roles, regardless of the individuals' current positions and job functions.

In practice, initiation of Service delivery roles often acts as an informative filter. Individuals who need the full press of change leadership support and a time allowance to shift their mindset to one more supportive of the direction that the IT organization is moving begin to stand out. At the same time, prior to beginning a Services Transformation, it is important for senior IT leaders to understand that not every member of their organization today will represent a strong resource in support of the post-Services Transformation IT organization. This unfortunate reality is true regardless of the success those individuals currently enjoy.

The individuals fulfilling the various Service delivery roles will face another key challenge. Recall that the Service delivery team is expected to advocate for their customers across the various IT assets, resources, processes, and budgets that ultimately enable the capabilities delivered by a Service. Without the right messaging and support from IT leaders, this can often lead to a case of "responsibility without authority." In other words, in such scenarios, a role such as a Service Owner accepts accountability for driving value for their business customers only to encounter stiff resistance or unwillingness from various IT resources to support these requirements. To avoid this scenario, individuals facilitating Service delivery roles must be recognized across the IT organization as representing the needs of the business, and as such should receive top priority and support from the rest of the organization. This is a critically important aspect of the cultural shift to an ITaaSO.

When the IT organization and Transformation team initially announce and then launch the first-ever Service delivery roles, they should anticipate a common set of questions and concerns to be quickly raised across the IT organization:

- Do the new Service roles mean a reorg, either now or in the future?

- Are we hiring new staff to fill these roles?

- Do the new roles override existing job functions that will lead to layoffs?

- How will these roles impact me?

The first question was addressed previously, and Cisco recommends that change leadership teams make an effort to highlight messaging that the Services Transformation is org-agnostic and does not require any departmental reorganization to facilitate. In fact, Cisco recommends avoiding any level of reorg before or during the Services Transformation to speed implementation. That is not to say that organizational changes will not be required in the future to best optimize the support of the ITaaSO and its transition to Fast IT. An ITaaS-based Service delivery framework, along with the longer journey to Fast IT, should be expected to inform the optimal structure of the IT organization over time.

There is also no requirement to hire new staff. Remember, Service delivery roles represent a set of responsibilities that augment, not replace, existing job functions. Newly introduced Service responsibilities should not in any way replace the requirement for any functions performed today. While workloads of individuals facilitating Service delivery roles will increase, most IT organizations find they can support the additional effort without a need for increased headcount. Recall from an earlier section that the IT organization should anticipate that the level of effort associated with Service delivery should decrease over time as processes mature and higher degrees of automation are leveraged. The advertised goal of the IT organization should be to facilitate these new Service roles and responsibilities and achieve the value outcomes of the Services Transformation by developing, supporting, and promoting individuals across the current organization.

The question of how the Service delivery roles impact individuals across the IT organization is a great opportunity to address the need for all job functions to prioritize support for the delivery of IT Services. IT leaders should also consider leveraging the opportunity to solicit volunteers for future Service delivery roles. In short, the response to this common question provided by the transformation team and senior IT leaders should be to emphasize new areas of focus and opportunity rather than drastic changes to an existing job function.

Change Leadership Recommendations

The announcement and initiation of Service delivery roles often equate to the "grand opening" for the Services Transformation Program and a new approach to Service delivery for the IT organization. Although at various points many IT and business stakeholders have likely been engaged in support of developing the ETC map or vetting the Service portfolio, the broader IT organization is unlikely to have been exposed to key messaging for the Services Transformation. This is one of the reasons we encourage the CIO and change leadership teams to begin broad and consistent messaging in support of the Services Transformation early.

The goal of change leadership in this phase of the Services Transformation Program is to ensure the first major interactions across the IT organization are successful. Change leadership needs to preempt any widespread concerns of the IT organization by quickly communicating the many considerations and proactively providing answers to common questions related to Service roles and responsibilities. Cisco strongly recommends that transformation teams consider the concerns that news of the new roles and responsibilities can lead to by preparing material to communicate the details of these roles and address questions and concerns. This material can take the form of widely distributed FAQs, handouts, and town halls led by senior leaders. A thoroughly detailed Service delivery roles handbook can be one of the most effective artifacts for distribution and is widely remembered years later by Cisco IT teams as "the day we knew this was for real."

Change leadership teams also play an important role in supporting the success of individuals facilitating the various Service delivery roles. Training materials and sessions can not only help these individuals achieve early success but also ensure each is engaging customers in a consistent manner. Promoting plans to support and reward successful Service delivery volunteers can also play an important role in incentivizing positive views of taking on these new responsibilities.

How to Design and Tailor Service Delivery Roles

Although the remainder of this chapter provides a comprehensive look at the Service delivery roles and responsibilities defined by Cisco's ITaaS framework, it is important that IT Transformation teams understand how to adapt these roles to their own IT organization. Transformation teams can rename or modify any of the standard roles, shift and realign the responsibilities aligned to a role, or do a combination of both.

When IT Transformation teams are modifying the roles and responsibilities, Cisco strongly recommends that they adhere to the following key principles:

- While Service delivery roles can be removed or consolidated, the full range of responsibilities identified by the ITaaS framework must be supported and aligned to one or more remaining Service delivery roles.

- The roles and responsibilities of Service Owners defined by the ITaaS framework should remain intact due to their importance to the operation and success of the Service delivery framework.

The initial principle is intended to ensure that everything that needs to be done is in fact done is retained. As you will learn shortly, the many roles defined by the ITaaS framework are apt to be consolidated by smaller IT organizations, and potentially even outright excluded from adoption in some cases. When this happens, it is critical that transformation teams carefully review the responsibilities that were attributed to that role by the framework and ensure each is realigned to another Service delivery role planned for adoption. Although the best adoption and implementation of roles may differ between IT organizations, the responsibilities required to operate the Service delivery framework largely remain the same. Similar to leaving several bolts loose or missing altogether from an assembled piece of furniture, failing to account for the functions and responsibilities of the ITaaS framework can leave the resulting IT Service delivery framework unstable and with the potential to fall apart when any significant weight (stress) is applied to it at any time in the future.

The latter principle is intended to act as cautionary advice based on years of experience. Think of the basic roles and responsibilities of Service Owners as a linchpin of the ITaaS framework. The upcoming section detailing the roles and responsibilities of Service Owners makes their importance to the framework clear, but you should understand that the allowances for modifying roles and responsibilities which act as an advantage in tailoring the ITaaS framework can actually act as a disadvantage when applied to the role of Service Owner. In practice, the role and core responsibilities of Service Owner are simply best left intact, and adopted in much the same way for any size of IT organization. Actual updates to the role of Service Owner in successful Services Transformations typically entail adding any number of responsibilities to the role stemming from consolidation and modification of other roles. As a best practice, consider that any responsibilities identified by the ITaaS framework should default to the role of Service Owner unless explicitly aligned to another role.

The size of the IT organization and parent enterprise business provides one of the clearest indicators for how best to update Service delivery roles and responsibilities. The various standard roles defined in this chapter represent a best practice reference in support of a large-scale global enterprise and IT organization. These many and varied roles all play an important part in operating the Service delivery function across a large-scale global company with complex operations, but can and will prove difficult to adopt within smaller enterprises. Smaller enterprises should anticipate the need to consolidate several of these roles, and several may not prove as applicable regardless of the size of the enterprise.

Note that transformation teams should take care not to attempt to completely rework the standard roles and responsibilities. These roles have been used to great effect across Cisco's own complex, global IT organization as well as for Cisco customers of different sizes and across different industries. Treat the adoption of Service delivery roles and responsibilities as an alignment practice, and not an overhaul.

Changing the names of the roles defined by the ITaaS framework can offer a simple alternative for easing deployment. IT organizations may have implemented roles using similar names to those in the ITaaS framework, in which case it is a matter of ensuring proper alignment of responsibilities and how the roles interact with other Service delivery roles and the broader Service delivery framework.

Regardless of how closely the final Service roles match that of the ITaaS framework, transformation teams need to review, finalize, and then socialize across the IT organization a document formally detailing each of the roles and responsibilities. The goal is to provide a detailed reference for individuals across the IT organization as well as those actually fulfilling a Service delivery role. The CIO and senior business leaders should review and approve this document prior to the transformation team distributing.

Service Delivery Roles and Responsibilities

This section reviews the Service delivery roles defined by the ITaaS framework. Each role is associated with a set of responsibilities key to the successful operation of the Service delivery function and achieving the value outcomes of the ITaaS framework. The standard Service delivery roles are

- Service Owners
- Service Executives
- Service Architects
- Service offering managers

We also discuss the responsibilities of an IT Service management team or Service management office. Likely already present in the IT organization and actively involved in the Services Transformation Program, this functional team is responsible for administering the many tools, artifacts, and processes associated with the adoption of the ITaaS framework for IT Service delivery.

Recall that each Service delivery role should be aligned to a level of the Service delivery taxonomy and is ultimately responsible for effectively leveraging the capabilities of the multitier hierarchy for Service delivery. The recommended alignment of the standard Service delivery roles recommended by Cisco's ITaaS framework are illustrated in Figure 7-1.

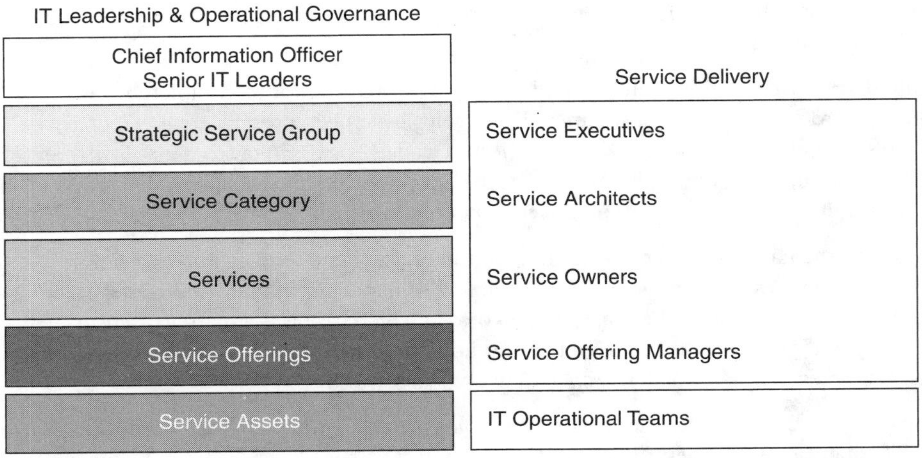

IT Leadership & Operational Governance

	Service Delivery
Chief Information Officer Senior IT Leaders	
Strategic Service Group	Service Executives
Service Category	Service Architects
Services	Service Owners
Service Offerings	Service Offering Managers
Service Assets	IT Operational Teams

Figure 7-1   *Service Roles Taxonomy Alignment*

Service Owners

No other Service delivery role receives the level of visibility and emphasis within Cisco's ITaaS framework as that of the Service Owner. Services represent the pinnacle of the ITaaS framework, and within the context of a single Service, no supporting role has more impact on the successful management and delivery of a Service and the value it provides. This is a result of the role's primary responsibility for acting as the general manager of a Service. Within the broader context of the framework, no Service delivery role is more pivotal in driving successful engagement with the business and widespread adoption across the enterprise or in leading the way for a new culture of IT.

> **Service Owner Role:** Service Owners are accountable for the end-to-end delivery and management of a Service and for the value the Service provides to the IT organization and enterprise business.

To evaluate this description in detail let's first consider what is implied by end-to-end management and delivery of a Service. End-to-end delivery implies that a Service Owner is ultimately accountable for the ongoing delivery of all technical capabilities associated with a Service and ensures they are available when needed and perform as required by the customer. This means delivery of technical capability requirements across all Service offerings as well as proactively assuring availability of capabilities required by the business customer in the future. Accountability for Service delivery rests with the Service Owner, regardless of any Service offering managers responsible for a specific offering, or technical teams or managers who may be responsible for operating various Service assets involved in enabling the technical capabilities of the Service.

Just because a set of required technical capabilities is delivered does not mean they have necessarily added value for the enterprise business. In fact, if the total costs to deliver the capabilities at the scale and performance required are too high, the Service may have actually provided no value at all while draining resources. The Service Owner is accountable for ensuring the Service delivers value at all times and identifies opportunities to increase that value, typically by reducing operating costs, scaling and improving existing capabilities, or introducing new transformative capabilities. It is also important that Service Owners and IT leaders think of Service value as a constantly rising bar and not a single, static milestone that is achieved and then simply maintained.

Service Owners are the sole IT resource accountable for the delivery and value of a Service. They forfeit the right to point fingers or pass blame to other segments of the IT organization. This is why it is important for IT leaders to communicate the prioritization of support for Service Owners across the IT organization and to nominate Service Owners with the right entrepreneurial mindset.

The General Manager of a Service

The responsibilities and lines of accountability associated with a Service Owner role can represent a significant shift in priorities and philosophies around IT Services for most IT professionals. Even senior managers and directors with prior education in business management can hesitate to fully embrace a mindset that prioritizes the needs of the business ahead of technology. To best articulate the ideal behavior and mindset of a Service Owner, Cisco recommends candidates think of themselves as a general manager or CEO of a small company, which is their Service.

A general manager or CEO of a company needs to create, maintain, and constantly critique a complete business plan. This person needs to fully understand the value proposition of the business (Service) and its customer base. Is the "company" delivering capabilities that reflect the needs of the customer base, and how are those needs likely to change in the future? A general manager considers the current and future demand for Services and has one or more options for scaling if needed. This person also wants to ensure the company is operating efficiently, and that Service assets are actively utilized, plans are in place to decommission idle assets, and investments can be made to improve the efficiency or decrease ongoing costs of Service operations.

A general manager should also be aware of any dependencies the business has for delivering a Service, such as materials for the supply chain. Within the context of the ITaaS framework, this means any capabilities consumed from another IT Service via a Service chain.

How would Service delivery be impacted if these capabilities failed to be available or perform as needed? Can any steps be taken to minimize the impact of these dependencies?

A CEO also needs to consider all potential sources of competition. IT organizations and especially Service Owners must realize they do, in fact, face competition for delivery of IT Services within the enterprise. As we discussed in Chapter 1, today's IT organizations are facing the threat of irrelevancy from combinations of Shadow IT and public cloud Services. Awareness of the very real opportunities to bypass their own IT organizations and obtain the capabilities their teams need to operate successfully is growing and is often viewed as a more flexible and cost-effective alternative solution.

The best strategy for heading off competition is to acknowledge it, understand and actively measure and compare differences between the offerings, and finally clearly communicate a better value case to the customer. This remains true within the context of today's IT organizations, and Cisco's ITaaS framework aids Service Owners in comparatively measuring potential sources of competition and demonstrating a better value proposition. This can largely be accomplished by leveraging the ITaaS framework to establish the IT organization as a trusted advisor that alleviates the business of the burdens of technical expertise and management while innovating on their behalf. The ITaaS framework enables a number of strategies and tools to further support value positioning against sources of competition, such as practices for Service performance benchmarking detailed in Chapter 8, "Measuring IT Service Performance." It is the Service Owner, however, who is responsible for leveraging these strategies to successfully engage the customer base with a clear understanding of alternative solutions for obtaining technical capabilities and contrasting the value their Service provides today and in the future.

A CEO has to ask the hard questions of a Service, and one of the hardest questions for IT Service Owners is often, "Can I achieve better value for the enterprise and my customers by procuring the technical capabilities they need from outside my own IT organization?"

Every ITaaS Service Owner needs to consider this decision and reevaluate it on a regular basis. IT organizations have the same options available for consumption of technical capabilities as their business customers. The Service Owner is accountable for providing a set of technical capabilities at a desired level of performance to the customer base in the most efficient and reliable means necessary. In today's environments, achieving this goal may mean leveraging a mix of vendors, partners, and public cloud Services to augment the capabilities of the current IT organization. Many Service Owners are initially hesitant to make use of these options based on concerns that the choice could negatively impact their IT organization, when in fact the mutual decision of numerous Service Owners can drive key improvements to the IT operating model that otherwise would have been missed. Renegotiating vendor or partner agreements for broader scale, demonstrating clear investment needs for internal infrastructure and teams to facilitate required capabilities, and shuffling resources for optimal utilization are just a few examples. The key is that Service Owners "leave no stone unturned and nothing unanswered" when it comes to the value their Service delivers and the efficiency with which it is operated.

Above all, a CEO maintains a vision for the company. This vision reflects the many details, considerations, and hard questions the CEO is continuously evaluating, and charts a course for the company (Service) in support of achieving higher levels of value for the IT organization and enterprise business. This vision, shared equally and openly with the customer base and the resources supporting the Service, establishes a sense of commitment, support, and even loyalty never before associated with IT Service consumption. Service Ownership within Cisco's ITaaS framework and the company CEO share more similarities than do any IT roles today, and the ITaaS framework provides the necessary tools and strategies for a Service Owner to communicate and realize this vision. The challenge for IT organizations lies in identifying the strongest candidates to fulfill the role of Service Owner and then demonstrating the type of mindset for IT Service delivery that the IT organization wants to empower and support them in.

Service Owner Responsibilities

Service Owners are unique from other Service delivery roles in that they are often not only responsible but also accountable for many aspects of Service delivery. While many of the responsibilities shown in the following list can be shared with various other Service roles, the Service Owner must ultimately accept accountability for the end-to-end delivery, efficient management, and value the Service provides, each of which is directly impacted by the many responsibilities listed. The primary set of responsibilities associated with the Service Owner role include

- Understanding the priorities, goals, and requirements of the customer base including any business processes and associated outcomes supported by the Service

- Identifying the customer base and key customer stakeholders

- Assigning and approving all associated Service delivery roles in support of the Service (Service Architect, Service offering managers)

- Organizing the Service, including designating any Service offerings

- Proactively identifying and recommending technical solutions that can enhance customer productivity or business outcomes

- Developing, managing, and optimizing the processes for measuring Service performance and strategies for correlating technical metrics to impact on business outcomes

- Providing communications for any significant outages impacting Service capabilities and ensuring any post-incident investigation accurately reflects the impact to business outcomes and the broader enterprise

- Facilitating the desired Service performance levels through engagement of IT functional teams as required (operations, engineering and development, etc.) including scale, security, and resiliency needs

- Developing, managing, and optimizing the process for accurately reporting the total costs of delivering a Service (TCO)

- Making all Service investment decisions, including justification and prioritization, and reviewing with customer stakeholders, Service Executives, IT leaders, and especially the enterprise architecture practice as needed

- (When applicable) ensuring the functionality and management of a Service chain, including the development of a consumption-based cost distribution process and cost reporting to other IT Services, and the development of strategies for chaining of Service metrics

- (When applicable) agreeing to a Service chain and engaging Service Owners to review, understand, or challenge cost and metrics chaining processes

- Maintaining the Service capability roadmap in conjunction with the Service Architect, including overall quality, accuracy, and alignment to customer needs and architectural strategy

- Reviewing, authorizing the release of, and communicating the availability of new capabilities

- Proactively ensuring that Service capabilities can scale and are available as negotiated with customer stakeholders

- Establishing, communicating, and managing the expectations and requirements for any vendors, partners, or public Services leveraged in support of Service delivery

- Preparing, reviewing, and presenting regular Service Reviews or Service checkpoints with the CIO, senior IT leaders, and customer stakeholders

Also note that the Service Owner, as a result of accountability, is required to take on the responsibilities of any Service delivery support role not assigned. For example, if no Service Architect is associated with the Service, the Service Owner assumes all responsibilities associated with the role of Service Architect.

Also note that it is possible, and common in many ITaaS deployments, for individuals to fulfill the role of Service Owner for multiple Services. In many cases, these are some of the earliest Service Owners supporting Service pilots as part of the Services Transformation Program who are able to extend their expertise as additional Services are on-boarded and core processes such as costing and performance are automated.

In more limited cases, individual resources within the IT organization act in the role of Service Owner as well as Service Executive. In these cases, the Service Executive overseeing a strategic grouping of Services additionally acts as the Service Owner for one or more of those Services. The primary concern is to remember the accountability and level of responsibilities associated with the Service Owner role, and not to sacrifice the value that role drives at the cost of spreading a successful resource too thin. Dual Service delivery assignments become more sustainable as the Service delivery framework matures.

From the Diary of an ITaaS Consultant

Here's a pro tip: If you want your Services Transformation to demonstrate value outcomes and make a strong impression on IT and business leaders, you have to choose the first-ever Service Owners carefully and then give them the support that they need to be confident.

Not successful, *confident*. I chose this word because the truth is that confidence is the single ingredient I've seen consistently lead to successful Service Owners. It may not always be present at first, and you need to build it up. Encourage a sense of ownership and creative entrepreneurship. Guide these Service Owners in thinking like CEOs and prioritizing value delivery to their customer base. Show them how to leverage the strategies within the ITaaS framework to communicate the value of the Service in terms that resonate with the customer. Never just throw them to the wolves; make sure they are prepared. Have them present mock communications and Service Reviews while you role-play a skeptical business leader and challenge their approach and choice of topics.

As Service Owners build their confidence, they actively embrace the stewardship of their IT Service and, just as importantly, the accountability that it entails. Just be sure to choose the right individuals to devote your time to developing.

Service Owners and Service Types

The role of individual Service Owners differs slightly based on the type of Service they are managing. These differences are important for transformation teams and IT leaders to understand and for candidates to carefully consider when deciding on accepting the role.

Service Owners for Business Operations Service types are closer to the enterprise business than any other Service delivery roles. Their Services provide technical capabilities that directly enable the enterprise to operate, and as such, they need to actively develop an understanding of the business processes and outcomes enabled by their Service. This includes an understanding of how those processes and outcomes affect business outcomes. The processes for measuring and reporting Service performance also differ somewhat from other Service types and require the Service Owners to actively develop strategies for linking technical metrics to business outcomes. Business Operations Services almost always participate in Service chains as they consume foundational technical capabilities from other IT Services. This requires that Service Owners understand and approve the processes for chaining costs and metrics to their Service. These individuals are also required to lead business-facing Service Reviews and checkpoints with senior business leaders.

Because of the widespread consumption of technical capabilities delivered by Enterprise End-Customer Service types, their associated Service Owners should typically expect to prepare and present Service Reviews internal to the IT organization. In these IT internal Service Reviews, the CIO, senior IT leaders, and Service Executives for the Service represent and advocate for the enterprise customer base. Senior business leaders and stakeholders outside the IT organization can quickly become a part of Service Reviews whenever it regards significant positive or negative impact to their capabilities. Like all members of the IT organization, Service Owners should develop an understanding of how their Service indirectly supports the operation of the enterprise, but are not required to develop a focused, in-depth understanding of specific business functions or cultivate relationships with specific business leaders. There are still requirements for these Service Owners to develop tailored strategies for measuring and reporting Service performance, potentially translating technical metrics to impact on resource productivity.

Many Service Owners for Technology Foundation Services have the added responsibilities of developing and continuously seeking opportunities to optimize cost-chaining processes because many of these Services support Service chains. These Services also have the least requirements for understanding specific business functions and relationships because the capabilities they provide indirectly support productivity and operations across the enterprise through Business Operations and Enterprise End-Customer Services. As such, they primarily present IT internal Service Reviews that are likely to include the CIO, senior IT leaders, and the associated Service Executive in attendance. In addition, fellow Service Owners often represent the most challenging stakeholder group because they are accountable for Services that rely on capabilities delivered by Technology Foundation Services for the delivery and value of their own Service.

Service Delivery Support Roles

The Service Owner role often receives the largest amount of focus as a result of its significance to the value delivered by any given IT Service. It is also commonly the first role introduced, and as a larger population of the IT organization adopts or witnesses the Service Owner role and mindset in action, IT Transformation teams often find implementing the remaining Service delivery roles that much easier.

Although these roles may not receive the same level of attention as that of the Service Owner, it is important that transformation teams and senior IT leaders understand that the responsibility sets associated with each are critical to the successful adoption of the ITaaS framework and its ability to generate value for the enterprise in the long term. This is why the Service Owner is tasked with facilitating the execution of any responsibilities for roles that are not filled.

Service Executives

Service Executives are most commonly aligned to Strategic Service Groups and enable an important range of capabilities for the ITaaS framework by providing a strategic level of Service planning, management, and executive-level customer engagement for a set of related Services. In practice, this role's associated responsibilities leverage the mechanisms enabled by the ITaaS framework's multitier Service hierarchy to drive even greater value for the IT organization and enterprise business.

> *Service Executive* **Definition:** Service Executives support executive-level business relationships and provide a strategic level of oversight, planning, and strategy for a related set of IT Services, and are accountable for facilitating target outcomes across the Service group as directed by the CIO or customer stakeholders.

A more general description of Service Executives is that they are responsible for looking at a larger segment of the Service landscape. While Service Owners provide much-needed focus on the delivery and value of individual Services, Service Executives provide a level of oversight, ensuring that Services are aligned to a broader strategy.

In practice, Service Executives need to understand the overall performance, costs, and plans for each of the Services in their Service group. With this level of oversight, they would be expected to identify and investigate trends across the Service group—for example, if the quality Service metric category for multiple Services goes down. An individual Service Owner is unlikely to realize the presence of a widespread issue beyond the Service, but with a Service Executive role in place, these trends are highlighted and the proper actions taken. This same oversight should be applied to Service capability roadmaps, avoiding duplication, identifying opportunities for reuse, and prioritizing capability investments across a set of Services. Finally, this oversight includes identifying the need for and proposing additional new Services to the portfolio, either in support of a new set of capability requirements from the customer or growing scale and complexity of an existing Service, potentially warranting the transition of a current Service offering to a standalone Service. Service Executives are also responsible for reviewing and approving situations in which Services should be discontinued.

Service Executives act as the executive-level leaders of the Service delivery function, bridging strategy and planning from the CIO or other enterprise business leaders to the numerous Service Owners and Services across the IT organization. In real-world ITaaS deployments, Service execs often find themselves juggling strategies from both. For example, a chief operations officer (COO) could choose to launch an initiative to optimize the supply chain with specific goals for increasing the speed of processes. At the same time, the CIO wants to minimize capital expenses (CAPEX) for the remaining year while also targeting a 5-percent reduction in Run the Business (RtB) costs per Service group. In this example, an IT Service Executive would communicate the requirements to the Service Owners across the Service group, ultimately identifying a mix of Services that can contribute to each of the desired outcomes.

Senior leaders and CIOs are unlikely to have the time to engage all the Service Owners needed to relay strategic directives. This is often the case for Service Reviews as well, as we've hinted previously that every Service should present these on a regular basis. Although Chapter 10, "Communicating IT Service Value," provides a complete strategy for Service Reviews, we can safely assume that most CIOs do not have the time to regularly attend reviews for all Services. Instead, many Service Owners present to their Service Executive, who then develop a summary-level review of their Service group to the CIO and, in some cases, may elect to have selected Service Owners present as well. The role of Service Executive provides a strategic level of aggregation for the responsibilities associated with Service delivery in the same manner that the Service taxonomy aggregates and organizes Services within the portfolio.

Another important set of relationships for Service Executives is with the other Service Executives. Facilitating information exchange between Service Executives enables an efficient, high-value communications pathway between individual Services. This information exchange can run the gamut from identifying capabilities for reuse, to escalations on delivery, strategic alignment, or partnered efforts to facilitate outcomes directed by the CIO.

Again, this exchange is something that can be effectively achieved only through strategic aggregation, as a pool of 40–60 Service Owners in most enterprise IT organizations would find it hard to effectively exchange information. Service Executives in most ITaaS deployments typically number between 4 and 6, and can more readily facilitate information exchange. A closely knit group of Service Executives, in lockstep with a CIO, is key to facilitating the strategic end-to-end management of the Service landscape.

The final and likely most active set of relationships for Service Executives to be mindful of is with the managers and directors of functional teams and resources across the IT organization. These relationships are leveraged in a similar manner to Service Owners: to advocate for the needs of the customer across various technical teams and infrastructures. Service Executives simply advocate for multiple Services and maintain relationships with their peer executives on the consumer side.

Whenever we consider the accountability that must be accepted by Service Executives, it is to facilitate outcomes across a set of Services as directed by the CIO or executive business leaders, and this is where the Service Executive role, in practice, can drive significant value for an IT organization and enterprise. The role is uniquely positioned to identify opportunities across a set of Services to facilitate the directive and ensure the target outcomes are achieved by the desired dates.

The responsibilities of a Service Executive include

- Providing strategic oversight and management for a Strategic Service Group

- Managing any associated executive-level business relationships

- Reviewing and managing summary-level information on Service performance and Service costs, identifying and investigating trends, and understanding the impact to the Service group

- Developing and presenting summary-level Service Reviews/checkpoints to the CIO and executive business stakeholders

- Identifying, developing, and utilizing strategic levers to facilitate target outcomes across the Service group as directed by the CIO or executive-level customer stakeholders

- Prioritizing investment allocations across the Service group

- Providing oversight of Service roadmaps across the Service group

- Proposing new Services or the discontinuation of existing Services within the Service group as required

- Working with the CIO and other Service Executives to manage the Service portfolio end-to-end

Execution of the Service Executive role differs only slightly based on Service type, with each Service Executive's role mirroring the others much more closely than Service Owners managing different Service types. Service Executives overseeing Business Operations Service groups are responsible for regular, ongoing executive-level business relationships. Similar to Service Owners, Service Executives managing Service groups of Enterprise End-Customer or Technical Foundation Service types primarily interface with the CIO through IT internal reviews but may be required to engage senior- and executive-level customers on occasion.

Service Architects

Service Architects play a crucial role within the ITaaS framework. Similar to how Service Executives act as a type of bridge between executive leaders and Service Owners, Service Architects act as a bridge between an IT Service and the enterprise architecture practice.

The significance of this role can be highlighted by recalling the need for a Service to continuously adapt in an agile manner to support the needs of the business to compete in rapidly changing marketplaces. At the same time, the capabilities delivered by each and every IT Service should align completely to the broader strategies of the enterprise.

> *Service Architect* **Definition:** Responsible for the end-to-end architecture of a Service and the alignment of that Service architecture to the broader enterprise architecture, planning and development of Service strategy alongside the Service Owner, and accountable for enabling systemic Service capabilities as directed by the Service Owner.

In practice, the Service Architect works alongside the Service Owner to understand the Service's current alignment to the business and identifies opportunities to improve, as well as understand and prepare to deliver the future capability requirements of the customer. From this point, the Service Architect then ensures that the current and planned architectures adhere to the broader enterprise architecture and business strategies while supporting requirements for scale and availability.

Although these core responsibilities are strategic in nature, the Service Architect can also play a tactical role in supporting the execution of strategies through architectural changes that achieve specific outcomes for the Service. As a minor example, consider a scenario in which the Service Owner needs to improve the level of a metric category for Service performance to continue delivery at agreed-to performance levels. In this example, the Service Architect could review the architecture to identify and recommend possible changes, which when approved would lead to the Service Architect working with the Service Owner and likely one or more Service offering managers to implement any required changes. In real-world IT environments, this means working across any number of IT functional teams. The key is that the Service Architect is regularly involved in tactical planning and execution of changes to the Service in support of specific, systemic outcomes for Service capabilities.

A broader and more common example of the Service Architect role involves supporting directives and initiatives passed from executive leaders to a Service Executive. The sample scenario provided in the Service Executive section provides a case in which executive leaders set targets for optimizing the supply chain while the CIO additionally sets targets for cost reduction. All these targets were passed to and reviewed by the Service Executive, who was ultimately accountable for facilitating those outcomes across a Service group. In practice, the Service Executive would actually be required to work closely with one or more Service Owners and the associated Service Architects to identify and then successfully execute options for facilitating these desired outcomes.

The engagement of Service Architects by Service Executives is common, and results from the practice of most Service Architects overseeing the architecture for a group of related Services. This is why the Service Architect role is commonly aligned to the Service category level of the taxonomy. Recall that Chapter 4, "Service Delivery Taxonomy and Definition of a Service," highlighted a best practice adopted through many ITaaS-based Service transformations of aligning Service groups at this level architecturally. Doing so allows a single Service Architect to oversee a group of Services with closely related architectures, and from there, a Service Executive oversees a strategic level set of Services of one or more architectural groups.

The Service Architect role varies between Service types, with Service Architects for Technical Foundation Services likely leaning more heavily on existing information from an enterprise architecture practice. Service Architects overseeing Business Operations Service types, however, likely need to further develop a view of their underlying Service architectures to best facilitate their responsibilities.

Cisco's ITaaS framework does not currently include a defined methodology or processes for Service architecture, outside of recommending a general approach for Service Architects. Be sure not to confuse a Service architecture as a specific slice or segment of an existing, large-scale enterprise architecture. Instead, remember to think of a Service architecture as modeling the linkage of various technical infrastructures, systems, teams, and processes to a Service capability set. This model then enables Service Architects to deliver the same value at a Service level that is commonly achieved at the IT organization and enterprise level through an EA practice.

Any successful framework for enterprise IT Service delivery must allow for Services end-to-end across an enterprise to respond in an agile way to the needs of the business. At the same time, this framework must ensure that a rapid pace of changes doesn't duplicate existing capabilities and ultimately remains aligned to a broader enterprise architecture and business strategy. While Cisco's ITaaS framework supports this capability, it is the Service Architect role which is accountable for execution of this important function.

Service Offering Managers

The broad set of responsibilities and the significance of the accountability associated with the Service Owner role can constitute a significant commitment for an IT resource. Why not get that person some help?

As the title implies, the role of Service offering manager works within a specific IT Service to support a Service Owner. Think of this role as the tactical counterpart to a Service Owner. If we compare the Service Owner to that of a general manager, the Service offering manager represents the various managers and directors ensuring that specific segments of the general manager's vision and strategy are achieved.

> *Service Offering Manager* **Definition:** The Service offering manager is responsible for supporting a Service Owner via tactical operation of specific aspects of a Service, commonly aligned to a Service offering, and held accountable for outcomes as directed by the Service Owner.

Despite what the name implies, limiting the role to the management or delivery of a specific Service offering can constrain the value that the role can provide to the Service Owner, the Service, and its customers. It is often best to allow the individual(s) fulfilling the role to provide value across the Service in any way possible. In that regard, the standard name attributed to the role by the ITaaS framework can be misleading. In fact, this is one of the most commonly renamed roles during an ITaaS deployment. Potential name might include Service Support Manager, Service engineer, or as some Cisco Services customers have come to reference it, "the Service Owner's little helper." Regardless of how an IT Transformation team chooses to designate the role, the key is to understand that its purpose is to enable a level of attention, focus, and follow-through to be applied to specific details of a Service that a Service Owner alone may struggle to provide.

In practice, a Service offering manager's support of a Service and Service Owner could take on many forms; the focused management of one or more Service offerings is just one common example. The role could also be leveraged to investigate, optimize, and even manage a specific component of the Service in the long term, such as a process for performing outbound cost chaining or ramping up the availability of analytics to measure Service impact on business outcomes. Individuals in these roles may also be called on to oversee programs to introduce or to discontinue capabilities within the Service. They may also find themselves conducting very tactical management of Service assets or other aspects of the Service.

The possible responsibilities associated with the Service offering manager role are shown in the following list. The actual responsibilities are likely to vary between Services and ultimately be directed from the Service Owner:

- Execute the management and delivery of one or more Service offerings

- Manage or optimize a specific Service strategy or process such as the Service performance or cost modeling

- Manage IT catalog requests mapped to the Service via the Service catalog and their associated details such as SLAs, metrics, availability, or one-time and recurring costs

- Provide project management or support of Service development

Note that whereas Service Owner, Service Executive, and Service Architect roles tend to be fixed, with the same individual facilitating for the longer term, Service offering managers tend to be more fluid. In some cases, these individuals develop an expertise that can be applied across numerous Services, such as development and optimization of processes for outbound cost chaining. In fact, it is common for a Service offering manager to lend support for several Services.

As a best practice, remember that Service offering managers are the most flexible of the Service delivery roles and make use of them to support the desired outcomes of a Service. Teams can expect the most common responsibilities to be the focused management of one or more Service offerings, but be aware of the significant level of flexibility afforded by the role to support an IT Service.

Service Management Office

A Service delivery framework is supported by numerous strategies, processes, tools, and artifacts, all of which must continue to be maintained and administered, and must evolve with the strategies for Service delivery. Many IT organizations today leverage an IT Service management team to oversee the management and administration of tools and processes supporting IT Services. In fact, they likely represent a large segment of the IT Transformation team and are actively involved in the design and implementation of the new Service delivery framework. The ITaaS framework refers to this function as the IT Service Management Office.

As the Services Transformation Program progresses, this same team is responsible for the general planning and management of the Service delivery platforms and processes. Similar to Service delivery roles, these responsibilities are not considered to require a dedicated team but to augment the responsibilities of an existing IT Service management team. In many cases, this simply means a continuation of prior responsibilities that were executed by the IT organization already—for instance, management and administration of a Service portfolio.

The responsibilities for managing the Service delivery model include

- Developing and maintaining a plan and strategy for the Service delivery framework and function, including ongoing optimization and automation of processes, reviewed with the CIO, senior IT leaders, and Service Executives

- Ensuring that the adoption of any changes to the Service delivery framework are reflected by tools, artifacts, and processes end-to-end

- Managing and publishing any and all documents supporting Service delivery, including a Service delivery roles handbook

- Administering and managing the Service portfolio and any platforms used to host it

- Managing the Service catalog platform and associated customer interface portals such as corporate e-stores

- Managing and optimizing IT Service cost modeling strategies and processes in partnership with IT finance

- Managing and optimizing strategies, processes, and tools for IT Service performance measurement and reporting

- Managing any tools supporting Service capability roadmapping

- Managing and administering the Enterprise Technical Capabilities (ETC) map

- Overseeing, planning, and executing information exchange between tools, artifacts, and processes associated with Service delivery and other Service management platforms (ticketing systems, application portfolios, asset databases, CMDBs, and so on)

Behind the Scenes of the Cisco IT Services Transformation

Cisco defined its Service delivery roles by first understanding the complete set of responsibilities that had to be carried out by the Service delivery function. From there, it developed and refined a view of how to divide those responsibilities across a set of roles. Once it had defined an initial set of roles, the question shifted to understanding the types of skills each needed to have, with lots of heavy lifting on being clear on "this is what you do in this role." The *IT Service Roles Handbook* was developed and then published; it laid out the roles and expectations, while in parallel training and support material were being developed, including cost accounting, to ensure Service Owners could manage their TCOs.

Years prior, Cisco IT had advanced an initiative to adopt roles defined by popular IT Service management standards, like Service manager and Service leads. However, the program was not well thought out and had to be unwound. Looking back, the issue came down to a lack of true Services and designating Services end-to-end. Additionally, it had been tied to a traditional organizational, solid-line ownership. You were successful if you owned all the budget and all the people, but in the new model, it was less about that and you now owned a Service. Even if you didn't necessarily own all the people, you were still held accountable. Cisco removed finger pointing that was based on what you owned.

At first, no one took accountability, so the CIO said, "You are accountable. If you own this Service—even if you don't own all the people of the Service or own all of the assets—you own it, and you are responsible for delivering it across the board and taking accountability for the value it delivers." That really helped us move from where we came from (finger pointing) to, "Hey, if I finger point, I'm not going to be successful. I need to influence everything." It made us run more like a competitive business end-to-end. Cisco had a strong leader and vision driving it from the top down, backed by a clear message that these are what the roles are and this is how it fits with you.

As a Service Owner, you had to report on things. You had to say what was working on a quarterly basis. So you had opportunities every quarter to highlight partnerships that were working and those that had challenges. This approach created a cultural change that was driven from the top. The CIO was very vocal that Service Owners were the people being held accountable and were responsible for things. That message helped changed the culture that it wasn't whom you reported to, but it was who owned the Service. Sometimes the most successful work happens when you can lead through influence, as compared to leading by "Hey, I'm the boss, and you are going to do what I say you do."

Service Owners presenting to the CIO quickly learned that finger pointing was not acceptable and that outcomes were the goal. So, if you were an owner of a Service like Corporate Network that other Services depended on, that created pressure to work on continual improvement and not just on reliability, like where we came from, but also against the new metrics as well (customer experience, risk, leverage, speed, and so on).

One resource shared a personal account of his time as an initial Service Owner. "I was the Service Owner for video. Something we wanted to do was to make Cisco a video-based company. Not just selling video but to use it internally and make video a Service. I started a project to drive video pervasively across the company, initially intended to drive Cisco to 'eat its own dog food.' Soon after, I had the opportunity to present that Service to the CIO. The reply I received from the CIO was, 'My expectations of you are not just to increase sales and eat our own dog food; I want you to deliver business outcomes.' That's what I was being held accountable for. That message changed my perception of how I did things and created a goal in my mind for an initial target outcome, which was now focused on actual adoption and driving actual use of video. This led me to do things like remove phones and other things from conference rooms and only have a video system (which also saved money for those rooms). People didn't know how to use it. We actually put on the video unit, 'Hey, I am a phone; I can make a phone call.' What we saw was the dramatic increase in video across the business we had been seeking."

Summary

Cisco's ITaaS framework built on a community of people who transition the framework from theory into practice and realize the value outcomes for Service delivery, lead the way in forging trusted advisor relationships with business customers, and accelerate the cultural shift of the IT organization. Transformation teams should be aware of the impact that early candidates can have on the long-term success of the Service delivery framework and remain conscious of a series of considerations and challenges that they are likely to face during early deployment of Service delivery roles.

The ITaaS framework defines the following set of standard Service roles and responsibilities:

- Service Owners are accountable for the end-to-end delivery and management of a Service and for the value the Service provides to the IT organization and enterprise business.

- Service Executives support executive-level business relationships and provide a strategic level of oversight, planning, and strategy for a set of IT Services. They also are additionally accountable for facilitating target outcomes across the Service group as directed by the CIO or customer stakeholders.

- Service Architects are responsible for the end-to-end architecture of a Service and the alignment of that Service architecture to the broader enterprise architecture, planning, and development of Service strategy alongside the Service Owner, and accountable for enabling systemic Service capabilities as directed by the Service Owner.

- Service offering managers are responsible for supporting a Service Owner via tactical operation of specific aspects of a Service, commonly aligned to a Service offering, and held accountable for outcomes as directed by the Service Owner.

Chapter 8

Measuring IT Service Performance

It is impossible to determine the value of an individual Service without considering Service Performance, and since the final determination of Service value relies on the customer, a view of Service Performance must be developed that resonates with the customer base and considers the impact of Service Performance on business outcomes. To create that view, an individual Service has to measure performance specific to the capabilities it delivers and the goals and priorities of the stakeholders. At the same time, it is equally impossible for IT and business leaders to conduct strategic planning across the Service landscape without a strategy for reporting Service Performance consistently across all Services. In short, IT organizations need a single strategy that can effectively measure all aspects of an IT Service, support consistency across Services, be highly customizable to individual Services, and also resonate with customer stakeholders.

This mix of competing challenges and complexities is why few IT organizations have leveraged end-to-end Service Performance strategies in the past, instead often only considering isolated aspects of performance, such as the number of problem tickets raised. As you will soon learn, managing and planning the future of a Service without considering a well-rounded view of performance can create risk for the IT organization and enterprise, decrease customer satisfaction even after significant investments, and lead to many other unintended consequences.

Cisco's ITaaS framework includes an end-to-end Service Performance strategy capable of addressing these requirements by leveraging a two-step process. The first step requires every Service to aggregate large sets of metrics into a series of strategic Service Metric Categories equally familiar to both IT and business leaders, while the following step correlates the impact of those metrics on business outcomes.

This chapter first describes the many considerations and requirements for a Service Performance strategy. With these considerations in mind, we introduce the ITaaS framework's Service Performance strategy and review it in detail. From there, we share best practices for planning, reporting, managing, and evolving the strategy over time.

When brought to light and examined as a whole, the many details and intricacies of Service Performance merge to tell a story. The ITaaS framework's end-to-end Service Performance strategy helps Service Owners and IT leaders interpret that story, share it with their customers, make a truly informed determination of the value that a Service delivered, and then plan for its future confident in the fact they are now able to understand the impact of those decisions over time.

Service Performance Considerations

The most immediate consideration for IT leaders and Transformation teams is to distinguish between measuring Service Performance and measuring the operation and characteristics of the underlying technical platforms used to deliver a Service. Chapter 1 used the example of a ride-sharing or taxi Service that failed to deliver a value to the customer (failing to pick up or deliver the customer on time) even though the tire pressure and oil temperature (operational characteristics of the platform used to deliver the Service) were fine. Measuring operational aspects of the technical systems and infrastructure will remain an important function of IT, but a strategy focused on measuring the performance of capabilities enabled by those platforms and delivered through an IT Service is also required if IT and business leaders hope to understand the value of a Service and conduct informed planning.

A strategy for Service Performance encompasses many elements, with Service Metrics representing the topic most readers will immediately associate. The following section will look at considerations specific to Service Metrics, but it is important to understand first that an overarching strategy has to be in place to guide the collection, aggregation, and use of those metrics at both the individual Service level and at a strategic planning level across larger groups of Services.

Besides acknowledging the many aspects of a Service Performance strategy it is important to also clearly establish the purpose and goal that the strategy is intended to support, so that we know how to best leverage those many elements. The purpose of the Service Performance strategy is to aggregate, report, and manage Service Metrics with a goal of creating a well-rounded view of performance that resonates with both IT and business leaders to support a qualification of the value delivered by a Service. In support of that goal our strategy should help to answer these key questions specific to a Service:

■ Were the required technical capabilities available and did they perform as needed to allow customers to achieve their desired goal, and how did the performance of the Service impact business outcomes?

■ Did the delivery of the Service meet all operational requirements agreed to by both customer stakeholders and the IT organization, and are these the proper requirements for future delivery?

■ Did the delivery of the Service create value for the business?

The reality is that without a well-rounded, complete view of Service Performance, any planning decision risks unintended consequences, and any determination of Service value is incomplete. The ITaaS framework seeks to address this issue by creating visibility to and then driving accountability across all aspects of Service Performance end-to-end. Later sections provide examples and highlight the importance of change leadership strategies to demonstrate and reinforce the use of the end-to-end Service Performance strategy to influence decision making at different levels of the IT organization.

Service Metrics Considerations

A Service Performance strategy focuses heavily on the aggregation and interpretation of Service Metrics, but what exactly are Service Metrics?

A metric is simply a measurement of something, captured at a specific point in time, or in some instances over a selected period of time. IT professionals are no doubt most familiar with technical metrics, which measure aspects of technical assets such as hardware and software. While the Service Performance strategy obviously considers a great many of these, it must also look at nontechnical metrics that can provide insight to aspects of Service delivery such as the customer experience. Limiting Service Metrics to technical metrics alone will never provide IT and business leaders with a complete view of Service Performance.

Any metric, technical or nontechnical, that provides insight to the operation of a Service is a candidate Service Metric. The challenge for many IT professionals first leveraging the ITaaS framework's Service Performance strategy is isolating and collecting metrics that truly reflect an aspect of Service delivery. Developing a set of metrics for Services requires careful review of those metrics already available to the IT organization as well as very likely introduction of new tools and platforms and at times even relying on manual collection of data.

To support the intended goal of creating valuable information, metrics must be given context. Simply gathering a series of measurements adds little value until they are paired with context that shapes an understanding of what these measurements mean for the delivery of the Service. Does a measurement that was captured for the Service indicate positive or negative performance? What was the goal for the metric, and how far did it miss or exceed the target outcome? How significantly has the metric changed over time and why? Baselines, targets, benchmarks, and trending are all part of the context that shapes the value of the information that a metric provides.

Finally, consider that not all metrics are relevant to all stakeholders. In fact, the most appropriate set of metrics to report varies depending on whether the performance review is aimed at IT or business stakeholders, the leadership level, and even change relevant to the timing, circumstances, and current priorities. It is important for the Service delivery team to maintain visibility to all applicable Service Metrics at all times, while understanding that only specific views of performance are appropriate for different customers and circumstances. The ITaaS framework's taxonomy and the introduction of IT Services as a layer of abstraction together create multiple opportunities for Service delivery teams to develop different views of IT Service Performance, while at all times maintaining full visibility to all relevant metrics to a Service.

Prioritizing Both Consistency and Customization

For a Service Performance strategy to support any level of strategic planning across the Service landscape, much less create an opportunity to engage stakeholders and contribute to a qualification of Service value, it must provide IT and business leaders with a consistent view of performance across Services. Planning at a strategic level is an impossible task whenever each Service reports performance using a significantly different approach.

At the same time, the IT Service landscape represents the delivery of a vast range of technical capabilities across an equally diverse group of stakeholders, each with its own unique elements and priorities. Delivery teams have to exercise a high degree of flexibility when aggregating metrics for an individual Service in order to develop a well-rounded and accurate view of that Service's unique performance. Monitoring and reporting only a set of metrics that can be applied across all Services means delivery teams aren't looking at the right things. This means Services are difficult to manage efficiently, struggle to focus on the priorities of their customer base, and increase the risk of unintended consequences introduced by planning decisions made without complete visibility of Service Performance.

For a Service Performance strategy to enable strategic planning, while at the same time allowing each Service to be efficiently managed and align to the needs and priorities of the customer base, the strategy must somehow prioritize both consistency and customization of metrics for every Service. Here again, the ITaaS framework's introduction of IT Services as a layer of abstraction between a customer base and the complexities of the IT organization delivering those capabilities provides an opportunity to do exactly that.

Managing an End-to-End Service Performance Strategy

Another key consideration for an end-to-end Service Performance strategy is how to ensure the strategy is supported and successful over time. This includes everything from providing delivery teams with the capabilities they need to measure Service Performance to publishing and evolving standards over time.

First, consider that platforms for metrics reporting available in today's IT organizations are largely focused on the operation of technical systems and infrastructures and unlikely to provide Service delivery teams with all the capabilities they need to measure Service Performance going forward. There is the potential that new systems and platforms will be required to support reporting of both technical and nontechnical Service Metrics. Note that although platforms that enable new reporting capabilities are likely to be required, Service delivery teams still leverage data from existing platforms for technical metrics and finance data, and it is important that the strategy take care not to duplicate capabilities or metrics data. Instead, the strategy should consider the availability of capabilities for Service Performance dashboards, which can pull metrics data from new and existing platforms into a central reporting platform for Service delivery teams.

An interesting consideration is that we now have requirements for a set of related technical capabilities, which means there is likely justification for a new IT Service or Service offering. In fact, most IT organizations adopting the ITaaS framework do exactly that, creating a Service that gathers requirements for reporting metrics, such as measurement frequency, reporting capabilities, and data retention and security requirements, and then managing platforms that can enable the required capabilities.

IT organizations must also consider how to achieve widespread and successful adoption of the Service Performance strategy, along with how to evolve it over time. This requires a central authority accountable for managing the Service Performance strategy and ensuring it can facilitate the expectations of IT and business leaders, diverse stakeholder groups, and yet still be manageable by Service delivery teams now and in the future.

Developing an initial end-to-end Service Performance strategy can be a challenging task for IT Transformation teams. Ignoring these considerations could prevent the strategy from ever being widely adopted and at risk of being abandoned before it ever achieves any level of value outcomes for the delivery of Services. Failing to proactively manage the overarching Service Performance strategy can leave Service delivery teams without the capabilities they need to facilitate the expectations of the strategy and over time allow the strategy to diverge from its intended purpose and goals for Service delivery.

Overview of the ITaaS Service Performance Strategy

The Service Performance strategy leveraged by Cisco's ITaaS framework establishes a set of strategic Service Metric Categories that are standardized across all Services. These various categories serve to create a well-rounded view of Service Performance consistent across Services, while at the same time still allowing Service Owners to actively leverage any number of metrics relevant to their Service.

The following sections examine this strategy in full, beginning with a review of the Service Metric Categories and tactics for developing and leveraging each. Business Operations Services take the additional step of correlating Service Performance to impacts on business outcomes. We also describe recommendations for managing the strategy, best practices for leveraging it in practice, and guidance for change leadership.

This end-to-end strategy achieves the intended purpose and goals of the Service Performance strategy while also proactively addressing the many considerations highlighted in previous sections. It can represent a significant effort for IT Transformation teams to develop and depends on Service Owners and Service Executive communities to demonstrate its value and drive widespread adoption. Even when plans for the Service Performance strategy have been completed, transformation teams and IT leaders should expect the capabilities and outcomes of the strategy in practice to be limited initially. The capabilities and value outcomes it contributes to the Service delivery function will increase over time as the strategy matures, and as with all aspects of a Service delivery framework, will need to evolve over time to maintain alignment to the needs of the business and drive continuous value creation.

Service Metric Categories

The purpose of Service Metric Categories is to aggregate large sets of Service Metrics into a consistent set of categories end-to-end across the Services landscape. The categories should establish visibility to aspects of Service Performance that are familiar to both IT and business leaders and are always standard across all Services.

Service Owners should actively monitor any metric relevant to the delivery of their Service, but they must associate every metric with a single metric category. This does not mean that every metric actively monitored by Service Owners is shared with every stakeholder. There could be dozens or even hundreds of relevant Service Metrics, depending on the Service. In reality, the Service Metrics that are reported in any given instance likely represent only a small subset of the metrics that are actively monitored by the Service delivery team.

In addition to Service-specific metrics, the IT Transformation team and later Service Management Office, in partnership with IT leaders, will publish a set of key performance indicators (KPIs) for each metric category. These KPIs should be capable of adoption across all Services whenever possible. This provides an additional level of consistency by standardizing a set of Service Metrics common to each metric category. Note that in some cases, a group of Services simply may not be able to adopt one or more metric category KPIs effectively. Rather than forcing these Services to manage inconsequential data, customized KPIs can be created for the Services. Customization of metric category KPIs should be minimized whenever possible, limited to a Service Group (Service Category or Strategic Service Group) rather than a single Service, and always subject to review and approval by the Service Management Office, relevant Service Executive, and IT leadership team.

Some Service Performance strategies leverage KPIs as a subcategory underlying the metric category and then allow Service Groups to determine the best metrics and processes to qualify the particular KPI. For example, KPIs for resiliency, compliance, and security may be defined for the Risk metric category consistent across all Services; however, different groups of Services may associate different metric and processes for qualifying each of these.

By leveraging a common set of Service Metric Categories along with a standardized set of core metrics (KPIs) within each, the Service Performance strategy establishes a level of consistency required for strategic planning by IT and business leaders. At the same time, allowing the inclusion of additional metrics (each still associated with a metric category) ensures Service delivery teams have the flexibility to monitor all relevant aspects of Service Performance and share these measurements whenever necessary.

Cisco's ITaaS framework currently defines the following five Service Metric Categories (note that Service cost is the final remaining component of Service value and is the subject of Chapter 9, "Modeling the Total Costs of IT Service Delivery"). Upcoming sections look at each of these metric categories in detail and highlight potential data sources and examples of the information each can provide.

- **Quality:** Provides an overall measurement of the operational performance of the Service and the effectiveness and availability of the technical capabilities it delivers

- **Leverage:** Measures the scale and utilization of technical capabilities and the level at which capabilities are actually being consumed

- **Speed:** Measures the time to respond to customer requests for technical capabilities already delivered by the Service and the time to develop and introduce new capabilities and achieve a target rate of adoption

■ **Risk:** Measures overall risk to the ongoing delivery of technical capabilities and ensures Service delivery continuously manages risks associated with the IT organization and enterprise business operations

■ **Customer Experience:** Examines aspects of Service delivery from the perspective of the customers consuming the Service

These categories establish a well-rounded view of Service Performance. Just as important, these strategic categories are independent of any direct technical references, instead representing aspects of Service Performance that are familiar considerations to business leaders evaluating any Service. This allows each and every Service delivered by IT to deliver a consistent view of Service Performance that quickly becomes recognizable to IT and business leaders.

After developing a level of experience with these metric categories in practice, some IT organizations may choose to refine and optimize these initial categories. Cisco urges caution when doing so because changes to the metric categories can fundamentally alter the visibility of Service Performance currently available and also act as a reset for any historical trending of data. Cisco IT and other IT organizations adopting the ITaaS framework have over time made refinements and optimizations to these categories to better facilitate the unique needs of their Service delivery function as they transition to a Fast IT operating model. That said, these five core categories continue to successfully serve numerous IT organizations and offer an ideal proven starting point for any Services Transformation.

From the Diary of an ITaaS Consultant

Based on my experience, the ITaaS framework's strategy for Service Performance has to be seen in practice before it can be truly appreciated. In fact, most Service Owners quickly pull together Service Metrics for Quality built from technical metrics most familiar to them and associate initial metrics with the Leverage category. After that, however, most pay little attention to developing informed views of the remaining categories. Guidance and encouragement from the transformation team or IT leaders may result in perfunctory attempts at filling a category with data, but Service Owners still rarely dedicate in-depth consideration to what the information in these categories can tell them about the Service. This is likely to remain the status quo, up until a creative Service Owner (perhaps with the right encouragement from the transformation team) makes a breakthrough high-value demonstration of a metric category like Speed, Risk, or Customer Experience while engaging the customer base.

Once this happens, it kicks off a positive feedback loop in which other Service Owners attempt to replicate the success, spurring further interest and engagement with stakeholders, leading to further development and leverage of metric categories across individual Services. When working with IT Transformation teams, I dedicate a significant amount of time sharing real-world examples to justify the recommended strategies for Service Performance. I've learned, however, that nothing beats a few early and highly visible examples of metric categories leveraged to highlight a previously unknown aspect of the Service or to justify a major investment to encourage Service Owners to begin aggressively developing their individual Service Performance strategies.

Sexy slideware and dedicated chapters in a book can only do so much to raise awareness of the value potential for an end-to-end Service Performance strategy. During Service pilots, transformation teams should actively attempt to facilitate opportunities to "make it real" for their IT organization and business stakeholders. That's how to foster widespread adoption for a Service Performance strategy in real-world IT organizations.

Quality

As a Service Metric Category, Quality is the one most familiar to today's IT professionals, encompassing Service Metrics that immediately come to mind for many with a background in IT support or Service management. This metric category is also the most aligned with the Service Performance strategy's goal for understanding whether the technical capabilities delivered by the Service were available and performed as necessary when required by the stakeholders.

Evaluating the quality of technical capabilities delivered by a Service requires capturing any instances where circumstances prevented the use of the capabilities and then clearly understanding what each circumstance was and its cause. Another key aspect of quality is to understand the severity of any issues, their level of recurrence, how long the issue took to resolve, and whether impact occurred from planned maintenance performed by IT teams. Existing standards and practices for IT technical operations, including processes for incident and problem management and change management common in IT organizations today, heavily inform the development of the Quality metric category for most Services.

The Quality metric category serves to answer these types of questions:

- Were the technical capabilities available when they were needed?

- Did the technical capabilities perform as needed?

- How often was the availability and performance of technical capabilities impacted?

- What was the cause of the impact?

- Has the issue been known to happen before?

Examples of Service Metrics commonly included in the Quality metric category include

- Total number of IT support cases linked to the Service

- Breakdown of case severity levels (totals for each severity level)

- Total time the capabilities were impacted or unavailable

- Recurrence of issues

- Restoration times

- Percentage of cases resolved inside/outside of an SLA

- Percentage of high-severity cases resolved inside/outside of an SLA

- Number of cases resulting from scheduled changes

- Total downtime attributed to scheduled changes

Sources of data to support these Service Metrics are often readily available in many of today's IT organizations. Feature-rich Service management platforms and enterprise ticketing systems can provide a wealth of information to Service Owners. The key effort for Service Owners is to review these metrics and determine whether they truly reflect the availability and performance of the capabilities delivered by the Service or of the underlying technical platforms and infrastructures. In some cases, the Service Owner simply needs to filter metrics that are currently reported based on applicability. In other cases, monitoring processes may be updated or new monitoring and associated reporting provisioned.

From the Diary of an ITaaS Consultant

Quality is one of the foremost metric categories demonstrating the need for Service Owners to reexamine what constitutes a Service Metric. Many of the Service Metrics they initially propose often provide little insight to the availability of capabilities delivered by the Service and instead simply offer stats on technical platforms that likely to mean little to stakeholders. IT Transformation teams need to actively challenge Service Metrics proposed for this category during Service pilots and to guide Service Owners in refining these metrics to reflect the actual technical capabilities being delivered by a Service. I should also warn that development of Service Metrics for this category often leads to the initial occurrences of Service delivery teams passing requirements to the broader IT organization, as Service Owners engage IT operations teams to establish new monitoring processes, workflow logic, and reporting. Updating ticketing systems to map reporting to specific Services is a prime example.

Diligently working through these considerations has the benefit of shifting the mindset of early Service Owners, and shifting their focus to metrics that measure capabilities rather than technical platforms and infrastructures. As a prime example of the type of thinking that transformation teams need to foster, I often challenge Service Owners with this question: If an application falls in a data center when no one is using the capabilities that it enables, does the customer make a sound?

The Service Metrics associated with the Quality metric category are largely the same across all Service types. The key consideration for Service Owners with regard to Service type is that initial data sources for Service Metrics can often be readily applied to Technology Foundation Services because they deliver capabilities directly enabled by technical infrastructures. All other Service types require careful review and customization to monitoring and processes, and are more readily applicable after reporting platforms can be made Services-aware. Also, note that Service Metrics from the Quality metric category are regularly chained from Technology Foundation Services to other Service types.

KPIs for the Quality metric category are easier to establish end-to-end across all Services than KPIs for other categories. Cisco recommends five KPIs focusing on incident, problem, and change management specific to the capabilities delivered by a Service:

- **Incident Management (Three KPIs):** Total number of Service support cases, total high-severity cases, and total downtime

- **Problem Management:** Number of recurring high-severity issues

- **Change Management:** Total Service downtime resulting from scheduled changes

The type of information afforded by the Quality category may at first seem similar to that available within most IT organizations today, but transformation teams must remember that the purpose is to measure quality from the point of view of the Service. When launching initial Service Performance strategies, IT organizations that assumed their technical infrastructures were running at a high degree of operation may be surprised to find that the introduction of a Service-centric view of quality paints a much different picture, potentially highlighting grievances previously expressed by the customer base but never acted on. Think of quality as the baseline for the Service; if performance measurements begin to trend negatively, IT has a problem.

Leverage

Leverage helps delivery teams and IT leaders understand the level of consumption for capabilities delivered by the Service, while also actively monitoring the numbers of assets and other elements involved in the delivery of those capabilities. The Leverage metric category creates visibility to the scale and availability of Service capabilities and the effective use of underlying Service assets. It can influence a culture that identifies opportunities for reuse rather than new-build for similar customer and capability requirements. Above all, the Leverage metric category ensures that Services are "right-sized," managed efficiently, optimized over time, and that the IT organization is not expending resources and investments to deliver capabilities that are rarely used.

The Leverage metric category serves to answer these types of questions:

- What is the current and historical consumption of capabilities delivered by the Service, and what should the ideal target consumption be?

- How many customers rely on each of the capabilities that the Service delivers?

- Is there enough scale and quantity for each capability to support current and future customer demand?

- Is the Service overdelivering, or is there a significant footprint of idle Service assets that could be scaled back to reduce Service costs?

- Does the demand and customer base justify the total costs associated with a given capability?

- Is there a unit cost that can be associated with the Service? How does it compare with the rest of the industry, and how can I drive it down?

- Do the metrics in this category highlight the presence of any low-cost/high-benefit capabilities that could be prioritized?

The first priority when developing this category is to identify Service Metrics that can establish visibility to the scale at which capabilities are being delivered, the level at which they are being consumed, and finally the anticipated requirements for future consumption. Note that after Service cost modeling processes are established, Service Owners can often develop an understanding of the costs associated with delivering the different capabilities associated with their Service. These metrics obviously differ quite significantly between Service types and even individual Services, and the types of planning and decision making they enable vary as well.

Leverage metrics for Enterprise End-Customer Services are often easy to identify, such as the number of laptops or smartphones and subscribers currently delivered. For these Services, the Leverage metric category can help Service Owners evaluate the need for specific capabilities or even Service offerings. For example, devices with a small customer base could be discontinued, saving on associated support costs and transitioning customers to a more popular device or offering. Alternatively, demonstrating a large customer base for a specific capability can justify ongoing operational costs or even new investment.

Technology Foundation Services primarily utilize the Leverage metric category to ensure infrastructures are scaled appropriately. Service Metrics providing insight to network bandwidth utilization, available storage, and utilization of cloud resources are all prime examples. Leverage is regularly highlighted by these Service Owners to justify investment to scale these large infrastructures.

Service Owners for Business Operations Services are likely to struggle at first to identify appropriate Service Metrics, and the Leverage category may not receive as significant a focus over time for these Service types. That said, the category should still be actively developed for these Services, and the category does provide actionable insight that at times is quite significant. Consider that these Services exist as a direct result of existing requirements to enable business processes, and as such, they should not be subject for discontinuation simply because of a limited customer base. When costs are associated with the capabilities, however, the metrics captured by the Leverage category take on a new meaning. As an example, consider senior stakeholders, previously supportive of a costly platform deemed a requirement for their team to execute a daily process, presented with data demonstrating that the platform is, in fact, accessed only once a month by several resources. The key consideration is that information established by the Leverage metric category sheds new light on capabilities delivered by these Services that can support joint IT and business planning. It helps IT clearly demonstrate what the right move for the enterprise is, whether that is investment approval or the discontinuation of a capability.

From the Diary of an ITaaS Consultant

A common real-world example I highlight for Leverage involves a Service for mobile devices with three Service offerings reflecting smartphones from different manufacturers associated with different carriers. Each Service offering is associated with carrier and support contract costs.

After developing an initial report for Leverage, the Service Owner noticed that over 90 percent of the customer base leveraged one of two popular smartphone types, leaving just under a dozen customers who were unwilling to migrate from the rarely-used third option, which required a $100,000 yearly expense for support. After a review of these findings with senior IT and business leaders in a joint Service Review, the decision was quickly made to discontinue the seldom-used offering, with business leaders personally instructing their resources to immediately transition to one of the remaining options.

The key consideration to highlight with this example is that without the ITaaS framework and Service Performance strategy, this very obvious outcome could have been very difficult to achieve. The need to migrate from a costly solution leveraged by a dwindling customer base would have been driven by an IT manager interfacing with any number and level of customers, each likely to resist and even escalate any attempt by IT to discontinue their Service. Had an IT manager simply forced these customers to transition, it would have only sunk customer satisfaction with the IT organization. Instead, a Service Owner and senior IT and business leaders all clearly understood and agreed to a course of action for the Service and provided their support in communicating requirements for change to the customer base.

Leverage can be one of the most difficult metric categories to establish standardized KPIs for. Whenever possible, Service Owners should attempt to establish a specific unit delivered by their Service or by a Service offering. Doing so allows for the introduction of a Service Leverage index, which considers the current level of unit consumption against a target consumption. As we have already established, however, not all capabilities can easily be reduced to a consumable unit, and forcing Services across the board to adopt this approach ultimately invests effort and resources to create inconsequential data. Enterprise End-Customer Services can often effectively leverage units of consumption, while other Service types often adopt different tactics for KPIs. Some IT organizations adopt a Red/Amber/Green (RAG) status or similar strategy early on to indicate that Service Leverage has been reviewed, optimized, and accompanied by key Service Metrics specific to each Service that can support validation of this assessment. Best practices for RAG statuses are discussed later in this chapter.

Data sources for Leverage Service Metrics are commonly available in today's IT organizations. Asset databases, infrastructure management platforms with inventory reporting capabilities, application portfolios that track licensing and installations, log files reporting number of logins and access, and any number of spreadsheets capturing manually collected data are all likely available to be mined for valuable information.

Leverage can provide Service Owners with powerful justification for investment approvals when it establishes dangerously low levels of available capacity alongside growing demand. Leverage also ensures Service Owners are alerted to scenarios where Service assets are simply being underutilized and precious assets and resources can be saved by right-sizing capabilities. When combined with the total costs for Service delivery, leverage can initiate fact-based conversations and planning between IT and business leaders that was not possible before.

Speed

Speed is a metric category that quickly becomes a focus area for IT and business stakeholders when Service Owners have achieved desired levels of quality and then right-sized their Services through the Leverage metric category. Achieving a high level of success in this area correlates directly with customer satisfaction and in supporting the enterprise business success in rapidly changing marketplaces. It can also drive improvements across the IT operating model, including processes for change management and investment and architectural reviews.

Speed Service Metrics establish visibility to the time required to deliver established capabilities, which refers to the repeat delivery of matured capabilities previously delivered by a Service, such as the time to provision and deliver a common laptop model to a new hire. For Business Operations Services it also looks at how capabilities impact the duration of business processes and examines how investment and innovation can increase the speed at which those processes complete. Finally, Speed Service Metrics evaluate the time it takes to develop and introduce new capabilities and then achieve a target rate of adoption.

The Speed metric category serves to answer these types of questions:

- How long does it take to deliver a common customer request, and how does that compare with other IT organizations?

- What is the primary contributor to the length of time to deliver a capability? Can that aspect of Service delivery be removed or optimized in any way?

- Why has the time to deliver a capability been increasing the past few quarters? Are resources and assets a bottleneck?

- How long does it take the customer to complete a specific business process today, and how can the IT organization help complete the process faster?

- Are some of the processes in use across the IT organization adding unnecessary delay to the delivery of established or new capabilities?

- How long is the average development, test, and release cycle for software-enabled capabilities? Are there practices or emerging trends that could improve development and release cycles?

The general Service Metrics compiled by this category are similar across Service types, with the exception of Business Operations Services, which are likely to also trend process completion times. Some metrics are available initially from Service management and ticketing system platforms that can report the length of time from when a request was submitted until it was delivered. Although these platforms offer definitive measures of time, Service Owners should never hesitate to include estimated measurements, such as the length of time a proposed capability awaited its turn for review in an approval board process. Although there may be some initial resistance to estimating the duration of IT internal processes, it serves to highlight the impact they have on delivering capabilities and customer satisfaction and often leads to formal processes for documenting these times. Note that program and project managers can also be valuable sources of information when documenting the speed of developing and introducing new capabilities.

The standard Service Metrics and KPIs for speed are

- **Existing Capability Delivery:** Cycle times, time to provision/deliver

- **New Capability:** Process and cycle times, time to capability, time to adoption

- **Business Process Execution Times:** Time to complete selected business processes

For Existing Capability Delivery Service Metrics, while "time to provision" represents the total from the time the request was submitted to delivery, cycle times represent the time required to complete a specific step in the overall process. As an example, a Service for enterprise computing that manages delivery of laptops would measure the time to provision as the time from when the request was submitted to when the laptop was actually delivered to the customer. Within this process are multiple cycle times, such as the time to ship and receive the laptop, and for the laptop image and standard applications to be loaded. It is critical that cycle times be measured as well as the total process times because this allows Service Owners to identify opportunities to reduce capability delivery times by optimizing specific cycle times. In our earlier example, the time to provision may be reduced by improving the cycle time associated with receiving the laptop by switching vendors.

From the Diary of an ITaaS Consultant

Laptop provisioning has provided a number of real-world examples to highlight the need to measure both total provisioning and delivery times as well as incremental cycle times, plus the need to continuously evaluate whether the Service delivery teams are measuring the right things.

In one such circumstance, an IT organization was reporting a brisk delivery time for new laptops, but in reality the process required extensive effort by the customer to configure the laptops and this time was not measured. The complexity resulted in extensive support tickets, and customer satisfaction was never ideal. The Service Owner made the decision to incorporate the customer configuration period into the time to deliver measurement and then advocated for a complete overhaul of the build process, preload customization options, and even customer instructions. The cycle time and total time to deliver initially rose it eventually dropped significantly, reduced related support tickets to near zero, and increased customer satisfaction all without any significant investment or effort by the IT organization.

Measuring speed for the introduction of new capabilities typically requires some additional effort. Transformation teams should review and document a general process for establishing a time to capability measurement and allow individual Service Owners to update the process for a specific capability or Service when required. In general, a measurement for time to capability includes consideration of the following phases: review and proposal, approval, test and develop, first availability, and a separate metric for target adoption achieved. Not all phases are required in every time-to-capability calculation, and others, such as for large-scale development efforts, may be able to include additional phases. Also, as a best practice, Service Owners should understand the size and scale of the request so that simple and small-scale requests for new capabilities are not unfairly compared with large-scale and highly complex efforts.

The pace at which an IT organization can deliver established capabilities and develop new, likely transformative capabilities and get them into the hands of their business customers is a key factor in future marketplaces and supporting Fast IT. A transformative capability capable of disrupting the marketplace loses its value potential for an enterprise if it takes the IT organization months longer than competitors to incorporate it into business operations. The Speed metric category raises awareness for these considerations across the IT organization, highlighting opportunities to improve Service delivery.

Risk

The Risk metric category boasts a significant value outcome for the IT organization and enterprise business. It creates visibility to and then drives a broad community of resources to take ownership for risk-related aspects of Service delivery. Responsibility for the many aspects related to the risk of Service delivery, such as resiliency, compliance, and digital and physical security, cannot be limited to a few dedicated security resources. Strategies for managing risk must be supported by a broad community, at all levels, across the IT organization as well as the customer base consuming the Service. Service Performance strategies that fail to thoroughly consider risk during planning can leave the capabilities delivered by the Service, the IT organization, and potentially even the broader enterprise business vulnerable.

The Risk metric category serves to answer these questions about Service delivery:

- What is the level of resiliency associated with the technical capabilities delivered by the Service?

- Is the current level of resiliency in line with customer requirements?

- Is there an agreed-upon disaster recovery plan?

- Are the Service assets leveraged to enable the technical capabilities still supported, reliable, and secure?

- Does the delivery of the Service fully adhere to all applicable industry and government regulations?

■ Does the delivery of the Service fully adhere to all company standards and practices?

■ Are all aspects of Service delivery secure?

Service Metrics for Risk come in many forms and vary significantly between Service types and individual Services. Cisco recommends establishing the following KPIs and then encouraging Service Executives, Service Architects, and Service Owners to develop Service Metrics that support an evaluation of each across a related group of Services:

■ **Resiliency:** Considers the survivability of capabilities and the ability to restore each within a defined time frame

■ **Compliance (Standards and Audits):** Provides a measurement of the Service's adherence to company, industry, and government requirements

■ **Support and Lifecycle Management Compliance:** Grades the reliability of Service assets leveraged to enable the Service and measures the level of available support based on the product lifecycle

■ **End-to-End Security:** Provides a measurement of all applicable security considerations for the ongoing delivery of the Service, including both physical and digital security

To produce a quantifiable measurement for these KPIs, some Service Performance strategies have developed processes that define a specific set of Service Metrics across a Service Group, assigning weights to each as input to a calculation that produces a percentage-based measurement. As an example, if four Service Metrics have been standardized for a security KPI, equally weighted they would result in a 75 percent score if one of the metrics was not successfully addressed. Other strategies have simply adopted an RAG status indicator reflecting Amber for a single requirement not met, and Red for more than one. In some cases, a valuable metric for risk may be a simple check box—for example, confirming that a particular audit was completed. In this case, the Service Owner should be able to produce the results of the audit if requested. The key is for the Risk metric category KPIs to provide an indication that the Service delivery team has conducted a thorough evaluation of the Service across each area and determined whether issues need to be addressed and that each measurement can be supported and is actionable.

The first priority when building the resiliency KPI should be to provide an indication that the current target requirements for different aspects of Service resiliency have been reviewed with and preferably signed off by senior stakeholders. Many Service delivery teams find they are actively overdelivering initially. Further, when costs are later associated with Service delivery, many stakeholders begin to reassess their requirements for resiliency. From there, resiliency should consider the required level of survivability for the capabilities delivered by the Service, such as the ability to immediately direct access to another instance of the capability. This KPI should also consider instances in which the capabilities are rendered unavailable—for example, during major disasters—and the requirements for restoring each. These metrics should also consider whether a plan is in place to accomplish the restoration and if the plan has been tested within an agreed-to time frame.

Compliance Service Metrics are intended to ensure that the Service recognizes and successfully adheres to all applicable standards and audit requirements, including those required by the IT organization, enterprise business, industry, or government. This requires Service Owners to identify applicable standards, understand their requirements, and translate those requirements to the delivery of their Service. These could range from industry standards such as ISO or SOX compliance to enterprise and IT organization–specific standards such as leveraging specified platforms. As an example, consider a Service providing technical capabilities to hazardous areas, with requirements that all local Service assets be rated intrinsically safe (Class-1/Div-1 or Div-2). The key is that Service Owners consider not only IT standards but also the standards that apply to business processes that their Service is enabling and understand how the technical capabilities they deliver impact these requirements.

The support and lifecycle management–related Service Metrics are intended primarily to reflect the status of hardware and software Service assets within their support lifecycles and grade their reliability. These Service Metrics should indicate whether proper levels of support are facilitated through support contracts, partners, vendors, or specially trained IT teams. They also examine the impact of product lifecycle on Service Assets and highlight assets and infrastructures prone to failure. The key is to understand the level and type of support required and ensure that it is available, while quality measures the success of the support model in practice.

End-to-end security means exactly what it says: Service Owners are responsible for considering every aspect of security related to the delivery of their Service. This includes Service Metrics that likely immediately come to mind for many IT professionals, such as confirmation that Service assets have had the latest security patches applied; are compliant with operating system, platform, and antivirus standards; and have been subjected to any intrusion detection or security scans applicable in the reporting period. These Service Metrics should also confirm that best practices for application and platform administration are adhered to, such as role and access management, password requirements, and configuration standards. Many of these requirements will be driven by a central digital security team.

A well-rounded consideration of security also includes considerations not so common to most Service Owners, such as the presence of physical security. This may span badge access to secure areas hosting Service assets or even requirements for security cameras for review of any unauthorized access. Consider a Service that delivers Industrial/Production Control System (ICS/PCS) capabilities to manufacturing floors. Uninterrupted delivery of these capabilities should ensure that risk of locally launched attacks (via USB or similar) or simple physical interference to local devices by unauthorized personnel is considered and managed.

These various groupings of Risk Service Metrics vary to a limited degree based on Service type, but many ITaaS deployments are able to leverage similar KPIs and associated processes across most of the Service landscape. Business Operations Services obviously reflect additional process- and industry-specific metrics associated with compliance, while Technical Foundation Services and Enterprise End-Customer Services include a more extensive set of Service Metrics with a technical focus. Data sources for these metrics vary from automated reports and analytics, manual compilations of audit results, and even in-person verification of security measures.

Customer Experience

No topic within the Service Performance strategy causes more initial resistance and angst from IT professionals yet offers the potential for truly understanding the impact and value that a Service delivers than the Customer Experience metric category. It often requires an end-to-end strategy of its own and takes longer to implement effectively than the other Service categories. It also typically requires capabilities for metrics and reporting that may not be currently available within the IT organization, but as these challenges are overcome, it establishes visibility to an aspect of Service Performance unique from any other metric category.

Customer Experience seeks to establish a view of key aspects of the Service directly from the customers who consume and rely on the technical capabilities it delivers for their own productivity and success. Although Service Owners and senior stakeholders have to carefully review, vet, and weigh the feedback gathered prior to taking action, the reality is that until this input is sampled across the broader customer base, it represents a potential blind spot for Service delivery and planning.

Customer Experience helps IT organizations understand the Service from the customer perspective:

- Was the customer base satisfied with the overall delivery of the Service? Do they believe it creates value for the enterprise?

- Did the capabilities perform as desired? Were they reliable?

- Were the capabilities delivered by the Service easy to access and use?

- Was the Service ultimately useful? At the end of the day, did it help a customer to be productive or execute business processes?

- Is there a need for additional differentiation in capabilities, such as localization to a specific team or region?

- Is there broad agreement across the customer base that capabilities could be improved? If so, in what area?

- What else can IT do to help?

Similar to risk, Cisco recommends leveraging KPIs as subcategories that encourage Service Owners to develop the following Service Metrics capable of establishing visibility:

- **Performance:** Measures whether Service capabilities are available and accessible when needed and perform as required to enable their intended functions

- **Service Experience:** Seeks to understand whether Service capabilities are designed and implemented in a manner that provides a positive experience for customers

- **Value/Usefulness:** Attempts to measure the overall sense of impact and value the Service provides to productivity or execution of business processes

- **Satisfaction:** Attempts to gauge the overall sense of fulfillment and gratification with the Service

- **Improvement Opportunities:** Collects open-ended comments, which encourages continuous feedback on Service capabilities and opportunities

At first, it may seem that these areas and the metrics compiled for each heavily duplicate aspects of Service delivery already monitored by the Quality metric category. This is actually a key aspect in the value that customer experience brings to a Service Performance strategy. Remember that Service Metrics supporting the Customer Experience category reflect the customer's perspective, whereas Quality relies on monitoring and reporting designed and provisioned by IT. In cases where the Customer Experience and Quality measurements for a Service are consistently out of sync, it is an indication to the Service Owner that further tuning is required in the processes that measure quality.

In fact, Service delivery teams are consistently surprised at the valuable information and opportunities identified through Customer Experience. While Service Reviews aim to bring a Service Owner together with senior IT and business leaders to understand Service value and plan Service strategy, these parties alone can never represent the complete customer base or consider all aspects of Service delivery at each level of an organization. Even with strong communications from both the Service Owner and IT and business leaders across the customer base, valuable feedback may not be heard. The Customer Experience metric category provides a path for that valuable information and insight to Service delivery to be collected, but also requires a strategy to carefully manage how the information is gathered, and then filter and weigh the input prior to incorporating as part of a broader Service plan.

As you have no doubt already guessed, compiling data and information for this metric-category is likely to involve surveys, and many IT and business stakeholders are often wary and cautious of anything resembling surveys. Surveys do not represent the sole source of information for developing these metrics, however, and with careful proactive planning, they can be leveraged effectively. Doing so requires the development of a formal strategy for collecting and managing the Customer Experience Service

Metric Category. The strategy should limit the total number of surveys and adopt best practices to proactively avoid common complaints. Above all, Service Owners must be allowed to act as gatekeepers responsible for managing the right type and frequency of surveys for their stakeholders.

Resistance to the idea of surveys most often originates from several historical challenges and missteps when leveraging them. First is a general sense of being presented with too many surveys. While the individual goals of these various surveys are no doubt well intended, the announcement of even more surveys as a result of the Services Transformation effort may leave segments of the customer base feeling overrun. Instead, IT Transformation teams should document all surveys currently in use across Service management and ticketing systems or other sources, and then develop a strategy to discontinue, replace, or integrate them as part of the end-to-end IT Service Customer Experience strategy.

Another recurring grievance is associated with a lack of perceived action after the submission of surveys, creating a sense that nothing will result from the time and effort taken to address a survey. As a general best practice, be sure not to survey feedback that you are incapable of addressing. This consideration highlights another value of the ITaaS framework's Service Owner role. Service Owners in an ITaaSO have significant leverage to advocate for their Service across the IT organization and therefore are responsible for demonstrating changes to the Service delivery strategy in response to Customer Experience metrics, along with illustrating improvements to the same metrics over time.

Although it may seem contradictory to our prior point, another key consideration for survey-based feedback is to make sure that Service delivery teams not immediately overreact to feedback, and instead carefully review all feedback and possible actions during Service Reviews with IT and business leaders. Service Owners should understand how broadly this feedback reflects the customer base and how it aligns to strategies previously agreed to with senior stakeholders. Overly reactive Service providers will find themselves constantly flipping from one strategy to the next as they erratically try to respond to the latest and loudest submission of feedback, often with little consideration to the financial impacts or an understanding of how feedback aligns to a broader enterprise strategy. That is not the type of behavior the Customer Experience metric category is intended to initiate. Customer experience alone does not drive Service strategy or investment decisions, or act as the final say on how well the Service is being managed. Service Owners leverage customer experience as one of many pieces of valuable information available to them to ensure that the Service creates value for the IT organization and enterprise business.

Consider that surveys can take many forms. In most IT organizations, they are likely already generated whenever closing a support or request ticket. In this case, these results need to be made available to the Service and Service Owner now linked to the request. Another option is gathering input from senior stakeholders at the conclusion of a Service Review. When doing so, Cisco recommends leveraging a minimal set of questions that can be quickly discussed and then documented by the Service Owner.

Service Owners should also work with senior stakeholders to identify a selection of key stakeholders capable of representing the different areas and interests consuming the Service. These stakeholders would agree to receive and carefully reply to a customized survey from the Service Owner once per reporting period. The ideal number of stake-holders is different depending on the size of the organization and Service type. Because Business Operations Services have a focused customer base, 5–10 stakeholders can typi-cally provide a broad sampling of feedback. Enterprise End-Customer Services, however, provide technical capabilities across the entire enterprise and, as such, may consider soliciting feedback from significantly larger groups.

This initial strategy provides Service Owners with three levels of data sources to begin shaping their Customer Experience metric category: leveraging ticket-based surveys that customers are likely already familiar with, customized surveys provided to key stake-holders, and finally feedback collected from senior stakeholders while concluding a Service Review.

Best Practices for Measuring Service Metrics

Cisco recommends adopting quantified measurements whenever possible for Service Metrics and KPIs—for example, simply reporting the total number of support cases, but this is not always possible. Scales and percentages are often leveraged as well; for example, a Customer Experience metric scored between 1 and 5, or 95 percent of all change requests were completed within the agreed-to SLA. One of the most popularly leveraged measurements in the absence of other options is the use of Red/Amber/Green (RAG status) indicators. They work incredibly well for the Risk metric category, reflect-ing the status of a series of audits or checks having been completed, and are leveraged heavily in the early stages of the Service Performance strategy while reporting capability requirements are still being identified and implemented.

While they offer a reliable temporary solution, these measurements also introduce chal-lenges for consistent use and interpretation. Therefore, Cisco recommends minimizing their use over time and driving long term to leverage quantifiable measurements for all Service Metrics. In many cases, teams fail to clearly define the three colored indicators or what measurements constitute assigning one value over the other. This leads to fur-ther complexity for interpreting the precise meaning of the reported metric. Typically, there is no standard for their use across the Services landscape, leading to inconsistencies and confusion between each Service. Finally, IT professionals tend to either constantly report an intermediate Amber status, implying that the Service has never warranted Red or Green, or to only ever report Green or Red. In other words, one Service Owner constantly reports that Service Performance is "not horrible but could be better," while another constantly reports "everything is absolute perfection, or is completely broken." Again, these reports result from a lack of established process and definitions leveraged by all IT Service Owners.

Cisco provides many ITaaS adopters with the reference definitions shown in Figure 8-1 for use with RAG status indicators. Remember that some level of customization and interpretation is always required at the Service level. The goal is to introduce a level of consistency and address the common issues we noted.

RAG Status	Definition	Service Impact Description	Resolution Details and Time frame	Visibility and Escalation
Effective	All required technical capabilities are actively being delivered from the Service and within parameters agreed to by business stakeholders	There are zero or more issues that have minor impact to the performance of service capabilities	Known fixes scheduled and/or applied within time frames agreed to by business stakeholders	A small number of customers have raised cases with no reason to escalate
Barriers	Technical capabilities deviated or are in danger of deviating from parameters agreed to by business stakeholders	One or more issues impacting the performance of capabilities for a limited number of customer	Resolutions have yet to be identified or have been or are in danger of being applied outside of target time frames	A growing customer base is being impacted by the performance and there is potential for escalations
Deficient	Technical capabilities have failed to be delivered within parameters agreed to by the business	One or more issues resulting from performance impacting a larger number of customer for an extended time or for complete disruption of Service capabilities	Resolution has not been identified, or cannot be delivered within customer required time frame, or requires significant costs or effort resulting in high-visibility escalations	A large number of customers are unable to leverage the Service capabilities and escalations have or will soon be raised

Figure 8-1   *Red/Amber/Green Indicators Definition*

We established earlier in this chapter that Service Metrics must be given context to provide meaningful information. Without context, metrics are nothing more than data points and do little to support a determination of Service value or strategic planning. Performance goals or targets, baselines, benchmarks, and trending all represent important context associated with Service Metrics.

Service Performance targets are crucial for driving continuous value. Sometimes referred to as plans or goals, they establish a target performance for an upcoming reporting period. These targets can be set by IT leaders, Service Executives, or in some cases senior stakeholders in support of a strategy or directive. The Service Owner should always be actively involved in determining targets, and all parties should agree that the targets are achievable. Consideration for new targets should also include the plans and support required to achieve the desired goal.

Where targets set a goal measurement that must be met or exceeded, a baseline may represent an initial measurement to improve upon or to establish a level below which a Service Metric cannot fall. Baselines are regularly associated with Service Metrics and KPIs for quality and speed, establishing acceptable times for delivery or restoration. Baselines can also be referred to as service-level agreements (SLAs), which are discussed further in Chapter 11, "Completing the Services Transformation."

Every metric category KPI must be associated with either a target or baseline. It is possible to use both; for example, some quality-related KPIs may have an established baseline as well as targets for improvements.

Benchmarking can have a broad meaning, but in the context of a Service Performance strategy, we are specifically referencing the comparison of a specific Service Performance measurement against the standard or average of that same measurement for another entity or industry as a whole. Benchmarking is a key component of the ITaaS framework's capability to allow IT organizations to demonstrate that they are providing competitive Services.

At the time of writing, benchmarking data for comparison against Service Performance as defined by the ITaaS framework is not widely available. Benchmarking should be used whenever possible, however, and continuous efforts made to identify and compare sources of benchmarking data for inclusion in the Service Performance strategy. Remember that a rapidly growing number of IT organizations are adopting Services end-to-end operating models and that more industry councils and standards are beginning to establish themselves. As industry adoption of end-to-end Services grows, so too will the availability of extensive IT Service benchmarking data.

Trending change in Service Metrics over time is most commonly associated with identifying issues such as slowly degrading quality or reliability. While this remains a key component of the ITaaS framework's Service Performance strategy, the real focus is on the ability to demonstrate the impact of investment and other strategic Service decisions. Service Performance strategies that do not consider a well-rounded view of Service Performance were historically constrained in understanding if a decision or investment was able to drive down costs or improve quality-related metrics. Now Service delivery teams can also demonstrate impact to Service speed, risk, leverage, and customer satisfaction, in addition to quality and costs.

How Service Metrics Translate to Business Outcomes

A key feature of Cisco's ITaaS framework is the ability to correlate IT Service Performance to impact on business outcomes. Leveraging the Service delivery framework to successfully demonstrate the IT organization's ability to do so is a critical step in establishing itself as a trusted advisor to the enterprise business.

But how exactly do IT Services and their Service Owners understand and demonstrate this correlation?

Recall that the design of IT Services within the ITaaS framework begins with a logical grouping of technical capability requirements. For Business Operations Services, these technical capabilities enable business processes, process groups, or functions across the enterprise business, including within the IT organization. The Enterprise Technical Capabilities map that was developed by the IT Transformation team as an input to the design of these Services captured a description of the processes supported by those technical capabilities and their intended outcomes. This means that Service Owners of a Business Operations Service have this same mapping of technical capabilities to processes and finally to business outcomes. As they develop a deeper knowledge of these processes, they can begin to correlate the impact of Service Performance to business outcomes.

The goal of the Service Owner is not to link every monitored Service Metric to one or more business processes or outcomes at all times. Changes in Service Performance may not impact business operations in every instance. The significance rests in the Service Owner, as a member of the IT organization, developing the capability of recognizing those instances where it does. Reactively, this may involve Service Owners understanding how business outcomes were negatively impacted and ensuring that IT communicates its understanding of the impact and intended resolution. Proactively, however, Service Owners can demonstrate how investment or changes in the technical capabilities improved business processes and related outcomes.

In practice, Service Owners can illustrate and communicate these events in numerous ways. During Service Reviews, Service Owners may highlight a metric, or set of metrics, and then visibly connect these to a business process listed on the side. In other cases, a Service Owner may provide a formal, regular report providing in-depth details. The key is that Service Owners regularly associate the business processes and outcomes supported by their Service alongside the standard Service Performance strategy.

Reasons to Chain Service Metrics

Another key component for understanding all aspects of Service Performance is realizing how the performance of a Service delivering capabilities consumed by other Services can, in turn, impact the performance of those Services. The Service chaining mechanism of the ITaaS framework allows Service delivery teams to clearly demonstrate these cases and highlight the need for investment and support for Services that may otherwise receive limited priority from senior business leaders.

The core concept involves a Service, typically a Technology Foundation Service, chaining one or more metrics up to a Business Operations or Enterprise End-Customer Service. There are no rules for when metrics have to be chained out to other Services, only that the Service receiving a chained metric is actively consuming capabilities from the underlying Service, and both Service Owners agree to the decision to chain the metric and on how it will impact the receiving Service's performance.

One or more metrics could be chained for different reasons, but the most common is to illustrate accurately how degraded performance levels reported by a Technology Foundation Service truly impact other Services. An easy example is a data center or private cloud infrastructure leveraged by an Application Hosting Service. A large segment of this infrastructure has been allowed to go beyond its end-of-life date, meaning that risk of failure is rising while support is likely no longer available. The application hosting capabilities delivered by this Service are actively consumed by a number of Business Operations Services, and the capabilities they deliver, in turn, are at higher risk of impact. When metrics are chained, these Services could demonstrate the increased risk and likely prioritize support for upgrading the infrastructure.

Service Metrics from each of the metric categories can all be chained, and each can tell a different story. The key is that the mechanism allows Service delivery teams to effectively communicate very real dependencies as another key aspect to strategic Service planning.

End-to-End Service Metrics Interpretation

To get the most value out of the ITaaS framework's Service Performance strategy, Service Owners need to consider the meaning of performance measurements across metric categories rather than thinking of these Service Metrics as isolated within their respective category. The ITaaS framework's Service Performance strategy tells a story at both the micro and macro levels, and it is important for Service Owners to interpret each.

As an example, let's again consider an Application Hosting Service, leveraging an aging infrastructure to deliver its capabilities, resulting in negative Risk metrics. Before prioritizing an investment, however, consider the Leverage metric category, reflecting that although the Service is reporting higher risk, the capabilities it provides are barely being used by the customer base, possibly due to public cloud offerings. This could indicate that while hardware failures may occur more often, there is plenty of idle capacity in which to restore the capabilities and further inform the appropriate timing and level of investment. Alternatively, if the Leverage metrics all reflected high consumption of capabilities with little capacity left, this could help bolster a request for prioritized investment approval.

The addition of the total costs for Service delivery adds yet another component to these conversations. In fact, the addition of costs allows the IT organization and customer base to literally witness the impact of investment or reduction of operating costs across various metric categories.

It is important that Service Owners look across metric categories and consider the end-to-end picture. In some instances, a set of metrics viewed in isolation is given a completely different context when considered as part of the broader performance of the Service.

Dashboards and Scorecards

Even in the presence of large-scale Service management platforms with feature-rich reporting, Service Owners are still likely to leverage a number of platforms and data sources to develop each of their metric categories. With so many data sources, it is important for the Service Performance strategy to provide Service Owners with a capability to efficiently review Service Performance and share with stakeholders.

A Service Performance dashboard, or scorecard, provides the Service Owner and stakeholders with a strategic-level view of Service Performance. This is a critical capability for effectively communicating Service Performance. However, many adopters of the ITaaS framework have opted to initiate their Service Performance strategy and begin refining their preferred strategy and mechanics prior to heavily investing in a dashboard, and instead leverage manually built slides and graphics as an interim solution.

Most Service Performance dashboards strive for some type of top-level single-page view, displaying each of the five metric categories and a number of their associated KPIs, trending, and targets along with Service TCO. Although it may be difficult to achieve, a single-pane overview of Service Performance is a powerful tool for providing at-a-glance review and identifying which metric categories have missed targets or fallen below baselines. At the same time, some teams can quickly find themselves in a quagmire, attempting to develop a one-page overview of Service Performance that contains all vital information but yet is still readable and presentable.

From the Diary of an ITaaS Consultant

I often describe the value and desired functionality of a performance dashboard by comparing it to the dashboard in your vehicle. On your vehicle dash are metrics that are always visible, like the fuel gauge or the speedometer. There are also numerous metrics displayed only when a measurement falls below its baseline, such as a low-tire pressure indicator. In still other cases, some metrics are displayed only when needed and require further investigation to determine the underlying cause for the alarm and best corrective action, such as when the Check Engine light comes on.

Using our vehicle dashboard as a reference for our ideal performance dashboard, we know that stakeholders look for some values every time, such as the Service TCO, and some level of indication that the strategic-level metric categories are all exceeding baselines and hitting targets for performance. They may also wish to see condensed trending data, or at a minimum an indicator, for whether KPIs have improved from the previous reporting period. If Service Owners determine there is a concern with a Service that needs to be discussed, they would highlight these concerns as well. The key is that not every Service Metric or KPI associated with a metric category needs to be displayed on the dashboard at all times; in fact, doing so often leads Service Owners to overlook critical performance information. Rather, the dashboard should allow stakeholders to quickly glance at key measurements while reserving space for use by Service Owners to highlight required metrics.

Just be sure that issues highlighted by the dashboard are discussed and actions agreed to. You don't want to commit the IT Service equivalent of ignoring the Check Engine light until the Service finally breaks down during an inopportune moment.

Tactics for Reporting and Presenting Service Performance

The Service delivery team's approach to reporting and presenting Service Performance has a significant impact on the success of the strategy. It is important that Service Owners consider their audience and the capabilities that the Service Performance strategy provides and when best to use them.

A mature Service Performance strategy should tell a complete and accurate story for stakeholder groups at different levels and both inside and outside the IT organization. The ITaaS framework's Service Performance strategy provides all the tools to do so; Service Owners need only consider what metrics are relevant to a given stakeholder and their priorities. Service Owners should be proactive, anticipating how the recent performance of a Service relates to the priorities and concerns of the stakeholder in question, and be prepared for the questions they are likely to receive.

General strategies include beginning with a Service dashboard, then highlighting a metric category and potentially KPIs of interest before progressing into detail. Service Owners should always remember to interpret metrics end-to-end and illustrate how changes in cost or a metric category affected others, and always demonstrate how Service Performance impacted business outcomes.

Service Owners should also remember that they are responsible for highlighting any potential issues with Service delivery for IT leaders and senior stakeholders. To encourage this, however, all parties must remember that the purpose and goal of the Service Performance strategy is to enable informed decision making, and not to lay blame. Under no circumstances should they fear reporting negative Service Metrics, so long as they thoroughly understand why a metric is poor and have a plan to improve it.

Service Performance Change Leadership Strategies

Introducing Service Performance can be a complex effort for everyone involved and is especially challenging for the Service Owners. Change leadership efforts conducted prior to initiating Service Performance strategies, along with continued support of Service Owners, which includes the review and optimization of the initial strategy, ensure that Service Performance fulfills its intended purpose and the goals for the Service delivery framework.

It is important to remember that Cisco's Services Transformation Program initiates the development of the Service Performance strategy at the same time that Service pilots are initiated. This way, the developing strategy can be actively tested across early Services and inside mock Service Reviews, granting IT Transformation teams the opportunity to witness their proposed strategy in practice. This approach allows newly initiated Service Owners and transformation teams to refine the strategy within the IT organization before engaging the first senior customer stakeholders.

Training material that communicates the value of the end-to-end strategy, including each of the metric categories, should be developed quickly and provided to Service Owners. This material should be updated regularly to incorporate value outcomes that result from the strategy, helping illustrate for future Service Owners how the strategy has benefited their own IT organization and enterprise. Valuable tactics include sharing and reviewing best practices for reporting and presenting Service Performance, along with forums that bridge fellow Service Owners together to share lessons learned.

Care should be taken not to set expectations too high for initial Service Performance strategies. IT Transformation and Service Performance strategy teams typically focus on developing one to two metric categories at a time. It is not uncommon for some of the earliest views of Service Performance to use placeholders for some KPIs or even metric categories and for those Service Metrics reported initially to change over time as new monitoring and reporting capabilities are introduced and feedback is incorporated. Associating metrics with Quality and Leverage metric categories is often the easiest, while Customer Experience and Risk categories are typically more challenging, commonly requiring additional capabilities and development of KPIs and processes to calculate them. Remember also that key metric context, such as trending, is likely to be limited and to be reset often as processes are optimized throughout the Services Transformation Program. Service Performance is a strategy that begins slow, matures over time, and continuously improves with the right leadership.

Service Performance Strategy Management

An end-to-end Service Performance strategy represents a large and complex effort for the IT Transformation team and Services Transformation Program to design and implement. This strategy is still in its infancy by the completion of the Services Transformation, and requires that Service delivery teams, the Service Management Office, and IT leaders continue to support the value that IT Services provide.

Post Services Transformation, primary ownership for the strategy transitions to the Service Management Office, which accepts ongoing responsibility for two key aspects of Service Performance. The first is to ensure that Service Owners and delivery teams across the IT organization have the capabilities they need to measure and report Service Performance in the most efficient manner possible. This is commonly accomplished through a Service, with a member of the SMO acting as Service Owner, and ensuring efficient delivery of these technical capabilities to the customer base, in this case fellow Service Owners. Just like all Service Owners, they should not only seek to understand and continuously align Service delivery to the needs of their customers but also proactively identify opportunities to enhance or transform those capabilities on behalf of the customer base.

The second area of responsibility for the SMO is in managing, publishing, monitoring, and when required updating Service Performance standards for metric categories and their related KPIs. This includes developing and managing documentation and training, as well as ensuring that current standards are practiced effectively and add value to all Services and Service Groups. We've stressed throughout this book the need for the Service delivery framework, including its Service Performance strategy, to evolve over time, and the SMO is responsible for driving this evolution and refining based on feedback from the Service delivery community and IT and business leaders.

From the Diary of an ITaaS Consultant

I've witnessed numerous IT organizations get overly hung up on tools, prioritizing their desire for flashy dashboards fully automated by feature-rich platforms over the information that is already available to them and the conversations it can enable. At the same time some of the most successful Service Reviews I've ever witnessed were presented on slides that were built manually, and all based on information sourced from manually built spreadsheets.

While the SMO leads the effort to develop new reporting capabilities, Service delivery teams should have confidence in whatever tools they have. Focus on the information available and what it can tell you, even if it's on sticky notes, and then have a conversation with your customers.

Behind the Scenes of the Cisco IT Services Transformation

The Cisco IT team began by defining metric categories, asking themselves, "What are those things that we need to consistently care about across the Services?" (Looking back, this was something that was missing a lot of times from Service management.) From the top down, here are the key things we care about consistently across all Services from the perspective of both IT and business leaders. Instead, most Services prior had ended up with a bunch of individual metrics that could not be measured across the organization and they all cared about different things. The decision to roll these all up to a consistent set of metric categories and KPIs was instrumental to the success of the accountability framework.

Cisco IT designated a central group that developed the top-level metrics. One thing that's important with metrics is to be consistent. You don't want to change your metrics every six months because you would have no history. At the same time, you are not going to get the metrics perfect the first time. Even with the initial categories defined, it was still difficult and things changed dramatically at times. At first, the focus was cost while others were ignored; next was risk. It evolved. You start small and start basic so that people can understand, and then you build on it.

One IT leader described the initial experience, "Yes, we had folks who couldn't or didn't want to change. I was one of those in the middle. I was a technologist. I came from a technology background. I loved technology, and I thought, "I don't get this." After doing it for a year, reporting on these new metrics, I began saying to myself, "Hey, my success is not going to be judged on whether I have the latest version of hardware or database software. My success is going to be measured on real metrics, and by the way I am going to be accountable for those metrics..." That was sort of refreshing. And what was nice was that if you delivered on your metrics, you were rewarded."

Nobody wants to do the wrong thing, everybody wants to do the right thing, but they don't know what the right thing is. Until you put in very tangible metrics and tangible actions against those metrics, you're not going to get a holistic move. The metrics being Service-based initiated the change in behavior by first changing the entire perspective.

Cisco IT witnessed firsthand how the addition of a metric category, like risk, could influence outcomes for the IT organization and behaviors of the Service delivery teams. As one person stated, "Our security leaders and teams had advocated for years but could not get security pervasively across the company by themselves. Once risk was added as a metric, it forced Service Owners to take responsibility and to report on it, and before long, we had pervasive security across the organization. So, the lesson learned there was that people were starting to model their processes around the newly prioritized perspective around Services.

Summary

The ITaaS framework's Service Performance strategy creates visibility to all aspects of Service Performance, enabling individual Services to be managed efficiently while understanding the value they deliver. It allows performance of a Service to be communicated in terms that resonate with a customer, and is capable of illustrating the Service impact on business outcomes. It also enables strategic planning across the Services landscape, and for IT and business leaders to understand the impact of those decisions over time.

The strategy accomplishes this by granting Service Owners flexibility to monitor all metrics relevant to their Service and then aggregating each of these metrics into Service Metric Categories familiar to both IT and business leaders that create a well-rounded view of Service Performance. The following metric categories are defined by the ITaaS framework:

- **Quality:** Provides an overall measurement of the operational performance of the Service and the effectiveness and availability of the technical capabilities it delivers

- **Leverage:** Measures the scale and utilization of technical capabilities as well as the level at which capabilities are actually being consumed

- **Speed:** Measures the time to respond to customer requests for technical capabilities already delivered by the Service, as well as the time to develop and introduce new capabilities and achieve a target rate of adoption

- **Risk:** Measures overall risk to the ongoing delivery of technical capabilities and ensures Service delivery continuously manages risks associated with the IT organization and enterprise business operations

- **Customer Experience:** Examines aspects of the Service from the perspective of the customer stakeholders consuming the technical capabilities

Service Owners for Business Operations Services have the added responsibility of correlating the impact of Service Performance measurements on business outcomes. This can be done by incorporating information captured in the Enterprise Technical Capabilities map and leveraged in the initial design of the Service.

Many additional aspects of the Service Performance strategy must also be addressed. Targets, baselines, benchmarks, and trending should be associated with all Service Metrics to provide context that shapes information for planning. The ability to chain selected Service Metrics provides the IT organization with a valuable tool for accurately illustrating how the performance of one Service can impact others. To leverage the full potential of the ITaaS framework's Service Performance strategy, Service Owners must not only consider Service Metrics and metric categories in isolation but also consider how each metric and category links to and impacts one another. A key capability for managing and reviewing Service Performance is the availability of a dashboard, capable of providing an at-a-glance overview of Service Performance. The Service Management Office needs to support a Service Performance strategy, ensuring that Service Owners have the capabilities they need to measure and report Service Performance and that the standards and overall strategy evolve over time.

Chapter 9

Modeling the Total Costs of IT Service Delivery

What reason do enterprise business leaders have for continuing to accept the operating costs of a particular business unit? What reason would they have for prioritizing, much less approving, investment costs in the same business unit? Furthermore, why would a business unit such as an Enterprise IT organization choose to leverage a Service-based view of its budget in addition to the departmental- and program-based views traditionally favored?

The answers to these questions act as the foundation for the ITaaS framework's Service costing strategy. By now, you should recognize that understanding the total cost of Service delivery is a critical component of Service value communications. A consideration of these fundamental questions informs the design of an ideal Service costing strategy as well as its overarching value to the IT organization and enterprise beyond measuring the business value created by individual IT Services.

This chapter begins by reviewing these questions and concepts to clearly establish a purpose and goals for the IT Service costing strategy. From there, we highlight a range of considerations, including historical challenges as well as common missteps committed by IT organizations that can delay, derail, and drastically limit the benefits of a Service costing strategy. We review several basic finance concepts that inform and can support an IT Transformation team's understanding and development of the resulting strategy. The process for modeling the total costs of Service delivery may seem simple in theory but can quickly become problematic in practice as teams attempt to align cost elements from complex real-world IT budgets. As such, we also review best practices for navigating the most difficult elements of implementing Service costing, such as cost distributions, and strategies for leveraging and improving the strategy over time.

The goal of this chapter is not to provide a comprehensive review of the many significant topics relevant to managing IT budgets, nor does it aim to act as an introduction to finance concepts such as depreciation or cost types. After all, one of the goals of the ITaaS framework's Service costing is to greatly expand responsibility for managing costs by partnering Service delivery teams with IT leaders, IT Finance teams, and managers who own the underlying budgets today.

Purpose and Goals for IT Service Cost Modeling

To understand the purpose of assigning costs to Services, we need to first consider why an enterprise business invests in and accepts the operational costs of a business unit like the IT organization. In Chapter 1, "The Case for IT Transformation and IT as a Service (ITaaS)," we reviewed how an enterprise organization relies on lines of business to operate its core business and drive outcomes, while relying on supporting business units to provide specific capabilities either to the lines of business, other BUs, or the enterprise as a whole (such as tax reporting). We established that each of these business units, including the IT organization, held obligations to the enterprise to support business outcomes while operating efficiently.

An enterprise accepts the operational costs of a BU because it provides Services and capabilities required to enable business outcomes, and it approves investments in the BU to receive additional value. The key consideration is that if an enterprise business can acquire the same Services and capabilities in support of desired outcomes at a better value from outside the enterprise, the business unit is not needed. Likewise, if there is no demonstrable value-add associated with a proposed investment, or prior investments have failed to achieve their intended value, the enterprise has no need to fund additional investment in a BU.

Business units are ultimately responsible for validating the conditions that justify these costs, but common department- and program-based views of an IT budget do not reflect the costs of providing required capabilities. That is where Service costing comes in. The purpose of Service costing, then, is to create a view of IT spend that distributes both operational and investment costs to Services to demonstrate that long-term value is being created through investments, and verify that operational costs are being leveraged to support business outcomes.

In addition to this goal, the strategy also seeks to expand the community of responsibility for managing IT costs effectively. At present, the management of spend within the IT organization is likely limited to IT leaders and managers with departmental budgets or those overseeing a project or program. By establishing processes that model the total costs for Service delivery and responsibility for improving Service value, the strategy partners budget owners with a broader community of Service delivery teams to drive cost efficiencies across all areas of the IT operating model.

Considerations for IT Service Costing

IT leaders have traditionally understood the need and benefits of Service costing, but effective strategies have been difficult to adopt, primarily due to Services historically being designated for only limited segments of IT's operations, rather than end-to-end.

Service costing is a complex and challenging effort for any business unit, and IT organizations face the added complexity of relying on multiple tiers of shared systems and infrastructures to deliver a Service; these systems require unique processes to fairly distribute those costs to develop an accurate model of the total cost of ownership.

With such an important capability of the IT Service delivery function already difficult to implement, the IT Transformation team must remain conscious of key considerations related to Service costing and not make the effort any more challenging than it already is. This section highlights a number of missteps that I've seen committed on repeat occasions by IT organizations that ultimately derail, delay, or further complicate IT Service costing strategies. Besides leveraging these lessons learned, this chapter also reviews a series of considerations that inform and shape an ideal Service costing strategy.

One of the most common missteps made by IT leaders is to progress a Service costing strategy to an advanced stage prior to having completed end-to-end Service design. Attempting to develop and implement Service costing processes when large segments of the IT Service portfolio have yet to be designated carries the risk of those processes being incompatible with Services introduced later, leading to significant rework of complex processes. It also commonly results in those Services that have been designated reflecting inflated TCOs as numerous cost elements are assigned to them that would have been attributed to other Services had they been defined. Consider also that any significant changes in the Service landscape, likely to occur while vetting the portfolio, can cause major disruptions to the distribution of cost elements. Minor changes to the Service landscape, such as those that will occur as the IT organization optimizes the Service delivery function over time and introduces or discontinues Services to maintain alignment with business requirements, do not represent the same level of risk or impact to these processes.

There is often a significant amount of pressure to execute Service costing as quickly as possible, often as a result of IT leaders' desire to review costs with dissatisfied stakeholders or to win approval for budget increases or investments. It is critical that IT Transformation teams resist any pressure to begin development, much less implementation of Service costing, prior to having finalized the initial Services portfolio. When necessary, transformation teams may consider prioritizing Service pilots based on a desire to review their associated costs, so long as all parties acknowledge that these Service costs are likely to fluctuate as the team tests and refines the processes throughout the pilot phase.

IT organizations are also likely to introduce a significant amount of pressure to demonstrate cost reductions from Service costing even while the strategy is still in development or in the early stages of implementation during Service pilots. Chapter 1 highlighted the tendency for IT organizations to develop a tunnel vision–like fixation on cost reductions, often prioritizing a reduction of costs over an understanding and improvement of value. Pressuring IT Transformation teams or early Service Owners to prioritize cost reductions only results in planning based on limited information and distracts from the complex effort of designing and refining the quality of the Service costing process itself. I want to stress that cost reductions, along with optimizing the end-to-end efficiency of IT spend, will occur. However, it must be allowed to happen naturally as a result of the informed decision making enabled by well-designed Service costing and Service Performance strategies. Also, remember that following Cisco's Services Transformation Program creates numerous opportunities for cost reduction and optimization of resources, as described in earlier chapters.

Chapter 1 also highlighted a growing reliance on the presentation of large amounts of costing data to stakeholders. This "shock-and-awe" type strategy stems from a misperception that questions and concerns regarding the costs of technical capabilities delivered by the IT organization can be addressed by responding with large amounts of data. While significant levels of costing data that can be generated by increasingly popular IT finance platforms are certainly helpful to IT leaders and Service Owners in managing costs, customers typically just want to understand the major elements contributing to the cost of a Service rather than be presented with mounds of information to sort through and attempt to understand. Also remember that if customers are upset at higher than expected costs, pushing pages of data will not resolve the issue.

This consideration underscores a key requirement for Service costing strategies: they must be capable of generating informed but understandable views of Service costs for presentation and review with customers. The ITaaS framework's introduction of IT Services as a layer of abstraction creates an opportunity to generate an informative yet simple model of Service costs, while the Service delivery team maintains visibility to the many processes and cost elements that make up these models.

A closely related consideration that often distracts transformation teams designing a Service costing strategy is the tendency to become obsessed with accuracy. Let's be clear: accuracy is important, but 100 percent accuracy is not truly achievable with Service costing, nor is it our goal. Upcoming sections introduce cost distributions and cost-chaining processes, all of which involve the need to reflect shared costs across Services. We discuss best practices for driving high levels of accuracy, but it is important to understand now that these will never be perfectly accurate, and attempts to achieve complete accuracy will only result in more complex processes and costing models. Consider for a moment that most IT organizations can typically achieve a high level of accuracy, exceeding 85–90 percent, with a few short months of costing work. The result is processes that produce cost models that are easy to review with customers and provide "at-a-glance" understanding of cost makeup and trends. There is no proven solution for how far to take efforts to improve accuracy because each enterprise represents a unique scenario. As a general best practice, teams should obviously strive for every bit of accuracy possible without sacrificing the simplicity of the resulting Service cost models. Also, always remember that accuracy can be improved over time as tools and processes evolve.

While the Service costing strategy may allow for less than 100 percent accuracy, it demands 100 percent transparency. Transparency is key to fostering trust in the IT organization. While a primary goal of the Service costing strategy is to create simple yet informative models of the total cost of Service delivery, this does not mean that additional detail is never shared with stakeholders. Exactly the opposite is true. Full details on the elements of the IT budget assigned to the Service either directly or through cost distributions, the processes used to chain indirect Service costs, and any other details of interest should all be presented and reviewed with stakeholders on request. IT leaders are often surprised at the level of support they receive for Service costing strategies by simply emphasizing transparency. It rarely takes long for stakeholders to put their trust in the IT organization's strategy for measuring Service costs and begin focusing on their relevant Service cost models and the planning they enable rather than concerning themselves with dozens of minor details regarding the development of the models.

Kicking off an effort to develop a new strategy with related processes and responsibilities for managing IT spend can obviously raise concerns. That is why it is important for IT leaders and Transformation teams to remember to regularly communicate a key aspect of the Service costing strategy—that it represents a separate, parallel view of IT spend and does not impact any currently existing views or ownership of IT budgets. Service costing does not impact existing IT finance processes, or departmental or investment budgets. In other words, it represents a view of IT spend through a new lens rather than a modification to existing processes. Consider highlighting this message as an important aspect of change leadership for Service costing, as significant concerns and resistance can be raised as IT Transformation teams begin engaging IT finance and other resources to develop the Service costing processes.

Finally, consider that, historically, the entirety of IT spend was managed by a small community of managers, directors, and senior leaders, along with possibly an IT finance team. Typically, they leveraged processes focused on vetting investment costs or managing costs within a functional or departmental budget. Besides providing these resources with a new view of IT spend aligned to the costs of delivering Services, the strategy also expands the responsibility for these costs to the wider Service delivery community. Although Service Owners do not own a budget as a result of owning a Service, they nonetheless play a critical role in influencing the use of numerous budgets that impact their Service. Responsibility for managing costs in an end-to-end Services organization is shared by a broad community of resources rather than left to a small group of senior leaders.

IT Service Costs versus Cloud Services Costing

We need to address one last point of potential confusion. The costs and billing reported for the consumption of popular cloud Services (IaaS, PaaS, SaaS), either public or private, should never be confused as a Service costing strategy for an end-to-end Services organization. Although each may be referenced as reporting the costs of a Service, in reality, an organizational Service costing strategy has to be able to account for many more elements than consumption of cloud infrastructure resources.

The previous statements were not intended to imply that the capability to generate highly accurate and informative consumption-based billing for cloud resources is not important to IT leaders. In fact, these cost reporting capabilities will continue to provide valuable information to IT managers and will also help fast-track complex processes within the Service costing strategy aimed at accurately chaining indirect Service costs, which are described in an upcoming section. Billing for cloud services is valuable but should not be confused with a strategy for modeling the total costs of Services within an end-to-end Services organization.

Essential IT Finance Concepts

In an ideal world, Service Owners possess all the proactive and innovative traits detailed in Chapter 7, "Service Delivery Roles and Responsibilities," along with a basic understanding of finance concepts like depreciation or fixed versus variable costs. At the same time, it is possible for an otherwise ideal candidate Service Owner to possess these key traits but lack a foundational knowledge of finance topics. In this case, it is better to leverage those traits and to provide the finance background through training and knowledge sharing. Many change leadership functions work closely with IT finance and other resources to develop valuable training modules specifically for this purpose.

Providing an introduction to these concepts is best left to other experts, but several concepts commonly at play in IT finance heavily influence and can help transformation teams understand the mechanics of the ITaaS framework's Service costing strategy, and they are reviewed in the following sections.

The Different Views of an IT Budget

It is important that IT Transformation and future Service delivery teams be aware of common methods of viewing and managing IT spend independent of Services. Although they primarily work with the cost elements associated with their individual Service TCO, this background helps delivery teams understand how their TCO is built up and how strategies applied at the Service level can impact the underlying IT budget.

Service costing begins with the IT budget, which is built from debit and credit entries in the company's general ledger (GL) and assigned to the IT organization. These entries include the costs of any software or hardware purchases; bills for support costs and maintenance fees; and any costs for external Services, consulting, or labor. They also include the costs of all IT personnel resources and travel and training costs. Finally, the budget commonly reflects any departmental cross-charges—for example, from a facilities department reflecting the costs of maintaining office space used by the IT organization (the data source for these cross-charges may be separate from the GL). Think of this as the first and most complete view of IT spend. Note that this initial view of IT spend can sometimes be referred to as a CIO statement, a bill of IT, or other designations. The accuracy of the IT budget ultimately affects the accuracy of Service TCOs, but this is beyond the scope of the IT Transformation team and Services Transformation Program. In fact, the IT budget itself, its accuracy and data sources leveraged for input, its organization and presentation, and many other related concerns represent a significant topic of interest for IT leaders and the industry but are beyond the scope of this chapter.

While IT finance teams and the senior-most IT leaders may work directly with the IT budget at times, its format is rarely helpful for the broader community of IT leaders in managing and reporting costs. Instead, the information in the IT budget is commonly presented and managed through different views, the most common of which is the departmental or functional view of the budget. In this view, the IT budget is distributed out to specific teams, functions, cost pools, and dedicated budgets within the IT organization. This is the view of costs that most IT professionals are familiar with. For example, a network engineer likely understands their direct manager has a budget for headcount and training, and that there is a cost pool where the costs of network-related hardware and software costs are assigned. These views are easy to understand due to their close relation to the functional and organizational structure of the IT department and are highly effective in supporting ownership of costs and related strategies by managers and individual contributors.

Another equally common view of costs is a program or project view of IT investment costs. These views are often used to manage the costs of IT programs or projects, many of which span numerous IT teams and functions. This allows IT leaders to review investment costs, typically approved to scale or transform existing capabilities, separate from the operational costs associated with maintaining the capabilities delivered today.

Each common view of IT spend offers different benefits but is incapable of reflecting how IT costs are leveraged to deliver Services or resonating with stakeholders struggling to understand the costs and value of technical capabilities they consume. To provide this information, the IT organization requires another view of IT spend that accurately distributes IT costs to IT Services in an easy-to-understand model.

Chargeback versus Showback Policies

As IT organizations struggled to rein in spending, many adopted different policies intended to manage costs. One of the most common was chargeback policies, sometimes referred to as billback. The core concept was to charge, via departmental cross-charges or similar, enterprise customers and business units for their consumption of IT products and Services. This approach helped shift the approval and ownership of costs to the stakeholders, and successfully encouraged more involvement and careful decision making across the customer bases that previously may have demanded the latest technologies with little regard to the cost burden placed on IT and ultimately the enterprise business. It also helped the IT organization demonstrate the tiered costs for delivering specific technical capabilities that, in turn, relied on shared architectures and established visibility for IT leaders of those stakeholders responsible for driving costs.

These policies also introduced new challenges, however, and one of the most significant was the practice of some IT organizations to continue setting higher and higher targets for the billing out of costs, in some cases even attempting to completely zero-out the IT budget. The inherent problem with this approach was that it unnecessarily inflated the costs associated with technical capabilities, often so significantly as to be completely unexpected by the customer and indefensible by IT.

It also created scenarios in which shared resources had to be scaled to support growing demands, and those costs were often the burden of the customer that submitted the most recent request. As an example consider a Line of Business seeking to implement a new platform being held responsible for the full costs of a network upgrade because the current bandwidth cannot support the added traffic levels. Also, note that the accuracy and reporting capabilities of IT budgets were often still maturing, which made it even more difficult for IT to justify the costs that were being billed out.

From the Diary of an ITaaS Consultant

I've actually come across IT chargeback and costing processes that resulted in excess of $4,000 per quarter for the ownership of a laptop. These costs were built from a bottom-up cost model (detailed in a later section) and chargeback policy with high targets for billback to customers. This meant the costs that could be directly aligned to the ownership of the laptop were combined with numerous other cost elements in the IT budget that were divided across various assets and capabilities.

As one stakeholder rightly pointed out, it would have been cheaper to just buy a new laptop each quarter. While this is an extreme example, it illustrates the types of situations that arise as policies for charging out costs become disconnected from fair and accurate measurement of consumption of resources.

In my experience, stakeholders are more than willing to accept a limited degree of higher costs for delivery and support of technical capabilities from their own IT organization. Whenever these costs far exceed any expectations and fail to be justified, however, it causes significant frustration, sows distrust, and can even lead senior business leaders to begin evaluating opportunities to bypass IT in favor of external support.

It is important to note that Cisco's ITaaS framework and Service cost modeling can be leveraged without moving away from chargeback policies. They also provide a more fair and accurate view of Service costs that can help the IT organization bring costs within expectations through transparent modeling and processes, helping to address challenges commonly associated with chargeback policies.

At the same time, the ITaaS framework also supports what is commonly referred to as a showback policy. In this approach, the IT organization retains ownership of all costs but reviews (shows) the costs of each Service with relevant stakeholders, agreeing to the value achieved by those costs and planning future Service requirements and associated costs. Stakeholders still share in the responsibility for ensuring their teams' requirements for technical capabilities justify the value to the enterprise. They still work with Service delivery teams to justify costs and make careful investment decisions. After all, no leader wants to be seen as driving up enterprise costs without justification or as not supporting efforts to optimize spend.

Showback policies are gaining in popularity but are not required to understand the total costs of delivering a Service within the ITaaS framework. The key to understand is that a mature strategy for Service costing leveraged by an end-to-end Services organization can support either policy.

Bottom-up versus Direct + Chained Costs Models

As the adoption of chargeback policies spread, IT organizations needed a way to determine the costs of delivering technology and the costs of underlying shared resources, which led to the implementation of bottom-up cost models. Bottom-up cost models can vary significantly, depending on exactly how an IT Service is defined and the actual costs within the IT budget that are encompassed by the cost model. The goal of these models was primarily to distribute the costs of shared assets and resources to an IT Service. In effect, the cost of a Service became the sum of costs charged to it by different levels of shared IT resources. A basic illustration of this approach is shown in Figure 9-1.

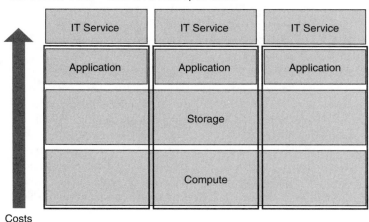

Figure 9-1 *Bottom-Up Cost Model*

These models were limited by Service design principles, often forced to distribute large costs to support chargeback targets, and struggled to accurately base the cost at each level on actual consumption. Instead, they relied on straight division of those costs across all Services regardless of consumption levels. This approach results in artificially inflated costs and an often large, single pool of costs assigned directly to a Service, leaving IT customers struggling to understand many of the details of unexpectedly high charges to their departments.

The Service costing model within the ITaaS framework tweaks the bottom-up approach, instead leveraging what is recognized as a direct Service costing with cost-chaining model. This model begins with a calculation of all direct Service costs, which might include the costs of hardware (including depreciation), software, support, and other costs attributed specifically to that Service. Next, IT Services chain a portion of their direct costs to other IT Services that consume the capabilities they deliver. An overview of this concept is shown in Figure 9-2.

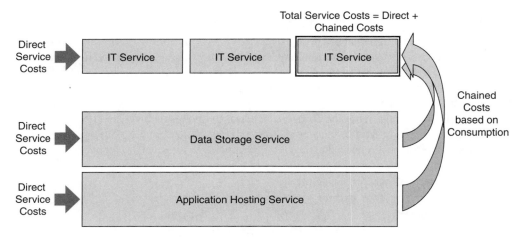

Figure 9-2   *Direct Service Costing with Cost Chaining*

These illustrations, while accurate, may not provide a clear distinction between the two approaches, but as we review the complete details of the ITaaS framework's Service costing strategy, we'll find the mechanics and results of the two are significantly different. From a customer standpoint, in fact, there is a considerable difference. Customers are presented with an immediate view of the direct costs for their Service, made up of cost elements that are easy to justify and that stakeholders are likely familiar with and actively anticipating. Beside these direct costs, stakeholders are presented with a separate block of costs chained from other IT Services tied directly to the consumption of shared systems and infrastructures.

Cost Distributions

Enterprise businesses and the various business units that make them up are complex organizations, with complex finances. The IT organization is no less complex, and has the added challenge of leveraging multiple tiers of shared resources and assets to deliver a Service. As such, any effort to model the total costs of Service delivery relies on some level of cost distributions. When leveraged correctly, this simple concept of dividing portions of a single cost element to multiple Services can help develop a transparent, understandable build-up of costs that all stakeholders can agree to. When best practices are ignored, however, cost distributions can unnecessarily inflate Service costs, decrease transparency, frustrate stakeholders, and lead to mistrust of the IT organization. It is important that IT Transformation teams consider these best practices when developing the core processes for Service cost modeling.

The most important principle for employing cost distributions is to first ensure that a proposed distribution is justified and preferably agreeable to all relevant stakeholders. If the assignment of a portion of costs to a given Service cannot be justified, it should not be assigned. Service Owners should be involved in any proposal and ultimately accept any distribution of costs to their Service.

Once the decision has been made to distribute a cost across multiple Services, consider if an option exists and whether it would be more applicable to perform a weighted distribution versus an equal division of the costs across the Services receiving the distribution. Weighted distributions can provide a more accurate assignment of costs and can leverage various inputs such as time cards or ticket counts, or may simply involve a pair of Service Owners agreeing to split the costs 75 percent and 25 percent between their respective Services. Just remember not to expend too much effort or introduce too much complexity in an attempt to drive levels of accuracy. Often stakeholders prefer a directionally correct weighted distribution rather than complex processes and formulas.

It is important that IT leaders and Service delivery teams remember to consider the potential impact of changes in the Service portfolio to existing cost distributions. For example, if a cost is divided equally across four Services, and two of those are discontinued in a reporting period, the TCO of the remaining Services will spike for no other reason than that the distribution calculation updated. This is why it is also equally important to thoroughly document all cost distributions as part of the Service costing strategy.

It is also important to refrain from distributing entire cost pools, especially those representing significant costs. Instead, reduce the dollar amount of the cost pool to the lowest amount possible by directly assigning any elements within the cost pool that can be to specific Services. This approach ensures first that we're distributing only necessary costs, and second that we understand exactly what the costs are in any cost pool distributed to multiple Services.

IT Service Cost Modeling

With the purpose and goals of Service costing along with key considerations actively in mind, we can now introduce the ITaaS framework's IT Service cost modeling strategy. First, we provide an overview of the strategy and foundational principles; then we provide a detailed look at each of the processes involved in building an IT Service total cost of ownership (TCO) model.

To build a model of total Service costs, let's once again leverage a two-step approach. The first step involves assigning all direct Service costs. This is accomplished through the distribution of 100 percent of the IT budget across the IT Services defined in the portfolio, with all Service costs assigned to one of two blocks of our eventual three-block Service TCO model. These first, Direct Service costs block are as follows:

- **Run the Business (RtB):** Direct Service costs associated with operating and maintaining the technical capabilities delivered by the Service today

- **Change the Business (CtB):** Direct Service costs associated with scaling or transforming technical capabilities delivered by a Service

After all direct Service costs have been assigned, the second step involves any Services that deliver capabilities consumed by another Service (most commonly Technology Foundation Services) are required to develop a process for chaining appropriate costs to that Service based on consumption of capabilities. Cost-chaining processes for all required Services may take some time to mature and should be subject to review and optimization efforts regularly as new management and reporting capabilities are introduced; this ensures the most accurate consumption-based costs are being chained out. Costs chained to a Service are assigned to an indirect Service cost block, sometimes referred to as the Run the Business Indirect (RtB-I) costs, and the total of these three blocks represents a model of the Service TCO.

When beginning work on a Service costing strategy, IT Transformation teams need to engage senior IT leaders and IT finance teams, along with potentially enterprise finance and accounting departments when necessary. Collaborating with these resources ensures IT Transformation teams leverage the most accurate and complete version of the IT budget, along with all other sources of relevant costing information (investment budgets and so on). The last thing any team wants is to invest extensive time and effort only to find that the data sources they were building their processes and models from were incomplete.

Direct Service Costs

Our first major effort for Service costing is to assign costs from the IT budget (and potentially other sources) into one of two direct Service cost blocks of our Service TCO model, designated as either Run the Business (RtB) or Change the Business (CtB). After all parties have agreed to the proper Service to align a cost element to, the determination of RtB versus CtB is often fairly simple, as any costs associated with a program or project can typically be allocated to the CtB block, and the majority of all other costs go to the RtB block.

Earlier, we stated our goal was to assign 100 percent of costs from the IT budget to Services, but the ITaaS framework includes an option for separating out a segment of costs from the IT budget into an IT retained costs pool. Think of the IT retained costs pool as a special placeholder, ideally temporary, within the Service-based view of IT finances, where costs can be set aside rather than assigned to any Services. This optional process is not required or necessary for all IT organizations, and should be leveraged only when needed and approved by senior leaders. The retained costs pool was introduced after working with numerous IT organizations whose budgets included costs with special circumstances. Some of these special circumstances included large-scale acquisition costs and merging of companies and their IT organizations. In practice, these costs were quite significant, temporary (presence in the budget not expected to exceed one year), and incredibly complex making fair assignment of costs to any set of IT Services difficult along with likely distorting the TCO of these Services. Instead whenever the CIO or other senior IT leaders report on their spending, they can present the strategic Service view beside the IT retained costs.

The effort of assigning cost elements from the IT budget can become quite complex. Whenever possible, assign 100% of a cost element from the IT budget directly to a single Service. Cost distributions are required and should adhere to the best practices described earlier. These distributions can be simple, such as an application license fee leveraged equally by two Services, in which case the Service Owners for each should agree to split the costs 50/50. Weighted distributions can also be leveraged, such as

50 percent of the costs to one Service and another 25 percent to two additional Services. Transformation teams may be surprised with how quickly Service Owners can propose and agree to an accurate distribution of many cost elements. Remember that the distribution of costs should be as fair and accurate as possible, and as such, teams may decide that some cost distributions will be adjusted each reporting period based on various data inputs. For example, the costs of a specialized IT support team may be allocated each period to Services based on the ticket counts, time reporting, or other methods reflecting the level of effort that the team dedicated to a particular Service.

Run the Business Costs

Run the Business (RtB) costs reflect costs of the day-to-day operation of the Service. Following are some of the most common cost elements assigned from an IT budget to this block of a TCO model:

- **Hardware:** Includes one-time charges for equipment that is not capitalized and depreciated over time

- **Software:** Includes licensing or renewal fees

- **Capital Depreciation:** Includes allocation of depreciated expenses in line with capital depreciation policies based on dollar amount and expense type

- **Support Costs:** Includes the costs of any support agreements or maintenance contracts

- **External Services:** Includes charges for vendors, contractors, or other external Services

- **Headcount:** Reflects the costs of personnel resources supporting the delivery of the Service

- **Departmental Cross Charges:** Includes expenses charged to the IT organization from another enterprise BU, for example, from a facilities department

RtB costs regularly receive a more significant level of scrutiny than any other block in our TCO model. A key consideration for RtB costs is that they represent the ongoing costs of delivering a set of technical capabilities at a specific level of performance. These costs should not be expected to change significantly from one reporting period to the next, especially if the Service Performance or scale of delivery has not changed. When they do change, Service Owners are responsible for identifying the source of the change and either justifying the cost or managing the cost out of the TCO model if they feel it is not applicable.

Even beyond examination of any fluctuations, RtB costs within a TCO model often receive the most scrutiny. Aggressive targets are set, and benchmarking against industry peers has to be actively examined. When a cost element is assigned to their TCO, Service Owners should immediately adopt a sense of ownership and responsibility for managing these costs. Here again, a Service Owner needs to take on the role of a general manager, asking hard questions. Are these costs absolutely necessary? Is there a way to invest in order to reduce these recurring costs? Is there another way to procure the support needed to deliver the same capabilities at the required levels of performance and scale while reducing costs? Could scale or performance be reduced? These are just some of the questions that Service Owners should be asking themselves as they review their RtB costs.

Change the Business Costs

Compared to their counterpart direct cost block for RtB, CtB costs are often much simpler to identify and then assign to Services. The reason is that these costs are traditionally associated with investment programs or projects that have been subject to extensive review prior to approval, and cost assignments to specific Services can typically be facilitated without extensive distribution processes. Costs in this block of the TCO often are broken down by program and project, and the costs and regular updates on the project can typically be provided to the Service Owner by the applicable project manager. The common exception to this is when investment costs are approved to support scaling or upgrading IT assets independent of a formal project.

The real question is, what exactly constitutes the cost of changing the business? Here again, IT Transformation teams and senior IT leaders have a strategic decision to make regarding their cost strategy.

The traditional use of this component of the Service TCO model was to reflect instances of investment where the capabilities delivered were being transformed. This approach drastically narrows the focus of this cost block, as approved investment to scale or upgrade capabilities that exist today are then associated with the RtB cost block. As an example, using this approach, costs to upgrade or scale traditional data center switching infrastructure that exists today would be allocated to the RtB block, while costs to introduce a fully virtualized switching environment constitute a transformation of the capabilities and as such would be accounted to the CtB block. The advantage to this focus is that IT and business leaders can more easily identify and then follow the successful use of investment dollars that would be approved for the purpose of improving Service delivery rather than simply scaling existing capabilities. Looking at our virtualized switching investment, for example, an IT leader would expect to see these costs drive improvement in Service Performance over time, particularly in the speed metric category. Also, consider that some expenses for scaling or growing business capabilities are already accounted for in the RtB cost block or are otherwise difficult to separate. For example, consider a cloud Application Hosting Service with an offering for public cloud hosting that results in a regular bill for Services from the cloud provider based on consumption and would simply increase or decrease in line with the scale of capabilities. At the same time, this strategy can sometimes lead to debate, and even cases of overthinking what constitutes a transformation of technical capabilities. For example, if the costs for introducing the virtual switching environment were only for a small test environment, does the first large-scale deployment count as CtB? What about the next?

Another method is to differentiate costs for scaling capabilities, that is, "growing" the business, and "transforming" the business. Some adopters have leveraged the costs associated with growing the business either as a subset of CtB or RtB costs, or even established them as a third block of direct Service costs in their TCO models.

Although all these approaches represent legitimate considerations and options, I commonly encourage keeping the strategy as simple as possible during the initial Services Transformation and then updating it at a later date if doing so has a high degree of value add. Keeping it simple means simply associating any and all investment costs with CtB. This makes establishing the CtB cost block easier because it simply reflects any approved investments and avoids any overthinking of what constitutes a CtB cost. In addition, Service Owners can still actively track and report the impact of specific investments on performance or operating costs which are commonly the most significant concerns.

Regardless of how your organization defines the specific use of the CtB cost block, it still needs to also establish a policy for how to reflect capital depreciation over time. The most common approach is to reflect the first period of depreciation for a Service asset in the CtB block before then moving all remaining depreciation expenses to the RtB stack.

The key consideration for CtB costs is that they should always reflect a desired impact for the Service. As many IT organizations complete their Services Transformation and mature and integrate their enterprise architecture practice, they adopt new investment policies. These policies often require architectural approval for all IT investment, which in turn links to desired outcomes for specific IT Services.

Indirect Service Costs

Chaining costs to another Service to accurately reflect a consumption of capabilities is a critical step in accurately reflecting the total costs of Service delivery, influencing behavior, and supporting informed costing decisions. At the same time, it is not a step that should ever be assumed or taken lightly. Poorly implemented indirect Service cost assignments can artificially inflate Service TCOs and raise questions and concerns across the customer base. As such, we should review several considerations before we begin developing processes for cost chaining.

First, remember not to confuse indirect Service costing with departmental chargeback policies. We are not charging the customer; we're chaining costs from one IT Service to another in an effort to accurately reflect the total costs of Service delivery. The TCO of a Service is not reduced by chaining out costs. Those direct costs remain the same because they are the costs associated with operating the Service. The difference is that a portion of those costs appear in the TCO models of additional Services as a result of their consumption of capabilities. This is an important consideration when rolling-up the costs of multiple Services, as there is potential to duplicate cost elements, and it will be discussed in a later sections.

A candidate Service for cost chaining should adhere to these fundamental criteria:

- There is an ongoing consumption of technical capabilities from one IT Service by another IT Service.

- A process for chaining out costs based on the consumption of capabilities can be achieved accurately and agreed to be the Service Owners.

- The justification for cost chaining, along with the process used to calculate the costs, can be presented and understood by the customer base at a strategic level (regardless of how complex the underlying process may be).

If a cost-chaining process is overly complex, requiring significant effort with little hope of future automation, and is unable to produce a defensible calculation of consumption-based costs, it is likely best to consider simply not chaining the costs. Service Owners should consider not only whether there is a consumption of capabilities taking place but also whether the complexity and effort to chain the costs and the dollar amounts that result from the chaining processes provide value to the Service value conversations across the broader portfolio.

A common example of this consideration is a Corporate Network Service, which provides network access to resources for end customers across the enterprise. At first, this may seem like a prime Service for chaining costs, and there are commonly selections of reporting on consumption of network resources, such as WAN link utilization, already available. In practice, however, accurately measuring consumption of network resources across the enterprise requires significant investment and quickly becomes many times more complex than originally anticipated. Many IT organizations opt not to chain out these costs.

Services that ultimately perform cost chaining are primarily made up of Technology Foundation Services, although some select Enterprise End-Customer Services also can make strong cases for cost chaining. Regardless of Service type, the process for calculating the costs to be chained are unique to each Service. These processes are developed and managed by the Service Owner of the Service chaining out the costs, but Service Owners who reflect these chained costs in their indirect Service costs should review the chaining processes regularly.

Cost chaining provides Service delivery teams with additional capabilities beyond simply reporting the total costs of a Service. It can be leveraged to influence behavior, helping IT leaders shift a customer community to a preferred offering. For example, an Application Hosting Service may find itself required to continue delivering a "non-virtual/bare-metal hosting" Service offering for customers who have so far refused to allow their applications to be hosted in a virtual environment. This, however, results in increased support costs for infrastructure teams, and the cost chaining can be used to reflect these increased costs in comparison to the traditional virtual environment-based Service offerings, which should over time encourage customers to leverage the cheaper, virtualized hosting offerings.

Overview of Cost-Chaining Processes

Developing processes for cost chaining can range in difficulty. This section reviews key guidelines and considerations for developing these processes.

The first consideration should be to clearly define the capabilities that are being consumed. By defining a unit of consumption, Service Owners can drive toward developing a unit cost, at which point the chained costs simply equal the number of units consumed in a reporting period multiplied by the unit cost. Note that whenever applicable for a Service, units of consumption would be tracked in the leverage metric category of the Service Performance strategy.

Deriving a unit cost requires first determining the appropriate amount of direct Service costs to chain out, which depends on the specific cost elements. Remember that there is no requirement to chain out 100 percent of a Service's TCO, and that Service Owners should be encouraged to chain out only those cost elements directly related to delivering the unit of consumption. Unit cost is determined by dividing the total costs to be chained out by the number of units delivered.

Note that once a unit cost is determined, it should quickly become a focus, including trending, understanding changes to the costs, and identifying opportunities to reduce unit costs over time. Likewise, any changes to the calculation of unit costs, such as additional cost elements, should be highlighted.

Service Costing Strategies

Efforts in support of IT Service costing are not finished when the initial strategy is in place. Similar to the Service Performance strategy, ongoing efforts to optimize the strategy and supporting processes, tools, and capabilities are key to ensuring the strategy continues to support the evolving requirements of the Service delivery function and deliver value for the enterprise over time.

Leveraging newly available Service TCOs to look at the sum of costs associated with Service groups at each level of the Service hierarchy is an early focus because it provides Service Executives and IT leaders with a view of the costs across specific segments of the Service landscape. It is important when developing these strategic views of Service costs to consider the impact of indirect Service costs, which may not be appropriate to include in all cost rollups. Simply totaling up the TCOs for a selection of Services may be inaccurate, because it may duplicate costs that exist in the TCOs of Services that are then chained to another Service's TCO.

Another top priority is automation of the Service costing strategy, including cost-chaining processes when applicable, and reporting of strategic cost rollups. Macros and basic scripting can help reduce the effort required to build Service TCO models each reporting period and can reduce potential manual calculation errors. Long-term reporting capabilities—especially with graphical representations of Service TCO, historical trending, and any number of strategic Service cost views—allow Service Owners and IT leaders to quickly evaluate Service costs rather than requiring them to manually build a TCO model ahead of a reporting period.

Benchmarking provides another tremendous capability for cost comparisons and target setting, and the collection of data and correlation to Service reporting should also represent a priority for automation efforts. Unfortunately, sources for IT Service cost benchmarking data, similar to Service Performance, may be limited at first but can be expected to grow significantly as more and more IT organizations transition to an ITaaSO.

Always remember the importance of evaluating Service costs against different aspects of Service Performance. CtB investment should, in most cases, impact Service Performance, either by increasing speed, leverage, or quality, or minimizing risk. In those rare cases where CtB investment does not impact at least one aspect of Service Performance, it should be expected to reduce future RtB costs, and this should be carefully monitored and reported.

Here again, a great deal of responsibility is laid at the feet of the Service Owners. A significant amount of effort needs to be invested to thoroughly review initial costs assigned to a Service TCO and either accept them as allocated or review with IT Transformation and finance teams to identify a more appropriate Service to align the costs to. From there, Service Owners begin actively managing the complete Service TCO, which includes understanding any indirect Service costs, planning investments to facilitate future Service capabilities, and above all proactively seeking out opportunities to reduce the RtB costs associated with the Service. Looking ahead is just as important as looking at historical and current cost information. Service Owners should be able to anticipate shifts in the Service TCO from any number of inputs, such as identification of variable cost types in the RtB stack that will rise as the business scales operations.

Another closely related and key activity for Service Owners is to identify and potentially develop cost levers that can be used to facilitate any financial outcomes as directed by a CIO or Service Executive. Service Owners should know what mechanisms are available to them and understand if updates to their organization of the Service (via Service offerings, alignment of Service assets, and so on) can provide additional levers. An equally important consideration is how cost levers can be used to impact Service Performance. Can risk be further mitigated through an increase in CtB costs? What level of increase in RtB spend would have to be accepted to elevate quality to a new target level? Can both speed and leverage be improved through accepted increases in indirect Service costs? These are the types of questions that Service Owners need to be prepared not only to answer but also to facilitate.

In terms of what to expect for overall IT spend after the completion of the Services Transformation and a Service cost modeling strategy, most IT organizations can anticipate up to six months or more of cost reductions without the need of a formal target for reductions. This is the result of Service Owners facilitating their roles as general managers of a Service and taking on the responsibility for optimizing Service costs with the new visibility provided by the ITaaS framework. In the first months, Service Owners across the Service landscape are often actively identifying instances of duplication or other cost-saving opportunities as they take on management of the Service and build initial relationships with customer stakeholders.

As IT Services across the enterprise business are optimized and naturally occurring, cost savings begin to flatten; then IT leaders and Service Executives should be ready to leverage their strategic views of the IT Service landscape to begin setting specific targets for IT Service costs. One popular strategy is to challenge all Service Owners to reduce their RtB direct Service costs by 5 percent each year. Service Owners should also be actively challenged to demonstrate a reduction of report unit costs. Although these strategies may sound challenging for the Service delivery team, in reality, they should instill just enough pressure to drive teams to continuously innovate and consider all aspects of a Service in order to identify opportunities to meet cost targets.

Behind the Scenes of the Cisco IT Services Transformation

One Cisco IT leader remarked that the Services model worked where most have failed because it granted Cisco IT the ability to clearly see where all the IT funding was spent with regards to enabling business outcomes. The principle uncovered by Cisco IT was that the only way to do it was to move to an end-to-end Services organization.

The initial driver for Service costing was that IT had a substantial budget, yet huge portions of the budget were based around running the business, and no one could really say definitively where the money was going or what outcomes it was supporting. All the leaders could point to their budgets and say, "This is how I'm spending my money." We knew where the money was organizationally, but the CIO couldn't look at these different budgets and understand the total costs to deliver an outcome. IT leaders were driving people crazy with constantly evolving processes and more and more complex spreadsheets, all just trying to answer this question.

Cisco IT eventually found that it was impossible to do based on traditional departmental views of the budget, with one individual claiming the transformation came about when someone said, "So why don't we flip this thing over and look at it through a Service lens," even as large numbers of people were against it. "Even when we knew the answer rested in distributing costs across an end-to-end Services model, we failed and restarted, failed again, and restarted. My advice now is try and find people that have done it and copy them!"

Cisco knew it wanted to understand costs as either Change the Business or Run the Business. RtB was keep the lights on and CtB was to enable, and there were many debates about how exactly to populate each. The foremost goal was always understanding and then optimizing those RTB costs while the next was making sure that CTB investment equaled optimization of running the business costs.

"Creating a cost model was like sticking a needle in your eye," with all the spreadsheets and meetings, which fed the resistance of "when do I get back to doing IT stuff?" The cohorts and the change management team combatted this attitude by rewarding good behaviors. It took Cisco IT years, not months, to develop the initial cost models. Debates raged over who would decide what's part of each bucket, how granularly to divide costs. It was more difficult in part because we were not in a green field; we were repairing the plane while it was in the air. We had to start working with the business and working with finance and infrastructure teams to work on the costs.

Summary

The purpose of the ITaaS framework's Service costing strategy is to create a parallel view of the IT budget aligned to Services that are supporting business outcomes, with a goal of justifying operational costs, demonstrating the impact of investment, and significantly expanding responsibility for managing IT spend across the Service delivery community.

IT Transformation teams must remain conscious of many considerations, including historical challenges related to managing IT spend along with common missteps made by IT organizations that can negatively impact a Service costing strategy. It is also important for transformation teams to consider IT finance principles such as chargeback and showback policies, and how these topics and the strategy for Service costing can influence one another.

The ITaaS framework's Service costing strategy distributes 100 percent of the IT budget across the Service landscape. It establishes a three-block TCO model for each Service—created by first distributing all cost elements within the IT budget to Services defined in the portfolio (direct Service costs)—and allows for a portion of these costs to be chained to another IT Service to reflect the consumption of capabilities (indirect Service costs). These three blocks are

- **Run the Business (RtB):** Direct Service costs associated with operating and maintaining the technical capabilities delivered by the Service today

- **Change the Business (CtB):** Direct Service costs associated with scaling or transforming technical capabilities delivered by a Service

- **Indirect Service Cost (RtB-I):** Costs chained to another IT Service to reflect the consumption of technical capabilities

Cost chaining should be performed only when a process can be developed without extensive effort or investment, and when doing so adds value to the Service delivery function. Each Service that performs cost chaining is required to manage a process to assign costs based on consumption, which typically pivots on a per-unit cost.

The Service costing strategy can deliver higher levels of value as it is optimized over time by automating and improving costing processes and providing strategic views of Service costs. Also, remember that as initial cost savings driven by the Services Transformation taper off, IT leaders should begin actively prescribing cost-reduction targets to Services and Service groups.

Chapter 10

Communicating IT Service Value

While it is important to generate an initial view of Service value, based on costs and performance relative to the customer perspective, it is equally important to develop a strategy for communicating that view, refining it, and prepare the Service to continue creating business value well into the future. We have alluded to IT Service value conversations throughout almost every chapter of this book. In a sense, the many components of the Service delivery framework introduced throughout have all been leading to this discussion.

This chapter will begin by exploring considerations for Service value beyond costs and performance relative to the capabilities being delivered. From there, we review the ITaaS framework's overarching strategy for communicating Service value and how that strategy should evolve over time. Best practices for structuring and leading these reviews are also detailed alongside tactics to employ over time to ensure the IT organization continuously improves its approach to communicating Service value.

Throughout this book, we've emphasized the need to establish a purpose and goal for all major aspects of the ITaaS framework, and the strategy for Service value communications is no different. More than ever before, the IT organization needs to establish itself as a trusted advisor to the enterprise business through the delivery of value Services. Strong relationships are built through effective communication and reinforcement of trust overtime. The purpose of the Service value communication strategy is to establish a forum for IT leaders, Service Owners, and stakeholders to engage in constructive conversations regarding the delivery of an IT Service, with a goal of agreeing to the value that Service creates for the business and planning future Service requirements.

Considerations for IT Service Value

What makes an IT Service valuable? More appropriately, what are the characteristics for the delivery of an IT Service that create value for the customer consuming it? As you consider these questions, be sure to think not in terms of your personal role and career as an IT professional, but as a customer stakeholder.

A determination of Service value is ultimately decided by the customer, not the Service provider. Whenever we reference the communication of IT Service value throughout this book, we are not implying that this represents the final qualification of value. Instead, our goal is for the IT organization to communicate an initial view of Service value for the purpose of initiating a conversation with the customer to refine that initial view.

The key is that for these value alignment conversations to be effective, the initial proposed view of Service value must be presented in terms that resonate with the customer, and it should be somewhat close to that the customer's interpretation of value. We can't expect customer stakeholders to engage with us when we're approaching the concept of Service value from dissimilar viewpoints, focusing on different aspects of value qualification, and ultimately presenting a completely unfamiliar interpretation and level of Service value.

As the Service provider, the IT organization is responsible for developing a strategy for measuring and communicating Service value in a manner that resonates with and fosters engagement with the customer base. This first task requires IT to develop a central concept of IT Service value capable of framing successful conversations with customers. Once defined, this concept of value informs the types of strategies and capabilities the supporting Service delivery framework has to support.

The ITaaS framework's definition of Service value was established throughout early chapters of this book. Service value is a consideration of the total costs of delivery for a set of required technical capabilities at a desired level of performance, weighed against the impact of those capabilities on business outcomes. With this definition established, we know that our ideal IT Service delivery framework has to be capable of aligning IT Services to the delivery of required technical capabilities. It also must include strategies for measuring Service Performance and modeling the total costs of Service delivery.

Now we are able to look back at the many aspects of Cisco's ITaaS framework—the strategies, considerations, and updates to existing philosophies for Service design—and to finally grasp the end goal that it has been building to. Every foundation and concept we've laid has been in support of merging the concept of IT Service value across IT and its stakeholders and providing IT with the means to measure, communicate, manage, and improve that value.

Developing a shared view of Service value requires that Service Owners and IT leaders be receptive to customer feedback. Service Owners should expect to receive some level of feedback counter to their initial value assessment. When provided, this feedback should be actively incorporated going forward as the Service Owner continues to develop further familiarity with stakeholder operations and priorities.

At the same time, our Service Owners and IT leaders are not simply passive listeners. Our goal is to establish a trusted advisor relationship with our enterprise business, not a "trusted Service provider pushover." This means striking a balance between advocating for the customer base across the IT organization and helping customers understand the efforts, costs, and assets leveraged behind the scenes of the Service and at times limitations for what IT can realistically support.

Communication and review of IT Service value can take place anytime, anywhere, and at any level of the enterprise. In fact, as Service Owners develop deeper and more trusted relationships across their customer base, they should anticipate increasingly frequent engagement as business leaders begin to actively consider and involve IT Services when formulating their own strategies. While customer-initiated Service conversations reflect growing trust in the IT organization, it is also the responsibility of IT to proactively initiate regular, organized conversations both internal to IT and with senior business leaders to review IT Service value and plan future Service delivery requirements.

A Strategy for Communicating IT Service Value

The Service value communication strategy of the ITaaS framework establishes a formal structure for the review of Service value with stakeholders. Within this strategy, Service Reviews act as the initial, primary vehicle for driving consistent and highly productive Service value conversations.

The purpose of Service Reviews is to generate a detailed information report for and, in most cases, facilitate a live conversation with three key parties to refine the initial view of Service value provided by IT and then plan future Service delivery. Although some Services may simply share the report and then incorporate feedback, the effects of having these three distinct parties present at the same table on a regular, recurring basis (typically quarterly), supported with the right information, working through an agenda focused on assessing and continuously improving IT Service value, cannot be understated. These parties include

- **Service Delivery Team:** The Service Owner, Service Executive, Service Architect, and any Service offering managers as required

- **IT Leadership:** Relevant IT leaders up to and potentially including the CIO

- **Service Customer Stakeholders:** Representatives for customers of the Service who actively consume and rely on the technical capabilities delivered by the Service either for productivity, business operations, or delivery of another IT Service

The Service Owner carries a significant level of responsibility with regard to Service Reviews, including ensuring the right mix of customer stakeholders and IT leaders is present. The customer stakeholders for a Service vary based on Service type. For Technology Foundation Service types, this effort is often simplified because the stakeholders are primarily represented by fellow IT professionals acting as Service Owners for Services consuming capabilities from the Service being reviewed.

Enterprise End-Customer Services, however, provide technical capabilities that enable productivity across the enterprise. As such, identifying a representative group of stakeholders can be challenging. In many cases, these reviews are hosted as IT internal-only Service Reviews, with stakeholders across the enterprise attending whenever major proposals are anticipated or when significant issues and concerns have arisen surrounding the capabilities delivered by the Service. Identifying an ideal mix of stakeholders is of the utmost importance for Business Operations Service types, because these stakeholders rely on the capabilities they consume through IT Services to operate and achieve business outcomes. In many cases, these individuals cannot be successful without IT's support. Senior leaders for teams that rely on these Services for their operations are the most obvious, but it can be equally important to include resources from various areas and levels of a BU.

It is also important that the Service Owner bring together all relevant IT leaders. Although the presence of the CIO is preferred for select Services, it is rarely possible in all cases. When not available, an empowered designee such as a Service Executive must be present. Also, note that it may be necessary to include Service Owners from chained Services, along with managers and directors across the IT organization who oversee the management of resources, assets, processes, and budgets that enable the Service. While the Service Owner can speak for these IT internal parties when necessary, it is always ideal to have these parties at the same table on a recurring basis especially when aspects of Service delivery that their resources enable represent a focus of conversation. As an example, the presence of a functional manager for a specialized IT support team may be required as part of a three-way discussion around improving Service quality, either by optimizing processes or adding additional resources to the support team.

Although the exact makeup of these three parties is likely to change over time it is important that all three be represented, even if an IT leader needs to advocate on behalf of the customer base, such as for an Enterprise End-Customer Service. Remember that the earliest Service Reviews—those conducted during the Service pilot phase of the transformation program—are likely to be hosted with restricted participation as the transformation team and first-ever Service Owners refine their approach and material.

With the ideal participants at the table, the next requirement of the Service Owner is acting as a conversational bridge between IT and the Service stakeholders. Remember, while IT leaders are actively managing teams, budgets, and processes to enable any number of IT Services, the Service Owner is responsible for acting as the general manager of the individual Service being reviewed, and as such represents the most knowledgeable subject matter expert. The Service Owner owns the agenda and acts as both a translator and mediator as the conversation progresses through a review of Service Performance, cost, and finally planning.

Structuring a Service Review

In this section, we introduce the basic template for Service Reviews, which we recommend IT Transformation teams begin with and then optimize over time:

- Top of mind
- Key Service topics

- Service Performance review

- Review of Service TCO

- Capabilities roadmap

The Service Review structure as shown is intended foremost to allow for the high-level examination of all aspects of a Service. In most cases, this report is built in slides and then submitted for review by IT and business stakeholders. Service Owners may choose to omit either of the first two segments, but Service Performance, Service TCO, and an updated capabilities roadmap are always required.

The "top of mind" segment is best treated as "what keeps me up at night." It's an opportunity for a Service Owner to raise awareness for any topic necessary, and I regularly encourage Service Owners to take advantage of it. Use bold statements here and dive right into the most-challenging conversations first. Topics shared in this segment should be considered "need to know" for all stakeholders.

The "key Service topics" section acts as an open-format opportunity for Service Owners to share brief updates on programs, projects, or activities that impact the Service but that do not necessarily require extensive review or conversation. Service Owners are generally allowed two to three pages or slides to cover these topics but should not go in depth or be overly technical on any topic. Additional information can always be shared or reviewed outside the Service Review when necessary; this segment is intended strictly as an informational update on Service-relevant but not Service-critical topics.

The review of Service Performance should open with the performance dashboard, which may involve either an imported graphic or a link to a live Service Performance dashboard platform display. The key is that stakeholders are provided a strategic overview of Service Performance via a top-down look at the five Service Metric categories and their associated KPIs, targets, benchmarks, and baselines. From there, all Business Operations Services should provide an additional section of content that links applicable Service Metrics to their impact on business processes and outcomes. In the initial one to two years after introducing Service Reviews, this section can easily generate an extensive amount of conversation, and it is not uncommon for Service Owners to include additional pages focused on a specific metric category and any number of Service Metrics that impact the overall KPIs.

The three-block TCO model is another requirement for any Service Review submission because it adds an additional layer of conversation to Service Performance. Here again, Service Owners may choose to include additional slides or pages detailing each of the three cost blocks.

Finally, the Service capabilities roadmaps, introduced in Chapter 5, "Mapping Enterprise Technical Capability Requirements," are reviewed and updated. This section of the review should always highlight the introduction or discontinuation of Service capabilities and not technical project or asset lifecycle roadmaps. Although early Service Reviews are likely to focus on performance and costs, this section is still required for all submissions. Over time the focus will shift predominately to this section and likely give way to dedicated Service architecture reviews, but it is critical that the opportunity to engage the three parties in conversation on capability planning be established from the earliest Service Reviews.

Establishing a Process for Service Reviews

A strategy for Service Reviews should include a formal process, approved by the CIO and senior IT leaders, establishing expectations for information, formatting, frequency, and reporting of Service Reviews. For example, the process may require all Service Owners to develop a Service Review information pack using a specified template that includes a time-stamped Service Performance dashboard and the TCO for the reporting period, among other information requirements.

Some enterprises leverage a two-stage submission. In this process, all Service Owners submit their Service Review documents, which are then reviewed and approved by the Service Executives, IT leaders, and CIO, before a subset (typically customer-facing Business Operations Services) is then copied to an additional location accessible by customer stakeholders. The submission process and deadlines should also be included and are based on the Service reporting periods. Many enterprises leverage quarterly Service Review periods, but some have adopted additional strategies that include mechanisms by which a Service can be designated as mission-critical and subjected to a higher frequency of Service Reviews and additional reporting requirements.

Generation and submission of a Service Review do not necessitate a formal three-party presentation and review of the content. In other words, any number of Service Reviews may be generated and then shared to all stakeholders for review; but they may not warrant hosting a formal three-party review session in-person or via conference. Although the importance and long-term value of hosting a three-party review of a Service cannot be understated, it's unrealistic to expect a presentation and three-party review of each and every Service defined in the portfolio. Recall that the total number of Services can scale from 15 to 150, depending on the size and complexity of the enterprise, making it impossible for IT to facilitate such a large number of meetings before the next reporting period is reached. IT and business leaders across the enterprise may simply not have the bandwidth in their schedules to participate in a large number of three-party Service Reviews. With this in mind, it is important to develop an idea for the number of Service Reviews, both customer-facing and IT internal, that can be supported for a given reporting period and then review a series of considerations to prioritize those Services that need to host a live Service Review and three-party conversation.

The Service Review process should establish criteria that trigger a live Service Review—for example, missed performance targets or overrun cost forecasts that prioritize specific Services for review. Service precedence with the customer base and senior IT leaders obviously provide an additional consideration for hosting Service Reviews, such as a Service on-boarding new capabilities deemed critical to success in the marketplace. Although these Services are easiest to identify and schedule sessions for, criteria must be established for Service Owners to proactively escalate their Service for review at any time they deem it necessary. With such a large landscape of Services, there has to be an efficient way for Service Owners to submit Service Review information packs to distinguish between "situation normal" and "we need to talk." In short, there are three considerations for identifying Services as candidates for scheduling and hosting three-party Service Reviews:

- Service visibility/priority based on IT or business leader input

- Reporting criteria (missed targets, costs exceeding 5 percent of forecast, and so on)

- Service Owner–initiated review

In some circumstances, a Service may be required to host both an IT internal and then a customer-facing Service Review. These scenarios should not be limited to IT leaders hoping to preview content prior to presenting to customers. Rather, this approach is leveraged to respect the separate yet equally important priorities for leaders in IT and the business. For example, the scheduled time for a customer-facing Service Review may be easily consumed by stakeholder focus on a specific Service offering or the performance related to a specific capability. At the same time, the CIO may wish to dig into strategies for reducing direct Service costs or evaluate how shifting personnel resources may impact select metric categories. Allowing for the option of split Service Reviews for different stakeholder groups ensures each group can accommodate the aspects of a Service most important to it.

The target length of Service Reviews represents another element in the broader strategy, and determines how many can host live conversations rather than simply gathering feedback on submitted reviews by the three parties. In the long term, effective Service Reviews can be hosted in a 20-minute time frame. While it may sound like a minimal amount of time, as all three parties become familiar with the format, Service Performance dashboard, TCO model, and capabilities roadmap, the conversations become more focused. In fact, some IT organizations leverage strategies for IT internal Service Reviews that call for a number of Service Owners to facilitate 5–10-minute sessions purely focused on addressing key aspects of the Service raised by stakeholders ahead of the session. Note that customer-facing Business Operations Service Reviews, when hosted, should typically target a minimum 20-minute session. The key to remember is that there is no magic time frame, and these numbers are purely prescriptive for long-term expectations. It is important to remain flexible and keep the focus on the goal of facilitating constructive conversations about IT Service value.

The Service pilot workstream of the Services Transformation Program is key in formulating, testing, and fine-tuning the approach, templates, and supporting tools (automated reporting of costs, performance, and so on) for Service Reviews. The customer base for a given Service is unlikely to become fully accustomed to the IT organization's new approach to Service delivery and Service Reviews until they've participated in a number of sessions, but it is important that these reviews begin as effectively as possible.

Following is a sample initial process for IT Service Reviews. Although these processes are typically hosted as a formal document managed by the Service management office, the process is presented here in simple list format that can be tailored before developing and publishing a formal process document:

- The reporting period for Service Reviews is quarterly, based on the corporate calendar year.

- Service Reviews provide a complete analysis of key aspects of the Service for the recently closed quarter.

- All Service Reviews are published to the shared folder x://IT Service Reviews/ QXYXX corresponding to the appropriate quarter and year.

- Service Reviews must use the most recent template posted to the shared folder x://IT Service Reviews/Template.

- All Service Reviews must be published to the shared drive by the end of the first week following the close of the quarter.

- Service Owners managing Services that meet any of the following criteria should proactively alert their senior stakeholders:

    - TCO exceeded a percentage of forecast

    - A Service Performance metric category KPI falls below baseline

    - Negative impact to capability roadmaps (identify the reason)

- Service Executives and IT senior Service stakeholders have one week to review the published Service Reviews and request follow-up actions or Service Review presentations that will be scheduled by the IT Service management team.

- Service Reviews are published to IT external stakeholders for review by the beginning of the third week after quarter close, and they have up to two weeks to request a follow-up or Service Review presentation that is scheduled by the IT Service management team.

In practice, this basic process means Service Owners are incredibly busy the first week after the quarter's close, even more so when relying on manual processes to generate Service Performance dashboards and Service TCO models. The process timeline has to be somewhat aggressive; otherwise, key input and Service planning decisions may not take place until well into the current quarter. Service Owners need to engage their Service Executives as early as possible and notify them of any Service topics likely to require review or presentation.

Service Review Best Practices

This section describes a number of strategies, tactics, lessons learned, and best practices for successfully implementing Service Reviews and realizing the value outcomes they are capable of creating. Although cost reductions, performance improvements, and roadmap planning may at first seem like the target value outcomes, in reality, the conversations that are initiated and the relationships between IT and its customer base are the real value outcomes of this topic.

Winning Early Support Through Service Reviews

As with earlier components of the Services Transformation Program, the initial success of transitioning Service Reviews into practice can either win broad support for the new approach to IT Service delivery or sow disenchantment and mute future interest for the transformation work. The proper change leadership strategies play a critical role in determining which path an IT organization finds itself on.

In earlier chapters, we established that Service pilots cannot simply focus on Technology Foundation Services and hide within IT internal-only Service Reviews. Instead, they should target sample Services across all three Service types and represent both IT internal and customer-facing Services. Change leadership teams work with the broader IT Transformation team to develop an initial proposal for candidate Services. From there, the change leadership team reaches out to potential customer stakeholders to gauge the level of willingness to support the first ever pilot Service Reviews.

This initial outreach should not be a simple request but instead include a well-crafted and concise communication describing the information contained in the Service Review, along with the advantages and goals of the three-party conversation. It should also stress the importance that participation in Service Reviews will have on shaping future Service delivery and the value it drives for the stakeholder in question.

When engaging potential stakeholders in support of the initial pilot Service Reviews, be sure to stress that these are early endeavors and that the feedback and lessons learned will be used to shape the longer-term strategy. It is important to set the expectation that the approach, format, and presentation may be rough at first but that IT and the Service Owner are actively seeking to improve and ensure they enable the most valuable review of a Service possible. As change leadership teams develop an outlook on appropriate stakeholders most willing to support and contribute constructive feedback, that information can be fed back to the broader IT Transformation team and help shape the sequence of pilot Services. Even with the understanding of stakeholders that the strategy will improve over time, it is still important that IT be thoroughly prepared. As such, transformation teams should leverage IT internal mock Service Reviews.

Take care not to internally rehearse these reviews for too long before engaging the stakeholder. It is important to host several internal-only (IT Transformation team and Service Owner) rehearsals just as with any presentation to get a feel for timing and content. Role-playing senior IT and business stakeholders can also help ensure a Service Owner is in the right mindset. After one to two rehearsals are complete, however, it's time to engage the stakeholders and test the approach. *Always remember the goal is to make a strong initial showing, and not a perfect showing; that's what the stakeholder input is for.*

From the Diary of an ITaaS Consultant

Helping IT Transformation teams and Service Owners prepare for the initial rounds of Service Reviews is by far one of the most entertaining aspects of any Services Transformation Program. At this stage in a transformation program, an initial shift in the mindset of the team for delivering IT Services has begun to set in as a result of the ETC mapping, Service design, and other efforts. Whereas these workstreams have acted as gentle introductions, rehearsing for and launching the first Service Reviews effectively push IT teams fully into the new philosophy for IT Service delivery.

Preparing Service Owners to think like their customer and to anticipate the questions, concerns, and priorities of a customer is where the real fun begins. I spend a lot of time in these rehearsals cutting off any topics that veer into technical operations, ensuring the presentation stays above the Service level, as we discussed in Chapter 4, "Service Delivery Taxonomy and Definition of a Service." I've even employed an annoying buzzer anytime a customer is referred to as anything but a customer or stakeholder. I may regularly interrupt a rehearsal, role-playing a senior customer stakeholder, asking, "What does any of this have to do with my team and my operations?" I'm not above quietly enlisting additional team members, even passing along scripted questions intended to catch the Service Owner off guard. This approach can be quite jarring to most newly indoctrinated Service Owners, but appointing several members of the IT Transformation team to play the role of a feisty devil's advocate is key to establishing the right mindset prior to engaging the stakeholders. Just be sure to always execute this exchange with an air of good-natured, constructive preparation for the real thing.

The goal is obviously not to be unnecessarily cruel or discouraging to these first-time volunteers to take on the responsibility of Service Owner, but the reality is that these Service Reviews set the tone for the new culture of IT Service delivery directly with the customer base. This change can be difficult, and a bit of a shock for some IT professionals, even for those who have been incredibly successful in the traditional technology-centric operation of an IT organization. In fact, it is at this stage in a transformation program when it may become clear that some individuals simply aren't willing to embrace a new mindset critical to Services Transformation and an eventual Fast IT organization. That said, it is important to bring along everyone possible. In that regard, after all the playful yet instructive rehearsals and after the initial presentation with stakeholders is done and the lessons learned are being compiled, be sure to take a moment to reward the team and acknowledge what's taking place with Service transformation and why.

I've found that happy hours work great too, both as a reward and a good opportunity to candidly acknowledge the impact of the team's efforts to the long-term success of the IT organization. Be sure to do the same for your teams.

Guidance for Service Owners

The two most important principles for successful Service Reviews are transparency and trust. Transparency has been emphasized for both Service Performance and cost modeling strategies but requires the Service Owner to demonstrate in practice through Service Reviews. Trust is earned over time, by the Service Owner facilitating desired outcomes, guiding stakeholders, and improving the value of the Service.

Whether presenting a live presentation or simply submitting a Service Review, Service Owners should always proactively prepare for the questions and concerns that the review is likely to raise with each stakeholder. *A golden rule for Service Owners with regard to Service Reviews: Never be caught off-guard by a stakeholder question in your Service Review.* To prepare for this, remember to think like the CEO of your IT Service.

Next, Service Owners should remain conscious of various tactics for successful Service Reviews. For example, with regard to topics you choose to include in the "top of mind" or "key Service topics" session, ask yourself, "What do I need from the stakeholder in regard to this topic?" In practice, the three-party Service Reviews would highlight these topics to achieve one of the following with stakeholders:

- **Escalation:** The issue requires escalation to the stakeholder, or support from the stakeholders is required to escalate the issue across other parties in IT or the business teams.

- **Decision:** A decision needs to be made or supported by the stakeholders.

- **Awareness:** The stakeholders need to remain actively aware of the topic for the remainder of the reporting period.

Always be clear about the needs. Also, never present a Service challenge or issue without accompanying it with a series of proposed recommendations to address the issue. When possible, include multiple options, highlighting strengths and constraints to each and making clear your recommended option and what is then needed from the stakeholders to move forward.

Above all, Service Owners should keep it simple and keep it focused on the capabilities provided by the Service and the outcomes they enable rather than on technology. You will have all manner of team and project meetings in which to delve into technical details, but the Service Review is a conversation focused on how technology impacts the stakeholder or business outcomes. Continuously ask yourself, "What does this mean to my customer? Why do they care?"

From the Diary of an ITaaS Consultant

As I've alluded to previously, the best reward when working with various teams is witnessing that cultural shift and the philosophies for IT Service delivery change, and this is always on full display throughout early Service Reviews. There is a point when the Service Owners not only get it but they adopt the new philosophy and then charge ahead with it, adding creative new ideas and spins to communicating IT Service value with little to no input or guidance.

In one instance, I had spent the previous week rejecting Service Reviews loaded with detailed technical architecture diagrams, a long-time "go-to" for IT pros to fill slides and presentation time. And yet while preparing a Service Review for a Technology Foundation Service, the Service Owner clicked to a slide fully taken up by an incredibly complex technical architecture diagram. There were dozens of icons and five times as many connections between each and just as many indecipherable labels. I was so caught off-guard by the graphic that before I was able to throw my buzzer at this particular Service Owner, he stated, "The only thing anyone here needs to understand about this drawing is that it's obviously and hopelessly complex, which is why before the next reporting period we're moving to this architecture." At this point, he clicked to another architecture diagram. This one included only a fraction of the icons, organized into layers with clear connections. "This simplification should decrease authentication times for your teams and address a range of other Service Performance metrics in quality and customer experience that we'll dig into on the following slides."

This Service Owner got it, and the clever approach had the desired impact on the audience when presented live. It also demonstrated that this particular Service Owner understood the need to minimize diverging into a discussion of technology and instead focus on how capabilities delivered by the Service would be impacted.

Guidance for IT Leaders

We should take a moment here to acknowledge the sheer opportunity and potential of the three-party Service value conversations. You now have an ideal mix of IT resources and stakeholders, along with a Service Owner acting as the general manager of the Service and able to leverage a complete strategy for measuring Service value, with a prioritized focus on how the Service impacts customers and business operations. That is a profound culmination of opportunities compared to the relationships in today's IT organizations. Take full advantage. It's a chance for all three parties to become equal partners in driving Service value that has historically not been available to IT leaders.

The questions and conversations you drive in early Service Reviews will shape longer term behanviors. Adopt a line of questioning that ensures Service Owners are looking at all aspects of Service Performance. Drive the Service Owners to continuously look for the next opportunity to increase Service value either through continuous reduction of Service costs or the introduction of transformative capabilities. IT leaders play an important role in setting the tone and expectation for Service Owners and Service delivery teams.

For business-facing Service Reviews, be prepared to engage wildly different concerns, goals, and priorities as you transition through enterprise lines of business and then corporate function business units (HR, finance, etc). Each has its own concerns, but you now have a distributed Service delivery team to track and manage these divergent priorities. Your main priority is how best to improve Service delivery end-to-end while always steering the IT organization like a competitive business.

General Service Review Guidance

I strongly recommend attempting to rotate through live three-party Service Review presentations for every Service at least once after a Service is designated. It is important for each Service Owner to get face time (or video-conference time at a minimum) with the stakeholders to begin developing these critical relationships.

Work with senior stakeholders to consider extending the audience and broaden the relationship base for the Service delivery team. There can be a disconnect between senior business stakeholders and their operational teams, which highlights another value opportunity for Service delivery teams to build new relationships. Historically, business teams may have raised alarms regarding various technical capabilities and escalated those issues to their leadership teams but then failed to notify those same leaders when an issue was addressed. While it is key to have senior stakeholders review submitted Service Reviews and present for any three-way presentations of the Service Review, consider adding various additional members of the business teams. Some have even added a rotating invitation of various managers and team leads. Adding this mix of insight into the already-robust three-party review of Service value can provide all-new levels of insight and opportunity to create additional value and build broader relationships with the business.

Consider openly publishing Service Reviews or allowing wide access to Service Performance and Service costing platforms, at least to view information that would be shared in a Service Review at the end of the reporting period. Assuring transparency and openly sharing details of IT Service delivery are essential building blocks for encouraging further cooperation with IT and use of IT Services, and will be key in the future Fast IT organization.

It is important to improve on all Service Reviews over time, and in support of this effort, the change leadership team should actively collect feedback from Service Review submissions and participate in any three-party reviews to collect and then share lessons learned. This feedback can also be key in shaping and prioritizing Service delivery and management platforms and tools. As always, the best way to improve is to begin as strong as possible, be open to feedback, and then get even better over time.

Evolving Service Value Conversations

The implementation of Service Reviews represents a significant milestone in a Services Transformation and establishing the IT organization as a trusted advisor over time. Just like the Service portfolio and other aspects of the ITaaS framework, it must be subjected to continuous improvement strategies and allowed to evolve over time to continue to create value for the IT organization and enterprise business. Having a long-term vision for how the strategy can evolve will help IT leaders monitor the current approach and anticipate when best to consider changes.

Up to this point, we have focused on individual Service Reviews. Even if it is not prioritized for a live presentation and conversation, this means each Service in the portfolio submits a Service Review to IT leaders and stakeholders and incorporates feedback.

There is an incredible amount of Service optimization, cost savings, performance improvement, and customer satisfaction to be realized by simply focusing on individual Service Reviews for upward of 16–24 months or longer. This is simply a natural result of making use of the ITaaS framework's Service design to whittle away duplication, align current and future capabilities, achieve desired levels of performance, and finally support informed cost planning through an understandable Service TCO. During this time, Service Owners and Service delivery teams forge close partnerships, and planning and operation of IT Services naturally become more fluid and agile.

Over time, however, what was initially an incredible outreach by the IT organization to completely transform its approach to Service delivery becomes a well-appreciated but expected model for operation. As trust is built, informal communication begins to flow in both directions on a regular basis, outside of formal Service Reviews. Eventually, what were once highly interactive Service Reviews now may become tedious reviews of details already well known across all parties. In other words, the IT organization is now actively fulfilling its role and meeting the expectations of a basic Service provider, which means it's now time to create additional value.

One of the first stages of evolution is likely to be the introduction of strategic Service Reviews and related presentations, relying on Service Executives to conduct a review of related Services for the most senior IT and business leaders. Fully detailed Service Reviews are still generated for every individual Service, which a Service Executive then leverages to develop the strategic Service Review. Some Service groups may rely only on the presentation of a strategic Service Review, only on individual Service Reviews, or a mix of both.

At some stage, IT leaders need to consider transforming the core Service Review process. This task typically takes the form of branching traditional Service Reviews into Service checkpoints and Service architecture reviews.

Service checkpoints act like a Cliffs Notes version of a Service Review. Their success relies on the principle that all parties are familiar with the Service delivery framework and the information commonly discussed in a Service Review. This means that only specific aspects of a given Service need to be reviewed and allows Service delivery teams to schedule Service checkpoints as blocks of time during which Service Owners address requested topics in 5–10 minute blocks.

As IT Service delivery and alignment are improved over time, the focus of Service value conversations between a Service Owner and stakeholder shifts from Service Performance and costs to future Service requirements and the identification and development of transformative technical capabilities. In other words, the conversations take a natural shift toward Service architecture. By introducing formal Service architecture reviews, IT organizations can support this focal shift. Formal strategies for Service architecture reviews also ensure that while IT responds in an agile manner at the Service level to capability opportunities, overall alignment to the broader enterprise architecture strategy is maintained.

This is accomplished by again fostering a three-party conversation, this time between the customer stakeholders, key members of the enterprise architecture team, and the Service delivery team, including the Service Owner and obviously the Service Architect.

Note that formal reviews for a single Service may be warranted in some cases but can quickly become a burden. Here again, we can leverage the Service taxonomy model and host Service architecture reviews at a strategic level, working through a group of related Services in one session. This approach grants the EA team the high-level visibility it needs to maintain a consistent architecture and provides another source of information for Services in another Service group seeking similar capabilities.

The key is that IT leaders and the Service delivery team view IT Service value conversations as a continuously evolving formal and informal communications strategy. These conversations lay the foundation for strong relationships between IT and the enterprise business, but like any relationship, it's important to keep the conversations meaningful and interesting.

Summary

Effective communication and constructive review of the value an IT Service provides are long-sought-after capabilities for today's IT organizations, and a great deal of Cisco's ITaaS framework represents a support structure for facilitating these conversations and the relationships they can foster. A strategy for IT Service value communication should acknowledge the importance of both formal and informal conversations between IT and business stakeholders and the Service delivery teams (Service Executives, Service Architects, and Service offering managers). The core of the formal strategy revolves around Service Reviews but should evolve over time to include Service checkpoints and Service architecture reviews.

A formal process should be adopted that streamlines the submission, review, and presentation of Service Reviews with three distinct parties: the Service delivery team, IT leadership, and customer stakeholders. Service Owners play a significant role in the preparation and delivery of Service Reviews and must be thoroughly prepared to engage their stakeholders. Change leadership plays an important role in introducing Service Reviews and winning further support for the three-party Service value conversations and overarching Services Transformation Program.

The basic structure of a Service Review, shown here, provides a blueprint for successful Service value conversations:

- Top of mind
- Key Service topics
- Service Performance review
- Review of Service TCO
- Capabilities roadmap

Both Service Owners and IT leaders should remain conscious of the opportunity and potential created by the three-party conversations, and ensure they take every advantage to align IT Service delivery to the current and future needs of the customer base and continue to deliver higher levels of value to the enterprise business.

Chapter 11

Completing the Services Transformation

At this stage of the Services Transformation Program, all major components of the ITaaS framework have been implemented and are likely in the process of being optimized, but there is a lot more work yet to be done in order to finalize the Service delivery function of the IT operating model. With that in mind, this chapter acts as a primer for the broad and extensive efforts associated with the final phase of Services Transformation.

We begin with a review of the final phase, Phase 3, of the Services Transformation Program and its distinct workstreams. Although the efforts outlined in this section may not strike IT Transformation teams as significant as designing a Service taxonomy or portfolio, they are nonetheless critical to the long-term success of the Service delivery framework and represent a significant series of parallel efforts for the IT organization.

This review segues naturally into a top-down review of the many strategies, processes, and tools that ultimately support a complete enterprise IT Service delivery framework. Many of these were popularized by popular Service management standards and are common in today's IT Organizations. Some, such as an asset database or application portfolio, have not been discussed yet and will not be impacted largely by the ITaaS framework but will nonetheless play an important role in Service delivery. In some other cases the ITaaS framework necessitates a reevaluation of the purpose and best value contribution of a common tool to the new Service delivery framework. IT Service Catalogs in particular will be shifted to play a key role in associating a flexible range of information with customer request portals and ensuring those requests are mapped back to a Service while allowing the Service portfolio to remain a strategic Service planning tool.

A common theme throughout this chapter is for the IT organization to become fully "Services-aware." This means potentially updating any number of processes and tools across IT to include support for Service mappings, and considering how to ensure that those that cannot be updated can still be linked to Services. After all, how can IT truly consider itself to be an end-to-end Service organization if large segments of its operations aren't Service-aware?

The Final Phase of Services Transformation

Looking back at our review of Cisco's Services Transformation Program in Chapter 2, "Introducing Cisco's ITaaS Framework and Transformation Program," we emphasized that Phase 3 represented a considerable amount of parallel work to bring the framework for Service delivery together. In addition to ongoing change leadership, which is very active during this phase, the Services Transformation Program establishes three distinct work packages:

- End-to-End Service Reviews

- Service Delivery Optimization

- Service-Aware Organization

The work package for end-to-end Service Reviews entails onboarding every remaining Service defined in the portfolio. Onboarding a Service covers designating a Service Owner and associated Service delivery team, who are then tasked with pulling together a Service-unique performance strategy and the Service TCO. At this stage in the transformation program, the processes for developing these Service elements should be well refined, and faster to mature for an individual Service. Be sure to leverage not just the IT Transformation and change leadership teams but also the now-experienced first waves of Service Owners and Service delivery teams. These IT professionals have unique and valued experience in truly owning a Service and engaging IT and business stakeholders. Note that teams managing similar Service types always support the best collaborative guidance. Change leadership materials and messaging at this stage should also be well refined; now it is simply a matter of scaling those efforts across the remainder of the Service landscape.

Service delivery optimization represents another significant effort. It acts as a stimulus to begin finalizing, documenting, and optimizing the processes and tools that have been developed thus far. Optimization should focus heavily on efforts to automate processes and reporting for Service Performance and Service TCO, and especially generating summary-level reporting for Strategic Service Groups for use by Service Executives and IT leaders. Several rounds of Service Reviews should have now been presented and hosted and lessons learned collected, incorporated, and shared. This is an ideal time to update and refine all the strategies and processes developed thus far, before then documenting and publishing the most up-to-date standards. Here again, the IT transformation team should not represent sole ownership for these many tasks but should instead act as oversight. An underlying goal is to transition the ongoing life of the Service delivery framework from the IT Transformation team to the Service management office and broader IT organization.

Finally, the Service-aware organization work package acts as an explicit call to action for moving all aspects of the IT organization and its operations to be mapped back to Services. At this stage, all core strategies and processes for the new IT Service delivery framework are in place and rapidly expanding to include Services end-to-end across the enterprise, which in turn allows for the opportunity to begin aligning the whole of the IT organization to the continuous delivery and optimization of those Services. A common effort within this workstream is to update or augment existing processes and tools to become "Service-aware," meaning that reporting and other elements of various platforms supporting IT operations can be mapped to one or more Services defined in the portfolio. As an example, consider an application portfolio or IT asset database and the value of having the elements documented by these platforms mapped to Services, which enables reporting by Service or Service group. Many of these existing tools and platforms can be updated with Service mappings through existing optional or extensible data fields, but others may require export and external processing to apply Service mappings.

Operating as an end-to-end Services organization entails a great deal more than simply the addition of Service mappings to tools to ensure they are Service-aware whenever possible. While the ITaaS framework distributes responsibility for Service delivery and ownership across a wider community of the IT organization, every member of the IT organization should now recognize the focus on Services. This is true even if they are not directly associated with a Service delivery role defined by the ITaaS framework. IT personnel purely focused on operations or support still need to understand that they are part of an organization that is mobilized for the delivery of business value through IT Services. The change leadership team, along with support and engagement from the CIO down across all levels of leadership, play a critical role in establishing this mindset. At this phase of the transformation program, there should be a significant number of achievements, success stories, and role models to point to in order to justify the adoption of this mindset. The underlying goal of this workstream is for everything possible in the IT organization—its people, its strategies, its processes, and its tools—to become Services-aware.

Overview of a Complete IT Service Delivery Model

This book has covered a number of strategies, processes, tools, and even roles and responsibilities for IT Service delivery but is still well short of providing a comprehensive review of every potential supporting element of an enterprise IT Service delivery function. Instead, only those elements unique to Cisco's ITaaS framework have received focus so far, but it is important for us to consider the overall framework for IT Service delivery and the necessity for Service-aware tools and reporting. This section also looks at several best practices for leveraging these elements specific to supporting Service delivery based on the ITaaS framework.

Consider Figure 11-1, which lays out a basic overview of the major tools and artifacts likely present in today's IT organizations in support of Service delivery and a potential flow of information between each.

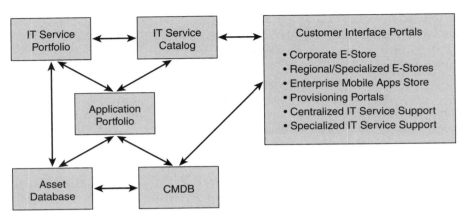

Figure 11-1 *IT Service Management Tools Landscape*

From the Service portfolio, we can derive a complete set of IT Services and Service offerings responsible for delivering technical capabilities end-to-end across the enterprise. Some of these technical capabilities are available for customers to request or subscribe to through various customer request portals. These potential requests are aggregated into an IT Service catalog and associated with additional information, while maintaining their Service mapping, before then being made available directly to the customer base via those subsequent customer portals. Several upcoming sections provide complete detail on developing a Service catalog, but the key to understand is that Service mapping must be maintained end-to-end. This means that when a customer request is made, it is associated with a specific IT Service offering, Service, and Service Owner.

Application portfolios are leveraged by IT organizations to inventory the hundreds of applications leveraged across an enterprise and associate each with relevant information. This information may include the license and support costs and associated details along with lifecycle information, technical information such as whether the application is hosted or a standalone installation on an end-customer device, and other application-specific details. In some deployments, the application portfolio may be linked to an asset database or even exist as a subset. A centralized inventory listing all applications deployed across the enterprise and key information allows an IT organization to administer the application landscape while protecting against widespread duplication of application assets.

Application portfolios create even further value within the ITaaS framework, assuming they can be made Service-aware. This will become clear as IT Transformation teams attempt to develop cost-chaining processes, as detailed in Chapter 9, "Modeling the Total Costs of IT Service Delivery." For example, consider the cost-chaining process for a cloud Application Hosting Service. The Service Owner likely has visibility to the resources consumed by specific applications, and separately has a process for calculating the cost of that consumption, but how would they know which Service to chain the costs of each application to? The addition of Service mappings to the application portfolio would support the proper assignment of these costs, along with reporting and numerous other valuable capabilities for Service delivery teams.

In addition to Service mappings, consider allowing for the inclusion of numerous additional fields, allowing Service Owners to leverage the application portfolio as a strategic tool. Some of the recommended fields include both summary-level and detailed descriptions of the application, and also a reference to the technical capabilities the application provides, potentially even linking directly to required capabilities identified within the ETC map. A later section reviews strategies for minimizing duplication of capabilities across the enterprise, and this information, maintained by Service Owners, is critical in supporting those efforts. Key information fields can also be associated with each application for Service Performance characteristics, allowing Service Owners to indicate requirements for IT operations teams to then facilitate. As an example, a Service Owner could indicate quality- and risk-associated parameters such as whether data should be backed up or encrypted. The important point is to recognize the potential of the application portfolio within the ITaaS framework not only as a valuable inventory but as a strategic tool supporting broader Service delivery and IT operations.

An IT organization should also employ an asset database or inventory platform for all IT assets. These inventory platforms allow the IT organization to track and manage all IT assets spanning applications, servers, data storage devices, networking equipment, and much more; and then associate each asset with relevant information that can be leveraged in a number of ways. Closely related to IT asset databases are configuration management databases (CMDBs), which inventory varying sets of configuration parameters associated with an IT asset at a given point in time.

Each of these tools can be closely associated with both technical operations and Service delivery functions of an IT operating model, and in fact can be invaluable for technical teams in support of Service Owners. CMDBs can be critical to investigations into decreasing levels of Service quality, and reporting made available from IT asset databases enables efficient lifecycle management reporting or security assessments that make up the Risk Service Metric category. Although the information maintained by these various tools can support both Service delivery and technical operations functions, this is true only if the information is accurate, which requires that IT teams adhere to strict processes and facilitate easy access for updating data.

Recall that in Chapter 6, "Service Design and Building the IT Service Portfolio," we established the IT Service portfolio as a strategic tool for IT leaders by restricting to some degree the content associated with it. The addition of Service mappings and other key information to existing tools like application portfolios and asset databases provides Service delivery teams with the valuable insight required to effectively manage Services without cluttering the Service portfolio. An end-to-end Services organization has to be supported by a complete set of Service-aware tools and processes, and although this section only looked at several potential considerations, it is critical that IT Transformation teams evaluate their complete environment and add functionality (awareness) for Services where needed.

Service Catalogs and Customer Request Portals

Many existing standards for IT Service management leverage an IT Service catalog. Within many of these standards the portfolio maintains a listing of active, retired, and pipeline or in-development Services, with those Services that are currently active representing the IT Service catalog. This IT Service catalog is then commonly leveraged to populate a corporate e-store, which customers across the enterprise can access to submit various IT requests. The technical capabilities available on these e-stores represent very specific and repeatable requests from the IT organization, such as provisioning and delivery of a specific model of laptop, installation of an application, or a request for IT administrators to reset a password.

Adoption of e-stores for facilitating matured, repeatable IT requests created a great deal of value for IT organizations and their customers as a broad range of requests could now be submitted, tracked, managed, and completed in significantly less time as backend workflows were optimized and automated. Their presence opened the door to wider adoption of self-provisioning systems leading to higher levels of customer satisfaction; they are still important today. It is important to remember however that IT requests capable of being hosted on various customer portals like an e-store represent only a small segment of the capabilities delivered by today's IT organizations, and that the central goal of the ITaaS framework is to designate Services end-to-end.

Besides a much broader range of Services at play there are other considerations necessitating the need for not so closely linking the portfolio, catalog, and an e-store. In order to properly present options to customers and manage backend workflow a significant amount of information typically needs to be associated with an IT request, ranging from pricing and build options to one-time and recurring costs, and even to specific SLAs. The type of information required will also vary significantly depending on the type of request. A solution is needed that allows for IT requests to be documented along with a large set of flexible information, while at the same time carefully restricting the information managed by the Service portfolio so that it remains a strategic tool.

Also consider that IT customers now need access to a wider range of technical capabilities that may not always be capable of being hosted on a single company wide e-store. Customers may need to access a special portal for loading enterprise mobile apps to smartphones and tablets, or to provision and launch several virtual machines (VMs) through a Cloud provisioning portal. Ideally a potential IT request should be capable of being hosted on one or more customer portals while not fully duplicating all of the information associated with it.

Another potential challenge is that the historically close relation of portfolio, catalog, and customer portal like an e-store can potentially create a platform dependency that in turn drives changes to the strategy for Service delivery. If the features and support on a given platform for a customer portal are changed, or the underlying platform itself, is changed out by the enterprise, it could drive changes to the catalog and portfolio rather than customer requirements for Service delivery driving changes for the underlying tools. *Tools should never be allowed to drive process or strategy for Service delivery (or any strategy for that matter).*

Cisco's ITaaS framework repurposes the Service catalog to a limited degree and updates its relationship with the Service portfolio and the expanding variety of customer portals used to submit IT requests. It accomplishes this by recognizing three distinct and separate levels for identifying, documenting, and then presenting requests for IT capabilities and support to enterprise customers:

- **IT Service Portfolio:** Documents all IT Services along with information required to establish a strategic overview of the complete IT Service landscape.

- **IT Service Catalog:** Provides a single, centralized document of all possible distinct and repeatable "IT catalog requests." These are defined as customer requests for IT technical capabilities or support, derived from a specific Service and Service offering, and associated with a flexible range of information allowing the request and associated workflow and reporting requirements to be hosted on one or more customer portals.

- **IT Customer Portals:** One or more portals host a selection of IT catalog requests derived from the Service catalog, allowing IT customers to search, review, and submit requests for technical capabilities.

In short, we have a list of IT Services, then a separate listing of the many potential requests for IT support or capabilities that could be derived from each Service along with flexible sets of information, and finally any number of customer portals that customers access to review and submit requests. The key consideration is that each serves its own unique purpose. The goal of the portfolio is to present a selective set of information at different levels of the Service hierarchy that provides the CIO and IT leaders with a strategic tool for managing the Service landscape end-to-end. This outcome cannot be achieved if the portfolio becomes cluttered with a wide range of technical information for managing specific IT customer requests. That is where the Service catalog comes in.

The primary goal of the IT Service catalog is to provide a complete listing of possible IT catalog requests and their associated Service mappings. The secondary goal is to support the documentation of a flexible range of details, information, and even options associated with a specific catalog request that can support its incorporation into common customer portals. There is no requirement to restrict the type of information that can be associated with an IT request; rather, it is more convenient for Service delivery teams to demonstrate flexibility in the data fields they support. The primary requirement is that each unique IT catalog request maintain its mapping back to a parent Service and Service offering. This ensures that a request submitted through any customer portal is ultimately linked back to the appropriate Service. When all potential IT requests have been documented, each can then be pulled into one or more customer request portals without the need for multiple catalogs or duplicating information or the catalog itself.

The distinction of a single catalog supporting multiple storefronts harkens back to the use of physical paper catalogs for department stores in prior decades. For example, a catalog was available and provided a complete listing of all items and merchandise, along with additional details such as pricing and sizing or color selection options. If customers wanted to acquire any of the items listed in the catalog, they had to either visit the store in person or potentially place an order by phone. In some cases, there were different levels of stores, some representing the full-scale department store, whereas other smaller stores focused on only select departments and items. Some items could be ordered only by phone or were available only during select times of year. The key is that the catalog acted as the definitive listing of all potential items. The ITaaS framework's recommended approach to a Service catalog is much the same, with the intent to support any number and type of portals for enterprise customers to submit their requests while also maintaining our Service mappings for reporting and management.

It is important to remember throughout these sections that although the prescribed approach supports multiple customer portals, Cisco still recommends providing as many customers as possible with a single starting point for initiating the largest range of requests possible. This may mean that customers are passed from a primary storefront to different portals and platforms to finalize the request. Direct access to these portals can still be supported for customers who know exactly what they want and do not wish to take the added steps of navigating from a central page.

Previous IT Service management standards established the Service catalog as a customer-facing tool, so you may be wondering if this updated approach adopted by the ITaaS framework changes that. Although the catalog is not necessarily intended as a customer-facing tool in the same manner as the actual request portals where customers submit their requests, there is no reason that customers could not browse or search the catalog directly to identify a specific request and verify the portals available for submitting the request. In other words, it can be made available to customers, but with proper implementation of customer request portals such as the corporate e-store, it won't be the first place customers think to look to submit a request for IT capabilities or support.

Now that we have detailed how the ITaaS framework repurposes and leverages these tools, the most important consideration is how much effort this new approach signifies for today's IT organizations.

The answer is that in most cases a high degree of rework or effort is not required. The various requests hosted on a corporate e-store today will be the same post-ITaaS implementation, so no major overhaul is required. The difference in the approach recommended by the ITaaS framework is primarily in decoupling the Service portfolio, and catalog and leveraging a single, centralized catalog to support multiple customer portals. In practice, this centralized catalog can often be built quickly by beginning first with a complete listing of things currently offered on the various customer portals managed by IT. Each element then needs to be mapped to a Service designated in the portfolio, and then the Service Owner for each Service should be allowed to review and propose additional catalog requests and associated information.

Corporate E-Store Design Best Practices

One of the most common IT customer portals is the corporate e-store, which allows IT customers to navigate and submit their requests for IT capabilities and support. This means that e-stores have a significant impact on customer experience and other aspects of Service delivery. As such, it is important to consider best practices for the design of these common customer interface portals.

The features and options available for design and implementation of an e-store are ultimately determined by the specific platform that the IT organization chooses to host its store. Some large-scale IT Service management platforms may combine capabilities for hosting the portfolio, catalog, e-store, and also technical support center. Most platforms on the market today should allow for linking to external request portals such as mobile app stores or technical support centers; thus, the e-store, with some minor configuration, is able to act as a single source for finding and submitting IT requests. The real challenge comes into how best to design the experience to allow customers to most quickly navigate to, find, and submit the most appropriate IT request for their requirements.

One of the most immediate selections that customers should be allowed to make is to indicate whether they need "IT technical support" or would like to request "IT products and services." In other words, is a capability you already use broken, or do you need something new? From there, we need to provide customers with the most intuitive path possible for submitting the appropriate request. The goal at this stage of organization is to strike a balance between multiple levels of categorization and the number of selections customers have to make before arriving at a specific request. On one hand, few customers want to navigate through more than a few categories before finding what they're after, but on the other hand, presenting too many choices at once may reduce the number of clicks required by customers but can also easily overwhelm and frustrate them. Cisco typically recommends teams consider the following top-level categories to begin with:

- Hardware
- Software
- Conferencing and Collaboration
- Infrastructure and Hosting
- IT Technical Support
  - Hardware
  - Software
  - Conferencing and Collaboration
  - Infrastructure and Hosting

As you can see, we leverage the same organizational categories, which provides consistency for customers in submitting requests for support or new capabilities. Second- and third-level categories can and should be introduced when applicable to reduce the number of selections presented at a single time, such as categories for "Video Conferencing" and "Phone Support" under "Conferencing and Collaboration."

Equally important to strong organizational design, however, are several features Cisco highly recommends for inclusion in any e-store deployment. The following features and options should also be presented to customers as early as possible after accessing the e-store:

- Search

- Most Common/Popular Requests

- Customer-Specific "Favorite" or Bookmarked Requests

- Open Requests

- Announcements

Poor search functionality will be quickly disregarded by customers, but strong search functionality can quickly become a "go-to" resource of choice for many customers in finding the appropriate IT request. Predictive text enables options to quickly autofill typing, which can be especially advantageous from mobile devices, and well-documented keywords captured by the Service catalog can help quickly initiate a search and find accurate results. In a large-scale enterprise with many wide-ranging varieties of potential requests submitted to the IT organization, a platform that boasts powerful search features provides customers with one of the fastest options available for selecting their requests. Search functionality is universally available on e-stores, but strong search functionality can be hard to find and requires effort on the part of the Service delivery teams to make the most valuable use of it.

Highlighting "Most Common" or "Popular Requests" is still far from a common feature but can be another powerful enabler for customers. The advantage of simply presenting the most commonly submitted IT requests to save customers time should be clear, but imagine having this feature dynamically update to reflect the most commonly submitted requests over the past hour. In the event of a widespread outage, customers are likely already frustrated, so you may as well save them the time of navigating through several levels of categories to find and submit their requests.

Another less commonly available feature is the capability for customers to save or bookmark their own most commonly submitted IT requests. This feature can save some customers a great deal of time if they find themselves regularly resubmitting a specific request, and it acts as an additional nicety common on many platforms today.

Finally, after accessing a centralized corporate e-store, customers should always be presented early on with the option of checking the status of existing requests while also receiving any key notifications via a news or announcements section. While this may seem like a lot to consider, note that all the recommendations in this section, including e-store features and primary categories, can easily be displayed on a single page. Following these core best practices can help driver higher levels of customer satisfaction across common Enterprise End-Customer Services.

Strategies for Optimizing IT Service Delivery

We've stated throughout this book that we would focus on implementing the ITaaS framework in practice, and this includes strategies and best practices for leveraging the framework for Service delivery when it's in place. A top-performance sports car has to be operated by an experienced driver who also knows how to eke out the highest levels of performance from that particular vehicle and configuration. You can think of the ITaaS framework in much the same way. Note that the goal of this section is to convey best practices for leveraging the new framework for IT Service delivery as a whole and tackle topics that simply could not be accommodated appropriately within previous chapters.

Leveraging Vendors for Value

Historically, an IT organization's use of vendors and partners to operate and deliver IT Services has amounted to some cost savings, although rarely as significant as originally planned, and typically at the expense of decreased customer satisfaction and overall lack of direct control over many aspects of Service Performance. Agreements with vendors supplying IT Service support and delivery traditionally revolved around defined priority levels and SLAs but closely followed the more technology-focused approach to Service design. We've now thoroughly established that this approach fails to recognize the impact of technology on business outcomes, the overall customer experience, or the many other strategic considerations for Service Performance adopted by the ITaaS framework. Common historical challenges faced by IT organizations are often made worse when outsourcing is initiated.

The answer is not necessarily to avoid outsourcing IT Service operations and delivery. In fact, achieving a state of Fast IT may ultimately require most IT organizations to leverage wide-ranging combinations of internal and external support. In some scenarios, market competitiveness may be decided by the IT organizations that can most nimbly and effectively blend the delivery of IT Services across all sources to achieve the desired outcomes. Effectively leveraging outsourcing in this manner requires IT organizations that have become an ITaaSO to take several important steps to leverage vendors as an opportunity to create additional business value.

The initial step should always be announcing to all vendors that you are now an end-to-end Services organization and reviewing in detail exactly what that means. Change leadership teams can lead reviews of the overall framework, including Service design principles, and introduce Service Performance and TCO strategies. From there, IT organizations should partner with their vendors to reevaluate when and how existing agreements can be reviewed to ensure that vendor support aligns itself to the same priorities for Service delivery. This effort is likely to include additional measurements and reporting for a wide range of IT Service characteristics. It is also critical that vendors understand the various Service delivery roles and treat the individuals in these roles with the same level of recognition as internal IT employees. This includes prioritizing the requests of Service Owners who are advocating for their customers. In other words, your partners and vendors have to become Service-aware. Note that as the vendors become more familiar with the Service delivery framework, they can often work closely with Service Owners to not only facilitate but accelerate aspects of Service delivery, such as speed.

Service Ownership must remain internal. This is true in all scenarios, even those where 100 percent of delivery is facilitated by vendors; the Service Owner should still be an internal employee. Although there is a long list of reasons for this stance, it all comes down to the mandate of Service Owners acting as general managers of the IT Service. If this final role is outsourced, the IT organization effectively transfers ownership of that Service and final accountability for the value it delivers outside of the organization. There really is no value to be gained from doing so. Just retain the role of Service Owner for internal employees even if the IT organization operates only a skeleton crew of resources who are all Service Owners, each managing multiple Services, while all remaining aspects of Service delivery are outsourced.

Beyond integrating vendors into the Service delivery framework, IT organizations can also create a Service to support vendor management strategies. It's not uncommon for enterprise companies to leverage a strategy and associated processes to manage and score the various vendors, and these would in turn obviously require various technical capabilities. Although it is unlikely to represent a high-effort or high-complexity Service, simply appointing a Service Owner to proactively identify tools and platforms that can deliver technical capabilities aiding in the management of vendors will prove invaluable for the enterprise and especially for the IT organization's eventual shift to Fast IT.

Operating an end-to-end Services organization requires that all vendors be Service-aware and play a supporting role in Service delivery. Without fundamentally transforming these relationships, Services supported by vendors can leave Service Owners with significant blind spots when attempting to rationalize costs and performance for IT Services, all while failing to address historical challenges with outsourcing. By integrating vendors into the Service delivery strategy and ITaaSO culture, along with initiating a Service to provide technical capabilities for scoring and managing vendor relationships, IT organizations actually can realize reduced operational costs while at the same time improving Service Performance categories, such as speed, and ultimately driving higher levels of Service value.

Delivering to External IT Customers

Throughout every chapter of this book, we have emphasized the ITaaS framework as prioritizing IT Service design and delivery in support of customers. We have primarily referenced these customers as those employees across the enterprise who leverage technical capabilities to be productive or to execute business processes. In reality, however, many of today's IT organizations also facilitate Service delivery for customers external to the enterprise. It's critical that the Service delivery framework acknowledge and facilitate these customers, seeking to align Service delivery and drive high levels of customer satisfaction similar to internal customers.

These external customers may have their own unique technical capability requirements, require the same capabilities as internal customers, or may require the same capabilities as internal customers but with different specifications for delivery or performance. In either case, the ITaaS framework can be leveraged to effectively support these customers, just so long as Service delivery teams stick to a few best practices.

Foremost among these practices is that simply because a customer is external does not equate to a requirement for a new, dedicated Service. All of our design principles remain intact. If a related set of technical capabilities is unique from those delivered by an existing Service today, and this capability set can be associated with a TCO model and Service Performance strategy that warrant the effort, a Service should be designated. Note, however, that the factors necessitating the creation of the Service have nothing to do with the customers being external, and that once created, internal customers could easily leverage those same capabilities.

If the capability requirements are the same as those from internal customers, the same Service can be leveraged for internal and external customers. If there is need for differentiation in the delivery of these capabilities, the Service Owner can create a Service offering. These capabilities may be delivered through secure portals and connections, but these are capabilities in and of themselves and do not represent a differentiation in the core capabilities.

IT organizations in the future may support a variety of customers both internally and externally. The ITaaS framework enables mechanisms for driving value across all these customers. Just be sure to use the capabilities of the framework rather than move away from the core Service design and delivery principles.

Preparing the Cloud Strategy for an ITaaSO and Fast IT

Something I actively anticipate nearing the end of every successful Services Transformation program is the IT organization's realization that its underlying strategy for Cloud will have to quickly mature and evolve in order to keep pace with the requirements being driven by the newly established landscape of IT Services and their delivery teams. In practice this is best described as the perceived bottleneck for supporting business outcomes that used to be generally associated with the IT organization itself is effectively moved downward to the enterprise IT cloud strategy.

I believe this happens as a natural result of the Services Transformation shifting focus to the capabilities being delivered by IT Services and establishing a framework capable of driving requirements for improving Service value across the IT organization. While a segment of the IT Services landscape will be free to progress these newly highlighted requirements with little constraint the sheer number of Services that ultimately rely on the enterprise IT Cloud strategy often create a deluge of requirements coalescing against a single IT strategy.

Besides a general awareness of the eventuality I recommend IT leaders and Service Delivery teams managing Services that deliver capabilities from the Cloud (Application or Data Hosting Services) proactively develop plans to rapidly improve both Leverage (for scale) and also Speed as part of their Service Performance strategies.

Embracing and Driving Self-Provisioning

As the IT organization completes its initial Services Transformation and begins transitioning to Fast IT, it is important for all Services to identify and adopt opportunities to provide their customers with a range of self-serve, self-help, and self-provisioning options for accessing and consuming technical capabilities. Chapter 12, "Fast IT—The Mandatory Future for Enterprise IT Organizations," provides a deeper look at Fast IT and the customer culture it seeks to foster, which revolves heavily around self-service, but the transition of technical capabilities to embrace self-servicing consumption by customers should not wait.

Remember that driving operational efficiencies across any aspect of Service delivery equates to value. If a combination of automation platforms allows the customer base to serve itself while providing Service Owners with the visibility they need, it not only serves to drive further value but also encourage broader Service adoption and higher levels of customer satisfaction.

Embracing Shadow IT

Chapter 1 introduced the concept of Shadow IT, along with the challenges and opportunities it creates for IT organizations and enterprises. In that same chapter, we established that Shadow IT was not something to be aggressively ferreted out by IT leaders but instead embraced through the ITaaS framework as one of many strategies for achieving a state of Fast IT.

Service Owners should immediately begin trying to understand where in their customer base Shadow IT efforts are taking place and especially why. The "why" should include an understanding of what capabilities the effort aims to enable and the perceived value. I want to stress that the role of the Service Owner is not to shut down a Shadow IT effort, but to understand the various reasons for its existence and to provide IT external stakeholder teams with any guidance or support necessary to minimize duplication and especially to avoid introducing risk to the enterprise. Another priority objective is to formulate and actively communicate how the effort could benefit from being transitioned to the IT organization and delivered successfully by leveraging the new framework for Service delivery. With the ITaaS framework in place, the capabilities often benefit from broadened consideration of Service Performance, especially speed, risk, and scale, which BU teams are typically not capable of supporting.

While the thought of abiding Shadow IT efforts may raise concerns for some IT leaders, we should consider the state of the IT and business relationship post-Services Transformation and anticipate how it is likely to impact Shadow IT efforts. The reality is that as an IT organization transitions to an ITaaSO the relationship between IT and the enterprise business begins to change, and the customer base begins to see their Service Owners as trusted advisors and the IT organization as a favored Service provider. Over time the customer base will likely initiate the transition of capabilities to the IT organization, while working closely in partnership with the Service delivery team as the need and opportunity for new capabilities arise.

Even as overall instances of Shadow IT give way to growing engagement and joint planning with the IT Service delivery teams, the business may still initiate Shadow IT efforts. If this occurs within the new IT and business relationship, there is potentially a very good reason for why it was initiated, which again is critical for the Service Owner to understand. Justification could range from constraints on the IT organization that prevented early development and deployment in time to capitalize on a market opportunity or even a lack of expertise required for early development. In some cases, it may have just begun as an innovative idea within the business that was considered to be too early in the proof of concept phases to engage the broader IT organization. Any of these factors bring us back to the recommendation of the Service Owner actively understanding the effort, providing support where needed, and preparing to bring the capabilities inside the ITaaS framework in the future if it proves a significant value for which the customer base wishes to scale and ensure performance.

As a final consideration, be mindful of the fact that a strategy for embracing Shadow IT initiatives is actually a key component of a Fast IT organization. Chapter 12 looks closer at the concept of transitioning Shadow IT to Customer-Initiated IT.

Considerations for the Completed Service Delivery Framework

Imagine yourself at the end of a lengthy and complex Services Transformation Program. The IT Transformation team has designed a set of IT Services end-to-end fully aligned to the support of business outcomes, and developed a series of strategies, processes, and tools for managing and understanding the value those Services deliver to the business. We've discussed how the Service Portfolio and strategies for communicating Service value should evolve over time, but IT leaders and Service delivery teams should now be thinking about some additional key considerations:

- How to leverage the ITaaS-based Service delivery framework to drive continuous value

- How to protect the long-term integrity and value of the Service delivery framework

It's important for the teams to take a step back at this point, survey the framework for IT Service delivery that has now been implemented, and consider its capabilities and opportunity for the IT organization and enterprise business as a whole. This is not unlike an engineering team that has spent over a year building a high-performance racecar. While the team members began with an overall purpose, goal, and specifications, they've since spent the past months alternating their focus between aerodynamics, steering and suspension, and engine design. Now that their car is complete and is a physical reality, it's important to consider the finished project as a whole, understanding how all the components complement one another and how best to operate the final vehicle that resulted from their design decisions. In the ITaaS framework, we now have a high-performance vehicle for delivering IT Services.

Some pro tips for getting the most out of your new vehicle for IT Service delivery:

■ Never forget that you face competition for delivery of IT Services to your business, and use every capability of the ITaaS framework to demonstrate value and competitiveness against other options for consuming technical capabilities.

■ Look at Service Performance categories individually, in relation to one-another, and also in relation to costs. Never forget that cost is only one aspect of overall Service value.

■ Don't forget to leverage the aggregation of IT Services at different levels of the Service hierarchy. Look for trends in costs, changes in performance, or common drivers for new capabilities.

■ Support communities for IT Service delivery roles. Encourage sharing of lessons learned, best practices, and recommendations for tools that can help these different roles be successful across the Services landscape.

■ Be prepared to invest in platforms that support the Service delivery function, especially reporting and automation of processes such as IT Service costing and other platforms that likely offer additional capabilities and benefits to the IT organization and enterprise. This is a major function of your IT operating model, be sure to invest in it as such.

Today's enterprise businesses and IT organizations are incredibly complex, and unique and challenging scenarios will arise for every IT Transformation team. When they do, it is important to understand and leverage the many capabilities and mechanisms available within the framework and broader IT operating model to develop creative solutions to these challenges. Do not begin sacrificing the principles that informed the design and development of the framework. Too many IT organizations react by compromising on the guiding principles for Service delivery they agreed to before initiating and investing heavily in their Services Transformation at the first sign of a challenging scenario. These compromises may not seem significant at first, but they add up quickly. Don't forget that the Service delivery framework acts as the foundation for Fast IT, and the last thing we want is to begin chipping away at that foundation.

Summary

The final phase of Cisco's Services Transformation Program represents a significant effort. Failing to see these activities through can limit the potential value created by the newly adopted framework for Service delivery, even leaving it ultimately crippled and of little value to the enterprise before it is even finished.

It is important to integrate the ITaaS framework with existing processes and tools for IT operations, such as asset databases, application portfolios, and configuration management databases. All these components of an IT operating model should be Services-aware, and developing a top-down view of how these tools and processes link to and feed one another is key in facilitating Service delivery and reporting.

The ITaaS framework necessitates a different approach to IT Service catalog design, which serves to enable any range and variety of future customer request portals while maintaining a mapping of all potential IT catalog requests back to IT Services. This three-level approach is as follows:

- **IT Service Portfolio:** Documents all IT Services along with information required to establish a strategic overview of the complete IT Service landscape.

- **IT Service Catalog:** Provides a single, centralized document of all possible distinct and repeatable "IT catalog requests." These are defined as customer requests for IT technical capabilities or support, derived from a specific Service and Service offering, and associated with a flexible range of information allowing the request, along with associated workflow and reporting requirements, to be hosted on one or more customer portals.

- **IT Customer Portals:** Host a selection of IT catalog requests derived from the Service catalog, allowing IT customers to search, review, and submit requests for technical capabilities.

The IT organization needs to review a variety of best practices and strategies for Service delivery, along with considerations for how the newly adopted framework for Service delivery impacts vendors, external customers, and Shadow IT. Finally, it is critical for IT leaders to step back and consider the capabilities of the Service delivery model as a whole and carefully consider how to drive continuous value and protect the integrity of the framework as they take their next steps toward Fast IT.

Chapter 12

Fast IT—The Mandatory Future for Enterprise IT Organizations

In the beginning of this book, we established that today's IT organizations must transform how their operations to Fast IT in order to not only maintain relevance but also to establish their place as transformative enablers of an enterprise business. Transforming how the IT organization designed, delivered, and communicated the value of IT Services was highlighted as a first step toward Fast IT by resolving long running challenges and firmly establishing IT as a trusted advisor to the enterprise business. A successful Services Transformation is a monumental feat for today's IT organizations, and also one that can create insurmountable value for the IT organization and the enterprise business—but it is only the beginning of your organization's journey to Fast IT.

The "concept" of Fast IT has been discussed at length by numerous sources, but what about in practice? That is to say, what does it look like in the day-to-day operation of a real-world IT organization? Here again, Cisco has extensive real-world experience gleaned from its own global IT organization. Instead, this chapter is intended to provide a brief introduction to concepts and principles associated with Fast IT in practice, such as continuous delivery and customer-initiated IT, and in doing so illustrate how the transition to an architecture-led, end-to-end Services organization acts as the foundation for Fast IT.

The Purpose and Goals of Fast IT

Chapter 1, "The Case for IT Transformation and IT as a Service (ITaaS)," introduced a series of drivers influencing the transformation of today's IT organizations to Fast IT organization; establishing that transformation was not simply a value-add opportunity but a mandatory requirement for IT organizations to justify their relevance to a future highly digitized enterprise business. In the very near future a major factor in the determination of a market leader will be which enterprise has the fastest and most efficient IT organization aligned to enabling its business.

These drivers were followed by a series of challenges, both historical and emerging, facing today's IT organizations that were preventing successful transformation to and operation as a Fast IT organization that had to be addressed first. Adoption of Cisco's ITaaS framework and transformation to an end-to-end Services organization, or ITaaSO, resolved these challenges, and in doing so established the IT organization as a trusted advisor to the business.

The purpose of Fast IT then, is to adopt new and evolve existing IT operating strategies with a goal advancing the IT organization from a trusted *advisor* to *transformative enabler* of the enterprise business through operational speed and excellence capable of embracing digitization and navigating instances of digital disruption, while also accelerating the development of transformative business capabilities. Adoption of Fast IT principles is the difference in an enterprise business responding to disruption in the future marketplace or acting as the disruptor.

The Concept of Fast IT

What is it about the idea of Fast IT that establishes it as the mandatory future for enterprise IT organizations? What does it mean for IT? What can it do for the business? Perhaps most importantly, what does it actually look like for an enterprise business in practice?

Fast IT can arguably encompass virtually all aspects of IT operations. The transition largely involves evolving the many functions carried out by an IT organization to become much faster as a reflection of IT's new role in enabling the business to keep up in rapidly changing digitized marketplaces. At the same time IT is increasing the speed of it's operations, it is also maintaining operational excellence. Efficiency, and overall contribution of business value, is never sacrificed for speed. It will also require the incorporation of new strategies such as continuous delivery, and DevSecOps, and more.

Practical execution of Fast IT operations are best demonstrated through regular, rapid innovation. Not just a single program however, but multiple parallel lines of innovation being actively driven at their own pace to enable new business models, capitalize on marketplace opportunities, and adopt new strategies. The entirety of IT operates in a manner that allows it to facilitate multiple lines of business, each with it's own goals, priorities, and timelines.

By imagining the day-to-day function of a Fast IT organization, you can begin to see how an Architecturally-led, end-to-end Services organization acts as the critical foundation. End-to-end Services allow IT to provide dedicated focus to each line of business it supports, and deliver value relative to the customer-base. It also allows innovation to progress in-step with individual Service opportunities. Architecture provides the overarching roadmap, ensuring investment and activities are ultimately aligned to support of the core business strategies; it establishes the outer guardrails that Services operate within. This foundation enables an operating model where IT stays in lock-step with the pace set by each segment of the enterprise business, rather than the business waiting for IT to enable its operations.

Similar to the Services Transformation, there is also a cultural aspect at play behind the scenes of these new and evolved operational processes required for IT organizations to realize the full benefits of Fast IT. Unlike the ITaaS framework, however, the culture of Fast IT extends beyond just the IT organization and encompasses a change in the culture of the enterprise business itself. There is a very real risk that in the presence of a true Fast IT organization that the enterprise business itself becomes a bottleneck. Fast IT requires fast business. Rather than considering only the culture of the IT organization we have to examine the overarching corporate culture of an enterprise benefitting from the presence of a Fast IT organization. Once we understand the future culture of the business and IT we can work backwards to understand the strategies leveraged by IT to help foster those outcomes.

Above all, the corporate culture encouraged by Fast IT is one that embraces and even seeks out change. Resources across the enterprise realize they operate within fluid marketplaces subject to digital disruption and appreciate the need to remain ready for rapid adaptation to these changes while also proactively developing their own transformative capabilities in hopes of leading marketplace disruption. These teams of IT and business resources truly understand and have likely witnessed or even participated in the development and introduction of new capabilities to business operations. This same mix of IT and business resources actively surveys the marketplace and technology landscape, seeking out ideas for new capabilities and remaining on the lookout for the earliest signs of new and potentially disruptive capabilities. These capabilities are, of course, delivered by IT Services, and as a result of the adoption of the ITaaS framework both IT and business have a clear understanding of the value to the business created by these Services alongside the future needs of the Service.

The equal embrace and anticipatory drive for change as a means of succeeding in the marketplace highlight another key aspect of the culture of a Fast IT organization, which is the regular, confident tolerance of risk as a necessity for responding to marketplace opportunities. That is not to say that risks to the enterprise are not carefully weighed against the potential for reward as always. Rather, the key is that Fast IT provides both IT and the business with a series of frameworks and strategies for managing risk at all stages, effectively establishing guardrails for the IT and business teams to freely operate within. In other words, the culture of Fast IT is one that is risk-tolerant rather than risk-averse.

The culture of Fast IT is one in which organizational boundaries hold less meaning for enterprise resources than they ever have historically. Where previously individual resources spent the majority of their time working within their local teams and departments, engaging other teams only in limited cases typically for projects, their daily activities now begin to shift toward working within any number of virtual teams that span functional teams and organizational departments. These dynamic, self-forming teams work across boundaries to support, optimize, and at times transform business outcomes closely reflecting the practice of the ITaaS framework in which Service delivery teams work across functional teams to deliver outcomes and drive value.

The culture of Fast IT is also one that is empowered and self-servicing. This aspect of the corporate culture will be driven by a broad landscape of IT Services that can be sought out and leveraged by IT customers with little-to-no formal IT resource engagement. The clearest example is always mobile app stores for major smartphone and tablet providers, where, in minutes, customers can actively search out, install, and test any number of apps delivered by any number of providers that fit their capability requirements. While far from every technical capability will be available on an app-store-like customer portal, the key is that a convergence of self-provisioning Services will have fostered a deeper sense of empowerment for customers. In practice, this means customers feel encouraged to experiment with different IT Services as needed, even evaluating aspects of capabilities originally intended for other operations that ultimately spur new ideas and innovation, without the need for direct, dedicated support from IT.

A final defining characteristic of the corporate culture driven by Fast IT is the expectations from both IT and the business for speed and agility across all aspects of IT operations in order to respond as quickly as possible to transformative opportunities or instances of digital disruption. Everyone in the enterprise recognizes IT as central to the daily operation of the business and its success in the marketplace and the need for IT to operate both quickly and efficiently. These across the board expectations will in turn drive continuous improvement. IT Service delivery teams closely embedded with lines of business now proactively drive efficiencies, and in those cases where needed customer demand drives improvement. The key is that in either case the IT Service delivery function based on Cisco's ITaaS framework provides IT and the business with the means for achieving these improvements. Services Transformation has established a solid foundation of IT Services, the value they deliver, and a framework for evolving those Services over time. In parallel the prior adoption of the ITaaS framework resolved historical and emerging challenges that were initially preventing broader IT Transformation and established IT as trusted advisors to the business. It also fundamentally shifted the culture of the IT organization to one that was more able to make the final leap to the to the corporate culture that facilitates Fast IT. In those enterprises where IT bypassed the Services Transformation however, the unchanged culture of IT, and the challenges and resulting gap between IT and business, is simply too far, and with no reliable bridge the two parties finally break apart at a time when competitors are evolving their own IT organizations to a role of transformative enabler.

Moving from Shadow IT to Customer-Initiated IT

In earlier chapters, we defined and provided examples of Shadow IT while establishing that in many cases its existence was born out of a sense that IT "just wasn't getting it done," which left the business teams to develop and manage their own capabilities required for success. Repeated demonstration that the IT organization didn't share the priorities, goals, and concerns of the customer base and was incapable of supporting the needs of the business in a timely, cost-effective manner led to continued growth of Shadow IT. In some cases, the combinations of Shadow IT and public cloud Services allowed some departments to entirely bypass the enterprise IT organization. While Shadow IT can expose the enterprise to risks, both known and unknown, we stressed that in most cases there was equal opportunity for the creation of significant value and that the goal of Cisco's ITaaS framework was not to eliminate Shadow IT. Post adoption of the ITaaS framework, customer-developed capabilities that have matured to the point of carrying risk for enterprise operations have likely been transitioned into the IT organization's Service delivery framework, and new capabilities are mostly developed in partnership with the Service delivery teams.

Even in this state, however, there is still value for not only abiding but also supporting customer-initiated development of capabilities. This is simply a reality for the future of enterprise operations dealing with digitization and digital disruption where marketplaces are constantly changing. Regardless of the success of the Service delivery team, the enterprise lines of business will always be closest to industry operations and trends; they will be most effective at identifying transformative opportunities and then progressing them through the earliest proof of concept stages prior to initiating major efforts in partnership with IT. Engaging IT Service delivery teams for each and every proposal, many of which will not proceed beyond initial proof of concept, is simply too slow.

Think of customer-initiated IT as equal parts your customer's idea factory, for brainstorming ideas and combining and revisiting previous proposals with new innovations; and a sandbox, for the early incubation and testing of these proposals to gauge their viability before engaging broader IT and business teams. In practice, customer-initiated IT can and will be initiated and then gestate in many different ways and in many cases will still involve IT resources in dynamically forming teams. The key is that the IT organization not be overly prohibitive in facilitating this sandbox, and to have strategies in place to closely partner with business teams at any stage in the development.

Uncovering Fast IT

The following sections will look at some of the components that enable Fast IT operations. As with any model, the building blocks are the most important, which for Fast IT means evolving the major functions common to IT organizations introduced in Chapter 2. Once these core functions can fully support Fast IT operations, IT can begin introducing and realizing value from new strategies like Continuous Delivery that drive further speed and efficiency.

The Building Blocks of Fast IT

Chapter 2 introduced three core functions common to all IT operating models, and these same common functions will act as the building blocks for Fast IT operating models, but will be required to evolve further in order to support the speed of future IT operations.

- IT technical operations
- IT Service delivery
- Enterprise architecture

The evolution of the technical operations function has already begun in support of the Services Transformation. IT technical operations teams are now actively facilitating requirements driven by Service delivery teams, and are also feeding information back to Service delivery in support of Service Performance strategies. This is far different from technical operations across many of today's IT organizations which focus purely on the operation of technical platforms in pursuit of SLAs and best practices driven by the IT industry with little regard for how those processes impact the business. Fast IT simply drives further requirements primarily in support of Service Speed (solution development and time to adoption) and Leverage (rapid scaling), which has to be supported by technical operations; otherwise, the function becomes a bottleneck. In practice this means further evolution of many processes for change-control while leveraging segmentation technologies to isolate risk.

Enterprise architecture practices will need to evolve further as well. The Services Transformation required no fundamental change to EA practices, instead leveraging end-to-end Services to establish a second level of architecture capable of progressing at a different speed than that of the overarching enterprise roadmap so long as it remained continually aligned to it. EA practices will nonetheless have to be fully matured in order to support Fast IT operations. Initiating Fast IT without a mature enterprise architecture practice capable of moving at the required speed will only break processes and duplicate architecture faster.

In practice, many of the standards and methodologies popular today for enterprise architecture may be too cumbersome and clunky to support the speed of change required for Fast IT. Instead, I often highlight the need for lightweight methodologies and associated processes that I refer to as "Fast Architecture." Fast Architecture should reflect the criticality of architectural alignment that still allows for progression at different levels at varying speeds; but its most important facet is that it be an agile practice that can support rather than constraing both Fast IT and by association "fast business". This means leveraging the simplest methodology possible while still successfully executing the function of linking technical architectures to business operations and leveraging that information to support the planning of rapidly evolving business strategies. While it is not specifically referenced as Fast Architecture by Cisco IT the underlying characteristics are the same; reflecting a lightweight and agile function capable of establishing a roadmap for architecture aligned to business strategy while not constraining IT and business operations as a consequence of the practice.

The IT organization's Service delivery framework will also have to be fully matured and optimized. Fast IT will require Service delivery teams to make use of every capability and strategic lever introduced by the ITaaS framework to quickly facilitate outcomes. Asking these teams to facilitate Fast IT strategies and requirements while strategies, processes, and tools for Service delivery are still maturing will always lead to a breakdown of the broader IT Transformation.

The Mechanics of Fast IT

With each of the core functions of an IT organization tuned to provide the foundations of Fast IT, the next area of focus is the specific strategies that truly enable Fast IT operations. In some cases this involves transforming specific strategies likely common to most IT organizations today, such as those dealing with Cloud and IoT. In other cases entirely new strategies developed with the intent of accelerating key aspects of IT operations are incorporated, such as those introducing continuous delivery practices.

The primary enterprise IT strategies that must be considered for enabling Fast IT are

- Continuous delivery, including DevSecOps
- Cloud
- Big Data
- Security
- Internet of Things (IoT)

The following sections will provide a brief introduction to continuous delivery and DevSecOps, while future Cisco content will provide dedicated examinations of how the remaining strategies evolve to support Fast IT.

Continuous Delivery

Introduction of continuous delivery strategies represents the next major step in the evolution of IT Service delivery. Note that continuous delivery strategies are commonly associated with development of new capabilities through software engineering and DevOps practices which are discussed next. Cisco IT however abstracts these principles from software development and applies them to end-to-end Service delivery. The intent of Cisco IT's Continuous Delivery strategy is to partner IT with it's business customers from the earliest conceptualization of a capability through the life of it's delivery and eventual discontinuation. It especially emphasizes the development and transition to operations of new capabilities for any given Service. Continuous delivery is seen as a broad strategy for the continuous creation of business value through IT Services.

Cisco associates the following set of principles with continuous delivery; you can think of them as another set of guiding principles that Service delivery teams are expected to abide by at all times:

- Build the right things
- Build things the right way
- Build things fast

By "things," we are referring, of course, to technical capabilities delivered through IT Services. While I have typically emphasized Business Operations Services when referencing development of new capabilities, in fact continuous delivery will apply to all IT Service types. Consider for instance that programmable infrastructures and segmentation practices will mean many Technology Foundation Services are actively provisioning infrastructures to support incoming parallel requirements from numerous other IT Services. Principles of Continuous Delivery are applicable across all Services.

There are three characteristics for executing continuous delivery:

- Continuous engagement
- Self-organizing dynamic teams with semi-autonomy
- Strong collaboration capabilities

Continuous engagement refers to the engagement of the customer base and key stakeholders by the teams responsible for delivering Services. Service Owners, Service Executives, and the wider Service delivery community will have at this point already established strong relationships and regular communications with the customer base. Continuous engagement emphasizes the ongoing engagement with the customer base throughout the development of a new capability. This approach is in contrast to the historical practices for developing new capabilities in which IT often gathered initial requirements from the customer before then working in isolation for an extended period of time to build and test the proposed solution. Only after the solution and new capabilities were completed would the IT teams present their work to the customer. The challenge with this approach was that requirements may have been misinterpreted or simply changed for any number of reasons, and the likelihood of changes in requirements was accelerated as a result of digitization and digital disruption across industries. Even following the adoption of the ITaaS framework and the trusted advisor status and relationships it establishes many Service delivery teams continue to follow the historical approach of isolated capabilities development.

Continuous engagement practices address this issue by encouraging constant engagement of key stakeholders throughout the development of a capability. The IT organization does not hope to avoid changes to requirements but instead anticipates and even welcomes them as a key element of ensuring that their efforts lead to the development of a capability that delivers valuable outcomes. This concept reflects a key characteristic of the corporate culture shaped by Fast IT practices, in this case one that accepts and even drives change.

Success for a continuous delivery strategy relies on the ability of individuals across functional teams and departments to self-organize into dynamic teams with the allowance to operate semi-autonomously. We established the willingness to participate across functional and organizational boundaries as a key part of the culture of Fast IT the adoption of the ITaaS framework for Service delivery, resources across the IT organization are already accustomed to working across functional boundaries to support business outcomes through IT Services. IT resources in one team may find themselves actively working within two or more cross-functional teams to facilitate outcomes for a number of different IT Services.

Over time, the transition to an end-to-end Services organization and eventual transition to Fast IT can flip the dynamic of how IT and business teams work within the enterprise. Traditionally, an IT professional may have spent 80 percent of their time working within their functional team and only 20 percent of their time working outside of that team, typically on formal large-scale projects. These percentages begin to shift as the ITaaS framework is implemented, and once a state of Fast IT is truly realized, they will have potentially flipped entirely, with IT professionals spending 80 percent of their time supporting various virtual teams and the remaining 20 percent within their formal organizationally assigned team.

Continuous delivery practices recognize and support the organic formation of these teams. Although formal team assignments and structure can always be leveraged, the culture of Fast IT is one in which this is rarely needed. Similar to Service Owners who adopt a general manager level ownership and accountability for their Service, IT professionals and even customer stakeholders who anticipate change as an opportunity to create value for the enterprise are often self-motivated. The small, agile teams required to pull together many capabilities are often self-organizing. This is especially true after a general structure for these teams has been demonstrated on several occasions, which is largely limited to establishing the Service Owner as the "product owner" responsible for engaging the correct stakeholders and setting expectations for the development of the capability when needed. The key is that by fostering the right mindset across the organization, individuals who identify a value opportunity are self-motivated and less concerned with departmental boundaries, and cross-functional teams will form organically as needed to deliver the capability opportunity.

One of the most important elements of support that can be provided by business and IT leaders for these self-organizing teams is a higher degree of autonomy than teams were historically allowed to operate with. Enforcing extensive review and approval processes makes sense when large-scale investments and effort are required but will only constrain and potentially demotivate the type of smaller-scale innovation we're seeking to foster. We should acknowledge that some, at times many, of these efforts will naturally be brought to an end by the same team that initiated the effort before it bears fruit. The team, especially adhering to continuous engagement practices with the Service Owners and stakeholders, may choose to discontinue development at any time if the idea proves not to deliver on the intended value. There is always value created by these efforts, however, whether it is nothing more than a new working relationship or highly valuable intellectual capital with a high chance of being leveraged in another future innovation. I personally witnessed an IoT solution picked up and abandoned on three separate occasions, undergoing minor evolutions each time, before becoming a now well-recognized and proven industry-changing solution. Grant these self-motivated, self-organizing teams a level of autonomy in which to innovate, and at times fail, knowing they are creating continuous value for the enterprise.

A strong collection of collaboration platforms is critical for enabling these teams. These teams should be able to quickly initialize a centralized hub for storing and sharing information, along with engaging the Service Owner and customer stakeholders. Failing to provide a broad landscape of reliable collaboration platforms to resources across the enterprise can be just as debilitating to these self-motivating, self-organizing teams attempting to drive innovative transformation of capabilities as extensive oversight and management.

Taking Services Beyond the IT Organization

Cisco's ITaaS framework transforms how today's IT organizations design and deliver Services, and introduces strategies for measuring the value those Services provide to the enterprise business. Why limit the framework to only IT Services?

Operations as a Service (OaaS) is a transformative business operations framework that adopts the model for IT Service delivery pioneered by Cisco's ITaaS framework to other critical enterprise business organizations, such as supply chain. The potential for Services is universal across enterprise business units. These business organizations share the same obligations to the enterprise business of supporting business outcomes and efficient operations as the IT organization, and can leverage the same basic framework for Service delivery to establish themselves as trusted advisors to their own customers.

While much of the value opportunity for adopting the ITaaS framework to other areas of a business are likely clear there is one aspect I find is often overlooked. So much focus has been placed on Fast IT that industry leaders have forgotten to consider what happens when the business itself cannot keep pace with the readiness of the IT organization. While this may be a welcome change for many IT leaders, in reality, the business has to evolve its practices as well to be able to benefit from digitization and navigate digital disruption.

Similar to Fast IT, the first big step in realizing fast business is to transform how that business delivers Services and measures the value of those Services relative to its customers.

Summary

Services Transformation through the adoption of Cisco's ITaaS framework provides the crucial foundation for IT Transformation to Fast IT. Fast IT represents a significant body of knowledge, and this chapter sought to provide an introduction to Fast IT and its most significant elements.

The goal of Fast IT is to advance the IT organization from trusted advisor to transformative enabler of the enterprise business by fostering enterprise digitization and responsiveness to digital disruption, while also accelerating the development and delivery of transformative business capabilities.

The corporate culture of an enterprise business benefitting from the presence of Fast IT organization is described as

- Embraces and seeks out change as an opportunity to create value

- Is risk-tolerant rather than risk-averse

- Shares a widespread self-Service mindset

- Sanctions customer-initiated IT as an evolution of Shadow IT

- Expects speed and agility across all activities and operations

Fast IT relies on the maturity and evolution of common IT functions for technical operations, enterprise architecture, and Service delivery. With these core building blocks in place several other IT strategies must be evolved alongside the introduction of new strategies that enable Fast IT:

- Continuous delivery, including DevSecOps

- Cloud

- Big Data

- Security

- Internet of Things (IoT)

The ITaaS framework for Service delivery is not strictly limited to IT Services. Operations as a Service (OaaS) is an evolving framework with the goal of adopting a similar framework for Service delivery and strategies for measuring Service value to other segments of enterprise business operations.

From the Diary of an ITaaS Consultant

By now, you have likely noted the absence of any diary entries throughout this chapter, and while I very much would have liked to include several, the point of these diary entries has been to share real-world experiences from my consulting career in guiding Cisco customers through their own Services Transformations. The reality is that at the time of writing, my prior experience has largely focused on Services Transformation, and my practical knowledge of Fast IT is still only beginning. Instead, I wished to use this final entry to thank you for your interest in the content of this book and to leave you with some final words of advice and encouragement for your Services Transformation.

IT Transformation to Fast IT is mandatory for today's IT organizations, and Services Transformation represents the first big step. Not only is it a significant and complex effort, but some of the core concepts and especially the cultural transition that are required can together raise significant concern for many IT professionals. I've witnessed everything from widespread resistance to progressing any aspect of the Services Transformation to full-out revolts by some individuals. As I stated in an earlier chapter, not all of today's IT professionals will thrive in the new culture of a Services-led IT organization, but we should take every step possible to leave the door open. That is why I wish to illustrate what an incredible opportunity IT Transformation represents not only for the IT organization as a whole, but for an individual IT professional.

Imagine for a moment what it's like to be a contributing member of an IT organization that is seen as a trusted advisor to the enterprise business. This is a future IT organization in which self-motivation, innovation, and the ability to work across organizational boundaries to achieve value for the company are fostered and rewarded. The organization that you're a member of is recognized as integral to the success of the business in the marketplace, and as such, your contributions mean that much more.

Services Transformation within your current organization will be a lengthy and at times difficult journey, but it's one that can be a lot of fun with the right team. Your enterprise business is filled with incredible opportunities and innovative professionals just waiting to partner with you. You'll be challenged to think in new ways, but you'll meet some great people and will certainly have some fun on the way. Just take my word for it: never underestimate the positive effects of getting a good team of people out for an in-person happy hour when things seem overly daunting.

I've never believed in luck. I believe strongly, however, in the capacity of talented, motivated individuals to achieve incredible feats, especially when supported by their leaders and environment. With that thought in mind, I leave you now to get to work. Enjoy the transformation!

Justin Mann

Cisco ITaaS Framework Reference Portfolio

Table A-1 includes a complete copy of the ITaaS framework's reference portfolio. This baseline Service portfolio was developed to help Cisco Services consulting teams fast-track customer IT Service and portfolio design effort, as well as to assess their proposed Service design against a real-world example. To do this, Cisco consulting teams identified common Services that consistently result from best-practice-based Service design across different industries.

A number of considerations are crucial for IT Transformation teams to remain conscious of in order to leverage this tool effectively. Above all, this reference portfolio is intended as a guide and example for IT Transformation teams. *Under no circumstances should the information provided in this section be allowed to supersede or replace proper Service design practices.*

We also want to stress that leveraging this reference material does not eliminate the need to vet and finalize the proposed portfolio per the recommendations in Chapter 6, "Service Design and Building the IT Service Portfolio." Failing to do so can lead to significant challenges for the transformation team and constrain the value outcomes.

This portfolio was developed to be industry agnostic and primarily focused on the designation of Technology Foundation and Enterprise End-Customer type Services common to most enterprises, although a number of Services enabling supply chain, sales, and several other common corporate functions have been included as sample Business Operations Services. These Services have been grouped into Service Categories and Strategic Service Groups closely following recommendations and naming conventions in Chapter 6. The portfolio includes just over 70 Services, and transformation teams supporting large-scale enterprises can assume that 20–30 additional Business Operations Services would be defined in order to support business processes across the enterprise. Some additional Enterprise End-Customer and Technology Foundation Services are also likely to be added, bringing the total Service count closely within the ranges recommended in Chapter 6. Note that smaller-scale enterprises should expect that their Services will map more naturally to the Service Categories found in this portfolio. In all cases, transformation teams can simply remove any nonapplicable Services.

Table A-1   *Reference Portfolio*

Strategic Service Group	Service Category	Services	Service Offerings
Business Enablement Services	Supply Chain Management	Product Supply and Transport	
Business Enablement Services	Supply Chain Management	Supply Chain Operations	
Business Enablement Services	Supply Chain Management	Supply Planning	
Business Enablement Services	Supply Chain Management	Ordering Services	
Business Enablement Services	Sales Management	Revenue Accounting	
Business Enablement Services	Sales Management	Sales Force Technologies	
Business Enablement Services	Sales Management	Pricing and Quoting Services	
Business Enablement Services	Sales Management	Customer Data Management	
Business Enablement Services	Sales Management	Partner Program Management	
Corporate Functions Services	Health, Safety, and Environmental	Health and Safety	
Corporate Functions Services	Health, Safety, and Environmental	Environmental Stewardship	
Corporate Functions Services	Health, Safety, and Environmental	Incident Response and Risk Management	
Corporate Functions Services	Health, Safety, and Environmental	Compliance and Audit Assurance	
Corporate Functions Services	Corporate Management	Legal	
Corporate Functions Services	Corporate Management	Policy, Government, and Public Affairs	
Corporate Functions Services	Corporate Management	Global Security	
Corporate Functions Services	Corporate Management	Property, Land, and Lease Management	

Strategic Service Group	Service Category	Services	Service Offerings
Corporate Functions Services	Finance	Accounts Receivable	
Corporate Functions Services	Finance	Corporate Accounting	
Corporate Functions Services	Finance	Demand Forecasting	
Corporate Functions Services	Finance	Financial Planning and Budgeting	
Corporate Functions Services	Finance	Fixed Asset Management	
Corporate Functions Services	Finance	Tax	
Corporate Functions Services	Finance	Internal Controls and Audit	
Corporate Functions Services	Finance	Investor Relations	
Corporate Functions Services	Procurement	Order Management	
Corporate Functions Services	Procurement	Payable and Expense	
Corporate Functions Services	Procurement	Procurement Service	
Corporate Functions Services	Procurement	Reverse Logistics	
Corporate Functions Services	Procurement	Global Inventory Management	
Corporate Functions Services	Procurement	Contracting	
Corporate Functions Services	Human Resources	Workforce Management	
Corporate Functions Services	Human Resources	Case Management	
Corporate Functions Services	Human Resources	Compensation and Benefits Management	

Strategic Service Group	Service Category	Services	Service Offerings
Corporate Functions Services	Human Resources	Employee Financial Service	
Enterprise Productivity and Collaboration Services	Enterprise Productivity	Corporate E-Store and Customer Interface Portals	
Enterprise Productivity and Collaboration Services	Enterprise Productivity	Laptops and Desktops	
Enterprise Productivity and Collaboration Services	Enterprise Productivity	Desktop Software	
Enterprise Productivity and Collaboration Services	Enterprise Productivity	Smartphones and Tablets	
Enterprise Productivity and Collaboration Services	Enterprise Productivity	Enterprise Printing	
Enterprise Productivity and Collaboration Services	Enterprise Productivity	Partner Learning and Development	
Enterprise Productivity and Collaboration Services	Enterprise Productivity	Employee Learning and Development	
Enterprise Productivity and Collaboration Services	Enterprise Collaboration	Email and Calendaring	
Enterprise Productivity and Collaboration Services	Enterprise Collaboration	Core Collaboration Technologies (Voice, Voicemail, etc.)	

Strategic Service Group	Service Category	Services	Service Offerings
Enterprise Productivity and Collaboration Services	Enterprise Collaboration	Conferencing	
Enterprise Productivity and Collaboration Services	Enterprise Collaboration	Social Collaboration Tools	
Enterprise Productivity and Collaboration Services	Enterprise Collaboration	Video Streaming and Multicast	
Enterprise Productivity and Collaboration Services	Enterprise Collaboration	Messaging	
Enterprise Productivity and Collaboration Services	Enterprise Capabilities	Enterprise Program, Portfolio, and Project Management Systems	
Enterprise Productivity and Collaboration Services	Enterprise Capabilities	Enterprise Program, Portfolio, and Project Management Systems	Enterprise Project Management
Enterprise Productivity and Collaboration Services	Enterprise Capabilities	Enterprise Program, Portfolio, and Project Management Systems	Enterprise Portfolio Management
Enterprise Productivity and Collaboration Services	Enterprise Capabilities	Enterprise Vendor Management	Local Vendor Management
Enterprise Productivity and Collaboration Services	Enterprise Capabilities	Enterprise Vendor Management	International Vendor Management

Strategic Service Group	Service Category	Services	Service Offerings
Enterprise Productivity and Collaboration Services	Enterprise Capabilities	Enterprise Operations and Process Management	Enterprise Change Management
Enterprise Productivity and Collaboration Services	Enterprise Capabilities	Enterprise Operations and Process Management	Business Process Management
Enterprise Productivity and Collaboration Services	Enterprise Capabilities	Enterprise Operations and Process Management	Business Intelligence
Enterprise Productivity and Collaboration Services	Enterprise Capabilities	Corporate Web Presences	xyz.com
Enterprise Productivity and Collaboration Services	Enterprise Capabilities	Corporate Web Presences	Intranet
Enterprise Productivity and Collaboration Services	Enterprise Capabilities	Corporate Web Presences	Extranet
Infrastructure Services	Platform and Development Services	Application and Web Services	
Infrastructure Services	Platform and Development Services	ERP Platform Hosting	
Infrastructure Services	Platform and Development Services	Database and Middleware Hosting	
Infrastructure Services	Platform and Development Services	Mobile Application Platform and Development	

Strategic Service Group	Service Category	Services	Service Offerings
Infrastructure Services	Platform and Development Services	Application Development, Testing, and Integration	
Infrastructure Services	Platform and Development Services	Database Reporting and Development	
Infrastructure Services	Digital Security	Data Protection and Security	
Infrastructure Services	Digital Security	Network Security	
Infrastructure Services	Digital Security	Platform Security	
Infrastructure Services	Digital Security	Application Security	
Infrastructure Services	Digital Security	Application Security	Application Scanning
Infrastructure Services	Digital Security	Application Security	Application Testing
Infrastructure Services	Digital Security	Identity Access and Management	Directory Services
Infrastructure Services	Digital Security	Identity Access and Management	Authentication and Authorization
Infrastructure Services	Digital Security	Identity Access and Management	Identity Services
Infrastructure Services	Cloud Services	Cloud Administration and Management Platforms	
Infrastructure Services	Cloud Services	Data Center Network	Local Server Load Balancing
Infrastructure Services	Cloud Services	Data Center Network	Global Server Load Balancing
Infrastructure Services	Cloud Services	Data Center Network	SSL Offload

Strategic Service Group	Service Category	Services	Service Offerings
Infrastructure Services	Cloud Services	Cloud Application Hosting	Public Cloud Hosting
Infrastructure Services	Cloud Services	Cloud Application Hosting	Private Cloud Hosting
Infrastructure Services	Cloud Services	Cloud Storage and Backup	Private Cloud Storage
Infrastructure Services	Cloud Services	Cloud Storage and Backup	Public Cloud Storage
Infrastructure Services	Cloud Services	Cloud Storage and Backup	Legacy Local and Offsite Backup Solutions
Infrastructure Services	Network and Connectivity Services	Corporate Network	Corporate Wireless
Infrastructure Services	Network and Connectivity Services	Corporate Network	Core Network Services
Infrastructure Services	Network and Connectivity Services	Corporate Network	Corporate WAN
Infrastructure Services	Network and Connectivity Services	Corporate Network	Guest Network
Infrastructure Services	Network and Connectivity Services	Partner Connections (Extranet)	
Infrastructure Services	Network and Connectivity Services	Home and Remote Access	Software VPN
Infrastructure Services	Network and Connectivity Services	Home and Remote Access	Home Office
IT as a Business Services	IT Operating Services	Enterprise Architecture Operations and Governance	Architecture Modeling Technologies

Strategic Service Group	Service Category	Services	Service Offerings
IT as a Business Services	IT Operating Services	Enterprise Architecture Operations and Governance	Architecture Methodologies and Governance
IT as a Business Services	IT Operating Services	Enterprise Architecture Operations and Governance	Architecture Design and Delivery
IT as a Business Services	IT Operating Services	IT Service Management	Service Planning
IT as a Business Services	IT Operating Services	IT Service Management	Portfolio Planning and Management
IT as a Business Services	IT Operating Services	IT Service Management	IT Service Costing (Dashboarding and Tools)
IT as a Business Services	IT Operating Services	IT Service Management	IT Service Reviews
IT as a Business Services	IT Operating Services	IT Service Operations	Service Performance Analytics
IT as a Business Services	IT Operating Services	IT Service Operations	Technical Support Platforms
IT as a Business Services	IT Operating Services	IT Service Operations	Monitoring and Management Platforms
IT as a Business Services	IT Operating Services	IT Service Operations	On-Site Support Tools
IT as a Business Services	IT Operating Services	IT Service Operations	Workload Automation

Index

C

D

E

F

R

S

T

U–V

W–X–Y–Z